# THE ART OF BIBLICAL INTERPRETATION

# BIBLE AND ITS RECEPTION

Rhonda Burnette-Bletsch, General Editor

*Editorial Board:*
Brennan Breed
Stephen R. Burge
Lesleigh Cushing
J. Cheryl Exum
Michael Rosenberg
Robert Paul Seesengood

Number 3

# THE ART OF BIBLICAL INTERPRETATION

## Visual Portrayals of Scriptural Narratives

*Edited by*
Heidi J. Hornik, Ian Boxall, and Bobbi Dykema

SBL PRESS

**SBL PRESS**
**Atlanta**

Copyright © 2021 by SBL Press

All rights reserved. No part of this work may be reproduced or transmitted in any form or by any means, electronic or mechanical, including photocopying and recording, or by means of any information storage or retrieval system, except as may be expressly permitted by the 1976 Copyright Act or in writing from the publisher. Requests for permission should be addressed in writing to the Rights and Permissions Office, SBL Press, 825 Houston Mill Road, Atlanta, GA 30329 USA.

Library of Congress Control Number: 2021944614

## Contents

Figures ............................................................................................................. vii
Abbreviations ................................................................................................ xv

Introduction
    Heidi J. Hornik, Ian Boxall, and Bobbi Dykema ............................... 1

1. Unsettling the Gaze: Bathsheba beyond Verse and Image
    Yohana A. Junker ............................................................................... 11

2. "I Am Come into My Garden": The Canticle of Canticles and the *Florilegium* of Philips Galle and Adriaen Collaert
    James Clifton ..................................................................................... 37

3. "I Sought Him Whom My Soul Loves": Symbol, Ornament, and Visual Exegesis of the Song of Songs in the *Saint John's Bible*
    Jonathan Homrighausen ................................................................... 67

4. Touch Me, Don't Touch Me—Peter, Jesus, and Mary: Painted by Scarsellino and Portrayed by Cornelius à Lapide
    Heidi J. Hornik ................................................................................ 103

5. The Vacant Girl: Bernardino Luini's Salome
    Ela Nuțu ........................................................................................... 135

6. Picturing the Parable of the Sower
    Christine E. Joynes ......................................................................... 163

7. "The Belated Return of the 'Son'": Thomas Hart Benton's *Prodigal Son*
    David B. Gowler ............................................................................. 181

8. Visualizing the Beloved Disciple in the Art of the Reclining Banquet
   Jeff Jay ..................................................................................................207

9. A Seat at the Table: Grant Wood's *Dinner for Threshers*
   Meredith Munson ...............................................................................243

10. Seeing Christ's Angel: Visual Exegesis of Revelation 10
    Ian Boxall............................................................................................261

Contributors.................................................................................................293
Ancient Sources Index................................................................................297
Authors and Artists Index..........................................................................303
Subject Index................................................................................................310

# Figures

**1.1.** Jean Bourdichon, illuminator, *Bathsheba Bathing*, 1498–1499. Tempera and gold on parchment, Leaf: 24.3 × 17 cm (9 9/16 × 6 11/16 in.), MS 79, recto. J. Paul Getty Museum, courtesy of the Getty Open Content Program.
**1.2.** Rembrandt Harmenszoon van Rijn, *Bathsheba at Her Bath*, 1654. Oil on canvas, 142 x 142 cm. Photo: Mathieu Rabeau. Musée du Louvre, Paris, France ©RMN-Grand Palais/Art Resource, NY.
**1.3.** Willem Drost, *Bathsheba with David's Letter*, 1654. Oil on canvas, 103 x 87 cm. Photo: Franck Raux. Musée du Louvre, Paris, France. ©RMN-Grand Palais/ Art Resource, NY.
**1.4.** Marc Chagall (1887–1985) © ARS, NY. *David and Bathsheba*. 1956. Lithograph, 35.8 x 26.5 cm. Photo: Gérard Blot. Musée National Marc Chagall. ©RMN-Grand Palais/Art Resource, NY.
**1.5.** Lorna Simpson, *Guarded Conditions*, 1989. 18 dye diffusion color Polaroid prints, 6 frames total (3 prints in each), 21 engraved plastic plaques, 17 plastic letters, overall: 214 x 376.6 x 4.1 cm. © Lorna Simpson. Courtesy of the artist and Hauser & Wirth.
**2.1.** Adriaen Collaert after Philips Galle, *Bouquet of Flowers*, ca. 1587–1589. Engraving, 26.4 x 17.6 cm; plate 3 of *Florilegium*; Sarah Campbell Blaffer Foundation, Houston, 2014.7.3. Photo: Museum of Fine Arts, Houston.
**2.2.** Adriaen Collaert after Philips Galle, *Title Plate*, ca. 1587–1589. Engraving, 26.4 x 17.6 cm; plate 1 of *Florilegium*; Sarah Campbell Blaffer Foundation, Houston, 2014.7.1. Photo: Museum of Fine Arts, Houston.
**2.3.** Adriaen Collaert after Philips Galle, *Sponsa and Sponsus*, ca. 1587–1589. Engraving, 26.4 x 17.6 cm; plate 2 of *Florilegium*; Sarah Campbell Blaffer Foundation, Houston, 2014.7.2. Photo: Museum of Fine Arts, Houston.
**2.4.** Adriaen Collaert after Philips Galle, *Roses*, 1587–1589. Engraving, 26.4 x 17.6 cm; plate 4 of *Florilegium*; Sarah Campbell Blaffer Foundation, Houston, 2014.7.4. Photo: Museum of Fine Arts, Houston.

**2.5.** Adriaen Collaert after Philips Galle, *Lilies*, 1587–1589. Engraving, 26.4 x 17.6 cm; plate 6 of *Florilegium*; Sarah Campbell Blaffer Foundation, Houston, 2014.7.6. Photo: Museum of Fine Arts, Houston.
**2.6.** Johannes Wierix, *The Virgin and Child in the Enclosed Garden*, 1606. Engraving, 27.5 x 31 cm; Metropolitan Museum of Art, New York, 53.601.18(94). Photo: Metropolitan Museum of Art, New York.
**2.7.** Theodoor Galle, *Reciprocal Invitation of the Bride and Bridegroom to Their Respective Gardens (Reciproca Sponsae Sponsique ad hortum suum invitatio)*. Engraving in Jan David, *Paradisus Sponsi et Sponsae* (Antwerp: Ex officina Plantiniana, Apud Ioannem Moretum, 1607); private collection. Photo: Sarah Campbell Blaffer Foundation, Houston.
**2.8.** Unknown artist, Bruges, The "Mors Vincit Omnia" Hours, ca. 1510, Book of Hours, use of Rome. Colors on parchment, ca. 11 x 8.5 cm; Sarah Campbell Blaffer Foundation, Houston, 2015.19. Photo: Museum of Fine Arts, Houston.
**2.9.** Adriaen Collaert, *Saint Lucy*, ca. 1600. Engraving, 19.5 x 15 cm; from *Martyrologium Sanctarum Virginum*; Yale University Art Gallery, 2011.53.1.105. Photo: Yale University Art Gallery.
**2.10.** Daniel Seghers, *A Garland of Flowers on a Carved Stone Medallion*, ca. 1650. Oil on canvas, 114.3 x 95.3 cm; Sarah Campbell Blaffer Foundation, Houston, 1977.4. Photo: Museum of Fine Arts, Houston.
**3.1.** Donald Jackson, *The Song of Solomon*. Poetry Scribe: Sally Mae Joseph; Prose Scribe: Susan Leiper; Hebrew Script: Izzy Pludwinski; Book Heading: Donald Jackson. 2006. From *The Saint John's Bible*. Gouache and ink on vellum, 15½ x 23½ in. Saint John's University, Collegeville, MN.
**3.2** (left and right). Donald Jackson, *Garden of Desire*, Scribe and Artist: Donald Jackson; Hebrew Script: Izzy Pludwinski. 2006. From *The Saint John's Bible*. Gouache and ink on vellum, 31½ x 23½ in. Saint John's University, Collegeville, MN. Saint John's University, Collegeville, MN.
**3.3.** Donald Jackson, detail of *Garden of Desire*. 2006. From *The Saint John's Bible*. Gouache and ink on vellum, page measures 15¾ x 23½ in. Saint John's University, Collegeville, MN.
**3.4.** Donald Jackson, *I Am My Beloved's*, Scribe and Artist: Donald Jackson; Hebrew Script: Izzy Pludwinski. 2006. From *The Saint John's Bible*. Gouache and ink on vellum, 31½ x 23½ in. Saint John's University, Collegeville, MN.
**3.5.** Donald Jackson, *Set Me as a Seal*, Scribe: Sally Mae Joseph; Hebrew Script: Izzy Pludwinski; Book Heading: Donald Jackson. 2006. From *The*

*Saint John's Bible*. Gouache and ink on vellum, 15¾ x 23½ in. Saint John's University, Collegeville, MN.

**3.6.** Donald Jackson, *Solomon's Temple* (1 Kings 8:1–66). 2010. From *The Saint John's Bible*. Gouache and ink on vellum, page measures 15¾ x 23½ in. Saint John's University, Collegeville, MN.

**3.7.** Donald Jackson, *Isaiah's Temple Vision* (Isaiah 6:1–13). 2005. From *The Saint John's Bible*. Gouache and ink on vellum, page measures 15¾ x 23½ in. Saint John's University, Collegeville, MN.

**3.8.** Donald Jackson, *Crucifixion* (Luke 23:44–49). 2002. From *The Saint John's Bible*. Gouache and ink on vellum, page measures 15¾ x 23½ in. Saint John's University, Collegeville, MN.

**3.9.** Donald Jackson, *Resurrection* (John 20:1–31). 2002. From *The Saint John's Bible*. Gouache and ink on vellum, page measures 15¾ x 23½ in. Saint John's University, Collegeville, MN.

**3.10.** Donald Jackson, detail from *Set Me As a Seal* (Song 8:6–7), Donald Jackson, *Set Me as a Seal, Scribe*: Sally Mae Joseph; Hebrew Script: Izzy Pludwinski. 2006. From *The Saint John's Bible*. Gouache and ink on vellum, page measures 15¾ x 23½ in. Saint John's University, Collegeville, MN.

**4.1.** Scarsellino, *Christ and Saint Peter at the Sea of Galilee*, ca. 1585–1590. Oil on canvas. 27¼ x 45¾ in. Credit Line: Harvard Art Museums/Fogg Museum, Bequest of Grenville L. Winthrop.

**4.2.** Scarsellino, *Noli Me Tangere*, ca. 1586. Oil on canvas, 74.5 x 93.5 cm. 1938E477. Photo: Franck Raux. Musee Magnin, Dijon, France. Photo Credit: © RMN-Grand Palais / Art Resource, NY.

**4.3.** Andrea di Bonaiuto, Vault. *Pendentive with Saint Peter's Boat*. Fresco (postrestoration 2003–2004). Spanish Chapel, S. Maria Novella, Florence, Italy. Photo Credit: Scala / Art Resource, NY.

**4.4.** *Christ Walking on the Water*. Gold coin of the Papal State with a value of 5 ducats (verso). Time of Pope Alexander VI (1492–1503). Gold, diam. 41 mm, weight 16.75 g. Inv. 18232173. Muenzkabinett, Staatliche Museen, Berlin, Germany. Photo Credit: bpk Bildagentur / (Muenzkabinett, Staatliche Museen, Berlin, Germany) / (Lutz Jürgen Lübke) / Art Resource, NY.

**4.5.** Albrecht Dürer, *Noli me tangere*. From the *Illustrated Bartsch*. Photo Credit: ARTSTOR. https://library-artstor-org.ezproxy.baylor.edu/asset/BARTSCH_6160090.

**4.6.** Benvenuto Tisi da Garofalo, *Noli Me Tangere*, ca. 1525. Oil on Canvas. Kunsthistorisches Museum Wien. Photo Credit: ARTSTOR. https://library-artstor-org.ezproxy.baylor.edu/asset/ARTSTOR_103_41822000570380.

**4.7.** Correggio, *Noli Me Tangere*, ca. 1525. Oil on panel transferred to canvas. 130 x 103 cm. Museo del Prado. Public Domain: https://www.wikiart.org/en/correggio/noli-me-tangere-1.
**4.8.** Alonso Cano, *Noli Me Tangere*, ca. 1640. Oil on canvas. 109.5 x 141.5 cm. Museum of Fine Arts, Budapest, Hungary. Public Domain: https://www.wikiart.org/en/alonzo-cano/noli-me-tangere.
**4.9.** Titian, *Noli Me Tangere*, ca. 1514. Oil on canvas.110.5 x 91.9 cm. National Gallery, London. Public Domain: https://www.wikiart.org/en/titian/do-not-touch-me-1512.
**5.1.** Bernardino Luini, *The Executioner Presenting Herodias with the Head of John the Baptist*, 1527. Oil on panel, 51 x 58 cm. Galleria degli Uffizi, Florence / Bridgeman Images. © 2019 Ministero dei Beni e delle AMinistero dei Beni e delle Attività Culturali e del Turismo—Gallerie degli Uffizi.
**5.2.** Bernardino Luini, *Salome with the Head of St. John the Baptist*. Oil on canvas, 62 x 55 cm. Musée du Louvre, Paris / Peter Willi / Bridgeman Images. © Musée du Louvre.
**5.3.** Bernardino Luini, *Salome Receiving the Head of the Baptist*, 1501–1515. Oil on canvas, 62 x 78 cm. Museo Nacional del Prado, Madrid. © Photographic Archive Museo Nacional del Prado.
**5.4.** Bernardino Luini, *Salome with the Head of Saint John the Baptist*, 1515–1525. Oil on panel, 62.23 x 51.43 cm. Museum of Fine Arts, Boston. Gift of Mrs. W. Scott Fitz. 21.2287. Photograph © 2019 Museum of Fine Arts, Boston.
**5.5.** Bernardino Luini, *Salome with the Head of Saint John the Baptist*, 1515–1525. Oil on panel, 62.23 x 51.43 cm. Museum of Fine Arts, Boston. Gift of Mrs. W. Scott Fitz. 21.2287. Photograph © 2019 Museum of Fine Arts, Boston. Detail.
**5.6.** Bernardino Luini, *Salome Receiving the Head of the Baptist*, 1501–1515. Oil on canvas, 62 x 78 cm. Museo Nacional del Prado, Madrid. © Photographic Archive Museo Nacional del Prado. Detail.
**5.7.** Bernardino Luini, *Salome with the Head of John the Baptist*, ca. 1525–1530. Oil on panel, 55.7 x 42.5 cm. Kunsthistorisches Museum, Vienna / Bridgeman Images. © KHM-Museumsverband.
**5.8.** Bernardino Luini, *The Conversion of the Magdalene*, ca. 1520. Oil on panel, 64.7 x 82.5 cm. San Diego Museum of Art, San Diego. Gift of Anne R. and Amy Putnam in memory of their sister, Irene / Bridgeman Images. © 2019 The San Diego Museum of Art.
**6.1.** Jacopo Bassano (Jacopo da Ponte), *The Parable of the Sower*, ca. 1560.

Oil on canvas. 139 x 129 cm. Museo Nacional Thyssen-Bornemisza, Madrid. Photo © Museo Nacional Thyssen-Bornemisza, Madrid.
**6.2.** Jean-François Millet, *The Sower*, 1850. Oil on canvas. 101.6 x 82.6 cm. Gift of Quincy Adams Shaw through Quincy Adams Shaw Jr. and Mrs Marian Shaw Haughton. Museum of Fine Arts, Boston. Photograph © 2021. Museum of Fine Arts, Boston.
**6.3.** Sir John Everett Millais (1829–1896), *The Sower* from illustrations to *The Parables of Our Lord*, engraved by the Dalziel Brothers. 1864. Wood engraving on paper. 140 x 108 mm. Tate, London. Photo © Tate.
**6.4.** Vincent van Gogh (1853–1890), *The Sower*, 1888. Oil on canvas. 64.2 x 80.3 cm. Kröller-Müller Museum, Otterlo, the Netherlands. Photograph © Kröller-Müller Museum, Otterlo, the Netherlands.
**6.5.** Oscar Roty, Five francs. Copper-Nickel. 29 x 2.09 mm. Private collection. Photograph © Christine Joynes.
**6.6.** Irish commemorative stamps. Centenary of the death of Thomas Davis. 1945. Ink on paper. 20 x 23 mm. Private collection. Photograph © Christine Joynes.
**7.1.** James Tissot, *The Parable of the Prodigal Son, No. II: In Foreign Climes. L'enfant prodigue: En pays étranger*. The Parable of the Prodigal Son series, 1882. Etching on laid paper; second state of two. 20 3/16 x 24 13/16 in. The Metropolitan Museum of Art, New York, NY. Photo Credit: The Elisha Whittelsey Collection, The Elisha Whittelsey Fund, 1968.
**7.2.** Albrecht Dürer, *The Prodigal Son amongst the Pigs*, 1496. Engraving, 9 3/4 x 3 15/16 in. National Gallery of Art, Washington, DC.
**7.3.** Rembrandt, *The Return of the Prodigal Son*, 1636. Etching, 6 1/4 x 5 1/2 in. Rembrandt House Museum, Amsterdam. Photograph by David B. Gowler.
**7.4.** Rembrandt, *The Return of the Prodigal Son* (detail), 1636. Etching, 6 1/4 x 5 1/2 in. Rembrandt House Museum, Amsterdam. Photograph by David B. Gowler.
**7.5.** Thomas Hart Benton, *Prodigal Son*, 1939. Lithograph, 10 1/8 x 13 1/4 in. Ackland Art Museum, The University of North Carolina at Chapel Hill. © 2019 T.H. and R.P. Benton Testamentary Trusts / UMB Bank Trustee / Licensed by VAGA at Artists Rights Society (ARS), NY.
**7.6.** Thomas Hart Benton, *The Departure of the Joads*, 1939. Lithograph, 12 7/8 in x 18 1/2 in. San Diego Museum of Art. © 2019 T.H. and R.P. Benton Testamentary Trusts / UMB Bank Trustee / Licensed by VAGA at Artists Rights Society (ARS), NY.

**8.1.** Fresco from the House of Chaste Lovers (IX.12.6), triclinium, west wall, ca. 35–45 CE, 63.5 x 74 cm. Pompeii. Photo: © Scala/ Art Resource, NY.

**8.2.** Fresco from Pompeii, mid-first century C.E., 44 x 48 cm. Naples, Museo Archeologico Nazionale 9015. Photo: © Erich Lessing/ Art Resource, NY.

**8.3.** Terracotta red-figure kylix, ca. 480 BCE, signed by Hieron, attributed to Makron, height 13.8 cm., diameter 33.2 cm. Metropolitan Museum of Art, New York.

**8.4.** Terracotta red-figure kylix, ca. 480 BCE, signed by Hieron, attributed to Makron, height 13.8 cm., diameter 33.2 cm. Metropolitan Museum of Art, New York.

**8.5.** *Opora, Agros, and Oinos at Dinner*, Syria (present-day Turkey), third century. Stone, glass, and lime mortar, 94½ x 124½ x 2½ in. (240 x 316.2 x 6.4 cm). The Baltimore Museum of Art: Antioch Subscription Fund, BMA 1937.127. Photograph by Mitro Hood.

**8.6.** Fresco on the north wall of the Tomb of the Diver. Ancient Greek, ca. 480–470 BCE, 195.5 x 79.5 cm. Museo Archeologico Nazionale, Paestum, Italy. Photo: © Vanni Archive/ Art Resource, NY.

**8.7.** Fresco on the south wall of the Tomb of the Diver. Ancient Greek, ca. 480–470 BCE, 193 x 79.2 cm. Museo Archeologico Nazionale, Paestum, Italy. Photo: © Vanni Archive/ Art Resource, NY.

**9.1.** Grant Wood, *Dinner for Threshers*, 1934. Oil on beaverboard, 20 x 80 in. Fine Arts Museums of San Francisco, © Figge Art Museum, successors to the Estate of Nan Wood Graham/Licensed by VAGA, New York, NY.

**9.2.** Johann Gottfried Saiter, after Paolo Caliari, called Veronese, *Marriage Feast at Cana*, seventeenth century. Engraving, 21 3/4 x 21 7/8 in. Harvard Art Museums.

**9.3.** Velázquez, *The Supper at Emmaus*, 1622–1623. Oil on canvas, 48 1/2 x 52 1/4 in., Metropolitan Museum of Art.

**9.4.** Leonardo da Vinci, *Last Supper* [with perspective lines], ca. 1495–1498. Oil on plaster, 15 ft 1 in x 29 ft. Santa Maria della Grazie, Milan. Perspective added by author.

**9.5.** Grant Wood, *Dinner for Threshers* [with perspective lines], 1934. Oil on beaverboard, 20 x 80 in. Fine Arts Museums of San Francisco. Perspective added by author.

**10.1.** Albrecht Dürer, *St. John Devouring the Book*, ca. 1498. Woodcut, 15 1/2 x 11 5/16 in. Metropolitan Museum of Art, New York, 40.139.6(10), Gift of Mrs. Felix M. Warburg, 1940.

**10.2.** Abingdon Apocalypse, *John Takes the Book* (ca. 1270–1275). Colors with gold on parchment; folio size 13 x 8 in. British Library, London, Add. MS 42555, fol. 27v. © The British Library Board.
**10.3.** Abingdon Apocalypse, *Massacre of the Innocents and Flight into Egypt*, ca. 1270–1275. Colors with gold on parchment; folio size 13 x 8 in. British Library, London, Add. MS 42555, fol. 28r. © The British Library Board.
**10.4.** Getty Apocalypse, *The Mighty Angel and John Forbidden to Write*, ca. 1255–1260. Tempera colors, gold leaf, colored washes, pen and ink on parchment; 12 9/16 x 8 7/8 in. Getty Museum, Malibu, MS Ludwig III.1, fol. 15. Photo Credit: Digital image courtesy of the Getty's Open Content Program.
**10.5.** Cloisters Apocalypse, *The Angel with the Book*, ca. 1330. Tempera, gold, silver, and ink on parchment; folio size 12 1/8 x 9 1/16 in. The Cloisters, Metropolitan Museum of Art, New York, 68.174, fol. 16r.
**10.6.** Jean Duvet, *The Angel Gives Saint John the Book to Eat*, 1561. Copper engraving, 15.3 x 20.9 in. Bibliothèque Nationale, Paris. Photo Credit: INTERFOTO/ Alamy Stock Photo.
**10.7.** William Blake, *The Angel of the Revelation* (ca. 1803–1805). Watercolor, pen and black ink, over traces of graphite, 15 7/16 x 10 1/4 in. Metropolitan Museum of Art, New York, Rogers Fund, 14.81.1.
**10.8.** Benjamin West, *A Mighty Angel Standeth upon the Land and upon the Sea*, ca. 1797. Oil on paper, mounted on panel; 21 1/5 x 31 in. Location unknown. Credit: The Picture Art Collection / Alamy Stock Photo.
**10.9.** Charles Wands after John Martin, *The Angel with the Book*, ca. 1839–1844. Engraving; 6 9/16 x 7 11/16 in. Victoria and Albert Museum, London, E.724-1968, Bequeathed by Thomas Balston through Art Fund. © Victoria and Albert Museum, London.

# Abbreviations

| | |
|---|---|
| AB | Anchor Bible |
| *ABD* | *Anchor Bible Dictionary.* Edited by David Noel Freedman. 6 vols. New York: Doubleday, 1992 |
| ACT | Ancient Christian Texts |
| *AgHist* | *Agricultural History* |
| AGJU | Arbeiten zur Geschichte des antiken Judentums und des Urchristentums |
| *AICMS* | *Art Institute of Chicago Museum Studies* |
| *A.J.* | Josephus, *Antiquitates judaicae* |
| *AJA* | *American Journal of Archaeology* |
| *AL* | *Arte Lombarda* |
| *Amat.* | Plutarch, *Amatorius* |
| *AncBio* | *Ancient Biomolecules* |
| ANT | Anglo-Norman Texts |
| *Antennae* | *Antennae: The Journal of Nature in Culture* |
| *Anth* | *Anthropozoologica* |
| *ArtB* | *Art Bulletin* |
| *ArtJ* | *The Art Journal* |
| ARTS | *The Arts in Religious and Theological Studies* |
| *ASAH* | *Assaph: Studies in Art History* |
| *AU* | *The Art Union* |
| AYB | Anchor Yale Bible |
| BBC | Blackwell Bible Commentaries |
| *BCMA* | *Bulletin of the Cleveland Museum of Art* |
| BEFAR | Bibliothèque des Écoles Françaises d'Athènes et de Rome |
| *BibInt* | *Biblical Interpretation* |
| BibInt | Biblical Interpretation Series |
| *Bibl.* | Apollodorus, *Bibliotheca* |
| *B.J.* | Josephus, *Bellum judaicum* |

-xv-

| | |
|---|---|
| *BMFA* | *Bulletin of the Museum of Fine Arts* |
| BN Neérl. | Bibliothèque Nationale Neérlandica |
| BMW | The Bible in the Modern World |
| BNTC | Black's New Testament Commentaries |
| BPSC | Biblical Performance Criticism Series |
| *BRec* | *Biblical Reception* |
| *BTB* | *Biblical Theology Bulletin* |
| *CA* | *Critica d'Arte* |
| ca. | circa |
| cat. | catalog |
| *Cat.* | Cicero, *In Catalinam* |
| CC | Continental Commentary |
| CEB | Common English Bible |
| cm | centimeters |
| *Dem. ev.* | Eusebius, *Demonstratio evangelica* |
| *Dial. mar.* | Lucian, *Dialogi marini* |
| *EM* | *Elseviers Maandblad* |
| EMCVA | Early Modern Catholicism and the Visual Arts |
| *Epigr.* | Martial, *Epigrammata* |
| *ERC* | *Explorations in Renaissance Culture* |
| *Erot.* | [Demosthenes], *Eroticus* |
| ESEC | Emory Studies in Early Christianity |
| exh. cat. | exhibition catalog |
| *Exp. Apoc.* | Tyconius, *Expositio Apocalypseos* |
| FC | Fathers of the Church |
| *GBA* | *Gazette des beaux-arts* |
| *GR* | *Geographical Review* |
| GSCC | Groningen Studies in Cultural Change |
| *Hist.* | Dio Cassius, *Historiae Romanae* |
| *Hist. mon.* | Rufinus, *Historia monachorum in Aegypto* |
| *Hypatia* | *Hypatia: A Journal of Feminist Philosophy* |
| *In Apoc.* | Victorinus of Pettau, *Commentarius in Apocalypsim* |
| *Inst.* | Quintilian, *Institutio oratoria* |
| *Int* | *Interpretation: A Journal of Bible and Theology* |
| *JAAC* | *The Journal of Aesthetics and Art Criticism* |
| *JBL* | *Journal of Biblical Literature* |
| *JHistSex* | *Journal of the History of Sexuality* |
| *JLS* | *Journal of the Lepidopterists' Society* |

| | |
|---|---|
| Jos. Asen. | Joseph and Aseneth |
| *JPGMJ* | *J. Paul Getty Museum Journal* |
| *JRS* | *Journal of Roman Studies* |
| *JSNT* | *Journal for the Study of the New Testament* |
| JSOTSup | Journal for the Study of the Old Testament Supplement Series |
| *Jupp. trag.* | Lucian, *Juppiter tragoedus* |
| *JWCI* | *Journal of the Warburg and Courtauld Institutes* |
| KJV | King James Version |
| *LS* | *Libyan Studies* |
| m. | Mishnah |
| *Metam.* | Ovid, *Metamorphoses* |
| *MFAB* | *Museum of Fine Arts Bulletin* |
| MIB | Masterpieces of the Illustrated Book |
| *MJBK* | *Münchner Jahrbuch der bildenden Kunst* |
| MM | Museum Monograph |
| *MMJ* | *Metropolitan Museum Journal* |
| MS BL 42555 | Manuscript 42555. British Library, London |
| MS BL 17333 | Manuscript 17333. British Library, London |
| MS BNF lat. 14410 | Manuscript lat. 14410. Bibliothèque Nationale, Paris |
| MS Lambeth Pal. 209 | Manuscript 209. Lambeth Palace, Liverpool |
| MS Ludwig III.1 | Manuscript Ludwig III.1. Getty Museum, Malibu |
| MS MMA | Manuscript 68.174. Metropolitan Museum of Art, New York |
| MS UL Mm.5.31 | Manuscript Mm.5.31. Cambridge University Library, Cambridge |
| *NHR* | *New Hibernia Review* |
| NICOT | New International Commentary on the Old Testament |
| NIV | New International Version |
| NJB | New Jerusalem Bible |
| *NLT* | *New Literary Theory* |
| *Noct. att.* | Aulus Gellius, *Noctes atticae* |
| NovTSup | Supplements to Novum Testamentum |
| *NP* | *The New Path* |
| NRSV | New Revised Standard Version |
| *NTS* | *New Testament Studies* |
| *OH* | *Oud Holland* |

| | |
|---|---|
| OTL | Old Testament Library |
| OTM | Oxford Theological Monographs |
| par(r). | parallel(s) |
| PCC | Paul in Critical Contexts |
| *PCQ* | *Print Collector's Quarterly* |
| PL | Patrologia Latina [= *Patrologia Cursus Completus*: Series Latina]. Edited by Jacques-Paul Migne. 217 vols. Paris, 1844–1864 |
| *PP* | *Pastoral Psychology* |
| *PRQ* | *Political Research Quarterly* |
| *PRSt* | *Perspectives in Religious Studies* |
| PSEMIF | Proteus: Studies in Early Modern Identity Formation |
| Ps.-Mt. | Gospel of Pseudo-Matthew |
| *RelArts* | *Religion and the Arts* |
| *Rhet.* | Aristotle, *Rhetorica* |
| *RSP* | *Rivista di studi pompeiani* |
| *Sat.* | Juvenal, *Satirae* |
| SBLSP | Society of Biblical Literature Seminar Papers |
| ser. | series |
| *SF* | *Social Forces* |
| SFG | Spanische Forschungen der Görresgesellschaft |
| SHA | Studies in the History of Art |
| *SHA* | *Studies in the History of Art* |
| SPP | Studies in Prints and Printmaking |
| StAM | Studies in Ancient Medicine |
| *Subl.* | Longinus, *De sublimitate* |
| *Symp.* | Plato, *Symposium* |
| THR | Travaux d'Humanisme et Renaissance |
| *Tim.* | Lucian, *Timon* |
| *ULC* | *Upper & Lower Case: The International Journal of Typographics* |
| UTH | UBS Technical Helps |
| *Vit. phil.* | Diogenes Laertius, *Vitae philosophorum* |
| *Vit. soph.* | Eunapius, *Vitae sophistarum* |
| VTSup | Supplements to Vetus Testamentum |
| *W86th* | *West 86th: A Journal of Decorative Arts, Design History, and Material Culture* |
| WestBC | Westminster Bible Companion |

| | |
|---|---|
| *WI* | *Word & Image* |
| WUNT | Wissenschaftliche Untersuchungen zum Neuen Testament |
| Yad. | Yadayim |

# Introduction

## HEIDI J. HORNIK, IAN BOXALL, AND BOBBI DYKEMA

While Jews and Christians have long been considered "people of the book," in our highly literate contemporary world this has often been assumed to mean primarily or even exclusively "people of the *written* book." Yet at least as early as the sixth century, with the Rabbula Gospels, and long before that in terms of wall paintings and material objects, Christians in particular have been at least as much people of the image. From first-century Palestine to global Christianity today, the sacred stories, hymns, poems, and teachings have been interpreted and shared in images as much as in text. In times and places where the majority of the populace was textually illiterate, images on walls, in codices and books, and in objects for liturgical and home use have been a key part of conveying the scriptural story.

Yet until recent decades, it was not at all uncommon for the academic disciplines of biblical studies and art history to be altogether separate from each other. It is increasingly gratifying to see biblical scholars learning the language and skills of visual exegesis and tracing the reception of biblical accounts through images, as well as art historians delving more deeply into the biblical and theological worlds of the images they study. In all cases, scholars are understanding that depictions of biblical texts are not merely illustrations but are themselves visual exegeses, offering commentary on, interpretation of, and added detail to the biblical text. This trend is reflected in the professional academic societies of both disciplines, but the Society of Biblical Literature has provided the strongest, and most fruitfully consistent, forum through the Bible and Visual Art program unit, begun in 2001. This volume reflects select contributions presented in recent sessions of the Society of Biblical Literature Bible and Visual Art program unit. As such, they represent the scholarly work of both art historians and biblical scholars, brought together to aid collaboration and dialogue between these two disciplines. Academic interpretive approaches such as sexuality and gender, reception history, visual exegesis, and intertextual relationships are explored, all maintaining an equal footing for both the image and the text.

Visual depictions allow a very different reading of a textual story, especially in their ability to emphasize particular moments or figures and to add layers of compelling detail through the use of color, light and shadow, composition, and scale. It is through the visual and not the textual record, for example, that we learn that Paul's encounter with a blinding light on the road to Damascus caused the apostle to fall off his horse; there is no horse in the textual account. Such details add life and color to the often barebones structure of biblical narrative, creating imaginative reconstructions of biblical people, places, and events. Many of these details become part of the tradition that surrounds the narrative for future generations of artists, both literary and visual.

As one of the first volumes in the Bible and Its Reception series of SBL Press, this volume must, first and foremost, attend to the way in which artists themselves have actualized the text in the production of visual images. This part of the exercise requires that we frequently examine a work of art in stylistic, historical, and iconographical terms. Erwin Panofsky, in his instrumental essay "Iconography and Iconology: An Introduction to the Study of Renaissance Art," first published in 1939 and still available in his *Meaning in the Visual Arts*, also significantly contributes to our methodological stream. Panofsky allows that "synthetic intuition [a sense of the meaning of the whole picture] may be better developed in a talented layman than in an erudite scholar."[1] Yet he warns against pure intuition because a work of art is a symptom of "'something else' which expresses itself in a countless variety of other symptoms, and we interpret its compositional and iconographical features as more evidence of that 'something else.'" Panofsky calls it "intrinsic meaning or content." Intrinsic meaning is "apprehended by ascertaining those underlying principles which reveal the basic attitude of a nation, a period, a class, a religious or philosophical persuasion unconsciously by one personality [a painter, for instance] and condensed into one work." Intrinsic meaning, therefore, will inform both the "compositional and stylistic methods" and "iconographical sig-

---

1. Erwin Panofsky, "Iconography and Iconology: An Introduction to the Study of Renaissance Art," in *Meaning in the Visual Arts* (Chicago: University of Chicago Press, 1955), 38.

nificance" of a painting.[2] The authors represented here tread down this challenging path to differing degree in order to situate each work of art in its cultural, political, and theological context and to attempt an evaluation of its intrinsic meaning.

John Shearman, an art historian, focuses the problem quite clearly: "It goes without saying, I would have thought, that we cannot step right outside our time, avoiding, as it were, all contamination by contemporary ideologies and intervening histories." Nevertheless, we also agree with Shearman's conclusion:

> Such inevitable imperfection ought not to be allowed to discourage the exercise of the historical imagination. In the same way it goes without saying that we will not reconstruct entirely correctly, but it is a sign of an unreflexive lack of realism to suppose that because we will not get it entirely right we had better give up and do something else not subject to error.[3]

In this first move of reception history, namely, to understand the way the artist has actualized or concretized the biblical text, we have been greatly assisted by another art historian, Paolo Berdini. Berdini thinks of the interpretation of the text as a "trajectory of visualization," which he labels "visual exegesis." In Berdini's words:

> The painter reads the text and translates his scriptural reading into a problem in representation, to which he offers a solution—the image. In that image the beholder acknowledges, not the text in the abstract, but the painter's reading of the text so that the effect the image has on the beholder is a function of what the painter wants the beholder to experience in the text. This is the trajectory of visualization, and the effect of the text through the image is a form of exegesis. Painting is not the simple visualization of the narrative of the text but an expansion of that text, subject to discursive strategies of various kinds.[4]

This volume offers a banquet of visual exegeses not only for biblical scholars, theologians, and art historians but also for working pastors and

---

2. Panofsky, "Iconography and Iconology," 30–31.

3. John Shearman, *Only Connect ... Art and the Spectator in the Italian Renaissance* (Princeton: Princeton University Press, 1992), 4–5.

4. Paolo Berdini, *The Religious Art of Jacopo Bassano: Painting as Visual Exegesis* (Cambridge: Cambridge University Press, 1997), 35.

armchair exegetes, as well as art-museum aficionados and those entranced by beauty in human artistic creation. The essays cover a wide range of biblical passages as well as artists and art mediums. The biblical sources are found in the Hebrew Bible and the New Testament ranging from the story of David and Bathsheba to the strange accounts in Revelation. The artistic mediums include painting, pottery, coins, and various works on paper including prints and codex illumination. Artists considered range in time and place from ancient Greece to the present day, through medieval France, Renaissance Italy, and the Dutch Golden Age, to the twentieth-century United States. Some scholars begin with an examination of various instantiations of depicting a particular biblical text, exploring their similarities and differences to shed light on how these accounts were understood and interpreted at particular places and moments in time. Several authors selected a particular work of art, not always overtly biblical in theme, as their starting point and explored the visual references to the biblical text. Still others have examined a biblical narrative in the context of the period and culture in which it was created to shed more light on the particulars of the staging and relationships within a single biblical episode. Postmodern art that problematizes both biblical accounts and the visual reception history is examined in interesting and provocative ways by several authors.

The essays proceed broadly in the order in which the respective biblical accounts treated appear in canonical Scripture. While each essay evidences particular scholarly expertise, the typical biblical exegete, theologian, or art enthusiast will find these essays accessible and approachable.

Yohana A. Junker's chapter surveys the visual tradition of portraying Bathsheba, wife of Uriah the Hittite and subsequently of King David (2 Sam 11; 1 Kgs 1–2). Junker critiques the dominant presentation of Bathsheba as seductress, an interpretation implicated in a patriarchal power dynamic that reduces Bathsheba's womanhood to fetishized erotic spectacle. She then considers how Marc Chagall's *David and Bathsheba* (1956) and *Bathsheba* (1962) mark a break in the art-historical tradition, reconfiguring Bathsheba's identity. The essay concludes with consideration of contemporary Black women artists Lorna Simpson, Carrie Mae Weems, and Lorraine O'Grady, whose oeuvres, juxtaposed with the Bathsheba narrative, confront the violence of the Eurocentric and heteropatriarchal gaze, and invite the viewer to complicate ways of reading Bathsheba's story.

Two contributors, one an art historian, the other a biblical scholar, explore the rich possibilities in visualizing the Song of Songs (Canticle of Canticles). While the Song forms part of the Hebrew Bible, it also functions as a transition to the New Testament, given the ancient Christian tendency of treating the book as an allegory of Christ and the church, or the Virgin Mary, or the human soul.

James Clifton's contribution focuses on the *Florilegium*, created in Antwerp around 1587–1589 by Adriaen Collaert and published by Philips Galle. The *Florilegium* consists of a series of twenty-four numbered engravings: a title plate, a scene of the Sponsus and Sponsa of the Song of Songs (Canticle of Canticles) in front of a garden, a bouquet of flowers in a vase, and twenty-one plates of various flowers with stems and leaves. The plate of the Sponsus and Sponsa, with its quotation of passages from chapters 2 and 5 of the Canticle, which suggests a different, though potentially overlapping, audience for the *Florilegium*, has been neglected. Clifton examines readings of the Canticle and images derived from it as profound allegories of the transformation of the soul through Christ and of the union of the soul with Christ, and argues that the *Florilegium* (including the floral plates) served devotional and meditative functions for some viewers. Generated in the lively mix of artists, scientists, and theologians of Antwerp's publishing world, the *Florilegium*, he proposes, is a hybrid work of art, science, and faith, in which mutually enhancing Scripture and botany are marshaled together to appeal to diverse viewers in a broad market.

Jonathan Homrighausen's essay on the same biblical book explores the complex intertextual relationships in the visual exegesis of the Song of Songs present in the *Saint John's Bible*, a modern version of the medieval illuminated manuscript tradition completed in 2011. Its treatment of the Song of Songs connects it most closely with temple symbolism and with Jesus's relationship with his disciples. Homrighausen shows how, in linking the Song with the temple, the *Saint John's Bible* draws a parallel between the intimacy of God's presence in the temple and the intimacy of the lovers in the Song. The Song's association with Jesus alludes to Jesus's encounter with Mary Magdalene in John 20:11–18 and suggests medieval Western liturgical traditions depicting the female beloved in the Song as the Virgin Mary, crying out for her son at the foot of the cross. In turn, this liturgical, canonical, and christological visual exegesis of the Song provokes the reader (or viewer, or pray-er) to read imaginatively, like their medieval forebears, constructing possible new meanings in the process. Homrighausen ably demonstrates the value, when considering the meaning(s) of this biblical book, of engaging its visual reception as a discussion partner.

Unsurprisingly given their narrative genre, the gospels have provided rich subject matter for artists across the centuries. Gospel texts are therefore well represented in this volume. Heidi J. Hornik examines two complementary narratives through the lens of the same artist, Ippolito Scarsella (1550–1620), commonly known as Scarsellino. Scarsellino was a Ferrarese artist who produced post-Trent religious paintings in the Mannerist style. He was considered among the Reformers in late sixteenth-century Italy, and his theological iconography anticipates the Baroque style of the next century. His two works in question, *Christ and Saint Peter at the Sea of Galilee* (Harvard Art Museums) and *Noli Me Tangere* (Musée Magnin, Dijon), focus on Christ's encounter with two gospel characters considered models for the penitent sinner in the post-Tridentine church: Peter (Matt 14:28–31) and Mary Magdalene (John 20:11–18). Hornik proposes that the writings of theological writer Cornelius à Lapide (1567–1637), most notably his *Great Commentary*, which draws heavily on the work of earlier commentators, serve as a valuable tool for interpreting these two penitent saints and the biblical narratives illustrated here. The dialogue between the two—Lapide's commentary and Scarsellino's images—richly illuminates these two vivid gospel narratives, one that encourages physical touch, the other eschewing it.

A gospel character is also the subject of the essay by Ela Nuțu. Nuțu examines visual interpretations of Salome, daughter of Herodias (Matt 14:1–12; Mark 6:14–29), regarded in popular perception as the epitome of the femme fatale, due not least to her portrayal in fin-de-siècle Decadent art. Such a view focuses on one aspect of a gospel text that is relatively silent about the girl's character and motives: her dance before Herod. In redressing the balance, Nuțu explores alternative depictions of Herodias's daughter, away from the dance, by Italian Renaissance artist Bernardino Luini (ca. 1480–1533). Nuțu argues compellingly, against some other interpreters, that Luini sets out to portray Salome not as a seductress, but as sweet and compliant, her gaze vacant. In his Vienna *Salome*, she is more akin to his Magdalene, furtive and impish, betraying the tainted innocence of a child on the precipice of adulthood, or, in Nuțu's words, "a spark of individuality."

The next two essays consider narratives within narratives, those vivid parabolic stories, so central to the teaching of Jesus, embedded in the gospel story. In her contribution, Christine E. Joynes discusses visual interpretations of the parable of the sower (Mark 4:1–20 and parr.), a parable with particular appeal to artists in the modern period. The well-known nineteenth-century images of Millet (1850), Millais (1864), and van Gogh (1888) are brought into dialogue, together with Oscar Roty's 1896 image of Marianne as sower, familiar from French coinage. Joynes argues that, despite superficial appearances, the sower is frequently shown as incompetent, indicating that the images are not intended to show the actual practice of sowing. She locates the popularity of this parable in the nineteenth century against the backdrop of social and political events and movements, and debates about the relationship between faith and reason and the historicity of the gospels. In doing so, she reflects on the dynamic relationship between text, image, and artist's context.

David B. Gowler's contribution concentrates on the subversive depiction of the prodigal son (Luke 15:11–32) by American artist Thomas Hart Benton (1889–1975). Benton's is an unusual visual interpretation of the parable, portraying the prodigal's return home without the joyful reconciliation explicit in the gospel text. Benton's prodigal has waited too long to return home; his father is long dead, the family house is in ruins, and bones are all that remain of the fatted calf. The possibility that Benton's image is autobiographical is explored, together with other reasons for his shockingly provocative interpretation of this parable's ending.

Though this volume prioritizes interpretations of biblical texts by visual artists, it is important to acknowledge that visual exegesis is not confined to art history. As biblical scholars, especially rhetorical critics, increasingly acknowledge, the world out of which the texts came and which shaped what the original audiences heard was also highly visual. Hearing or reading provoked the creation of mental images. Jeff Jay's contribution addresses this important dimension of biblical interpretation, bringing John's depiction of the Beloved Disciple, reclining "in the lap" or "on the chest" of Jesus (John 13:23, 25), into dialogue with the ancient iconographic motif of lap holding. This potent image of romantic, even erotic, love is part of the rich iconography of the banquet in ancient Mediterranean cultures, evoking images of intimacy, community, wine, the vine, and abundance. The same cluster of images coheres in John's Last Supper discourse (especially John 15). The multivalency of the image is explored in order to illuminate John's subversion of luxury, wealth, and prestige in favor of a discipleship of service and anticipated suffering, as well as the unique role of the Beloved Disciple in communicating his intimate knowledge of Christ's life and teaching.

The Last Supper, albeit in its more conventional Synoptic form (Matt 26:20–30; Mark 14:17–26; Luke 22:14–38), also appears in the essay by Meredith Munson. The precise connection to the gospel narrative, however, may not be immediately obvious. Her subject is *Dinner for Threshers* (1934; de Young Museum, San Francisco), by American artist Grant Wood. This decidedly odd depiction of the American Midwest is explored as a carefully encoded visual text of this artist's personal memory, as well as emblematic of a broader cultural memory, representative of an earlier time in American history viewed from the hardships of the Great Depression. Its resemblance to the predella of a triptych altarpiece, and its compositional arrangement, mirrors traditional visualizations of the Last Supper. This chapter moves beyond obvious similarities to explore Wood's appropriation of earlier models for his painting of dinner in rural America.

At certain periods in the history of Christian art, the book of Revelation has vied with the gospels for the honor of being the most visualized biblical text. The final contribution, by Ian Boxall, focuses on John of Patmos's vision of the mighty angel with the little scroll (Rev 10), a complex and ambiguous figure often identified by patristic and medieval commentators as Christ himself. Boxall compares a number of visual receptions of this passage, from different periods and cultural contexts, to illustrate both the challenges and the possibilities of visual exegesis. On the one hand, Albrecht Dürer's uncharacteristically stilted image of the angel in his *Apocalypsis cum figuris* (1498) reveals how even visual artists can struggle to present John's description effectively. By contrast, Jean Duvet's engraving published in 1561 and John Martin's 1837 *The Angel with the Book* explore with varying degrees of subtlety the nature of angelic vision and of John's inspiration. Similar exegetical subtlety, Boxall argues, can be detected in the illuminations of the passage in the Anglo-Norman Abingdon, Getty, and Cloisters Apocalypses, as well as William Blake's *The Angel of the Revelation* (ca. 1803–1805), the latter offering a novel interpretation of the seven thunders (Rev 10:3–4).

Appropriately for a book on the Bible and visual art, this volume is well illustrated. In each of the chapters, the primary work of art and the supporting images are illustrated in color. This enhances the accuracy of our object-oriented discussion. As the Bible and Visual Art program unit has contributed to the academic interdisciplinary discussion annually at the Society of Biblical Literature, it is hoped that this volume will showcase this contribution and provoke further scholarly publications uniting biblical studies and art history. The reader is additionally encouraged to seek out these works of art in situ and consider them anew in the light of these essays, as well as to consider anew the biblical passages with which they are in dynamic conversation.

Finally, we wish to thank Rhonda Burnette-Bletsch, Nicole Tilford, and Bob Buller at SBL Press for the fine production of this volume. We appreciate the thorough indexing done by Dr. John M. Duncan. The support of various resources from the College of Arts & Sciences' Associate Dean Kimberly Kellison and Dean Lee Nordt as well as the Department of Art & Art History, Baylor University, was critical to the completion of this volume.

## Works Cited

Berdini, Paolo. *The Religious Art of Jacopo Bassano: Painting as Visual Exegesis*. Cambridge: Cambridge University Press, 1997.

Panofsky, Erwin. "Iconography and Iconology: An Introduction to the Study of Renaissance Art." Pages 26–54 in *Meaning in the Visual Arts*. Chicago: University of Chicago Press, 1955.

Shearman, John. *Only Connect … Art and the Spectator in the Italian Renaissance*. Princeton: Princeton University Press, 1992.

# 1
# Unsettling the Gaze:
# Bathsheba beyond Verse and Image

YOHANA A. JUNKER

The visual arts have been—among a great number of other things—a means of understanding not only how humans make sense of the world by looking, but also how we frame such looking through the gaze. bell hooks reminds us that not every human inherently possesses the right to the gaze. Enslaved peoples, she writes, were punished for simply looking.[1] To cast one's eyes on something is, in some ways, a manner of exerting a particular kind of power, of dominion. And to paint or shoot (via camera) that which is gazed on is to have yet another degree of control, for the exchange is not reciprocal. This chapter looks at the tradition of representing Bathsheba in painting as part of a centuries-long visual framing of the biblical character as a seductress, who is denied the right to be included in a mutual exchange of speech, to quote Judith Butler, and to exercise her right to oppositional gaze, to paraphrase hooks.[2] I argue that Bathsheba's visual tradition not only locks her inside the pictorial schema of the enticing nude or bathing woman but also perpetuates the structural violence of heteropatriarchal power.

In the course of the chapter, I briefly survey some depictions of Bathsheba within Christian art that have established her as a seductress. Employing an art-historical method, I show how these paintings participate in a cisheteropatriarchal dynamic that asserts power and exerts

---

1. bell hooks, *Reel to Real: Race, Class and Sex at the Movies* (New York: Routledge, 2006), 254.

2. Judith Butler, *Senses of the Subject* (New York: Fordham University Press, 2015), 175–77; hooks, *Reel to Real*, 253.

control, reducing her womanhood to a fetishized erotic spectacle;[3] I go on to argue that Marc Chagall's *David and Bathsheba* (1956) marks a shift away from the tradition of rendering her as a temptress and takes an important step toward unsettling the traditional dominant gaze. In the last portion of the chapter, I suggest that the oeuvre of contemporary artist Lorna Simpson, along with works by Lorraine O'Grady and Carrie Mae Weems, offers corrective lenses through which to recuperate women's subjectivity and personhood in the visual arts. As hooks proposed, these artists stare back at their audiences and call forth a change in reality.[4] By unsettling our gazes, their works demonstrate how contemporary artists have challenged cisheteropatriarchal gazes, have refused to keep women enclosed within the frames of sexual objectification, and have invited viewers to develop an ethics of viewership that renders the audience accountable for questioning its own gaze. As a part of my analysis, I will also address how re-presentations of Bathsheba have done what philosopher Nelson Goodman calls worldmaking, functioning not simply as interpretations of reality but also as *creators* of realities.[5] In some ways, this chapter is a study of what William J. T. Mitchell terms the "lives and loves of images," raising questions of what claims images and the story of Bathsheba make on us, what questions they ask and how we are to respond to them, and what desires we cast on them.[6] In weaving these cross-threads that run deep through pictorial, historical, social, and political structures, I hope to demonstrate how the visual arts have affected our reading of Bathsheba in biblical text and how, in turn, these interpretations dialogue with contemporary issues.

## From *Nuditas Virtualis* to *Nuditas Criminalis*

In the Christian tradition, artworks have taken on multiple roles—at times functioning as means of retelling Bible stories, inspiring devotion, reinforcing political power, illustrating and regulating the interpretation

---

3. For a reflection on art-historical method as working toward making the impact of an artwork on the present legible, see Donald Preziosi's essay "Art History: Making the Visible Legible," in *The Art of Art History: A Critical Anthology*, 2nd ed., ed. Donald Preziosi (Oxford: Oxford University Press, 2009), 1–11.

4. hooks, *Reel to Real*, 254.

5. Nelson Goodman, *Ways of Worldmaking* (Indianapolis: Hackett, 1978).

6. William J. T. Mitchell, *What Do Pictures Want? The Lives and Loves of Images* (Chicago: University of Chicago Press, 2005), xv.

of sacred texts and doctrines, and restructuring the cultural identity of a community, among many other purposes. To David Morgan, such use of images is inevitable, for images play a major role in the mediation of "imaginary, linguistic, intellectual, and material domains" in the construction of reality.[7] As a result, religious images play a powerful part in the shaping of memory.[8] The iconography of Bathsheba is one such example that has concentrated a number of "related but abstract ideas into one symbol or image."[9] Early depictions of her character, as Sara Koenig's latest study demonstrates, portray her as a type for the church in patristic literature, a queen mother during the medieval period, and a seductress to David and a morally eroded character during the Reformation.[10] These roles emerge from the ways in which the text of 2 Sam 11 has been interpreted over the centuries and how these analyses overlay contemporary interpretations of Bathsheba both in the pictorial and textual tradition.

The story of how David encounters and pursues Bathsheba moves rather swiftly, with an overt economy of description. The passage that has informed most visual renditions of Bathsheba is 2 Sam 11:2–5, which reads:

> It happened, late one afternoon, when David rose from his couch and was walking about on the roof of the king's house, that he saw from the roof a woman bathing; the woman was very beautiful. David sent someone to inquire about the woman. It was reported, "This is Bathsheba daughter of Eliam, the wife of Uriah the Hittite." *So David sent messengers to get her, and she came to him, and he lay with her.* (*Now she was purifying herself after her period.*) Then she returned to her house. The woman conceived; and she sent and told David, "I am pregnant." (NRSV)

Though the entire chapter has twenty-seven verses, only verse 4, which I emphasize above, describes the king's physical contact with Bathsheba as an object of his sexual desire. The reader is thus left with no account of the characters' interiority, of how being fetched and laid with (and made

---

7. David Morgan, *Visual Piety: A History and Theory of Popular Religious Images* (Berkeley: University of California Press, 1999), 9.

8. See David Morgan and Sally M. Promey, eds., *The Visual Culture of American Religions* (Berkeley: University of California Press, 2001), 10–15.

9. Robin Jensen, *The Substance of Things Seen: Art, Faith, and the Christian Community* (Grand Rapids: Eerdmans, 2004), 50.

10. Sara M. Koenig, *Bathsheba Survives* (Columbia: University of South Carolina Press, 2018), 78.

pregnant from) affected Bathsheba's life. In similar ways, the tradition of visually representing Bathsheba has tended to dilute the impact of Bathsheba's rape narrative.

How, then, are we to picture Bathsheba with the insufficient information we are given in 2 Sam 11? And how is it that, despite such limited report, she has been repeatedly reduced to a depiction of an objectified woman for at least six centuries? Koenig shares the question: "The negative interpretations of Bathsheba do not represent the text, nor the earliest translations and interpretations. So what happened in the history of interpretation to swing the pendulum towards a negative characterization of Bathsheba?"[11] One of the clues in answering these questions is found in the understanding that biblical *and* cultural interpretations have filled in the gaps of the story to such an extent that the story is overlaid with biases that obscure our sense of what actually appears in the text and what does not.[12] Contemporary women scholars interpreting this story further underscore the issue. Deryn Guest reminds us that one "cannot consider the text of Bathsheba's bathing scene without being aware of its representations in western culture; the scene is already culturally loaded with erotic undercurrents."[13] Katharine Doob Sakenfeld urges us to realize that the portrayals of Bathsheba are not necessarily supported by the biblical text.[14] Tikva Frymer-Kensky also warns us that to read Bathsheba as enticing the king is not only to read what does not appear in the text; it is also dangerously connected to a victim-blaming attitude.[15] J. Cheryl Exum highlights the interplay between text and image, which has transmuted Bathsheba into a "kind of paragon of sensuality," "dramatically reinscribing the text's voyeuristic" and hetero-patriarchal gaze at the naked female body.[16] Exum reminds her readers that Bathsheba's rape takes place on philosophical grounds:

---

11. Koenig, *Bathsheba Survives*, 164.
12. Katharine Doob Sakenfeld, *Just Wives* (Louisville: Westminster John Knox, 2003), 71.
13. Deryn Guest, "Looking Lesbian at the Bathing Bathsheba," *BibInt* 16 (2008): 238.
14. Sarah Koenig, *Isn't This Bathsheba? A Study in Characterization* (Eugene, OR: Pickwick, 2011), 163.
15. Tikva Frymer-Kensky, *Reading the Women of the Bible: A New Interpretation of Their Stories* (New York: Schocken Books, 2002), 144–45.
16. J. Cheryl Exum, ed., *Between the Text and the Canvas: The Bible and Art in Dialogue* (Sheffield: Sheffield Phoenix, 2007), 10, 27.

Bathsheba's rape is semiotic; that is to say, her violation occurs not so much *in the story* as *by means of the story*. By denying her subjectivity, the narrator violates the character he created. By portraying Bathsheba in an ambiguous light, the narrator leaves her vulnerable, not simply to assault by David but also to misappropriation by those who come after him to spy on the bathing beauty and offer their versions of, or commentary on, the story. In particular, the withholding of Bathsheba's point of view leaves her open to the charge of seduction.[17]

In order to illuminate how the interpretation of Bathsheba has gone from a virtuous to a culpable character, I will briefly delineate some important shifts in her iconography from the medieval period to the twentieth century.

Artistic representations of Bathsheba in the Christian tradition grew in numbers during the Middle Ages and were found in primarily three genres: illustrated Bibles, books of hours, and Bibles moralisées.[18] In her latest and more detailed study of this minor character, Koenig explains that Bathsheba's iconography proliferated during this period through illuminated manuscripts. One of the earliest visual appearances of Bathsheba in paint happens in *Sacra Parallela*, which can be dated to 862, where she is depicted as bathing naked.[19] Mónica Ann Walker Vadillo explains that this image "marks a starting point for the development of this type of representation."[20] It is helpful for the contemporary reader to understand, however, that nudity in these manuscripts was closely related to the Christian idea of *Nuditas Virtualis*, "a symbol of purity and innocence" rather than one pointing toward "lust, vanity, and self-indulgent sin."[21] In the Morgan Picture Bible, Koenig's research further reveals, Bathsheba's bath is conflated with sexual intercourse. In a superior quadrant, she appears as a nude bathing woman. Right below, she is depicted having sex with David. If the reader looks back at the text, it becomes clear that such depiction takes on quite an imaginative license. The biblical account only describes a woman bathing and does not mention whether she was clothed.

---

17. Exum, *Between the Text*, 30–31.
18. Koenig, *Bathsheba Survives*, 56.
19. Koenig, *Bathsheba Survives*, 58.
20. See Mónica Ann Walker Vadillo, *Bathsheba in Late Medieval French Manuscript Illumination: Innocent Object of Desire or Agent of Sin?* (Lewiston, NY: Mellen, 2008), 20, cited in Koenig, *Bathsheba Survives*, 58.
21. Koenig, *Bathsheba Survives*, 89.

Fig. 1.1. Jean Bourdichon, illuminator (French, 1457–1521), *Bathsheba Bathing*, French, 1498–1499, Tempera and gold on parchment, Leaf: 24.3 × 17 cm (9 9/16 × 6 11/16 in.), Ms. 79, recto. J. Paul Getty Museum, courtesy of the Getty Open Content Program.

## 1. UNSETTLING THE GAZE 17

In the Book of Hours of Louis XII, Bathsheba is also exposed as a nude figure who is explicitly enticing. She is placed within an open-air bathing fountain within a luscious garden, surrounded by majestic architecture in the distance. Though she has her back to David, her eyes seem to be in search of the king. The king appears to gaze at her from a distant palace façade. Her long hair obstructs David's view of her nudity. The viewer, however, has total access to her frontal nudity: from face, to chest, to lower torso, and even to her labia, which are submerged in crystal-clear water. *Bathsheba Bathing*, an illumination in the book of hours from Rouen, France, circa 1510, has the biblical character in a similar position: onlookers have full view of her frontal nudity, except for the labia, which the artist chose to have her timidly hide behind her right hand. As John Harthan has put it, the illuminated manuscripts allowed artists to "safely give their patrons a mild erotic *frisson* by portraying nudity."[22] Hans Memling's panel *Bathsheba in the Bath* (1485) is strikingly similar to both illuminations done in the same century. In Memling's painting, Bathsheba's body is almost fully visible to viewers. Her back is protected by the linen a maid places over her shoulder.

In sixteenth–seventeenth century Netherlands, painters continued to produce works that were in tune with the "erotic *frisson*" described by Harthen. Prominent artists such as Rembrandt, Willem Buytewech, and Willem Drost continued to portray her as a seductress. Though their compositions represent a dramatic change from the illuminated manuscripts of previous centuries, they continue to fill in the gaps of the narrative with artistic licenses. For example, they add elements (that do not appear in the text) such as older maids tending to the bathing woman, a letter that is purportedly from King David, and objects that construe her as a vain woman. According to Eric Jan Sluijter, the addition of objects such as ointment jars, mirrors, and maids evoke conventions of a seductive theme, conferring on her attributes of vanity and sinfulness, which "would have been considered fitting for an image of a woman who is emphatically presented as adulterous."[23] Willem Buytewech's etching titled *Bathsheba Reading King David's Letter* (1616) features a silver plate engraved with the word *VANI-*

---

22. See John Harthan, *The Book of Hours* (New York: Crowell, 1977), 34, cited in Koenig, *Bathsheba Survives*, 74.

23. Eric Jan Sluijter, "Rembrandt's Bathsheba and the Convention of a Seductive Theme," in *Rembrandt's Bathsheba Reading King David's Letter*, ed. Ann Jensen Adams (Cambridge: Cambridge University Press, 1998), 54.

*TAS*, placed next to Bathsheba's back, which may be interpreted as a warning of the dangers of carnal indulgence.[24] Bathsheba's story was also used as one of the plates in a popularized visual series on the Ten Commandments, engraved by Maarten van Heemskerck. As the reader may have guessed, Bathsheba's sexual encounter with David illustrates plate 6—the "Thou shalt not commit adultery" commandment.[25] The old crone is yet another motif introduced to her depictions in the sixteenth century. It is associated with the figure of the "old procuress," a negative stereotype of a woman invested in corrupting young women and often depicted in the company other biblical figures connected with seduction, brothel scenes, and renditions of the prodigal son's excessive "carousing," as Sluijter puts it.[26]

Rembrandt's *Bathsheba at Her Bath*, from 1654, currently at the Louvre, has been widely lauded for conveying Bathsheba in a light that moves away from such stereotypes. In this masterpiece, Bathsheba is portrayed nude and in a seated position. The spectator's gaze meets only the left side of her face, which is slightly tilted to the right. Her melancholic countenance is pensive, as though she is not responsive to her surroundings. An older maid tends to her right foot, and yet Bathsheba seems absent, unaware. Bathsheba's right forearm reposes on her right thigh, which is crossed over her left knee. At this precise juncture, Bathsheba holds a letter in her right hand, which sharply contrasts with the dark hues of the rest of the composition. The letter and her body are the *chiaro* in the *scuro* of the large canvas. Her naked breasts and abdomen are in quasi-full view to the observer. Many contemporary interpreters of Rembrandt's 1654's nude painting understand this rendition as a rupture from the tradition of framing Bathsheba as the seductress and adulteress. Some posit that this painting marks a transformation of style for the artist, who, instead of creating compositions that defined the contours of form, was invested in creating works that disclosed "the most profound and essential aspects of human beings and their actions."[27] Berys Gaut argues that a morally charged story, filled with loss, violence, mourning, and hopelessness, could only be elaborated through Rembrandt's masterful depiction,

---

24. Sluijter, "Rembrandt's Bathsheba," 53.
25. Sluijter, "Rembrandt's Bathsheba," 51.
26. Sluijter, "Rembrandt's Bathsheba," 51.
27. Alejandro Vergara, *Rembrandt: Pintor de Historias* (Madrid: Museo Nacional del Prado, 2008), 47: "lo más profundo y esencial de los seres humanos y de sus acciones."

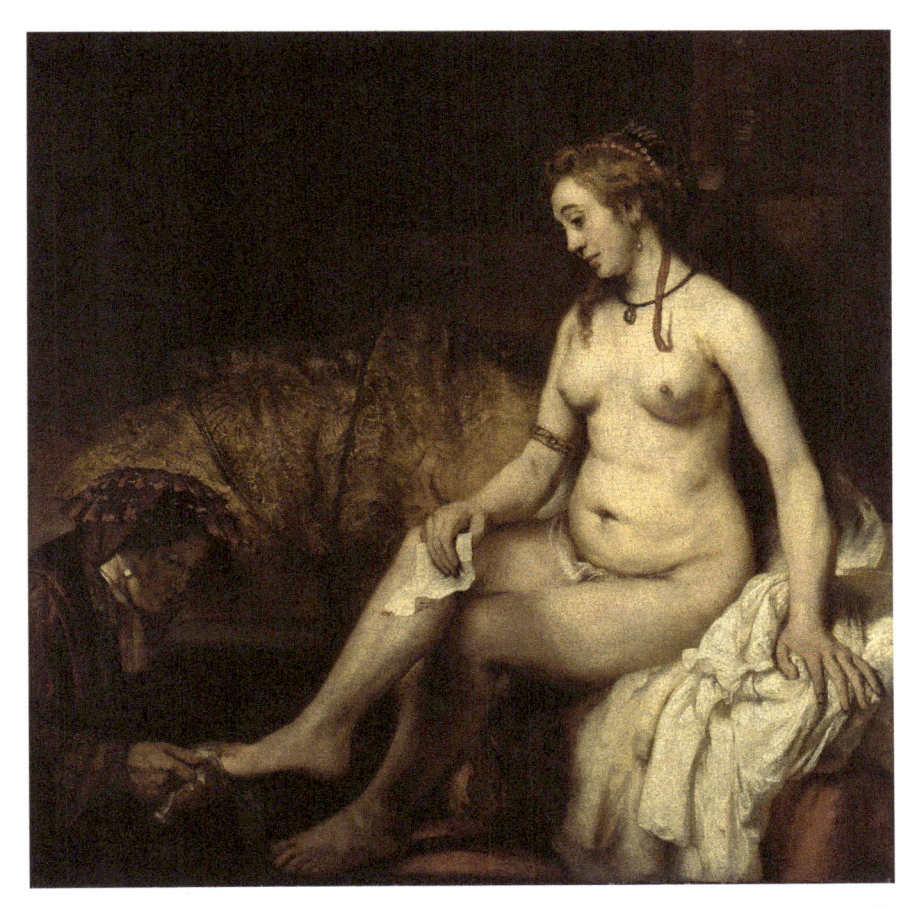

Fig. 1.2. Rembrandt Harmenszoon van Rijn (1606–1669), *Bathsheba at Her Bath*. 1654. Oil on canvas, 142 x 142 cm. Photo: Mathieu Rabeau. Musée du Louvre, Paris, France ©RMN-Grand Palais/Art Resource, NY.

which allows viewers to have a glimpse of the character's interiority.[28] Hélène Cixous decodes Rembrandt's Bathsheba as taking viewers on a journey of intimacy into "the land of the Heart," "the landscape of the interior Bible," a place of most primordial yearnings. It is as though "gone, behind her eyelids," Bathsheba in her absence and silence weighs heavy on viewers.[29]

---

28. Berys Gaut, *Art, Emotion and Ethics* (New York: Oxford University Press, 2007), 14.

29. Hélène Cixous, *Stigmata: Escaping Texts* (New York: Routledge, 1998), 5–19.

Despite these very poignant evaluations of the painting, the representation itself does not depart from the centuries-long construal of the biblical character as a sexualized and objectified woman. Our gaze still travels through the curves of her nude body, which is flanked by visual devices that have layered the biblical story with misconstructions of Bathsheba not as a victim but as a seductress. Gary Schwartz's meticulous documentary history and interpretation of this particular painting corroborates this assessment, as he explains that up until the nineteenth century "Bathsheba was nothing but a name for a complaisant woman with an irresistible body," an "emblem of sexual attraction and vanity."[30] Jean-Léon Gérôme's *Bethsabée* (1889) is a case in point. Though Bathsheba has her back to the viewers, she is still touching herself while she bathes, and both David and the audience are still watching: a most splendid painting and a most suggestive body.[31] Mieke Bal also indicates that Rembrandt's painting still participates in the interpretative tradition that has imposed on this image "a vague 'memory' that Bathsheba was responsible for her own rape."[32] Jean-Luc Nancy and Federic Ferrari agree that Rembrandt's naked, immobile Bathsheba is still silent, infantilized, and "wordless." As an "*ek-static*" figure, she is outside herself, "in a state of disorientation."[33] Completely outside her context—historical, biblical, and otherwise—she remains exposed to our gaze while being denied her right to speak.

Willem Drost (a pupil of Rembrandt's) also chose Bathsheba as the subject of one of his pieces, which has been described as his magnum opus. *Bathsheba with David's Letter*, which also dates to 1654, is part of the collection of the Musée du Louvre, where Rembrandt's painting is also housed.[34] The figures share commonalities: Bathsheba is seated and is beautifully adorned with necklace, earrings, and a headpiece. Her torso remains exposed; her hands hold David's letter. There are striking differ-

---

30. Gary Schwartz, "Though Deficient in Beauty: A Documentary History and Interpretation of Rembrandt's 1654 Painting of Bathsheba," in Adams, *Rembrandt's Bathsheba*, 192.

31. See J. Cheryl Exum's *Plotted, Shot, and Painted: Cultural Representations of Biblical Women* (Sheffield: Sheffield Academic, 2012), 34.

32. Mieke Bal, "Reading Bathsheba: From Master Codes to Misfits," in Adams, *Rembrandt's Bathsheba*, 126.

33. Jean-Luc Nancy and Federic Ferrari, *Being Nude: The Skin of Images*, trans. Anne O'Byrne and Carlie Anglemire (New York: Fordham University Press, 2014), 12.

34. Jonathan Bikker, *Willem Drost (1633–1659): A Rembrandt Pupil in Amsterdam and Venice* (New Haven: Yale University Press, 2005), 55.

Fig. 1.3. Willem Drost (ca. 1630–after 1680). *Bathsheba with David's Letter.* 1654. Oil on canvas, 103 x 87 cm. Photo: Franck Raux. Musée du Louvre, Paris, France. ©RMN-Grand Palais/ Art Resource, NY.

ences, however, that further accentuate her veneer as a seductress. Drost's Bathsheba appears half-length and wearing a white blouse that uncovers more of her body than it conceals. Her head, inclined to the left, leads the eyes of beholders right to her chest. The vivid illumination in the composition heightens the visibility of her dense, exposed left breast. Moreover, she is much closer to the viewer: her luring torso takes up the entirety of the pictorial field. Drost's painting suspends traditional ways of rendering Bathsheba as looking coyly away from David as well as any other onlooker. Here, she stares directly at her viewers. In Jonathan Bikker's analysis, Drost's departure from the pictorial tradition of his theme, during this time, was due to his proximity to sixteenth-century Venetian depictions of nobility, such as Palma Vecchio's *Courtesan*.[35] To the art historian, Drost's move speaks to his choice of visually intensifying the "qualities in Bathsheba that led King David to seduce her."[36] Her drooping eyelids suggests to viewers that Bathsheba is a willing receiver of David's actions.

That these portrayals are manifestations of enormous artistic prowess is undeniable. Yet, despite having traveled across different geographic locations and time periods, the voyeuristic invitation to gaze at her nudity remains. No painting of the biblical character thus far surveyed interrupts the one-way contact of the gaze. Though we may feel sympathetic to Bathsheba's situation, we do not turn away. As Exum argues, such normative renditions "do not permit the naked Bathsheba to leave her bath or the canvas."[37] The centuries-long tradition of placing women's bodies at the power of the male gaze suggests that there remains a recurrent need to challenge the ways the conventions of the Bathsheba type continue to etch certain biases toward the bathing biblical character. If the many Bathshebas were to exercise their right to subjectivity, what would they articulate in terms of the ways in which the gaps in the text should be filled? Would they challenge the hegemony of the white Western male perspective? Would she consent to permanently inhabiting a white nude body? These renditions of her as the nude temptress participate in an operation that not only obliterates the complexities of Bathsheba's narrative but also leaves viewers and readers without the proper apparatus to imagine the nuances of her story. Moreover, as interpreters, we fail to understand how her narrative encodes political hierarchies of power relations, conceals the violence of her rape, and dismisses the ways in which she grieved the deaths of her husband and first child. As Walter Brueggemann indicates, this is a story that stands in the threshold of "deep, aching psychology … and the most ruthless political performance."[38] Her representations should expose these tensions, not conceal them.

---

35. Bikker, *Willem Drost*, 57.
36. Bikker, *Willem Drost*, 57.
37. Exum, *Plotted, Shot, and Painted*, 43.
38. Walter Brueggemann, *First and Second Samuel* (Louisville: John Knox, 1990), 271.

Fig. 1.4. Marc Chagall (1887–1985) © ARS, NY. *David and Bathsheba*. 1956. Lithograph, 35.8 x 26.5 cm. Photo: Gérard Blot. Musée National Marc Chagall. ©RMN-Grand Palais/Art Resource, NY.

Marc Chagall's lithograph *David and Bathsheba*, which dates to 1956, may mark an essential shift in the ways Bathsheba has been historically depicted. In the composition, David and Bathsheba occupy equal surface area, and the nude bathing seductress is nowhere to be seen. Instead, both characters are placed into one conjoined head, while two images of ethereal figures hover over the two-in-one semblances. While Bathsheba looks away from the audience, David cannot escape our interrogatory gaze. Is Bathsheba signaling that portions of her story have been effaced and overlooked? Is she exercising some kind of resistance? This particular lithograph is quite distinctive from an etching by Chagall, from 1958, in which Bathsheba appears as the nude bathing woman while David enjoys full view of the scene from his rooftop. Why Chagall chose to depict the scene twice in dramatically different ways is a question for further assessment. Yet, one thing is fairly certain: the lithograph does breach the usual aesthetic distance David has enjoyed while removing Bathsheba from the position of the temptress. Her body is not exposed, and neither is her story. In a tale filled with ambiguities and conflict, the artist seems to be confronting the interplay between the dynamics of visibility and derealization, power and impotence, fixity and liberation.

Susan Sontag suggests that the exercise of looking at our looking is important when engaging with stories that are fraught with trauma and pain. Such visual narratives, she purports, must be approached with emotional freshness, ethical pertinence, and sincerity.[39] In the last portion of the chapter, I propose looking at the work of contemporary Black artists and scholars who are invested in revealing how audiences' gazes are complicit in perpetuating certain hegemonic ways of looking. In the twentieth and twenty-first centuries in the United States, Black artists such as Simpson, Weems, and O'Grady (along with scholars such as bell hooks and Wilda Gafney) have continuously challenged the cisheteropatriarchal gaze while refusing to keep women enclosed within the frames of sexual desire. hooks argues that in order for any tradition of representation of women to shift and unsettle, Black women's viewership and criticism *must* have a seat at the table.[40] Though referring to the cinematic art form, hooks contends that, in general, Black female spectators have been historically forced to develop "looking relations" within

---

39. Susan Sontag, *Regarding the Pain of Others* (New York: Farrar, Straus & Giroux, 2003), 104–13.

40. hooks, *Reel to Real*, 258.

artistic milieus that continue to erase their bodies and experiences. This present absence perpetuates a phallocentric (and white supremacist) construction of history and culture, indeed, of reality, where the category of women is not only meant to be looked at and desired but also abstracted. hooks writes, "Despite feminist critical interventions aimed at deconstructing the category 'woman' which highlights the significance of race, many feminist film critics continue to structure their discourse as though it speaks about 'women' when in actuality it speaks only about white women."[41] Inviting a further shift in the dynamic of the gaze, hooks asks viewers to develop an oppositional gaze: one that stands in resistance and disagreement with the construction of womanhood as object of a phallocentric gaze.[42] Such reading against the grain, as Annette Kuhn puts it, provides for women a resistance strategy of saying no not only to the "unsophisticated enjoyment" of culturally dominant images but, most importantly, to the "structures of power which ask us to consume them uncritically and in highly circumscribed ways."[43] Such spectatorship, as hooks puts it, goes beyond resistance to participate in a broad range of alternative looking attitudes that contest, interrogate, refuse, revise, and reclaim spaces for the construction of a radical female subjectivity.[44] In order to recuperate the position of the questioning subject, artists O'Grady and Simpson have developed works that unsettle and interrupt Western pictorial conventions around the bodies of Black women through a methodology that I see as attuned to what Gafney refers to as "the Womanist Framework."[45] That is, a methodology for looking at verse and image that asks questions about power, authority, voice, agency, inclusion, exclusion, and ethical responsibility. Taking these issues a bit further, Gafney encourages readers and viewers to ponder how contemporary experiences shape the reading of certain texts, and, in turn, notice how the formulations in the texts and images affect women today.[46]

---

41. hooks, *Reel to Real*, 264.

42. hooks, *Reel to Real*, 263.

43. Annette Kuhn, *The Power of the Image: Essays on Representation and Sexuality* (New York: Routledge, 1994), 8.

44. hooks, *Reel to Real*, 271.

45. Wilda C. Gafney, *Womanist Midrash: A Reintroduction to the Women of the Torah and the Throne* (Louisville: Westminster John Knox, 2017), 6.

46. Gafney, *Womanist Midrash*, 7–8.

## Unsettling the Gaze

What would contemporary interpretations and representations of Bathsheba that include Black women's perspectives read and look like? To Gafney, a good place to begin imagining such work is to admit that David raped Bathsheba. To the author, this is an important affirmation, for it exposes the asymmetrical power relation between David and Bathsheba. Gafney writes that though "the vocabulary of the biblical text is frustratingly ambiguous about whether the sex act between David and Bathsheba is consensual," it is highly improbable that she was in a position to refuse the order, for he holds relational, positional, and physical power over her.[47] Other questions a womanist interpretation would ask of the narrative include what kinds of experiences Bathsheba was afforded as a woman before, during, and after the assault. Did she have time to mourn her husband and child's deaths? Who was part of her support systems? Did she have a close family? How did her status of a "newly acquired" wife affect the way other women treated her in David's house? What would prove necessary for Bathsheba to live and flourish again, amid the wounds and wonders of her experience as a woman? Would she ever be able to escape the gaze that constructed her as the bathing seductress? Would she ever be able to exit the historic script in which a naked, "exceedingly beautiful woman" provoked the king?

Perhaps O'Grady's artworks *Gaze 1* and *Gaze 2* (1991) are compelling places to begin reimaging contemporary interpretations of Bathsheba. O'Grady explains that her commitment as an artist is to "*reclaim* black female subjectivity so as to 'de-haunt' *historic scripts*" and to establish agency for Black women.[48] The photomontage *Gaze 1* is of a black-skinned woman who stares into the viewer's eyes as interrogatively as defiantly. The woman is both aware and in control of her image. While regulating which parts of her body and interiority viewers will be able to access, she obstructs possible inspections for pleasure. For the artist, one of the Black woman's endeavors is to interrogate that precise cisheteropatriarchal—and white—gaze. The onlooker can only see the frontal part of her shoulder, neck, and face. No nudity, no sexual insinuation. In order to "win back

---

47. Gafney, *Womanist Midrash*, 214–15.
48. Lorraine O'Grady, "Olympia's Maid: Reclaiming Black Female Subjectivity," in *Art, Activism, and Oppositionality: Essays from Afterimage*, ed. Grant H. Kester (Durham, NC: Duke University Press, 1998), 281, emphasis added.

the position of the questioning subject," O'Grady maintains, social agency must be developed strategically. This must be done first with provocations "intense enough to lure aspects of her image from the depths to the surface of the mirror," and second to find pressure points—such as the hypersexualization of women's bodies—that call for Black women's perspective to "be reinserted into the social domain."[49]

Fig. 1.5. Lorna Simpson, *Guarded Conditions*. 1989. 18 dye diffusion color Polaroid prints, 6 frames total (3 prints in each), 21 engraved plastic plaques, 17 plastic letters, overall: 214 x 376.6 x 4.1 cm. © Lorna Simpson. Courtesy of the artist and Hauser & Wirth.

Simpson's oeuvre is one that ingeniously activates such pressure points. Her *Guarded Conditions* (1989) is composed of six large photographs with a full view of the back of a Black woman's body. Though their backs are turned to the camera, they do not entice viewers, as Gérôme's rendition

---

49. O'Grady, "Olympia's Maid," 283.

does. These identical women wear simple and loose white cotton dresses. Their crossed arms repose on their lower backs. Each figure is dissected into three horizontal planes. The inscriptions below their feet—which are made of plastic plaques used in offices—instead of displaying names, reveal the violence these women have been subjected to: "sex attacks" and "skin attacks." Simpson's work *You're Fine* (1988) also features the body of a Black woman, cloaked in a white garment, with her back to the audience. The reclining figure is chopped into four vertical planes with another set of white inscriptions: "You're fine. You're hired." Here, Simpson evidences the combined operation of white power that controls gender, race, and so much more. The shimmering golden plaques that flank the woman's image to the left and to the right allude to the kinds of scrutiny women are subjected to, which echo some of the ways Bathsheba's body has been surgically inspected over the centuries. They read: "Medical exam, blood test, reflexes, chest x-ray, eyes, ears, height, weight, Secretarial Position," and so forth. This work participates in the contemporary artistic effort of exposing the operations that have held Black bodies captive while denouncing visual culture's implication in constructing and maintaining racial and gender stereotypes and violence.

Weems's photographic series *From Here I Saw What Happened and I Cried*, for example, also exposes this violence through an installation consisting of almost thirty images of US enslaved peoples found in historical archives of universities and museums. Some of the photographs were commissioned by Louis Agassiz, a Swiss naturalist who, aided by a photographer, cataloged portraits of enslaved peoples to corroborate his theory of the racial inferiority of Africans.[50] "When we're looking at these images," Weems reports, "we're looking at the ways in which Anglo America—white America—saw itself in relationship to the black subject. I wanted to intervene in that by giving a *voice to a subject that historically has had no voice*."[51] Weems framed these photographs with added texts and portraiture frames that are meant to question our gazes. They feature phrases such as "you became a scientific profile," "a negroid type," "an anthropological debate," "descending the throne, you became foot soldier and cook," "drivers," "you became uncle Tom John & Clemmens' Jim," "For

---

50. Mary Warner Marien, *Photography: A Cultural History* (New York: Pearson, 2015), 40.

51. Carrie Mae Weems, audio interview for *MoMA 2000: Open Ends*, The Museum of Modern Art and Acoustiguide, 2000, https://tinyurl.com/SBL6703e.

your names you took hope and humble," "born with a veil you became root worker, juju mama, voodoo queen, hoodoo doctor."[52]

To art historian Nika Elder, Simpson's and Weems's work indexes and exposes the operations of stereotyping that continues to take place in the United States so unrestrainedly, revealing "all the subtle ways in which popular culture is implicated in its construction."[53] Another of Simpson's compositions, *Prefer, Refuse, Decide* (1989), a triptych of three Black women, contests these conventions and their implications for women. Simpson's figures face the camera frontally, though observers can only see their dressed torsos. Their arms repose loosely on the women's hips, except for the center panel, which interrupts the gaze. It reads "refuse" and features the woman's arms crossed and rested on her hips. Her closed fists guard her genitalia, sending waves of refusal and agency across the space. This woman is in no way "modestly" covering her genitalia as Bathsheba is in the depictions from the Rouen book of hours or Memling. She is simply saying no. Another of Simpson's works that rattles the gaze is *Waterbearer* (1986). Unlike Gérôme's hypersensual painting of a nude woman with her back to the audience, Simpson's denunciatory image features a Black woman with a loose white dress who pours water from two water jars—one metallic and one plastic. Below the image, a haunting phrase reads in all caps: "SHE SAW HIM DISAPPEAR BY THE RIVER, THEY ASKED HER TO TELL WHAT HAPPENED, ONLY TO DISCOUNT HER MEMORY." It is as though this woman (after having been violated) was asked to pour out her life in front of a jury, only to be met with denial of her narrative and experience. By interrupting the portrayals of the Black woman as an archetype of sensuality, Simpson's *Waterbearer* talks back to the viewer, implicates him in the gaze, and requires him to dismantle these centuries-long constructions of male encounter and representation of women's bodies.

If the audience were to interpret Simpson's work under the womanist framework proposed by Gafney, surely spectators would be challenged to diagnose how visual culture continues to read women's bodies as constrained by "oppressive norms of feminine beauty and behavior."[54] Though I am not arguing for the elimination of the category of the female nude

---

52. Carrie Mae Weems, "From Here I Saw What Happened and I Cried, 1995–1996, 33 Toned Prints," accessed 10 July 2020, https://tinyurl.com/SBL6703a.

53. Nika Elder, "Lorna Simpson's Fabricated Truths," *ArtJ* 77 (Spring 2018): 34.

54. Elder, "Lorna Simpson's Fabricated Truths," 36.

from art history and practice, I am inviting a reflection on the implication of such portrayals. The category of the female nude has been dramatically revised over the course of the last century, particularly in the context of the tension between passivity and agency. Until the nineteenth century, Sally O'Reilly clarifies, the female nude in art assumed a position of an idealized, mythical, biblical, or historical figure of significant stature in a particular society, and was fashioned as a symbol of beauty and sensuality, as well as a vehicle of voyeurism for white male eyes.[55] The impetus from artists such as O'Grady, Weems, and Simpson demonstrates that there are, indeed, ways of portraying women so as to confer them with subjective and agential power and visibility. The importance for contemporary audiences to examine, interrogate, and interrupt such portrayals if necessary cannot be sufficiently underscored. The recent publication *Rape Culture, Gender Violence, and Religion* exposes the complex roles that religious texts and belief systems, including visual ones, have played in perpetuating misconstructions that are closely linked to female sexualization, objectification, and victim blaming, as well as a naturalization of the aggressive cisheteropatriarchal power structures that allow for gender violence to continue to go on unobstructed.[56] Religions, the publication's many contributors assert, play a determining role in shaping worldviews of the faithful, which include attitudes toward gender. This is a fundamental conversation for a contemporary audience that in no small measure is affected by internalized gender bias, gender violence, and sexual abuse. In the wake of the #MeToo movement, which was created in 2006 by Tarana Burke to help victims of sexual abuse come forward, many women have been mobilized. As a result, accusations of sexual assault involving numerous high-profile public figures in politics and the entertainment industries continue to rise in numbers and exposure, from Roman Polanski to Clarence Thomas, Harvey Weinstein, R. Kelly, Bill Cosby, Woody Allen, Brett Kavanaugh, Brock Turner, Louis C. K., and the most recent prosecution of Brazilian religious leader João de Deus. De Deus's case has accumulated over five hundred accusations of sexual assault by female victims, all part

---

55. Sally O'Reilly, *The Body in Contemporary Art* (New York: Thames & Hudson, 2009), 17.
56. Caroline Blyth, Emily Colgan, and Katie B. Edwards, eds., *Rape Culture, Gender Violence, and Religion: Biblical Perspectives* (Cham, Switzerland: Palgrave Macmillan, 2018), 2.

of a culture in which nine out of ten victims of sexual abuse are women.[57] Transgender, genderqueer, gender-nonconforming, Black, and Indigenous women are at higher risk of suffering sexual assault in their lifetime.[58]

According to Lucinda Joy Peach, the law understands, benefits, and protects men from accusation, as the violence they perpetrate is seen as a form of male power. As Peach demonstrates, until recently, "the law considered it impossible for a husband to rape his wife, and thus did not allow prosecutions of marital rape."[59] Mark Whatley's study also affirms that the law continues to exert another form of institutional violence against women as it protects male rights and power while characterizing women as powerless and helpless, precisely the classification Bathsheba has received over the centuries.[60] Strikingly similar to Bathsheba's characterization are the studies performed as recently as the 1980s, which confirm that lawsuits have rampant victim-blaming rhetoric. The law fails to arrest, prosecute, and convict male perpetrators of sexual and domestic violence.[61] The further stereotype of women as victims who are too helpless or emotionally absent to reasonably take a course of action carries what Kathleen Ferraro calls the "cultural notion of deservedness."[62] As Peach concludes, not only does the law fail to recognize women as legitimate victims of violence and, further, implicate them in their assaults, but it also refuses to acknowledge women as subjects who could legitimately use violence in self-defense.[63] The current campaign for clemency for Cyntoia Brown is a case in point. Brown, now in her thirties, served a life sentence for having killed the man who *bought her to serve as a sex slave* when she was sixteen years old. Brown's fate was determined by Tennessee Governor Bill Haslam, who—in the course of my writing this chapter—granted the victim clemency and

---

57. Murillo Velasco, "MP-GO denuncia médium João de Deus por violação sexual e estupro de vulnerável, em Abadiânia," *O Globo*, 28 December 2018, https://tinyurl.com/SBL6703b. See also Cristina Rocha's *John of God: The Globalization of Brazilian Faith Healing* (New York: Oxford University Press, 2017).

58. RAINN, "Victims of Sexual Violence Statistics," https://tinyurl.com/SBL6703c.

59. Lucinda Joy Peach, "Is Violence Male? The Law, Gender, and Violence," in *Frontline Feminisms: Women, War, and Resistance*, ed. Marguerite R. Walker and Jennifer Rycenga (New York: Routledge, 2012), 58.

60. Peach, "Is Violence Male?," 58.

61. Peach, "Is Violence Male?," 59.

62. Kathleen J. Ferraro, "The Dance of Dependency: A Genealogy of Domestic Violence Discourse," *Hypatia* 11 (1996): 89.

63. Peach, "Is Violence Male?," 59.

released her from prison on August 7, 2019. Organizers, activists, scholars, and writers were fundamental in the process of bringing justice to Brown.[64]

Taken together, the art and scholarship surveyed in this chapter remind us that at the receiving end of these visual and textual codices there is the experience of particular women. As Bal points out, "The nude as a genre promotes a conflation between aesthetics and sexuality, and encourages a sexual response based on objectification; it assumes the woman is passive and precludes her engagement with the viewer."[65] Moreover, she warns, "the visual tradition informs (our readings of) the biblical story, not, at this point, the other way around."[66] That the pictorial tradition has taken interpretive license is understandable. What is of concern for womanist scholars, artists, and art historians who engage issues of asymmetrical relations of power is the assessment of how such centuries-old tradition has impeded a broader conversation of how art, standing at the other side of our gaze, has enabled these structures (and the men who populate them) to go unchecked, unimpeded, and unpunished. It has also blinded viewers to the actual impact these cultural constructions have in the lives of many women who continue to be traumatized, violated, and killed at the hands of gender and racial violence. In closing, the methodological move I propose is to read the text alongside images that challenge the traditional way of rendering Bathsheba and stimulate "the pressure points," to borrow O'Grady's language, of the narrative. Black women's aesthetics of denunciation and opposition, in conversation with womanist frameworks, provide valiant models that teach us to ask fundamental questions about our ways of worldmaking through the act of looking. Moreover, they reverse the one-way contact of reading and looking and demand change in behavior. A critical encounter with Bathsheba's iconography, informed by the methodologies proposed by Black women artists and scholars, would ask us to admit our complicity in keeping structures of power erect while asking us to surrender our discursive power so as to hear what Bathsheba's silence has voiced for so many centuries.

---

64. Christine Hauser, "Cyntoia Brown Inspires a Push for Juvenile Criminal Justice Reform in Tennessee," *New York Times*, 17 January 2019, https://tinyurl.com/SBL6703d.
65. Bal, "Reading Bathsheba," 122.
66. Bal, "Reading Bathsheba," 158.

## Works Cited

Bal, Mieke. "Reading Bathsheba: From Master Codes to Misfits." Pages 119–46 in *Rembrandt's Bathsheba Reading King David's Letter*. Edited by Ann Jensen Adams. Cambridge: Cambridge University Press, 1998.

Bikker, Jonathan. *Willem Drost (1633–1659): A Rembrandt Pupil in Amsterdam and Venice*. New Haven: Yale University Press, 2005.

Blyth, Caroline, Emily Colgan, and Katie B. Edwards, eds. *Rape Culture, Gender Violence, and Religion: Biblical Perspectives*. Cham, Switzerland: Palgrave Macmillan, 2018.

Brueggemann, Walter. *First and Second Samuel*. Louisville: Westminster John Knox, 1990.

Butler, Judith. *Senses of the Subject*. New York: Fordham University Press, 2015.

Cixous, Hélène. *Stigmata: Escaping Texts*. New York: Routledge, 1998.

Elder, Nika. "Lorna Simpson's Fabricated Truths." *ArtJ* 77 (Spring 2018): 30–53.

Exum, J. Cheryl, ed. *Between the Text and the Canvas: The Bible and Art in Dialogue*. Sheffield: Sheffield Phoenix, 2009.

———. *Plotted, Shot, and Painted: Cultural Representations of Biblical Women*. Reprint, Sheffield: Sheffield Academic, 2012.

Ferraro, Kathleen J. "The Dance of Dependency: A Genealogy of Domestic Violence Discourse." *Hypatia* 11 (1996): 77–91.

Frymer-Kensky, Tikva. *Reading the Women of the Bible: A New Interpretation of Their Stories*. New York: Schocken Books, 2002.

Gafney, Wilda C. *Womanist Midrash: A Reintroduction to the Women of the Torah and the Throne*. Louisville: Westminster John Knox, 2017.

Gaut, Berys. *Art, Emotion and Ethics*. New York: Oxford University Press, 2007.

Goodman, Nelson. *Ways of Worldmaking*. Indianapolis: Hackett, 1978.

Guest, Deryn. "Looking Lesbian at the Bathing Bathsheba." *BibInt* 16 (2008): 227–62.

Harthan, John. *The Book of Hours*. New York: Crowell, 1977.

Hauser, Christine. "Cyntoia Brown Inspires a Push for Juvenile Criminal Justice Reform in Tennessee." *New York Times*, 17 January 2019. https://tinyurl.com/SBL6703d.

hooks, bell. *Reel to Real: Race, Class and Sex at the Movies*. New York: Routledge, 2006.

Jensen, Robin M. *The Substance of Things Seen: Art, Faith, and the Christian Community.* Grand Rapids: Eerdmans, 2004.

Koenig, Sara M. *Bathsheba Survives.* Columbia: University of South Carolina Press, 2018.

———. *Isn't This Bathsheba? A Study in Characterization.* Eugene, OR: Pickwick, 2011.

Kuhn, Annette. *The Power of the Image: Essays on Representation and Sexuality.* New York: Routledge, 1994.

Marien, Mary Warner. *Photography: A Cultural History.* New York: Pearson, 2015.

Mitchell, William J. T. *What Do Pictures Want? The Lives and Loves of Images.* Chicago: University of Chicago Press, 2005.

Morgan, David. *Visual Piety: A History and Theory of Popular Religious Images.* Berkeley: University of California Press, 1998.

Morgan, David, and Sally M. Promey, eds. *The Visual Culture of American Religions.* Berkeley: University of California Press, 2001.

Nancy, Jean-Luc, and Federic Ferrari. *Being Nude: The Skin of Images.* Translated by Anne O'Byrne and Carlie Anglemire. New York: Fordham University Press, 2014.

O'Grady, Lorraine. "Olympia's Maid: Reclaiming Black Female Subjectivity." Pages 267–86 in *Art, Activism, and Oppositionality: Essays from Afterimage.* Edited by Grant H. Kester. Durham, NC: Duke University Press, 1998.

O'Reilly, Sally. *The Body in Contemporary Art.* New York: Thames & Hudson, 2009.

Peach, Lucinda Joy. "Is Violence Male? The Law, Gender, and Violence." Pages 58–72 in *Frontline Feminisms: Women, War, and Resistance.* Edited by Marguerite R. Waller and Jennifer Rycenga. New York: Routledge, 2001.

Preziosi, Donald. "Art History: Making the Visible Legible." Pages 1–11 in *The Art of Art History: A Critical Anthology.* 2nd ed. Edited by Donald Preziosi. Oxford: Oxford University Press, 2009.

RAINN. "Victims of Sexual Violence Statistics." Accessed 10 July 2020. https://tinyurl.com/SBL6703c.

Rocha, Cristina. *John of God: The Globalization of Brazilian Faith Healing.* New York: Oxford University Press, 2017.

Sakenfeld, Katharine Doob. *Just Wives.* Louisville: Westminster John Knox, 2003.

Schwartz, Gary. "Though Deficient in Beauty: A Documentary History and Interpretation of Rembrandt's 1654 Painting of Bathsheba." Pages 176–203 in *Rembrandt's Bathsheba Reading King David's Letter*. Edited by Ann Jensen Adams. Cambridge: Cambridge University Press, 1998.

Sluijter, Eric Jan. "Rembrandt's Bathsheba and the Convention of a Seductive Theme." Pages 48–99 in *Rembrandt's Bathsheba Reading King David's Letter*. Edited by Ann Jensen Adams. Cambridge: Cambridge University Press, 1998.

Sontag, Susan. *Regarding the Pain of Others*. New York: Farrar, Straus & Giroux, 2003.

Velasco, Murillo. "MP-GO denuncia médium João de Deus por violação sexual e estupro de vulnerável, em Abadiânia." *O Globo*, 28 December 2018. https://tinyurl.com/SBL6703b.

Vergara, Alejandro. *Rembrandt: Pintor de Historias*. Madrid: Museo Nacional del Prado, 2008.

Walker Vadillo, Mónica Ann. *Bathsheba in Late Medieval French Manuscript Illumination: Innocent Object of Desire or Agent of Sin?* Lewiston, NY: Mellen, 2008.

Weems, Carrie Mae. Audio interview for *MoMA 2000: Open Ends*. The Museum of Modern Art and Acoustiguide, 2000. https://tinyurl.com/SBL6703e.

———. "From Here I Saw What Happened and I Cried, 1995–1996, 33 Toned Prints." https://tinyurl.com/SBL6703a.

# 2
# "I Am Come into My Garden":
# The Canticle of Canticles and the *Florilegium* of Philips Galle and Adriaen Collaert

JAMES CLIFTON

The bouquet of flowers in a vase engraved by Adriaen Collaert, datable to the late 1580s, is thought to be the first independent print of such a floral arrangement and seminal for the subsequent development of painted flower pieces in the Low Countries (fig. 2.1).[1] It is independent in that it plays no part in a larger still-life, genre, or narrative composition. But it is decidedly *not* independent in that it is only one plate—the third, evident from the number at lower left—of a series of prints, called *Florilegium*. The *Florilegium* consists of twenty-four numbered engravings: a title plate (fig. 2.2), a scene of the *Sponsus* and *Sponsa* of the Canticle of Canticles in front of a garden (fig. 2.3), the bouquet of flowers in a vase, and twenty-one plates of various flowers with stems and leaves but no root structures, spread out evenly over each plate, with no overlap of forms (figs. 2.4–5). As the title page indicates, the series, which was dedicated to Giovanni de' Medici, was engraved by Collaert and published by his father-in-law, Philips Galle ("Ab Hadriano Collaert caelatum, et à Philip. Galleo editum"). Galle was also responsible for the design of the second plate at least (which is signed "Phls Galle inven. et excud. / Adrian. Collaert scalp.").

---

1. Sam Segal, "On Florilegia," in *Natural History & Travel*, cat. 279 (Amsterdam: Antiquariaat Junk, 2000), 14. Segal offers 1594 as a *terminus ante quem*, based on the apparent borrowings from the series by Nicolas de Bruyn ("On Florilegia," 19).

Fig. 2.1. Adriaen Collaert after Philips Galle, *Bouquet of Flowers*, ca. 1587–1589, engraving, 26.4 x 17.6 cm; plate 3 of *Florilegium*; Sarah Campbell Blaffer Foundation, Houston, 2014.7.3. Photo: Museum of Fine Arts, Houston.

Fig. 2.2. Adriaen Collaert after Philips Galle, *Title Plate*, ca. 1587–1589, engraving, 26.4 x 17.6 cm; plate 1 of *Florilegium*; Sarah Campbell Blaffer Foundation, Houston, 2014.7.1. Photo: Museum of Fine Arts, Houston.

Fig. 2.3. Adriaen Collaert after Philips Galle, *Sponsa and Sponsus*, ca. 1587–1589, engraving, 26.4 x 17.6 cm; plate 2 of *Florilegium*; Sarah Campbell Blaffer Foundation, Houston, 2014.7.2. Photo: Museum of Fine Arts, Houston.

Fig. 2.4. Adriaen Collaert after Philips Galle, *Roses*, 1587–1589, engraving, 26.4 x 17.6 cm; plate 4 of *Florilegium*; Sarah Campbell Blaffer Foundation, Houston, 2014.7.4. Photo: Museum of Fine Arts, Houston.

Fig. 2.5. Adriaen Collaert after Philips Galle, *Lilies*, 1587–1589, engraving, 26.4 x 17.6; plate 6 of *Florilegium*; Sarah Campbell Blaffer Foundation, Houston, 2014.7.6. Photo: Museum of Fine Arts, Houston.

The flowers in the *Florilegium* derive from herbals by the luminaries of Netherlandish botany: Rembertus Dodonaeus (Rembert Dodoens), Mathias Lobelius, and Carolus Clusius.[2] But the flowers are shown without their root systems and split into discrete blossoms. Significantly, the flowers are unidentified on the plates. Collaert's flower images cannot serve any serious, or at least complete, botanical purpose.

The inscription in the lower margin of the title plate addresses those "who favor little gardens" and extols the accomplishment of the artists, deploying a conventional—and rather overstated—comparison of nature and art: "Come ... and *graze* with your eyes on depicted little flowers: / in which there is in fact no liveliness, no greenness; / yet they are made by such an accomplished hand, / that if anybody were perchance to gather live ones, / he would almost estimate Nature to be conquered by art."[3] Several writers have suggested that the *Florilegium* was, in Ann Diels's terms, "aimed first and foremost at lovers of flowers and gardens [those who favor little gardens], but could equally well be used as a design repertory by artists and craftsmen."[4] This latter suggestion is readily supported by

---

2. The woodcut of *Rosa sativa* by Pieter van der Borcht in Dodonaeus's 1568 *Florum*, used as a model for one of the plates in the Galle-Collaert Florilegium (here fig. 4), may serve as an example. See Alexandra Wachtel, "Rembert Doedens," in *Prints and the Pursuit of Knowledge in Early Modern Europe*, ed. Susan Dackerman, exh. cat. (Cambridge: Harvard Art Museums; New Haven: Yale University Press, 2011), 192–99.

3. *Favete, adeste, qui favetis hortulis, / Pictosque ocellis flosculos depascite: / Queis nullus est quidem vigor, nullus viror; / Facti tamen sunt tam politâ dextrâ, / Vt si quis illis fortè vivos conferat, / Naturam ab arte p[a]enè victam censeat.*

4. Ann Diels, Marjolein Leesberg, and Arnout Balis, compilers and eds., *The Collaert Dynasty, Part VI: The New Hollstein Dutch and Flemish Etchings, Engravings and Woodcuts, 1450–1700* (Ouderkerk aan den Ijssel: Sound & Vision, 2005), lviii. See also J. G. van Gelder, "Van blompot en blomglas," *EM* 46 (1936): 81. He calls Collaert's *Florilegium* a "nuttige hulpbron voor schilders en ciseleurs"; he adduces the phrase *pictoribus, sculptoribus ... mire utilis et necessarius* (wonderfully useful and necessary for painters, engravers), which does not, however, appear in the *Florilegium*; rather, it appears on the title plate of the series, *Libelius varia genera piscium complectens*, engraved by Nicolaas de Bruyn and published by Frederick de Wit around 1594 (Hollstein 243; unnamed by van Gelder). Van Gelder was followed almost verbatim by Claus Nissen, *Die botanische Buchillustration: Ihre Geschichte und Bibliographie* (Stuttgart: Hiersemann Verlags-Gesellschaft, 1951), 1:68. Crispijn de Passe the Younger's *Hortus Floridus* (1614) was addressed to "Benigno florum ac omnium naturae ipsius elegantiarum amatori ac admiratori" (the kind lover and admirer of all elegant flow-

comparanda. For example, in the dedicatory epistle to Lady Mary Sidney in *La Clef des Champs*, published in London in 1586, Jacques le Moyne recommends his work as a pattern book for blazoners, painters, engravers, goldsmiths, embroiderers, weavers, and needleworkers.[5] Some of the

---

ers and nature itself). See Ilja M. Veldman, *Crispijn de Passe and His Progeny (1564–1670): A Century of Print Production*, trans. Michael Hoyle, SPP 3 (Rotterdam: Sound & Vision, 2001), 206.). At least one plate from the *Florilegium* (pl. 6, here fig. 2.5) was copied in Mughal India around the second decade of the seventeenth century. See Jeremiah P. Losty and Malini Roy, *Mughal India: Art, Culture and Empire: Manuscripts and Paintings in the British Library* (London: British Library, 2012), 135, 241 n. 219; Losty, "Further Light on Mughal Flower Studies and Their European Sources" (unpublished paper, 2014), https://tinyurl.com/SBL6703f, n.p.; Ebba Koch, "Flowers in Mughal Architecture," *Marg* 70, no. 2 (December 2018–March 2019): 25–33, esp. 26–27. The dedication to Giovanni de' Medici has suggested to Zygmunt Waźbiński that the *Florilegium* served as a manual for the Florentine Accademia del Disegno, of which he was patron. See Waźbiński, "Adriaen Collaert i jego *Florilegium*: Niderlandzkie źródła włoskiej szesnastowiecznej martwej natury," in *Ars longa: Prace dedykowane pamięci profesora Jana Białostockiego. Materiały Sesji Stowarzyszenia Historyków Sztuki, Warszawa, listopad 1998* (Warsaw: Ośrodek Wydawniczy Zamku Królewskiego w Warszawie, 1999), 249–68. The dedication has been used to date the series to 1587–1589, when Giovanni de' Medici was in the Netherlands, but it is worth noting that Galle dedicated several works to various Medici family members who were not at the time in the Low Countries; e.g., two different series of the *Passio, Mors et Resurrectio Dno. Nostri Iesu Christi* from the mid-1580s, with some plates engraved by Adriaen Collaert, one dedicated to Cardinal Ferdinando de' Medici, and one to Cardinal Alessandro Ottaviano de' Medici (Diels, Leesberg, and Balis, *Collaert Dynasty, Part VI*, lvii–lviii). A later edition of the *Florilegium* was published by Theodoor Galle, who took over the family workshop after 1600.

5. [Jaques le Moyne, dit de Morgues], *La Clef des champs, pour trouuer plusieurs Animaux, tant Bestes qu'Oyseaux, auec plusieurs Fleurs & Fruitz* ([London:] Imprimé aux Blackefriers, pour Jaques le Moyne, dit de Morgues Paintre, 1586), n.p.: "Or comme en ce siecle (esgoust de la malice des autres) il à pleu à Dieu nous donner icy vn heureux repos, accompagné de la lumiere de sa Parole sacrée, soubz le tres-heureux regne de sa tres-fidele, & nostre Tressérénissime ELIZABET a bon droit par sa Prouidence Royne de ces Pays, aussi nous à il concédé la réuolution des Arts suscitant pluseurs gentilz Esprits, qui se sont donnez la main pour communiquer aux autres ce qu'il luy à pleu leur impartir, en quoy i'ay volontiers & selon mon petit pouuoir tascé de les suyure en si louable entreprise, dressant vn petit Liuret ayant choysi d'entre les Animaux, quelque nombre de Bestes & d'Oyseuz des plus remarquables, non seulement de ceux qui se blasonnet Aux Armoires des Seigneurs: mais aussi qui sont plus [page] plaisans à l'oeil, & que l'Admirable Ouurier de Nature à mieux peins & bigarrez, ayant accompagné les dits Animaux d'autant des plus belles Fleurs & Fruitz, que i'ay pensé les

plates in the British Library's exemplar of this work—images of both animals and plants—have been scored or pricked for transfer, as have some impressions of the plates in Crispijn de Passe's *Hortus Floridus* of 1614.[6]

It is undoubtedly true that the *Florilegium* was intended to appeal to lovers of flowers, lovers of art, and even artists themselves. But it scarcely explains the second plate of the series, which is rarely reproduced and often not mentioned in discussions of the series (fig. 2.3). Drawn from the biblical Canticle of Canticles, it suggests another audience for the series, overlapping with the others.

Antwerp was the home to both the publishing house of Christophe Plantin and his heirs—the Officina Plantiniana—which was responsible for the publication of the works of Dodonaeus, Lobelius, and Clusius,[7] and the

---

plus propres, le tout apres le vif, lesquelz pouont seruir, à ceux qui ayment & desirent d'aprendre choses bonnes & honnestes, entre lesquelz il se trouue de la ieunesse, tant chez les Nobles que parmi les Artisans, les vns pour leur preparer en 'Art de Peinture, our Grauuer, les autres pour estre Orfeures ou Sculteurs, & aucuns pour la Broderie ou Tapisserie, & mesme pour toute sorte d'ourage à l'éguille, de toutes lesquelles Sciences la Portraiture est l'entrée, & sans laquelle nul ne peut venir à perfection." See also Segal, "On Florilegia," 17–19. Pattern books were produced in Europe as early as the 1520s. See Susan North, "'An Instrument of Profit, Pleasure, and of Ornament': Embroidered Tudor and Jacobean Dress Accessories," in *English Embroidery from the Metropolitan Museum of Art, 1580–1700: 'Twixt Art and Nature*, ed. Andrew Morrall and Melinda Watt, exh. cat. (New Haven: Yale University Press, for the Bard Graduate Center for Studies in the Decorative Arts, Design, and Culture, New York, and the Metropolitan Museum of Art, New York, 2008), 43. Such a function for engravings is explicit in John Taylor, *The Needles Excellency: A New Booke wherein are diuers Admirable Workes wrought with the Needle. Newly inuented and cut in Copper for the pleasure and profit of the Industrious*, 10th ed. ([London]: James, 1636). The figures on the title plate are set before a garden, and the book includes floral motifs (see Melinda Watt in Morrall and Watt, *English Embroidery*, 154–56, cat. 23). See also *The Therd Booke of Flowers Fruits Beastes Birds and Flies Exactly Drawne. With Additions by Iohn Dunstall* ([London]: Stent, 1661); Melinda Watt, "The Therd Booke of Flowers Fruits Beastes Birds and Flies Exactly Drawne," in Morrall and Watt, *English Embroidery*, 212–14.

6. Segal, "On Florilegia," 23. Veldman notes that the title page of the English edition is explicit that it was to aid flower painters (*Crispijn de Passe*, 206, 210–11). De Passe's chapter on coloring the flowers may be intended for hand-coloring the prints or for painting the flowers independently of the print.

7. On the publication of later botanical works in the Officina Plantiniana, see Jozef Lemli, "The Officinae Plantinianae in Antwerp and Leiden and Their Botanical Editions from 1589 until 1647," in *Botany in the Low Countries (End of the Fifteenth Century–ca. 1650)*, exh. cat. (Antwerp: Plantin-Moretus Museum, 1993), 57–59.

families of engravers and print publishers—Galle, Collaert, Wierix—who often worked with the Officina Plantiniana, as well as with each other. Professional ties were reinforced by familial ones. It is no surprise, then, that there is considerable cross-pollination of text, image, format, and genre among these highly productive and engaged publishers and engravers. And, of course, illustrated botanical texts constitute only a small fraction of the work produced by Plantin and his heirs, who were responsible as well for very important religious texts, often illustrated. Likewise, the Antwerp engravers were responsible for an enormous number of religious images of various types—scriptural, allegorical, instructional, and meditational—issued singly, in series, and bound in conjunction with texts. I suggest that Collaert's *Florilegium* is a hybrid work of art, science, and faith, generated in the lively mix of artists, scientists, and theologians of Antwerp's publishing world, and meant to appeal to diverse viewers in a broad market.

## Creation and Creator

A number of works published around the turn of the seventeenth century reminded the viewer that the botanical world was a divine creation.[8] Thus, for example, on the title page of the first volume of Clusius's collected works, the *Rariorum plantarum historia*, published "Ex officina Plantiniana" in Antwerp in 1601, Adam and Solomon appear with Theophrastus and Dioscorides, and the Creator is represented by the tetragrammaton in glory on high.[9] The first part of the inscription below it affirms the source

---

Potraits of Clusius and Dodonaeus appear on the title page of Emmanuel Sweerts, *Florilegium* (Frankfurt, 1612) and on the title plate of Crispijn de Passe the Younger's *Hortus Floridus* of 1614.

8. A brilliant introduction to and analysis of the relationship between religion and nature in the early modern period in the Netherlands is Eric Jorink, *Reading the Book of Nature in the Dutch Golden Age, 1575–1715*, trans. Peter Mason (Leiden: Brill, 2010). See also Klaas van Berkel and Arjo Vanderjagt, eds., *The Book of Nature in Early Modern and Modern History*, GSCC 17 (Leuven: Peeters, 2006).

9. The composition reappears as the title page of Rembertus Dodonaeus, *Stirpium historiae pemptades sex* (Antwerp: Ex Officina Plantiniana, Apud Balthasarem et Ioannem Moretos, 1616). It had not been used for the 1583 edition of Dodonaeus. See the title page to John Gerarde [sic], *The Herball or Generall Historie of Plantes* (London: John Norton, 1597). See Ronah Sadan, "Jacques de Gheyn II, Portrait of Carolus Clusius; Carolus Clusius and Pieter van der Borcht I, *Smilax aspera* (Bindweed) / *Rosa centifolia* (Hundred-petaled rose)," in Dackerman, *Prints and the Pursuit*, 200–203. The

of nature: "In each plant God placed his own powers" (*plantae cuique suas vires Deus indidit*). If nature as creation is a second order of being, knowledge of nature in itself is a secondary knowledge, at best only a means to a more important knowledge, as the second part of the inscription suggests: "and each plant teaches us his presence" (*atque praesentem esse illum, quaelibet herba docet*).[10] The knowledge, then, that one pursues would for some be not nature, not creation, but the Creator, God.

We find a rather more sustained tribute to the divine in Johann Theodor de Bry's *Florilegium novum*, published in three parts in De Bry's house in Oppenheim between 1611 and 1614.[11] In his prefatory letters

---

inscription on Jacques de Gheyn's portrait of Clusius, which was used in this book, attributes the source of virtues, skills, and talent (*virtus*, *genius*, and *ingenium*; "Virtute et genio non nitimur; at mage Christo / qui nobis istaec donat, et Ingenium")—implicitly Clusius's—to Christ. On Clusius, see Claudia Swan, "The Uses of Botanical Treatises in the Netherlands, c. 1600," in *The Art of Natural History: Illustrated Treatises and Botanical Paintings, 1400–1850*, ed. Therese O'Malley and Amy R. W. Meyers, SHA 69 (Washington, DC: National Gallery of Art, 2008), 63–81. The tetragrammaton appears also on the title page of Tabernaemontanus, *Neuw Kreuterbuch ...* (Frankfurt, 1588).

10. *Plantae cviqve svas vires Devs indidit, atqve praesentem esse illvm qvaelibet herba docet*. A version of the second half of the distich had appeared on a plate (part 3, no. 5) in the *Archetypa*, engraved by Jacob Hoefnagel after Joris Hoefnagel, 1592. See Thea Vignau-Wilberg, "Devotion and Observation of Nature in Art around 1600," in *Natura-Cultura: L'Interpretazione del mondo fisico nei testi e nelle immagini; Atti del Convegno Internazionale di Studi, Mantova, 5–8 ottobre 1996*, ed. Giuseppe Olmi, Lucia Tongiorgi Tomasi, and Attilio Zanca (Florence: Oschki, 2000), 48; Jorink, *Reading the Book*, 191. Vignau-Wilberg translates the inscription as, "God gave every plant its own force and every plant witnesses His existence" ("Devotion and Observation," 48). Brian W. Ogilvie translates, "God gave each plant its virtues, and every herb teaches that he is present." See Ogilvie, *The Science of Describing: Natural History in Renaissance Europe* (Chicago: University of Chicago Press, 2006), 317 n. 259. On a plaque below the title is "Virtvte et Genio," recalling De Gheyn's portrait of Clusius.

11. "Florilegium Novum, Hoc est: Variorum maximeque rariorum Florum ac Plantarum singularium urrà cum suis radicibus & cepis, Eicones diligenter aere sculptae & ad vivum ut plurimum expressae. New Blumbuch Darinnen allerhand schöne Blumen vnd frmbde Gewächs / mit ihren Wurtzeln vnd Zwiebeln / mehrer theils dem Leben nach in Kupffer fleissig gestochen zu sehen seind." See Johann Theodor De Bry, *Florilegium Novum, Hoc est: Variorum maximeque rariorum Florum ac Plantarum singularium urrà cum suis radicibus & cepis, Eicones diligenter aere sculptae & ad vivum ut plurimum expressae. New Blumbuch Darinnen allerhand schöne Blumen vnd frmbde Gewächs / mit ihren Wurtzeln vnd Zwiebeln / mehrer theils dem Leben nach in Kupffer fleissig gestochen zu sehen seind* (Frankfurt: De Bry, 1612–1614), "Dem WolEdlen / Gestrengen vnd Besten Herman zon und zu Kronberg," n.p.: "Es haben

to the dedicatee (Hermann von und zu Kronberg) and the reader (whom De Bry addresses as an "anthophilous reader and viewer" [*Ad Lectorem et Spectatorem Anthophilum*], likening us to flower-feeding insects), he repeatedly marvels at God's creation.[12] Apropos of the publication, he emphasizes flowers, "in so many and varied types, forms, sizes, and colors, that whoever takes account of such must say with the royal prophet David from Ps 111 (Ps 111:2): Great is the work of the Lord; whoever attends to it shall have pleasure therein."[13]

John Gerard, in the dedication of his book, *The Herball or Generall Historie of Plantes*, published in London in 1597, expressed similar sentiments and posited plants in particular as signs of the wisdom of God:

> Among the manifold creatures of God ... that haue all in all ages diuersly entertained many excellent wits, and drawen them to the contemplation of the diuine wisedome, non haue prouoked mens studies more, or satisfied their desires so much, as plants haue done, and that vpon iust and woorthie causes: For if delight may prouoke mens labour, what greater

---

sich bißher viel Gelehrter statlicher Leut hierin bemühet / daß sie solche Bücher zuwegen brächten / für anderen nenne ich Ehren Geschicklichkeit vnd angewendtes Fleisses wegen D. Carolum Clusium / Johannen Robinum vnd Petrum Valet / welchen ich theils in diesem Werck nachgefolget / damit solche Arbeit auch in Teutschland vielen bekant vnd zu nutz gemacht werde." He is presumably referring to the florilegium *Le Jardin du Roy très Chrestien Henry IV*, written by Jean Robin and published by Pierre Vallet in 1608, as well as to one or more of Clusius's published works. De Bry's title page, with its garden framed by a classicizing columniated structure, recalls Vallet's. Clusius and Lobelius flank Vallet's colonnade to the royal garden. (The title page remained virtually unchanged in Vallet's second edition of 1623.) The *Florilegium Novum* has a somewhat complicated publication history and varying configurations. The exemplar in Houston consists of prefatory matter and eighty-seven engravings of flowers and flowering plants, published in three parts in De Bry's house in Oppenheim in 1612 (first ed. 1611), 1613, and 1614.

12. "Es ist sehr weißlich von Gott dem allmächtigen Schöpffer vnd Allwissenden Regierer seiner so viel vnd mancherley creaturen geordnet / vnd fürsichtiglich angestellet / daß ob schon an einem jeden ort alles zubekommen ist / an einem jeden ort nicht alles wächset" (De Bry, "Dem WolEdlen," n.p.).

13. "Unter andern müssen wir gestehen / daß Gottes sonderbare Weißheit sich sonderlich erzeige / in dem herzlichen Blumwerck / welches die Natur selber zeuget / in so viel vnd mancherley Gattung / Gestalt / Größ / vnd Farben / daß / wer solches in acht nimpt / mit dem Königlichen Propheten David sagen muß auß dem 111. Psalm: Groß seynd die Werck deß Hernn / wer ihr achtet / der hat eitel Lust daran" (De Bry, "Dem WolEdlen," n.p.).

delight is there than to behold the earth apparelled with plants, as with a robe of imbroidered worke, set with orient pearles, and garnished with great diuersitie of rare and costly iewels? If this varietie and perfection of colours may affect the eie, it is such in herbes and flowers, that no Apelles, no Zeuxis euer could by any art expresse the like: if odours, or if taste may worke satisfaction, they are both so soueraigne in plants, and so comfortable, that no confection of the Apothecaries can equall their excellent vertue. But these delights are in the outward senses: the principall delight is in the minde, singularly enriched with the knowledge of these visible things, setting foorth to vs the inuisible wisedome and admirable workmanship of almightie God.[14]

Gerard's metaphor of the flower-covered earth as an embroidered robe calls to mind the suggestion that the *Florilegium* may have provided models for embroiderers. In drawing the *paragone* between nature and artists, however, he asserts that no one could ever match nature's array, thus drawing the exact opposite conclusion from that on the *Florilegium*'s title plate, which champions the artists in this competition.

For Gerard and many in the early modern period, knowledge of the natural world in and of itself is, at best, of secondary importance. Rather, knowledge of God is paramount.

Knowledge of God may be divided between a rational knowledge, available through an understanding of creation, and a suprarational knowledge, which is the result of spiritual union with God. This latter form of knowledge lies, strictly speaking, outside the study of the natural world, and yet natural imagery is sometimes employed to effect it. The *Florilegium* combines these forms of knowledge. Through it, I would

---

14. Gerarde, *Herball or Generall Historie*, n.p. On Gerard's illicit adaptation of a translation of Dodonaeus's *Pemptades* for this work, see Agnes Arber, *Herbals: Their Origin and Evolution; A Chapter in the History of Botany, 1470–1670*, 2nd ed. (repr., Cambridge: Cambridge University Press, 2010), 129–30. Gerard's dedicatory letter is not, however, anticipated in Dodonaeus's work. On Gerard and floral motifs in England more generally, see Andrew Morrall, "Regaining Eden: Representations of Nature in Seventeenth-Century English Embroidery," in Morrall and Watt, *English Embroidery*, 79–97. See also the quotation of Matt 6:28–29 on the title plate of Crispijn de Passe's series of engravings of plants, the *Cognoscite lilia: Cognoscite lilia agri qvomodo crescant non laborant, neque nent: attamen dico vobis ne Salomonem quidem in vniuersa gloria sua sic amic tum fuisse vt vnum ex his*. On the series, which was later reproduced as the "Altera pars" of Crispijn de Passe the Younger's *Hortus Floridus*, see Veldman, *Crispijn de Passe*, 82–83.

like to suggest that the pursuit of knowledge did not—does not, if you will—have a single goal, that knowledge could mean different things to different people, and that images could serve different purposes for different viewers.[15]

## Sponsa and Sponsus

In the Sponsa and Sponsus plate of the *Florilegium* (fig. 2.3), invented by Galle and engraved by Collaert, the couple appears in the immediate foreground before a formal garden that recalls those by Hans Vredeman de Vries in his *Hortorum viridariorumque elegantes & multiplicis formae* of a few years earlier.[16] Both wear floral crowns. As they look toward each other, she crosses her hands and genuflects, and he proffers a floral bouquet, comparable to those on the series title page and the third plate (figs. 2.1–2). Flowers are strewn on the narrow ground on which they stand, discretely placed, rather like the flowers arranged on the pages that follow. Inscribed below the image are two passages from the Canticle. First is 2:1–2: "I am the flower of the field, and the lily of the valleys. As the lily among thorns, so is my love among the daughters." Second is part of 5:1:

---

15. Kathleen Crowther-Heyck notes that the relations between religion and what we now call science in early modern Europe have been the subject of an ongoing scholarly conversation and that "historians have moved beyond questions of whether religion has hindered or helped scientific progress and have begun to examine the myriad ways in which natural knowledge was connected to piety and moral edification in the early modern period." See Crowther-Heyck, "Wonderful Secrets of Nature: Natural Knowledge and Religious Piety in Reformation Germany," *Isis* 94 (2003): 256.

16. The figures have been identified as Christ and Mary Magdalene by Marijnke de Jong and Irene de Groot, *Ornamentprenten in het Rijksprentenkabinet, I, 15de & 16de Eeuw* (Amsterdam: Rijksprentenkabinet, Rijksmuseum, and 's-Gravenhage: Staatsuitgeverij, 1988), 54; Ada Segre, "Le retour de Flore: Naissance et évolution des jardins de fleurs de 1550 à 1650," in *L'Empire de flore: Histoire et représentation des fleurs en Europe du XVIe au XIXe siècle*, ed. Sabine van Sprang (Brussels: La Renaissance du Livre, 1996), 179 (more precisely, "sainte Marie-Madeleine, la prostituée, en Flore"); Wachtel, "Rembert Doedens," 196. They are called "Christ and his bride Ecclesia" in Diels, Leesberg, and Balis (*Collaert Dynasty, Part VI*, 244). See Hans Vredeman de Vries, *Hortorum viridariorumque elegantes & multiplicis formae, ad architectonicae artis normam affabrè* (1583). On Vredeman de Vries and gardens, see Erik A. de Jong, "A Garden Book Made for Emperor Rudolf II in 1593: Hans Puechfeldner's *Nützliches Khünstbüech der Gartnereij*," in O'Malley and Meyers, *Art of Natural History*, 187–203.

"I am come into my garden, O my sister, my spouse, I have gathered my myrrh, with my aromatical spices."[17]

Since Christian antiquity, the Canticle had been read allegorically, with the Sponsus identified invariably with Christ, and the Sponsa variably with the church, the human soul, and the Virgin Mary.[18] The book was understood, in any case, to be a contemplative work, useful for seeking a spiritual union with—that is, a suprarational knowledge of—God.

The Canticle's imagery had long been used to evoke qualities of the Virgin Mary, especially the enclosed garden, and this association continued in late sixteenth- and early seventeenth-century Flemish prints, such as the engraving of the Virgin and Child in an enclosed garden by Johannes Wierix, dated 1606, which adduces passages from the Canticle (fig. 2.6; Cant 4:12; 5:1; 6:1). How we should interpret the figures in the *Florilegium* engraving is, however, less clear. In his commentaries on the Canticle, early seventeenth-century Jesuit Cornelius à Lapide explicates each passage in a different sense—"Of Christ and the Church" (*Ecclesia*); "Of Christ and the holy soul" (*anima sancta*); and "Of Christ and the Blessed Virgin"—varying the order from passage to passage according to which sense he felt was primary and citing a plethora of authorities for each.[19] The interpretations are not mutually exclusive, and the *Florilegium* composition may likewise invite multiple readings.

It may be instructive to compare Galle's image of the Sponsus and Sponsa before a garden with a more complex depiction of the subject that appeared in Jan David's *Paradisvs Sponsi et Sponsae* of 1607, published *ex Officina Plantiniana* for Galle. This Jesuit mystical emblem book, with a hundred engravings by Theodoor Galle, invites the votary to meditate on the soul's death through Christ's passion, and on renewed life in Christ through the virtues of the Virgin Mary.[20] The *Paradisus* uses the leitmotif

---

17. *Ego flos campi, et lilium convallium. Sicut liliam inter spinas, sic amica mea inter filias. Cantic. II. / Veni in hortum meum soror mea sponsa, mssui mijrrham meam cum aromatibus meis. Cantic. V.* English translations here follow Douay-Rheims.

18. For medieval readings, see Ann W. Astell, *The Song of Songs in the Middle Ages* (Ithaca, NY: Cornell University Press, 1990).

19. Cornelius à Lapide, *Commentarii in Canticvm Canticorvm* (Antwerp: Apud Iocabvm Mevrsivm, 1657).

20. *Paradise of the Bridegroom and the Bride, in which a Harvest of Myrrh and Spices Must Be Gathered from the Instruments and Mysteries of Christ's Passion, in order that We May Die with Him. And Marian Garland Divided into a Sevenfold Series of Titles, in order that We May Hasten toward the Fragrance of the Blessed Virgin and*

of a garden setting throughout and, like many botanical books and florilegia of the period, is itself presented as a metaphorical garden, that is, a garden on paper, as David puts it in his dedication to the archdukes Albert and Isabella (*chartaceo velut in campo*).[21]

The *Reciprocal Invitation of the Bride and Bridegroom to Their Respective Gardens* (*Reciproca Sponsae Sponsique ad hortum suum invitatio*) in David's *Paradisus* is keyed to the tripartite preamble to the work (fig. 2.7). David is explicit that the Sponsa signifies our soul (*anima*[*m*] *nostram, per Sponsam in Cantico significatam*), invited by Christ to the mystery of human redemption through his passion.[22] There are two gardens described by David and

---

*Christ Be Formed within Us*. On the *Paradisus Sponsi et Sponsae*, see Max Engammare, "Dans le jardin du bien-aimé. Illustration et exégèse du *Cantique des Cantiques* au XVIIe siècle," *Graphè* 8 (1999): 131–33; Ralph Dekoninck, *Ad imaginem: Statuts, fonctions et usages de l'image dans la littérature spirituelle jésuite du XVIIe siècle* (Geneva: Droz, 2005), 339–49; Walter S. Melion, "Meditative Images and the Portrayal of Image-Based Meditation," in *Ut pictura meditatio: The Meditative Image in Northern Art, 1500–1700*, ed. Walter S. Melion, Ralph Dekoninck, and Agnes Guiderdoni-Bruslé, PSEMIF 4 (Turnhout: Brepols, 2012), 32–60. It is worth noting that Galle, working with Benito Arias Montano, had previously engraved and published an allegorical treatment of the Sponsus and Sponsa as Christ and the Christian soul (albeit not drawn directly from the Canticle): the *Divinarum nuptiarum conventa et acta*, 1573. See Sylvaine Hänsel, *Der spanische Humanist Benito Arias Montano (1527–1598) und die Kunst*, SFG 2/25 (Münster Westfalen: Aschendorffsche Verlagsbuchhandlung, 1991), 100–18; Dekoninck, *Ad imaginem*, 334–38; Walter S. Melion, *The Meditative Art: Studies in the Northern Devotional Print, 1550–1625*, EMCVA 1 (Philadelphia: Saint Joseph's University Press, 2009), 39–43. For the Canticle of Canticles in the sixteenth century, see Max Engammare, *Qu'il me baise des baisers de sa bouche: Le Cantique des cantiques à la Renaissance; Étude et bibliographie*, THR 277 (Geneva: Droz, 1993); Engammare, "Dans le jardin."

21. On the *Jardin*, see Segal, "On Florilegia," 25. It is a trope that is also realized on the title pages of florilegia such as Theodor de Bry's *Florilegium Novum* and Pierre Vallet's *Jardin du Roy très Chrestien Henry IV* of 1608.

22. Jan David, *Paradisvs Sponsi et Sponsae: in qvo messis myrrhae et aromatvm, ex instrumentis ac mysterijs Passionis Christi colligenda, vt ei commoriamur. Et Pancarpivm Marianvm, Septemplici Titulorum serie distinctum: vt in B. Virginis odorem curramus et Christvs formetur in nobis* (Antwerp: Ex officina Plantiniana, Apud Ioannem Moretum, 1607), 1:n.p. Anticipating Cornelius à Lapide's imbricated interpretations of the Canticle, in the second part of the *Paradisus*, the *Pancarpium Marianum*, David also equates Mary with the Sponsa, as in Johannes Wierix's engraving (fig. 6), by quoting Cant 4:12 (*Hortus conclusus, soror mea, sponsa, hortus conclusus*) and apostrophizing, *Hortus es, ô Maria* (David, *Paradisvs Sponsi et Sponsae*, 2:136 [ch. 33, "Hortus Conclusus"]). See also the series of six engravings on the Canticle by Johannes Sadeler

Fig. 2.6. Johannes Wierix, *The Virgin and Child in the Enclosed Garden*, 1606, engraving, 27.5 x 31 cm; Metropolitan Museum of Art, New York, 53.601.18(94). Photo: Metropolitan Museum of Art, New York.

depicted in the accompanying engraving. Sponsa speaks from Cant 5:1 in her banderole at the background garden: "Let my beloved come into his garden, and eat the fruit of his apple trees" (*veniat dilectus meus in hortum suum: & comedat fructum pomorum suorum*). David describes this garden as simultaneously paradise, the human intellect (*animus humanus*), and the whole world. But, because of the guile of the serpent, it has become filthy (a punning *totus mundus, quantumuis immundus*), a woodland of malignant spirits (*silua spirituum malignorum*). The tree of the knowledge of good and evil stands in the center of the garden, but Adam and Eve are driven from it.

---

after Maarten de Vos, from 1590, in which Sponsa is identified with the Church (New Hollstein 132–17).

Fig. 2.7. Theodoor Galle, *Reciprocal Invitation of the Bride and Bridegroom to Their Respective Gardens* (*Reciproca Sponsae Sponsique ad hortum suum invitatio*), engraving, in Jan David, *Paradisus Sponsi et Sponsae* (Antwerp: Ex officina Plantiniana, Apud Ioannem Moretum, 1607); private collection. Photo: Sarah Campbell Blaffer Foundation, Houston.

In the foreground Christ the Sponsus invites us, under the name of the Sponsa (*nos sub Sponsa nomine inuitantem*) with the subsequent words of Cant 5:1 (also quoted in the subscription of the *Florilegium* composition and Wierix's *Virgin and Child in the Enclosed Garden*): "I am come into my garden, O my sister, my spouse, I have gathered my myrrh, with my aromatical spices" (*Veni in hortum meum, soror mea, sponsa: Messui myrrham meam, cum aromatibus*). This garden is planted with the instruments of Christ's passion, a bitter myrrh that, when harvested, can be transformed into aromatic spices. David frequently employs tropes of vision: "So let us go into the garden of the Lord's sorrows and contemplate all things with the eyes of an attentive spirit."[23] He asks the votary to create beautiful mental images of Christ's torment but also provides a hundred engravings in his book as prompts for such contemplation.

Needless to say, the Collaert-Galle *Florilegium* lacks the complex meditative apparatus of David's *Paradisus*. And David's particular emblematic use of the Canticle may be idiosyncratic and unrelated to Galle's composition, although David was probably, and Theodoor Galle was certainly, well aware of the *Florilegium*. In any case, we must acknowledge that the Canticle and images derived from it were read as profound allegories of the transformation of the soul through Christ and of the union of the soul with Christ, and that they served devotional and meditative functions. There is no reason to think that Galle's *Sponsa and Sponsus* in the *Florilegium* was not also to serve such a function, supported and enhanced in that function by the floral plates that follow it in the series.

The *Florilegium* composition obviously makes use of different imagery within the context of the garden of the Canticles than does the *Paradisus* composition, and it may provide a simpler, in any case certainly less articulated, devotional narrative. Whereas in Jan David's *Paradisus*, the dedicatees, Albert and Isabella, had been invited to pluck flowers from the garden of Mary's virtue and offer them as garlands to Christ, in Philips Galle's invention, it is Christ who presents the Sponsa with a bouquet of flowers.[24] The rest of the *Florilegium* supports this gesture. It is as if

---

23. *Eamus itaque in hortum Dolorum ipsius, & omnia attentis animi luminibus contemplemur* (David, *Paradisvs Sponsi et Sponsae*, n.p. ["Fax Praeambuli tertia"]; trans. Melion, "Meditative Images"). See the *Florilegium* title plate: *Pictosque ocellis flosculos depascite* (Graze with your eyes on depicted little flowers).

24. See the second plate of the De Vos-Sadeler series, in which Christ holds a bouquet of flowers in one hand and with the other offers Sponsa a fruit-laden branch.

the twenty-one plates of cut flowers provided Christ with his bouquet. They are also strewn on the threshold of the image, creating not only a further connection between the floral plates and the biblical scene but also a connection between the viewer and the bridal pair.[25] The viewer is also engaged through the *Florilegium*'s bouquet in a vase, which echoes Christ's proffered bouquet. Here the bouquet is an isolated, iconic image, and the viewer takes the place of the Sponsa in the narrative plate, to meditate on Christ's gift.

## Strewn Flowers

The flower plates of the *Florilegium* have been likened to the diverse flowers and other *naturalia* (among other motifs) that frequently appeared in the margins of late medieval illuminated manuscripts—surrounding miniatures or text—especially from the Ghent-Bruges school of the late fifteenth and early sixteenth centuries, which have themselves been seen more broadly as providing an impetus for the development of botanical and zoological illustration, as well as the independent still life (fig. 2.8).[26] Such

---

David's dedication reads: *Ex illa quidem, laborum poenarumque suaviamaros Salvatoris nostri manipulos, in mentis horreum colligetis; ex hac vero, omnigenis decerptis floribus, pancarpias pangetis corollas. Denique, ut eximiam utriusque vestrum in Deum eiusque Matrem pietatem augebitis; ita oneris vestri molem levari (vires & animos inspirante ipso Paradisi Domino & cultore) sentietis* (From that, indeed, you will gather in the granary of your mind bittersweet bundles of the sufferings and punishments of our Savior; from this, truly, you will make wreaths of plucked flowers of every kind. Finally, just as you may increase exceptional piety for both your God and his Mother, so you may feel the weight of the burden lifted [by the cultivator of Paradise, the Lord himself, inspiring your strength and souls]) (*Paradisvs Sponsi et Sponsae*, n.p. ["Serenissimis Alberto et Isabellae"]).

25. For a different use of strewn flowers—also ultimately deriving from the Canticle—see James Clifton, "'Lectulus noster floridus': The Flower-Strewn Bed and the Virgin's Womb," in *Marian Images in Context: Doctrines, Devotions, and Cults*, ed. James Clifton, Barbara Haeger, and Elliott Wise (forthcoming).

26. On the marginalia and their interpretation, see Thomas DaCosta Kaufmann and Virginia Roehrig Kaufmann, "The Sanctification of Nature: Observations on the Origins of Trompe l'oeil in Netherlandish Book Painting of the Fifteenth and Sixteenth Centuries," *JPGMJ* 19 (1991): 43–64; Jim Bennett and Scott Mandelbrote, *The Garden, the Ark, the Tower, the Temple: Biblical Metaphors of Knowledge in Early Modern Europe* (Oxford: Museum of the History of Science in association with the Bodleian Library, 1998); Anne Margreet W. As-Vijvers, "More than Marginal Meaning? The Interpre-

Fig. 2.8. Unknown artist, Bruges, *The "Mors Vincit Omnia" Hours*, ca. 1510, book of hours, use of Rome, colors on parchment, ca. 11 x 8.5 cm; Sarah Campbell Blaffer Foundation, Houston, 2015.19. Photo: Museum of Fine Arts, Houston.

Fig. 2.9. Adriaen Collaert, *Saint Lucy*, ca. 1600, engraving, 19.5 x 15 cm; from *Martyrologium Sanctarum Virginum*; Yale University Art Gallery, 2011.53.1.105. Photo: Yale University Art Gallery.

marginalia survived the early modern shift from manuscript illumination to printmaking and made frequent appearances in late sixteenth- and early seventeenth-century devotional prints by Flemish artists, including Collaert, which recall in scale as well as in format intimately sized illuminated books of hours. We find floral marginalia in several series by Collaert, including his *Life of the Virgin Mary* (*Virginis Mariae vita*), a suite of twenty engravings, and his *Female Martyr Saints* (*Martyrologium sanctarum Virginum*), a suite of twenty-five engravings (fig. 2.9).[27]

These marginalia have resisted precise interpretation, and their significance may vary greatly from one work to another, even within the oeuvre of a single artist. As Anne Margreet As-Vijvers has argued for Ghent-Bruges manuscript marginalia, though they may have been primarily decorative, the decoration generally "contains a symbolic element that is always implicitly present for the reader-beholder," and, since the majority of motifs are religious in their reference (including flowers), they "collaborate with the text of the book of hours," reminding the reader of "the transience of life on earth" and "eternal life in heaven."[28] Thus, the marginal flowers not only in Ghent-Bruges books of hours but also in late sixteenth- and early seventeenth-century Flemish prints were available to play a devotional and meditative role in conjunction with the images they border, in addition to whatever decorative function they may have had. The prints are thus comparable to the genre of religious garland paintings created by Jan Brueghel the Elder and Peter Paul Rubens—roughly contemporaneously with David's *Pancarpium Marianum* (that is, *Marian Garland*), the second part of the *Paradisus*—and subsequently developed

---

tation of Ghent-Bruges Border Decoration," *OH* 116 (2003): 3–33 (on flowers, see 6–7, 10–17). For their role in the development of flower painting, see Beatrijs Brenninkmeijer-de Rooij, *Roots of Seventeenth-Century Flower Painting: Miniatures, Plant Books, Paintings* (Leiden: Primavera Pers, 1996); Arthur K. Wheelock Jr., *From Botany to Bouquets: Flowers in Northern Art*, exh. cat. (Washington, DC: National Gallery of Art, 1999), 16–17. I am grateful to Barbara Haeger for her bibliographic suggestions.

27. As-Vijvers points out that strewing flowers was associated with the Virgin Mary in the late medieval period—for example, during Marian processions and Pentecost celebrations—although not exclusively so ("More than Marginal Meaning?," 6–7).

28. As-Vijvers, "More than Marginal Meaning?," 26. She recognizes and explores the marginalia's occasional meaningfulness: "The primarily decorative nature of the borders allowed room *to add* a signifying component where suitable or when the illuminator was inspired" (21, emphasis original).

by other artists, including Jesuit Daniel Seghers, far into the seventeenth century (fig. 2.10).[29]

Fig. 2.10. Daniel Seghers, *A Garland of Flowers on a Carved Stone Medallion*, ca. 1650; oil on canvas, 114.3 x 95.3 cm; Sarah Campbell Blaffer Foundation, Houston, 1977.4. Photo: Museum of Fine Arts, Houston.

---

29. On garland paintings, see David Freedberg, "The Origins and Rise of the Flemish Madonnas in Flower Garlands: Decoration and Devotion," *MJBK*, 3rd ser., 32 (1981): 115–50; Susan Merriam, *Seventeenth-Century Flemish Garland Paintings: Still Life, Vision, and the Devotional Image* (Burlington, VT: Ashgate, 2012).

In any case, it is likely that the flowers in the Collaert-Galle *Florilegium* also played a devotional role—at least for some viewers—in conjunction with the image of the Sponsa and Sponsus. The flower plates in the *Florilegium* have been loosed from a framing function around a central devotional image and dilated in the process to gain a much higher percentage of the pictorial field(s), but they remain tied to that image visually and iconographically. The *Florilegium* flowers could thus function much as floral marginalia had for a long time, in spite of its different format.

Some years earlier, Philips Galle had been explicit about the utility of printed images for devotional purposes. In the dedication to King Philip II of an emblematic series of prints on the Old Testament figure of David, with texts by Benito Arias Montano, Galle describes the publication as "eminently suited to be exhibited for the use and pleasure of pious students of the Catholic religion, and to be expressed and embellished by the diligence and industry of the art of engraving, furnished and exercised by me chiefly for the cultivation of piety."[30] The religious-minded, including those anthophilous readers and viewers "who favor little gardens," who "graze with their eyes on little flowers," might likewise gain use and pleasure from the engravings of the *Florilegium* in cultivating not only their piety but also their knowledge of God and his endlessly varied creation.

## Works Cited

Arber, Agnes. *Herbals: Their Origin and Evolution; A Chapter in the History of Botany, 1470–1670*. 2nd ed. Repr., Cambridge: Cambridge University Press, 2010.

Astell, Ann W. *The Song of Songs in the Middle Ages*. Ithaca, NY: Cornell University Press, 1990.

As-Vijvers, Anne Margreet W. "More than Marginal Meaning? The Interpretation of Ghent-Bruges Border Decoration." *OH* 116 (2003): 3–33.

Bennett, Jim, and Scott Mandelbrote. *The Garden, the Ark, the Tower, the Temple: Biblical Metaphors of Knowledge in Early Modern Europe.*

---

30. Quoted and translated by Walter S. Melion, "Benedictus Arias Montanus and the Virtual Studio as a Meditative Place," in *Inventions of the Studio: Renaissance to Romanticism*, ed. Michael Cole and Mary Pardo (Chapel Hill: University of North Carolina Press, 2005), 77.

Oxford: Museum of the History of Science in association with the Bodleian Library, 1998.

Berkel, Klaas van, and Arjo Vanderjagt, eds. *The Book of Nature in Early Modern and Modern History*. GSCC 17. Leuven: Peeters, 2006.

Brenninkmeijer-de Rooij, Beatrijs. *Roots of Seventeenth-Century Flower Painting: Miniatures, Plant Books, Paintings*. Leiden: Primavera Pers, 1996.

Bry, Johann Theodor de. *Florilegium Novum, Hoc est: Variorum maximeque rariorum Florum ac Plantarum singularium urrà cum suis radicibus & cepis, Eicones diligenter aere sculptae & ad vivum ut plurimum expressae. New Blumbuch Darinnen allerhand schöne Blumen vnd frmbde Gewächs / mit ihren Wurtzeln vnd Zwiebeln / mehrer theils dem Leben nach in Kupffer fleissig gestochen zu sehen seind.* Frankfurt: De Bry, 1612–1614.

Clifton, James. "'Lectulus noster floridus': The Flower-Strewn Bed and the Virgin's Womb." In *Marian Images in Context: Doctrines, Devotions, and Cults*. Edited by James Clifton, Barbara Haeger, and Elliott Wise. Forthcoming.

Crowther-Heyck, Kathleen. "Wonderful Secrets of Nature: Natural Knowledge and Religious Piety in Reformation Germany." *Isis* 94 (2003): 253–73.

David, Jan. *Paradisvs Sponsi et Sponsae: in qvo messis myrrhae et aromatvm, ex instrumentis ac mysterijs Passionis Christi colligenda, vt ei commoriamur. Et Pancarpivm Marianvm, Septemplici Titulorum serie distinctum: vt in B. Virginis odorem curramus et Christvs formetur in nobis*. 2 vols. in 1. Antwerp: Ex officina Plantiniana, Apud Ioannem Moretum, 1607.

Dekoninck, Ralph. *Ad imaginem: Statuts, fonctions et usages de l'image dans la littérature spirituelle jésuite du XVIIe siècle*. Geneva: Droz, 2005.

Diels, Ann, Marjolein Leesberg, and Arnout Balis, compilers and eds. *The Collaert Dynasty, Part VI: The New Hollstein Dutch and Flemish Etchings, Engravings and Woodcuts, 1450–1700*. Ouderkerk aan den Ijssel: Sound & Vision, 2005.

Dodonaeus, Rembertus. *Stirpium historiae pemptades sex*. Antwerp: Ex Officina Plantiniana, Apud Balthasarem et Ioannem Moretos, 1616.

Engammare, Max. "Dans le jardin du bien-aimé. Illustration et exégèse du *Cantique des Cantiques* au XVIIe siècle." *Graphè* 8 (1999): 123–62.

———. *Qu'il me baise des baisers de sa bouche: Le Cantique des cantiques à la Renaissance; Étude et bibliographie*. THR 277. Geneva: Droz, 1993.

Freedberg, David. "The Origins and Rise of the Flemish Madonnas in Flower Garlands: Decoration and Devotion." *MJBK*, 3rd ser., 32 (1981): 115–50.

Gerarde [sic], John. *The Herball or Generall Historie of Plantes*. London: Norton, 1597.

Hänsel, Sylvaine. *Der spanische Humanist Benito Arias Montano (1527–1598) und die Kunst*. SFG 2/25. Münster Westfalen: Aschendorffsche Verlagsbuchhandlung, 1991.

Jong, Erik A. de. "A Garden Book Made for Emperor Rudolf II in 1593: Hans Puechfeldner's *Nützliches Khünstbüech der Gartnereij*." Pages 187–203 in *The Art of Natural History: Illustrated Treatises and Botanical Paintings, 1400–1850*. Edited by Therese O'Malley and Amy R. W. Meyers. SHA 69. Washington, DC: National Gallery of Art, 2008.

Jong, Marijnke de, and Irene de Groot. *Ornamentprenten in het Rijksprentenkabinet, I, 15de & 16de Eeuw*. Amsterdam: Rijksprentenkabinet, Rijksmuseum, and 's-Gravenhage: Staatsuitgeverij, 1988.

Jorink, Eric. *Reading the Book of Nature in the Dutch Golden Age, 1575–1715*. Translated by Peter Mason. Leiden: Brill, 2010.

Kaufmann, Thomas DaCosta, and Virginia Roehrig Kaufmann. "The Sanctification of Nature: Observations on the Origins of Trompe l'oeil in Netherlandish Book Painting of the Fifteenth and Sixteenth Centuries." *JPGMJ* 19 (1991): 43–64.

Koch, Ebba. "Flowers in Mughal Architecture." *Marg* 70.2 (December 2018–March 2019): 25–33.

Lapide, Cornelius à. *Commentarii in Canticvm Canticorvm*. Antwerp: Aud Iacobvm Mevrsivm, 1657.

Lemli, Jozef. "The Officinae Plantinianae in Antwerp and Leiden and Their Botanical Editions from 1589 until 1647." Pages 57–59 in *Botany in the Low Countries (End of the Fifteenth Century–ca. 1650)*. Exh. cat. Antwerp: Plantin-Moretus Museum, 1993.

Losty, Jeremiah P. "Further Light on Mughal Flower Studies and Their European Sources." Unpublished paper, 2014. https://tinyurl.com/SBL6703f.

Losty, Jeremiah P., and Malini Roy. *Mughal India: Art, Culture and Empire: Manuscripts and Paintings in the British Library*. London: British Library, 2012.

Melion, Walter S. "Benedictus Arias Montanus and the Virtual Studio as a Meditative Place." Pages 73–107, 196–201 in *Inventions of the Studio:*

*Renaissance to Romanticism*. Edited by Michael Cole and Mary Pardo. Chapel Hill: University of North Carolina Press, 2005.

———. *The Meditative Art: Studies in the Northern Devotional Print, 1550–1625*. EMCVA 1. Philadelphia: Saint Joseph's University Press, 2009.

———. "Meditative Images and the Portrayal of Image-Based Meditation." Pages 1–60 in *Ut pictura meditatio: The Meditative Image in Northern Art, 1500–1700*. Edited by Walter S. Melion, Ralph Dekoninck, and Agnes Guiderdoni-Bruslé. PSEMIF 4. Turnhout: Brepols, 2012.

Merriam, Susan. *Seventeenth-Century Flemish Garland Paintings: Still Life, Vision, and the Devotional Image*. Burlington, VT: Ashgate, 2012.

Morrall, Andrew. "Regaining Eden: Representations of Nature in Seventeenth-Century English Embroidery." Pages 79–97 in *English Embroidery from the Metropolitan Museum of Art, 1580–1700: 'Twixt Art and Nature*. Edited by Andrew Morrall and Melinda Watt. Exh. cat. New Haven: Yale University Press, for the Bard Graduate Center for Studies in the Decorative Arts, Design, and Culture, New York, and the Metropolitan Museum of Art, New York, 2008.

Morrall, Andrew, and Melinda Watt, eds. *English Embroidery from The Metropolitan Museum of Art, 1580–1700: 'Twixt Art and Nature*. Exh. cat. New Haven: Yale University Press, for The Bard Graduate Center for Studies in the Decorative Arts, Design, and Culture, New York, and The Metropolitan Museum of Art, New York, 2008.

[Moyne, Jaques le, dit de Morgues]. *La Clef des champs, pour trouuer plusieurs Animaux, tant Bestes qu'Oyseaux, auec plusieurs Fleurs & Fruitz*. [London:] Imprimé aux Blackefriers, pour Jaques le Moyne, dit de Morgues Paintre, 1586.

Nissen, Claus. *Die botanische Buchillustration: Ihre Geschichte und Bibliographie*. 2 vols. Stuttgart: Hiersemann Verlags-Gesellschaft, 1951.

North, Susan. "'An Instrument of Profit, Pleasure, and of Ornament': Embroidered Tudor and Jacobean Dress Accessories." Pages 39–55 in *English Embroidery from the Metropolitan Museum of Art, 1580–1700: 'Twixt Art and Nature*. Edited by Andrew Morrall and Melinda Watt. Exh. cat. New Haven: Yale University Press, for the Bard Graduate Center for Studies in the Decorative Arts, Design, and Culture, New York, and the Metropolitan Museum of Art, New York, 2008.

Ogilvie, Brian W. *The Science of Describing: Natural History in Renaissance Europe*. Chicago: University of Chicago Press, 2006.

Segal, Sam. "On Florilegia." Pages 9–47 in *Natural History & Travel*. Cat. 279. Amsterdam: Antiquariaat Junk, 2000.

Segre, Ada. "Le retour de Flore: Naissance et évolution des jardins de fleurs de 1550 à 1650." Pages 174–93 in *L'Empire de flore: Histoire et représentation des fleurs en Europe du XVIe au XIXe siècle*. Edited by Sabine van Sprang. Brussels: La Renaissance du Livre, 1996.

Swan, Claudia. "The Uses of Botanical Treatises in the Netherlands, c. 1600." Pages 63–81 in *The Art of Natural History: Illustrated Treatises and Botanical Paintings, 1400–1850*. Edited by Therese O'Malley and Amy R. W. Meyers. SHA 69. Washington, DC: National Gallery of Art, 2008.

Sweerts, Emmanuel. *Florilegium*. Frankfurt, 1612.

Tabernaemontanus. *Neuw Kreuterbuch … Frankfurt*, 1588.

Taylor, John. *The Needles Excellency: A New Booke wherein are diuers Admirable Workes wrought with the Needle. Newly inuented and cut in Copper for the pleasure and profit of the Industrious*. 10th ed. [London]: Bloer, 1636.

*The Therd Booke of Flowers Fruits Beastes Birds and Flies Exactly Drawne. With Additions by Iohn Dunstall*. [London]: Stent, 1661.

Van Gelder, J. G. "Van blompot en blomglas." *EM* 46 (1936): 73–82, 155–66.

Veldman, Ilja M. *Crispijn de Passe and His Progeny (1564–1670): A Century of Print Production*. Translated by Michael Hoyle. SPP 3. Rotterdam: Sound & Vision, 2001.

Vignau-Wilberg, Thea. "Devotion and Observation of Nature in Art around 1600." Pages 43–55 in *Natura-Cultura: L'Interpretazione del mondo fisico nei testi e nelle immagini; Atti del Convegno Internazionale di Studi, Mantova, 5–8 ottobre 1996*. Edited by Giuseppe Olmi, Lucia Tongiorgi Tomasi, and Attilio Zanca. Florence: Oschki, 2000.

Vredeman de Vries, Hans. *Hortorum viridariorumque elegantes & multiplicis formae, ad architectonicae artis normam affabrè*. 1583.

Wachtel, Alexandra. "Rembert Doedens." Pages 192–99 in *Prints and the Pursuit of Knowledge in Early Modern Europe*. Edited by Susan Dackerman. Exh. cat. Cambridge: Harvard Art Museums; New Haven: Yale University Press, 2011.

Waźbiński, Zygmunt. "Adriaen Collaert i jego *Florilegium*: Niderlandzkie źródła włoskiej szesnastowiecznej martwej natury." Pages 249–68 in *Ars longa: Prace dedykowane pamięci profesora Jana Białostockiego; Materiały Sesji Stowarzyszenia Historyków Sztuki, Warszawa, listopad 1998*. Warsaw: Ośrodek Wydawniczy Zamku Królewskiego w Warszawie, 1999.

Wheelock, Arthur K., Jr. *From Botany to Bouquets: Flowers in Northern Art*. Exh. cat. Washington, DC: National Gallery of Art, 1999.

# 3
# "I Sought Him Whom My Soul Loves": Symbol, Ornament, and Visual Exegesis of the Song of Songs in the *Saint John's Bible*

## JONATHAN HOMRIGHAUSEN

All the Scriptures are holy, but the Song of Songs is the Holy of Holies.
—Rabbi Akiba, m. Yad. 3:5

In the current flowering of scholarship asking whether Christians should read the Song of Songs as literal love poetry or allegorical choreography to a divine dance between God and humanity, the visual reception of this beautiful poem is seldom invoked as a discussion partner. Yet as the most significant illuminated manuscript of the Christian Bible of the third millennium, the *Saint John's Bible* lends itself perfectly to this discussion. This ambitious Bible was commissioned in 1998 and completed in 2011 by Donald Jackson and his team of scribes and illuminators under the patronage and guidance of the Benedictine monks of Saint John's Abbey in Minnesota. Jackson and the scribes wrote its vellum pages with quills and traditional inks and pigments. Its art explicitly draws on the heritage of two millennia of Christian symbolism; its scriptural exegesis, guided by a team of biblical scholars and theologians, is inspired by patristic and medieval notions about and readings of Scripture. Its illuminations aim to be interpretations or visual meditations on the text.[1] By closely examining the Song

---

[1] This paper began its life as a talk at the Annual Meeting of the Society of Biblical Literature in 2017 and was expanded in Dorothy Verkerk's doctoral seminar on ornament. Gratitude is owed to those who accepted my paper and invited me to contribute to this volume, and to all who gave generous feedback on this paper along the way, including Donald Jackson, Michael Patella, Ellen Davis, Marc Brettler, Lucinda

of Songs illuminations in the *Saint John's Bible*, I aim to show the complexity of its literal and allegorical, spiritual and embodied reading of the Song.

The Song of Songs was one of the most significant and most commented-on biblical books of the medieval Latin Church.[2] It is also the most densely illuminated book of the *Saint John's Bible*, followed by Revelation. This poetic book's eight chapters record the speeches of two lovers as they share their honeyed discourse with one another; these chapters are loosely linked, with no clear narrative, though connected by the vivid imagery running throughout the poem. On a literal level, it may be read as secular erotic poetry between human lovers. However, until the modern era, the dominant reading of this poem has been not as love between humans but love between humans and God. Jewish tradition reads the man and the woman as God and Israel, and Christian tradition portrays them as Christ and the soul, or Mary, or the church. These allegorical interpretations are commonly reflected in visual exegesis, such as a historiated initial O in one twelfth-century manuscript in which Christ embraces Ecclesia, the personification of the church.[3] The rise in Marian devotion in the twelfth

---

Mosher, Andrea Sheaffer, Anne Kaese, Kathleen Maxwell, Dorothy Verkerk, and the editors of this volume.

All images copyright 2002–2011, *The Saint John's Bible*, Saint John's University, Collegeville, Minnesota USA. Scripture quotations are from the New Revised Standard Version of the Bible, Catholic Edition, Copyright 1993, 1989 National Council of the Churches of Christ in the United States of America. Used by permission. All rights reserved.

1. For background, see Michael Patella, *Word and Image: The Hermeneutics of the Saint John's Bible* (Collegeville, MN: Liturgical Press, 2013); Susan Sink, *The Art of the Saint John's Bible: The Complete Reader's Guide* (Collegeville, MN: Liturgical Press, 2013); Christopher Calderhead, *Illuminating the Word: The Making of The Saint John's Bible*, 2nd ed. (Collegeville, MN: Liturgical Press, 2015); Jonathan Homrighausen, *Illuminating Justice: The Ethical Imagination of The Saint John's Bible* (Collegeville, MN: Liturgical Press, 2018); Jack R. Baker, Jeffrey Bilbro, and Daniel Train, eds., *The Saint John's Bible and Its Tradition: Illuminating Beauty in the Twenty-First Century* (Eugene, OR: Pickwick, 2018).

2. E. Ann Matter, *The Voice of My Beloved: The Song of Songs in Western Medieval Christianity* (Philadelphia: University of Pennsylvania Press, 1992), 3.

3. Capuchins' Bible of St. Bertin, twelfth century, France (Paris, Bibliotheque Nationale Latin 16745), fol. 112v, found in Ruth Bartal, "Medieval Images of 'Sacred Love': Jewish and Christian Perceptions," *ASAH* 2 (1996): 96–97. See also Bartal, "'Where Has Your Beloved Gone?': The Staging of the *Quaerere Deum* on the Murals of the Cistercian Convent at Chełmno," *WI* 16 (2000): 270–89; Judith Glatzer Wechsler, "A Change in the Iconography of the Song of Songs in Twelfth and Thirteenth Century

and thirteen centuries led to Marian exegesis of the Song, as in the late medieval iconography of Madonna and Child in an enclosed garden such as Martin Schongauer's *Madonna of the Rose Garden* (1473).[4]

Unlike these medieval visual translations, the *Saint John's Bible* does not explicitly image the figures in the Song as Christ, Mary, or Ecclesia. But unlike many contemporary renditions of the Song, it also does not imagine the figures as *only* human lovers in erotic embrace.[5] Instead, it illuminates the Song of Songs not through any figural images of living beings but through symbols engaging with and drawn from the poetic sacred text. These symbols are strewn across the four bifolia (two-page spreads) of the Song: the first two focusing on the imagery of the garden and its connection to the temple and the church, and the second two featuring the imagery of lilies and lace connecting the Song with Christ. Symbolic ornament, or ornamenting symbols—here, they are one and the same—create a garden of desire framing the text exegetically and iconographically. It brings the reader/viewer into an *experience* of the dynamics of the Song's poetry—a reading not merely visual but, like its medieval predecessors, wholly embodied, even in the embodied forms of its calligraphied words and letters. Its spiritual reading, *lectio divina*, of the Song makes the text into a body itself—theologically, the word made flesh—highlighting the parchment materiality of this Bible.[6] This visual exegesis points beyond the tired literal-allegorical binary so often applied to the Song.[7]

---

Latin Bibles," in *Texts and Responses: Studies Presented to Nahum N. Glatzer on the Occasion of His Seventieth Birthday by His Students*, ed. Michael A. Fishbane and Paul R. Flohr (Leiden: Brill, 1975), 73–93.

4. Matter, *Voice of My Beloved*, 151–77. On the Song of Songs and *hortus conclusus* imagery, see Christina Bucher, "The Song of Songs and the 'Enclosed Garden' in Paintings and Illustrations of the Virgin Mary," in *Between the Text and the Canvas: The Bible and Art in Dialogue*, ed. J. Cheryl Exum (Sheffield: Sheffield Phoenix, 2007), 96–116; Brian E. Daley, "The 'Closed Garden' and the 'Sealed Fountain': Song of Songs 4:12 in the Late Medieval Iconography of Mary," in *Medieval Gardens*, ed. Elisabeth B. MacDougall (Washington, DC: Dumbarton Oaks Research Library, 1986), 254–78.

5. E.g., J. Cheryl Exum, "Seeing the Song of Songs: Some Artistic Visions of the Bible's Love Lyrics," in *Das Alte Testament Und Die Kunst*, ed. John Barton, J. Cheryl Exum, and Manfred Oeming (Münster: LIT, 2005), 91–127.

6. See, e.g., Ittai Weinryb, "Living Matter: Materiality, Maker, and Ornament in the Middle Ages," *Gesta* 52 (2013): 113–32.

7. On visual exegesis, see J. Cheryl Exum, "Toward a Genuine Dialogue between the Bible and Art," in *Congress Volume Helsinki 2010*, ed. Martti Nissinen, VTSup 148 (Leiden: Brill, 2012), 473–504.

## Presence and Absence, Geometry, and *Lectio Divina*

Turning to the opening page of the Song (fig. 3.1), the viewer finds herself lost in an abundance of ornament completely intermingled with the text. This motif continues and intensifies on the next bifolium (fig. 3.2). The complete intermingling of text and image here creates initial confusion for the reader: Which verses of the Song are being illuminated? On the second page, however, the top and bottom of the two-page spread direct the reader to focus on two key verses. At top, 3:1: "I sought him whom my soul loves; I sought him, but found him not"; at bottom, 4:12, "A garden locked is my sister, my bride; a garden locked, a fountain sealed."[8] These verses suggest that the first two double-page spreads of the Song visualize two passages in the Song: first, the woman speaking the presence and absence of her beloved in 3:1–5; and second, the overwhelming overflow of metaphor and imagery in the man's speech to and about his beloved in 4:1–15. To use Oleg Grabar's term, symbol and ornament work together to *mediate* the reader's experience of sacred text.[9]

While the Song as a whole has no clear narrative structure, it does have miniplots. One of these miniplots is 3:1–5, the woman's narration of her search for her lover by night. She wanders about the city to find him, failing at first, until she finally discovers him (v. 4). This might be read as either a dream sequence or a real event within this poetic world.[10] The Christian spiritual tradition, however, read it as an evocation of one's relationship with God, who sometimes feels present in prayer and other times seems absent; John of the Cross famously conveyed this in his spiritual-theological poem "The Dark Night."[11]

The first two bifolia of the Song of Songs capture this motif of presence and absence in their geometric patterns. While there is much going on in these pages, here we focus only on the half-circle patterns floating around

---

8. Unless otherwise stated, all biblical translations follow the NRSV.

9. Oleg Grabar, *The Mediation of Ornament* (Princeton: Princeton University Press, 1992), xxiv.

10. Othmar Keel, *The Song of Songs*, trans. Frederick J. Gaiser, CC (Minneapolis: Fortress, 1994); Roland E. Murphy, *The Song of Songs*, Hermeneia (Minneapolis: Fortress, 1990), 145; Tremper Longman III, *Song of Songs*, NICOT (Grand Rapids: Eerdmans, 2001), 129.

11. John of the Cross, *The Collected Works of St. John of the Cross*, rev. ed., trans. Kieran Kavanaugh and Otilio Rodriguez (Washington, DC: ICS, 2010), 353–460.

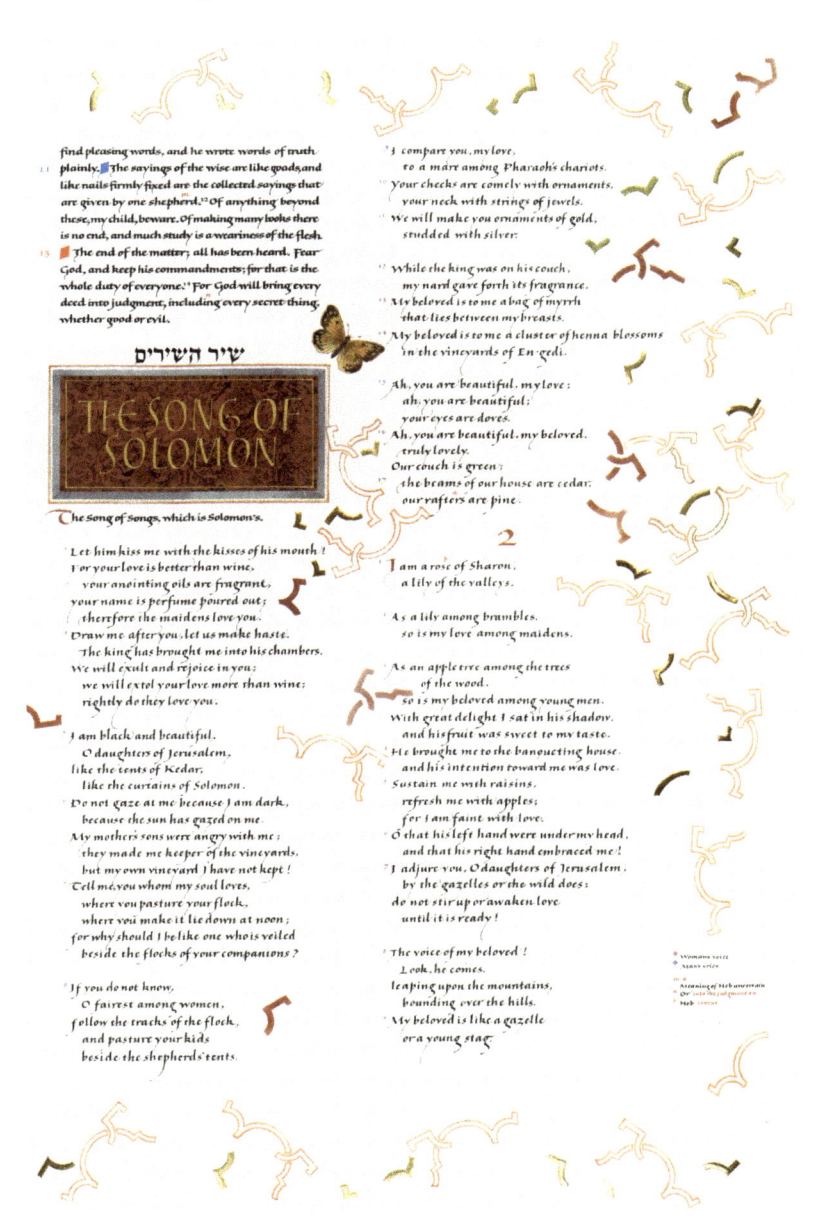

Fig. 3.1. Donald Jackson, *The Song of Solomon*. Poetry Scribe: Sally Mae Joseph; Prose Scribe: Susan Leiper; Hebrew Script: Izzy Pludwinski; Book Heading: Donald Jackson. 2006. From *The Saint John's Bible*. Gouache and ink on vellum, 15½ x 23½". Saint John's University, Collegeville, Minnesota.

Fig. 3.2 (left and right). Donald Jackson, *Garden of Desire*, Scribe and Artist: Donald Jackson; Hebrew Script: Izzy Pludwinski. 2006. From *The Saint John's Bible*. Gouache and ink on vellum, 31½ x 23½", Saint John's University, Collegeville, MN. Saint John's University, Collegeville, Minnesota.

## 3. "I SOUGHT HIM WHOM MY SOUL LOVES"

I SOUGHT·HIM · BUT·FOUND·HIM·NOT

in the streets and in the squares;
I will seek him whom my soul loves."
I sought him, but found him not.
The sentinels found me,
as they went about in the city.
"Have you seen him whom my soul loves?"
Scarcely had I passed them,
when I found him whom my soul loves.
I held him, and would not let him go
until I brought him into my mother's house,
and into the chamber of her
that conceived me.
I adjure you, O daughters of Jerusalem,
by the gazelles of the wild does:
do not stir up or awaken love
until it is ready!

What is that coming up from the wilderness,
like a column of smoke,
perfumed with myrrh and frankincense,
with all the fragrant powders
of the merchant?
Look, it is the litter of Solomon!
Around it are sixty mighty men
of the mighty men of Israel,
all equipped with swords
and expert in war,
each with his sword at his thigh
because of alarms by night.
King Solomon made himself a palanquin
from the wood of Lebanon.
He made its posts of silver,
its back of gold, its seat of purple;
its interior was inlaid with love.
Daughters of Jerusalem,
come out.
Look, O daughters of Zion,
at King Solomon,
at the crown with which his mother
crowned him
on the day of his wedding,
on the day of the gladness of his heart.

**4**

How beautiful you are, my love,
how very beautiful!
Your eyes are doves
behind your veil.
Your hair is like a flock of goats,
moving down the slopes of Gilead.
Your teeth are like a flock of shorn ewes
that have come up from the washing,
all of which bear twins.

and not one among them is bereaved.
Your lips are like a crimson thread,
and your mouth is lovely.
Your cheeks are like halves of a pomegranate
behind your veil.
Your neck is like the tower of David,
built in courses;
on it hang a thousand bucklers,
all of them shields of warriors.
Your two breasts are like two fawns,
twins of a gazelle,
that feed among the lilies.
Until the day breathes
and shadows flee,
I will hasten to the mountain of myrrh
and the hill of frankincense.
You are altogether beautiful, my love;
there is no flaw in you.
Come with me from Lebanon, my bride;
come with me from Lebanon.
Depart from the peak of Amana,
from the peak of Senir and Hermon,
from the dens of lions,
from the mountains of leopards.

You have ravished my heart, my sister, my bride;
you have ravished my heart with a
glance of your eyes,
with one jewel of your necklace.
How sweet is your love, my sister, my bride!
how much better is your love than wine,
and the fragrance of your oils than any spice!
Your lips distill nectar, my bride;
honey and milk are under your tongue;
the scent of your garments is like
the scent of Lebanon.
A garden locked is my sister, my bride,
a garden locked, a fountain sealed.
Your channel is an orchard of pomegranates
with all choicest fruits,
henna with nard,
nard and saffron, calamus and cinnamon,
with all trees of frankincense,
myrrh and aloes,
with all chief spices —
a garden fountain, a well of living water,
and flowing streams from Lebanon.

Awake, O north wind,
and come, O south wind!
Blow upon my garden
that its fragrance may be wafted abroad.
Let my beloved come to his garden,
and eat its choicest fruits.

·A·GARDEN·LOCKED·A·FOUNTAIN·SEALED·

the two bifolia as if blown about by the wind. As the viewer's eyes follow these patterns from left to right in the direction of reading, these patterns' variations depict the relationship of absence leading into presence in 3:1–5, leading into the total presence at the climax of 4:1–5:1, discussed below. They vary between being a lighter orange and a darker red, between being fully colored in or only in outline (a hint at absence and presence?), and in their proximity to the garden itself. Some smaller flecks are in gold, a signifier of God's presence in the *Saint John's Bible*, hinting at the full divine presence to come.[12] The next page exudes more sense of presence, as all of the geometric pieces are filled in, all are darker reds and browns, and they are more complete. The ornament, deliberately left incomplete, itself mesmerizes the reader into a meditative state.

They lead into the red, circular garden, which connects the motif (fig. 3.3). Jackson compares this to iron shavings gravitating towards a magnet,[13] though the geometric pattern may also be seen as blown about by the wind (see Song 4:16). At the center of the garden floats a scarlet circle inside its square walls; inside the pomegranate is a series of labyrinthine geometric patterns, which are the complete versions of those around this page and the page before. Within the garden itself, however, the pattern is left incomplete—what Ernst Gombrich describes as a "visual accent" that draws the viewer's attention to the breaking of a pattern, in turn bringing the pattern more fully to their awareness.[14] The viewer's eye naturally fills in the pattern by the "prognostic character of perception," our natural ability to fill in incomplete geometric patterns, thus drawing the viewer into the pattern ever more.[15] Perhaps the incomplete pattern hints that full consummation in our relationship with God is inarticulable in art or text, or not for this life at all.

The eye's tracing of the geometric patterns between the pages, around the page, and into the garden creates a meditative experience that lends itself to the *lectio divina* by which the medieval and modern monastic

---

12. Gold and gilding are an immense part of Jackson's technique and the *Saint John's Bible*'s theology. See Jonathan Homrighausen, "Words Made Flesh: Incarnational, Multisensory Exegesis in Donald Jackson's Biblical Art," *RelArts* 23 (2019): 240–72; Calderhead, *Illuminating the Word*, 130–33; Donald Jackson, "Gilding," in *The Calligrapher's Handbook*, 2nd ed., ed. Heather Child (New York: Taplinger, 1986), 177–98.

13. Calderhead, *Illuminating the Word*, 234.

14. Ernst H. Gombrich, *The Sense of Order: A Study in the Psychology of Decorative Art* (Ithaca, NY: Cornell University Press, 1979), 111.

15. Gombrich, *Sense of Order*, 107.

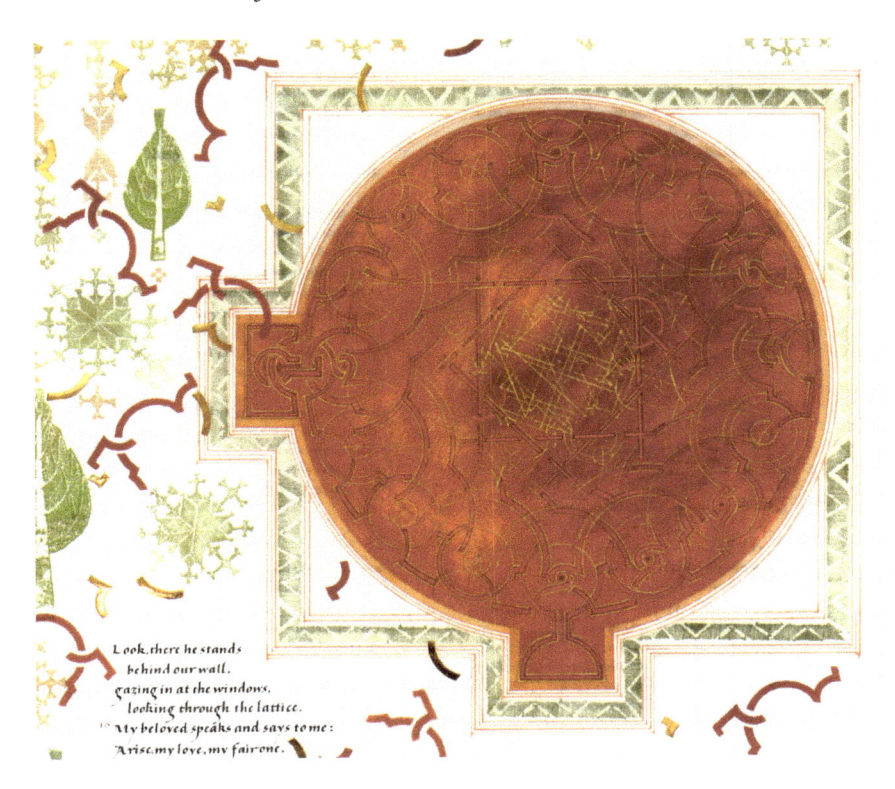

Look, there he stands
behind our wall,
gazing in at the windows,
looking through the lattice.
My beloved speaks and says to me:
Arise, my love, my fair one.

Fig. 3.3. Donald Jackson, detail of *Garden of Desire*. 2006. From *The Saint John's Bible*. Gouache and ink on vellum, page measures 15¾ x 23½". Saint John's University, Collegeville, Minnesota.

tradition engages Scripture. Indeed, the committee that gave Jackson theological guidance did its own *lectio* on each text before sending him its suggestions.[16] Most obviously, taking in the intricate ornament requires the reader to *slow down*, to ponder the words and images of this Bible slowly, a deliberate design choice in the making of this Bible.[17] But this is not merely because of the *amount* of ornament—it is also because of the specific geometric quality of the ornament. Scholars of insular manuscripts, those created in early medieval Britain and Ireland, have written

---

16. Patella, *Word and Image*, 12–13, 23–24; Calderhead, *Illuminating the Word*, 110–13.

17. Robert Moore-Jumonville, "Beauty Cannot Be Rushed: An Invitation to Contemplation from *The Saint John's Bible*," in Baker, Bilbro, and Train, *Saint John's Bible*, 43–58.

on the meditative quality inspired by the use of sacred geometry in manuscripts such as the Book of Kells, the Book of Durrow, and the Lindisfarne Gospels.[18] Discussing carpet pages such as folio 2v of the Lindisfarne Gospels (British Library, Cotton Nero D.IV), Benjamin Tilghman has written about how the use of "sacred geometry" may create a sense of flow in its artists, a loss of a sense of time, space, or identity.[19] I would add that viewers might experience the same mental state. As their eyes follow these geometric patterns around the page, as their minds fill in the patterns of the garden, they slowly ponder the full divine presence of the page and in the text, moving into that state of presence. The analogy between Jackson and insular manuscripts is affirmed by Jackson, who stated in a 1988 interview that the Book of Kells is one of his favorite artistic sources on which to draw.[20]

This slow, meditative reading is known in Benedictine and other monastic traditions as *lectio divina*. In *lectio divina*, the reader slowly ponders (*ruminatio*) the text, allowing it to begin a conversation with God in prayer. Reading the sacred text becomes not a mere means to information—monastic reading always has the end goal of deeper prayer and love for God.[21] Reading becomes a site of open-ended spiritual formation, focusing on experiencing and internalizing (often memorizing) the text rather than theorizing about it. Further, in *lectio divina* readers become active participants in the text, bringing their own conversation partners and free associations to the Bible drawn from other biblical texts, from the world around them, from their own experience.[22] Duncan Robertson shows, for example, how Bernard of Clairvaux's sermons on the Song of

---

18. Emmanuelle Pirotte, "Hidden Order, Order Revealed: New Light on Carpet Pages," in *Pattern and Purpose in Insular Art: Proceedings of the Fourth International Conference on Insular Art Held at the National Museum and Gallery, Cardiff 3–6 September 1998*, ed. Mark Redknap et al. (Oxford: Oxbow Books, 2002), 203–8.

19. Benjamin C. Tilghman, "Pattern, Process, and the Creation of Meaning in the Lindisfarne Gospels," *West 86th* 24 (2017): 3–28.

20. Marion Muller, "The Scribe Who Renounced the Pen," *ULC* 15.4 (November 1988): 4.

21. Jean Leclercq, *The Love of Learning and the Desire for God: A Study of Monastic Culture*, trans. Catherine Mizrahi (New York: Fordham University Press, 1982).

22. A great example of *lectio divina* inspired by the *Saint John's Bible* can be found in Matthew A. Rothaus Moser, "Should Bibles Be Beautiful? How Beauty Teaches Us to Pray," in Baker, Bilbro, and Train, *Saint John's Bible*, 26–42.

Songs are not a technical *commentary* on the text but an evocation of both his and his monastic community's personal engagements with it.[23]

Thus, the ornament lends itself to what the creators of the *Saint John's Bible* call *visio divina*, a prayerful meditation on the art, which is inseparable from the monastic *lectio divina* on the text which the art illuminates. And the symbols on these pages are tantalizingly ambiguous, open-ended enough to provoke that kind of *visio divina*.

## Image, Text, and the Abundant Garden

Once readers move their eyes away from the geometric patterns around the first two bifolia, they also notice a bewildering array of symbols, many drawn from the man's speech to his beloved in 4:1–5:1, from which the text at the bottom of the page is drawn: "A garden locked is my sister, my bride; a garden locked, a fountain sealed" (4:12). The abundant symbolism continues on the next two bifolia of the Song with brightly, warmly colored flowers, lace patterns, and text treatments. The overwhelming layout of symbols here is designed to overpower the reader in much the same way as the dense, intense metaphors of the text itself. Jackson's illuminations, then, invite the reader to *experience* the text more affectively. Following the *lectio divina*, the symbolism of these illuminations also brings the Song into conversation with other biblical narratives, specifically the temple traditions of ancient Israel and the crucifixion and resurrection scenes of the Gospels—thus reflecting medieval ecclesiological, christological, and mariological understandings of the Song.

The lovers' dialogue in 4:1–5:1 begins with a lengthy speech by the man (4:1–15). In this speech he praises the beauty of his beloved through a series of highly developed images and metaphors. At the end of his seductive speech, the woman invites him to "come to his garden, and eat its choicest fruits" (4:16), after which the man does so (5:1) in what many scholars see as the climax of the lovers' union, the Song's "most sensual pitch."[24] Many of the metaphors used to describe the woman's body are imagery of flora, fauna, or fine spices and oils; the overriding image then, is "a garden locked

---

23. Duncan Robertson, *Lectio Divina: The Medieval Experience of Reading* (Trappist, KY: Cistercian Publications, 2011), 156–203.

24. J. Cheryl Exum, *Song of Songs*, OTL (Richmond: Westminster John Knox, 2005), 173.

is my sister, my bride" (4:12). The metaphor of the garden, crucial here as it is crucial for the Song and the Old Testament more broadly, is also crucial for Jackson's artistic treatment of the Song.

If Jackson's illuminations of the Song on the first two bifolia are in the form of a garden enclosing the text, then this garden is rich indeed. Jackson surrounds and intermingles the text with a dense garden illumination around the page, between the columns of text, and at times even within the column of text, all echoing the piling up of metaphors in the poem itself.[25] The viewer's first glance at this page leaves them *overwhelmed*. Doing so echoes the few other places where such an explosion of visuals occurs, such as the eucharistic imagery (also an image of abundance!) of the *Loaves and Fishes* illumination (Mark 6:33–44, 8:1–10).[26] However, once the viewer shifts from a global perception of the whole ornament to a detailed analysis of its parts, its structure and symbolism become clear.[27] Anchoring the page is a light red-and-brown textile pattern inspired by those of Gujarat, India, with geometric shapes, camels, men and women, and even a large-plumed bird (a peacock?) and a weathervane.[28] Jackson explains that such textile patterns, which occur throughout his illuminations, represent "an endless urge to unite" as the fibers go in all directions; here, they also take on a bucolic appearance echoing the pastoral setting of the Song.[29] This decoration provides a kind of stability, an architectural frame, for the chaos it undergirds: stamped-on leaves of different sizes, shades, and slightly differing patterns, adding to the garden imagery in the text; and small crosses made up of four squares, echoing a motif used throughout the gospels illuminations. Far from reflecting the imagery in a wooden fashion, Jackson chooses very deliberate imagery that dialogues with it in interesting ways, focusing on

---

25. This imagery, particularly the basic identification of the symbols, is explained in Patella, *Word and Image*, 167–69; Sink, *Art of The Saint John's Bible*, 121–24; Calderhead, *Illuminating the Word*, 232–34.

26. Patella, *Word and Image*, 240–42; Donald Jackson and Saint John's University, *The Saint John's Bible: Gospels and Acts* (Collegeville, MN: Liturgical Press, 2005).

27. On perceptual shifts in seeing ornament, see Gombrich, *Sense of Order*, 95–101.

28. Donald Jackson has shared with me which specific textiles inspired this piece: John Gillow and Nicholas Barnard, *Traditional Indian Textiles* (London: Thames & Hudson, 1991), 94–95.

29. Donald Jackson, personal communication, 22 January 2019.

capturing the "imaginative field"[30] of the garden without visually rendering every metaphor in the man's poetic praises of the woman's beauty (4:1–15). Like a real garden, this balances stability, formality, and architecture with the chaos, movement, and spontaneous growth of living flora and fauna inhabiting a garden.[31]

On the next two bifolia (figs. 3.4–5), densely symbolic and colorful illuminations convey abundance and add a new visual theme: risk. This visual theme echoes the textual theme of risk in love, captured in the miniplot of the woman's beating by the city guards when she seeks her beloved (5:7–8), or in her refrain to the daughters of Jerusalem: "do not stir up or awaken love until it is ready!" (2:7, 3:5, 8:4). Around the text of 5:1–8:5 (fig. 3.4), Jackson places bright red flowers, either red lilies or roses of Sharon. The rubric for these flowers is provided in the text treatment: "I am my beloved's and my beloved is mine; he pastures his flock among the lilies" (6:3). To create the stems of these flowers, Jackson tipped the canvas and let the fresh, wet gouache run down the page, capturing the risk and danger inherent in love. He also dipped lace in paint and pressed it down with his hand. While the symbolism of the lace and the flowers is discussed more fully below, note already how these symbols construct a sense of duality reflecting the duality of man and woman in the Song. Jackson explains that he intended to convey a contrast between the delicate feminine lace and the "bold splatters" of the flowers.[32] Other contrasts are created within the lace, some of which is in bright gold and some of which is in light purple. The gold, as throughout the *Saint John's Bible*, refers to the presence of God. Given the significance of Solomon in the Song (1:1, 3:9, 8:12), the purple could signify him or a general sense of royalty for any reader of this text. Finally, two butterflies flit among the flowers—one purple, one golden yellow—and smaller flecks of gold burst out of several of the budded flowers. The visual motifs continue on the final page of the Song of Songs (fig. 3.5), which features smaller, golden flowers, gold lace, and a text treatment of Song 8:6–7. If the first two bifolia convey the entrance to the garden, here the reader-viewer is *in* the garden, smelling its flowers.

---

30. Phrase drawn from Jill M. Munro, *Spikenard and Saffron: The Imagery of the Song of Songs*, JSOTSup 203 (Sheffield: Sheffield Academic, 1995), 19.

31. Marilyn Stokstad, "Gardens in Medieval Art," in *Gardens of the Middle Ages*, ed. Jerry Stannard and Marilyn Stokstad (Lawrence: Spencer Museum of Art, University of Kansas, Lawrence, 1983), 18–35.

32. Calderhead, *Illuminating the Word*, 234.

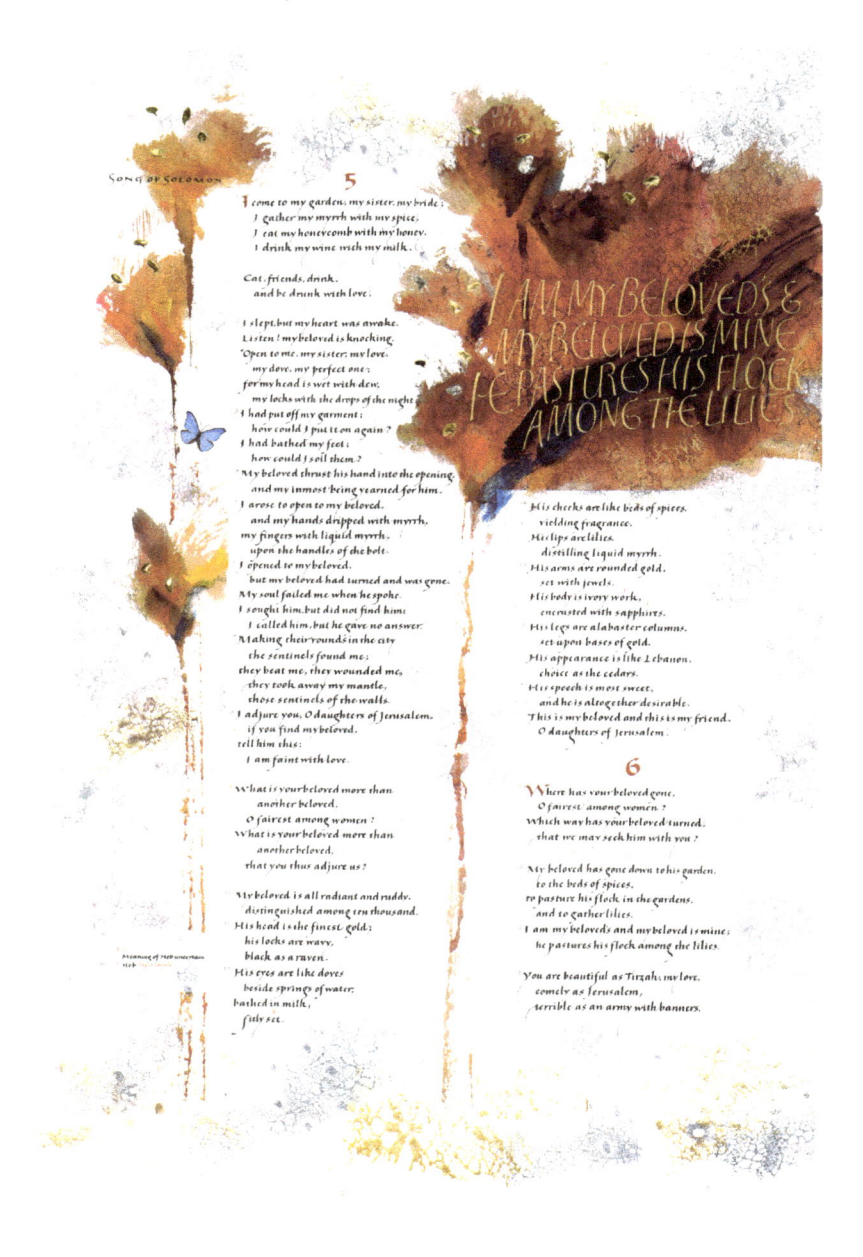

Fig. 3.4. Donald Jackson, *I Am My Beloved's*, Scribe and Artist: Donald Jackson; Hebrew Script: Izzy Pludwinski. 2006. From *The Saint John's Bible*. Gouache and ink on vellum, 31½ x 23½". Saint John's University, Collegeville, Minnesota.

Turn away your eyes from me,
 for they overwhelm me!
Your hair is like a flock of goats,
 moving down the slopes of Gilead.
Your teeth are like a flock of ewes,
 that have come up from the washing;
all of them bear twins,
 and not one among them is bereaved.
Your cheeks are like halves of a pomegranate
 behind your veil.
There are sixty queens and eighty concubines,
 and maidens without number.
My dove, my perfect one, is the only one,
 the darling of her mother,
 flawless to her that bore her.
The maidens saw her and called her happy;
 the queens and concubines also,
 and they praised her:
"Who is this that looks forth like the dawn,
 fair as the moon, bright as the sun,
 terrible as an army with banners?"

I went down to the nut orchard,
 to look at the blossoms of the valley,
to see whether the vines had budded,
 whether the pomegranates were in bloom.
Before I was aware, my fancy set me
 in a chariot beside my prince.

Return, return, O Shulammite!
 Return, return, that we may look upon you.

Why should you look upon the Shulammite,
 as upon a dance before two armies?

### 7

How graceful are your feet in sandals,
 O queenly maiden!
Your rounded thighs are like jewels,
 the work of a master hand.
Your navel is a rounded bowl
 that never lacks mixed wine.
Your belly is a heap of wheat,
 encircled with lilies.
Your two breasts are like two fawns,
 twins of a gazelle.
Your neck is like an ivory tower.
Your eyes are pools in Heshbon,
 by the gate of Bath-rabbim.
Your nose is like a tower of Lebanon,
 overlooking Damascus.
Your head crowns you like Carmel,
 and your flowing locks are like purple;

a king is held captive in the tresses.

How fair and pleasant you are,
 O loved one, delectable maiden!
You are stately as a palm tree,
 and your breasts are like its clusters.
I say I will climb the palm tree
 and lay hold of its branches.
O may your breasts be like clusters of the vine,
 and the scent of your breath like apples,
 and your kisses like the best wine
 that goes down smoothly,
 gliding over lips and teeth.

"I am my beloved's,
 and his desire is for me.
Come, my beloved,
 let us go forth into the fields,
 and lodge in the villages;
let us go out early to the vineyards,
 and see whether the vines have budded,
 whether the grape blossoms have opened,
 and the pomegranates are in bloom.
There I will give you my love.
The mandrakes give forth fragrance,
 and over our doors are all choice fruits,
 new as well as old,
 which I have laid up for you, O my beloved.

### 8

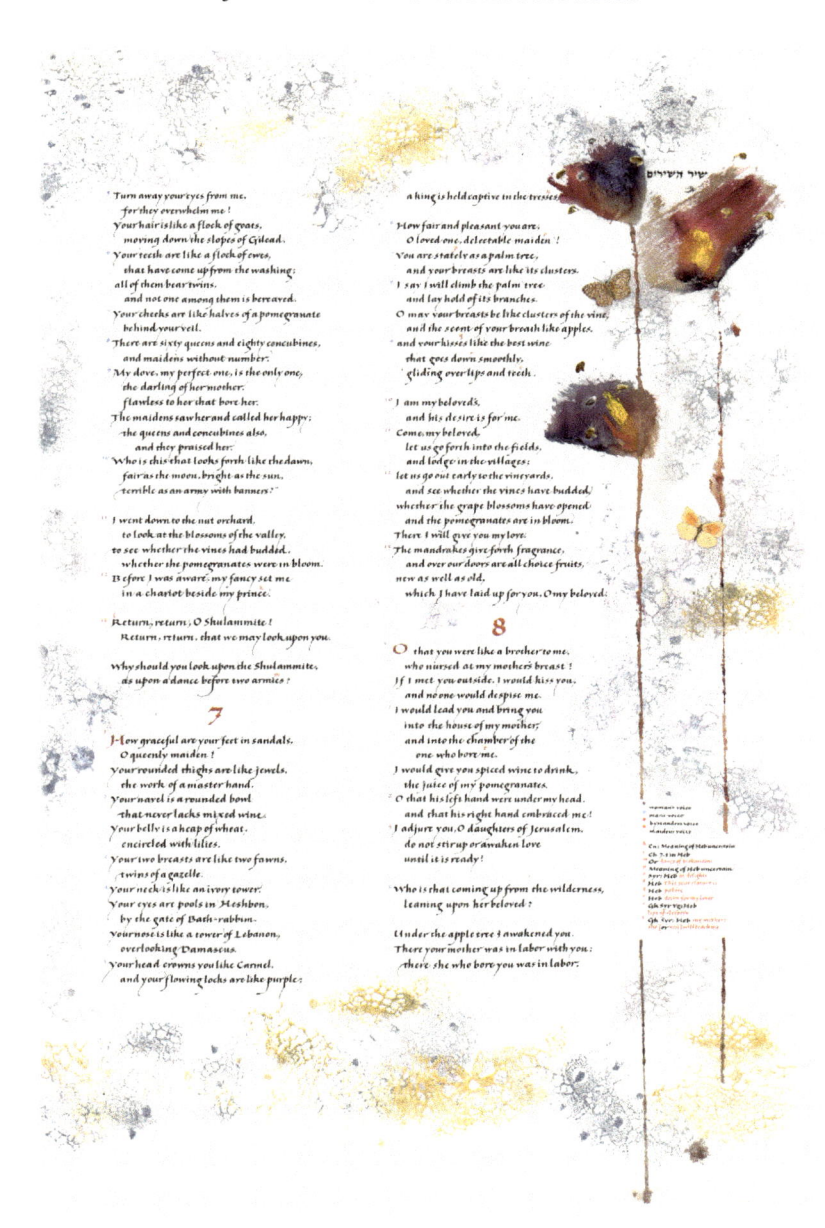

O that you were like a brother to me,
 who nursed at my mother's breast!
If I met you outside, I would kiss you,
 and no one would despise me.
I would lead you and bring you
 into the house of my mother,
 and into the chamber of the
 one who bore me.
I would give you spiced wine to drink,
 the juice of my pomegranates.
O that his left hand were under my head,
 and that his right hand embraced me!
I adjure you, O daughters of Jerusalem,
 do not stir up or awaken love
 until it is ready!

Who is that coming up from the wilderness,
 leaning upon her beloved?

Under the apple tree I awakened you.
There your mother was in labor with you;
 there she who bore you was in labor.

Fig. 3.5. Donald Jackson, *Set Me as a Seal*, Scribe: Sally Mae Joseph; Hebrew Script: Izzy Pludwinski; Book Heading: Donald Jackson. 2006. From *The Saint John's Bible*. Gouache and ink on vellum, 15¾ x 23½". Saint John's University, Collegeville, Minnesota.

In all four bifolia of the Song of Songs illuminations, symbolic ornament mediates the reader's experience of the marginal illuminations. The visual patterns overpower the reader with their busyness and color, underscoring the significance of this text. They also create a kind of climax within the *Saint John's Bible* as a whole, which can only be experienced when the reader engages the illuminations in the context of one of this Bible's bound facsimiles.[33] Ornament and symbol work together, however, not just for aesthetic effect but also to mediate the reader's experience of, their engagement with, the Scripture. Three of these symbols stand out as most significant: the pomegranate, the lily, and the lace. These symbols, and their allusions to other biblical illuminations and texts, point the reader to ecclesiological and christological understandings of the Song.

### The Pomegranate, the Garden Temple, and Ecclesiological Exegesis of the Song

Of all the symbols in the first two bifolia, the largest and most prominent is the deep-red pomegranate—a fruit with dense symbolic meaning in the Song of Songs, the Bible, and Christian art.[34] Here, it alludes to imagery throughout the *Saint John's Bible* of the temple and, typologically, the church. This pomegranate takes up half a page and has two square persistent calyxes inside a green-and-white patterned border. It is enclosed within a walled garden: "a garden locked." In the Song, the pomegranate is associated with the fertile beauty of the woman—"your cheeks are like halves of a pomegranate behind your veil" (4:3, 6:7). The woman promises her beloved that "I would give you spiced wine to drink, the juice of my pomegranates" (8:2) in the house of her mother; some read this as an allusion to her breasts.[35] Elsewhere in the Bible, the pomegranate

---

33. On climactic ornament in medieval illuminations, see, e.g., Robert G. Calkins, "Liturgical Sequence and Decorative Crescendo in the Drogo Sacramentary," *Gesta* 25 (1986): 17–23; Benjamin C. Tilghman, "Ornament and Incarnation in Insular Art," *Gesta* 55 (2016): 160.

34. Peter Murray and Linda Murray, *A Dictionary of Christian Art* (Oxford: Oxford University Press, 2004), 197; Lucia Impelluso, *Nature and Its Symbols* (Los Angeles: Getty, 2004), 145–48; Paul Corby Finney, ed., "Pomegranate," in *The Eerdmans Encyclopedia of Early Christian Art and Archaeology* (Grand Rapids: Eerdmans, 2017), 2:346–47.

35. Munro, *Spikenard and Saffron*, 86.

is described as one of the luscious fruits of Canaan (Num 13:23; Deut 8:8) and a key decoration in priestly garments (Exod 28:33–34) as well as temple architecture (2 Kgs 25:17) and decoration (1 Kgs 7:19, 7:22, 7:26).[36] In the ancient Near East it was known to have medicinal purposes.[37] In Greco-Roman myth, the pomegranate also symbolized resurrection, as in the myth of Persephone and Hades (e.g., the Homeric Hymn to Demeter; Ovid, *Metam.* 5.536; Apollodorus, *Bibl.* 1.5.3).

Both classical and Hebrew associations with the pomegranate feed into its use as symbol and ornament in late antique, medieval, and Renaissance Christian art. The pomegranate appears as a motif in several late antique mosaics, connoting immortality, paradise, and/or the many seeds of the faith.[38] This last idea is found in patristic and medieval authors who use the pomegranate as a symbol of the church: many seeds in one fruit.[39] This idea persists into the Renaissance: Cesare Ripa's *Iconologia* takes the pomegranate as a symbol of concord.[40] In the *Unicorn Tapestries* (Netherlands, ca. 1495–1505), the unicorn dwells inside an enclosed garden (*hortus conclusus*). The pomegranate tree above the unicorn (an allegory for Christ) symbolizes the lusciousness of the garden and perhaps the hope of eternal life. The pomegranate juice drips onto the unicorn, creating red splotches that look like wounds, symbolizing the wounds of Christ.[41] Thus, the red juice of the pomegranate is both resurrection *and* death. Likewise, the

---

36. Carol L. Meyers, "Temple, Jerusalem," *ABD* 6:360.

37. Robert Koops, *Each according to Its Kinds: Plants and Trees in the Bible*, UTH (New York: United Bible Societies, 2012), 64–66; Lytton John Musselman, *A Dictionary of Bible Plants* (New York: Cambridge University Press, 2012), 117–18; John F. Nunn, *Ancient Egyptian Medicine* (Norman: University of Oklahoma Press, 2002), 72, 152; Renate Germer, "Ancient Egyptian Pharmaceutical Plants and the Eastern Mediterranean," in *The Healing Past: Pharmaceuticals in the Biblical and Rabbinic World*, ed. Irène Jacob and Walter Jacob, StAM 7 (Leiden: Brill, 1993), 77.

38. E.g., J. M. C. Toynbee, "A New Roman Mosaic Pavement Found in Dorset," *JRS* 54 (1964): 14; Susan Pearce, "The Hinton St. Mary Mosaic Pavement: Christ or Emperor?," *Britannia* 39 (2008): 210; Norman D. Cowell, "Cyrenaican Church Floor Mosaics of the Justinianic Period: Decoration or Meaning?," *LS* 45 (2014): 87, 93.

39. Margaret B. Freeman, *The Unicorn Tapestries* (New York: Metropolitan Museum of Art, 1976), 131.

40. Cesare Ripa, *Iconologia, or, Moral Emblems* (London: Motte, 1709), 14.

41. Eleanor C. Marquand, "Plant Symbolism in the Unicorn Tapestries," *Parnassus* 10.5 (1938): 7–8; Adolfo Salvatore Cavallo, *The Unicorn Tapestries in the Metropolitan Museum of Art* (New York: Metropolitan Museum of Art, 2005), 19–28; Freeman, *Unicorn Tapestries*, 131–32.

pomegranate surfaces as a motif in several Renaissance *Madonna and Child* paintings from Italy and the Netherlands. Most commonly, Mary holds the pomegranate while Jesus reaches out his hand to draw some of its seeds.[42] For example, Sandro Botticelli's *Madonna of the Pomegranate* (ca. 1478–1490, Uffizi Gallery, Florence) features the infant Jesus eating of the pomegranate as if to symbolize both resurrection and the blood of the cross.

When he created the pomegranate in this illumination, Jackson was likely aware of many of the meanings of this fruit in Christian visual iconography from his lifelong interest in Christian symbolism. (His senior thesis from art school was an illuminated manuscript on the subject.)[43] Jackson builds on these associations of the pomegranate and adds another one consonant with biblical tradition: the association of this pomegranate in the Song of Songs with illuminations of the temple of Solomon elsewhere in the *Saint John's Bible*. The garden in the Song alludes to the temple, which brings us into a rich association of texts across Old and New Testaments.

The motif of the square-shaped temple of Solomon first appears in *Solomon's Temple*, illuminating the description of Solomon building the precisely ordered first temple and his ceremony opening the temple (1 Kgs 8:1–66; fig. 3.6).[44] The image includes the double-arched doorway to the Cathedral of Saint James at Compostela as well as an oscillograph of the monks of Saint John's Abbey chanting the Psalms, a motif found throughout the *Saint John's Bible* Psalter.[45] The purple hues of this illumination suggest Solomonic royalty, echoing the purple lace in the Song of Songs illuminations.[46]

The temple motif surfaces again in prophetic visions. Isaiah is called to his ministry in the temple (Isa 6:1–13), illuminated by Jackson. God, enthroned in the temple and attended by Seraphim, calls Isaiah to his prophetic ministry through a hot coal (fig. 3.7). Later, the motif structures Ezekiel's detailed

---

42. See, e.g., Frederick Hartt and David G. Wilkins, *History of Italian Renaissance Art: Painting, Sculpture, Architecture*, 7th ed. (Upper Saddle River, NJ: Prentice Hall, 2011), 234.

43. Homrighausen, "Words Made Flesh."

44. Information about this and following illuminations drawn from Patella, *Word and Image*; Sink, *Art of The Saint John's Bible*. For the 1 Kings illumination, see Donald Jackson and Saint John's University, *The Saint John's Bible: Historical Books* (Collegeville, MN: Liturgical Press, 2011).

45. Calderhead, *Illuminating the Word*, 202–9; Donald Jackson and Saint John's University, *The Saint John's Bible: Psalms* (Collegeville, MN: Liturgical Press, 2005).

46. Information about this and following illuminations drawn from Patella, *Word and Image*; Sink, *Art of the Saint John's Bible*.

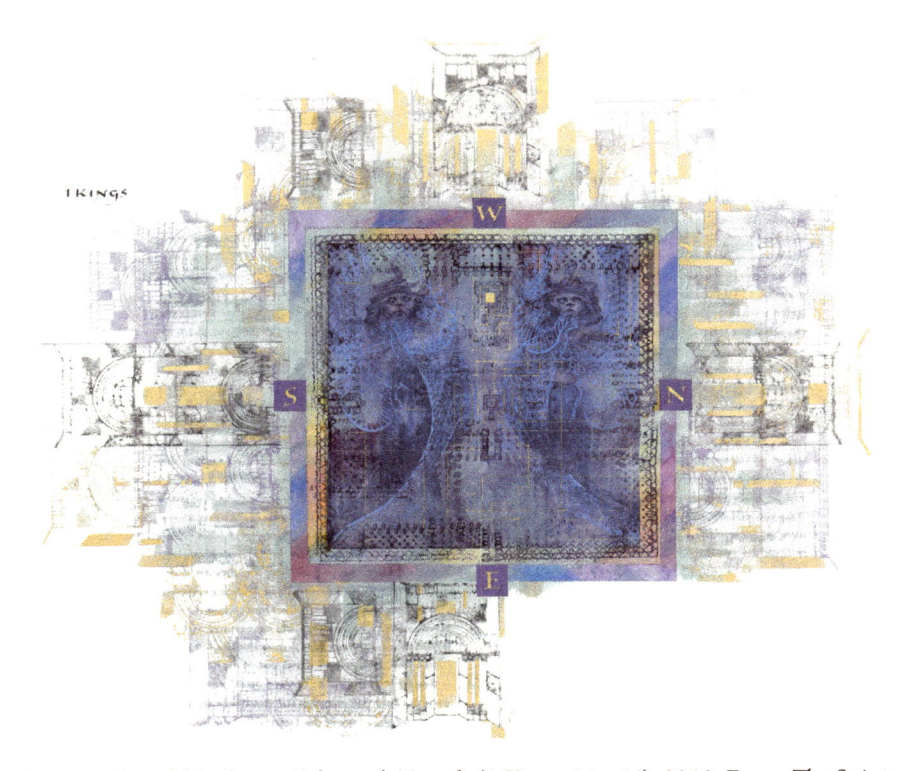

Fig. 3.6. Donald Jackson, *Solomon's Temple* (1 Kings 8:1–66). 2010. From *The Saint John's Bible*. Gouache and ink on vellum, page measures 15¾ x 23½", Saint John's University, Collegeville, Minnesota.

vision of the new temple (Ezek 40:1–48:35).[47] The background to this image is a rich, bright rainbow pattern—a frequent motif in this Bible, occurring here in the illumination to Ezekiel's valley of the dry bones, and in *every* illumination in the heavily illuminated book of Revelation. In every case, the rainbow indicates God's postflood covenant with Noah and promise to never again destroy humanity (Gen 9:16).[48]

The temple symbol appears again in Neh 8:1–12, which narrates the Israelites returning to Jerusalem and Ezra reading the Torah to them. The many squares and half-squares around the margins of the page represent the people of Israel returning from diaspora, about to rebuild their temple.

---

47. Donald Jackson and Saint John's University, *The Saint John's Bible: Prophets* (Collegeville, MN: Liturgical Press, 2006).
48. Patella, *Word and Image*, 80–81.

86                    JONATHAN HOMRIGHAUSEN

Those squares appear again in the penultimate illumination of the *Saint John's Bible*: John of Patmos's vision of the new Jerusalem (Rev 21:2–22:5). This illumination contains the rainbow pattern and the tree of life outside the city. In comparing the labyrinth motifs in the Song's garden and the labyrinth of the streets in the new Jerusalem illumination, Susan Sink points out that while the Song's tension between absence and presence makes the paradisiacal garden incomplete, in Revelation the full eschatological consummation of the God-human relationship closes the labyrinth.[49]

Fig. 3.7. Donald Jackson, *Isaiah's Temple Vision* (Isaiah 6:1–13). 2005. From *The Saint John's Bible*. Gouache and ink on vellum, page measures 15¾ x 23½", Saint John's University, Collegeville, MN.

---

49. Sink, *Art of The Saint John's Bible*, 121; Donald Jackson and Saint John's University, *The Saint John's Bible: Letters and Revelation* (Collegeville, MN: Liturgical Press, 2012).

Because of these rich symbolic resonances, every illumination in the *Saint John's Bible* must be viewed within the context of all of its illuminations, just as monastic *lectio divina* reads every biblical book in the context of Old and New Testaments.[50] In Jackson's illumination, the pomegranate startlingly has two calyxes. Perhaps this is a double pomegranate symbolizing the two lovers becoming one, or the concord of faith within the church. The left calyx seems to have a key, symbolizing the entrance to the locked garden—perhaps typologically St. Peter's.

In the Song, the garden is both the woman's body and the space—perhaps the *sacred* space—where intimacy takes place. It is no surprise that the *Saint John's Bible* picks up on textual cues linking the Song to the temple, the most sacred space in all of Israel, which is already a sacred space in biblical tradition.[51] The lovers' desire for intimacy in the Song is also the desire for intimacy with God in the house of the Lord. The cathedral doorway of *Solomon's Temple* represents the liturgy of the church, points to the temple as a type of the church, and takes part in a broader leitmotif of ecclesial symbolism in the *Saint John's Bible*, including symbols specifically of Saint John's Abbey and University and its distinctive Marcel Breuer architecture.[52] These ecclesial symbols draw on a long tradition of reading the Song as describing the love between God and the church, reflected in Gregory the Great and Bede's commentaries.[53] Since the *Saint John's Bible* is a Catholic Bible, sponsored and cocreated by a Benedictine monastery and meant to be a gift for the church and for the world, it is no surprise that ecclesial symbolism runs throughout.

### Lilies, Lace, and Christological Readings of the Song

While the pomegranate points to an ecclesiological understanding of the Song, the lilies and lace hint at a christological reading—pointing, gently,

---

50. Homrighausen, *Illuminating Justice*, 5–7.
51. Ellen F. Davis, *Proverbs, Ecclesiastes, and the Song of Songs*, WestBC (Louisville, KY: Westminster John Knox, 2000), 271; Edmée Kingsmill, *The Song of Songs and the Eros of God: A Study in Biblical Intertextuality*, OTM (Oxford: Oxford University Press, 2009), 155–78.
52. Homrighausen, *Illuminating Justice*, 8; Victoria M. Young, *Saint John's Abbey Church: Marcel Breuer and the Creation of a Modern Sacred Space* (Minneapolis: University of Minnesota Press, 2014).
53. Matter, *Voice of My Beloved*, 86–122.

to illuminations of the crucifixion and resurrection. The lace pattern in this illumination, created by pressing actual lace onto the page, alludes to the Song's attention to the woman's clothing as a marker of her hiddenness and inaccessibility to her beloved (e.g., Song 4:1, 4:3, 5:3).[54] Throughout the *Saint John's Bible*, indeed, ornate lace patterns symbolize the presence of women.[55] These symbols pick up on the small, easily overlooked square crosses in the previous bifolium, to the left of the pomegranate garden.

However, this particular lace pattern, with cross points, appears in only one other place in this Bible: *Crucifixion* (Luke 23:44–49; fig. 5.8). This features a purely golden Christ on the cross, askew as the world itself is topsy-turvy when God dies.[56] Behind Jesus, Jackson includes astronomical imagery, perhaps referencing the cosmic imagery on the torn temple curtain as described by Josephus (*B.J.* 5.212–214). The lace border evokes the presence of the women at the foot of the cross in all four gospels, especially Mary, the mother of Jesus, and Mary Magdalene (Matt 27:55–56; Mark 15:40; Luke 23:49; John 19:25–27).[57] While she is only implicitly present in *Crucifixion*, Mary Magdalene is given her spotlight in *Resurrection* (John 20:1–31; fig. 5.9). This illuminating focuses not on Jesus—we do not see his face—but on Mary Magdalene's face as she beholds him. Her bright red, elaborately ornamented dress boldly grabs the viewer's focus. In the illumination to John 1:35–51, *Call of the Disciples*, Jackson inserts a patch of Mary Magdalene's bright red dress at the edge, hinting that she might be counted among the disciples although she is not named formally as one of the Twelve.

With this connection to the crucifixion and resurrection made, the red flowers in the margins may hint further at Mary and/or Mary Magdalene at the foot of the cross. The special treatment given to Song 6:3—"I am my beloved's and my beloved is mine; he pastures his flock among the lilies [*šôšanîm*]"—gives a clue about the identity of the flowers. The *šôšan*, mentioned several times in the Song (2:1; 4:5; 5:13; 7:2), is typically translated "lily" and is seen as referring to the white lily, a flower associated in Christian tradition with Mary, mother of Jesus.[58] However, in

---

54. Munro, *Spikenard and Saffron*, 52–56.
55. Homrighausen, *Illuminating Justice*, 46–47.
56. Laura Kelly Fanucci, "Variation on a Theme: Intertextuality in the Illuminations of the Gospel of Luke," *Obsculta* 2 (2009): 27–28.
57. Homrighausen, *Illuminating Justice*, 62–66.
58. Koops, *Each according to Its Kinds*, 168–70.

Fig. 3.8. Donald Jackson, *Crucifixion* (Luke 23:44–49). 2002. From *The Saint John's Bible*. Gouache and ink on vellum, page measures 15¾ x 23½", Saint John's University, Collegeville, MN.

Fig. 3.9. Donald Jackson, *Resurrection* (John 20:1–31). 2002. From *The Saint John's Bible*. Gouache and ink on vellum, page measures 15¾ x 23½", Saint John's University, Collegeville, MN.

5:13 it is used to describe the man's lips, suggesting that this term can also refer to the red lily.[59] Similarly, in 2:1 the female lover describes herself as a *šôšan* in parallel with *ḥăbaṣṣelet*, a more obscure floral term, traditionally rendered as "rose of Sharon," though several other species have been proposed; it may be a red tulip.[60] Ultimately, the point is not achieving the impossible task of precisely identifying these obscure terms but noting the options available to the artist's imagination. The flowers in these margins may be red lilies; they may be roses of Sharon, or red tulips; or they may be nonspecific flowers.[61] Even so, this bright red resonates well with Mary Magdalene's bright red dress in *Resurrection*. Both lilies and roses often signify Mary, mother of Jesus—"there is no rose of such virtue."[62]

Finally, the two butterflies in this two-page illumination (there is another one atop the title, "Song of Songs") allude in general to a network of insect marginalia throughout the *Saint John's Bible*, including a half-page illustration of a monarch butterfly's life cycle at the end of Mark.[63] This illustration of a caterpillar, chrysalis, and butterfly, rendered by scientific illustrator Chris Tomlin, symbolizes the ordinary life, death, and glorified resurrected state of Christ, an association well known in Christian iconography.[64] Elsewhere in the *Saint John's Bible*, the butterfly is a symbol of angels, as in *Jacob's Ladder*.[65] What is this butterfly-Christ-angel doing in the Song of Songs? If the Song, on the surface, narrates human love, perhaps it serves as a reminder of the close connection between human love and the divine love that blesses, ordains, and sustains it.

These connections between the flowers, lace, and butterflies and the crucifixion and resurrection point to a series of allusions to the Song in John 20's resurrection scene previously noticed by other scholars.[66] John

---

59. See also Exum, *Song of Songs*, 113–14.
60. Koops, *Each according to Its Kinds*, 172–73; Musselman, *Dictionary of Bible Plants*, 123–24.
61. Previous studies of this illumination disagree too: Patella takes them as roses of Sharon; Sink describes them as lilies (Patella, *Word and Image*, 69; Sink, *Art of The Saint John's Bible*, 125).
62. Murray and Murray, *Dictionary of Christian Art*, 197.
63. Sink, *Art of the Saint John's Bible*, 241–42, 339–42.
64. Murray and Murray, *Dictionary of Christian Art*, 73; Vazrick Nazari, "Chasing Butterflies in Medieval Europe," *JLS* 68 (2014): 223–31; Eileen Yanoviak, "More than Marginal: Insects in the Hours of Mary of Burgundy," *Antennae* 26 (2013): 98.
65. Calderhead, *Illuminating the Word*, 197–98.
66. David M. Carr, *The Erotic Word: Sexuality, Spirituality, and the Bible* (New

places Jesus's death and crucifixion near a garden (19:41); both feature a female lover crying out for and seeking her beloved at night (see Song 3:1–4); and both feature the female beloved embracing her male beloved, though Jesus stops Mary Magdalene from touching him. More broadly, in the anointings of Jesus by Mary of Bethany (John 12:1–18) and Joseph of Arimathea (John 19:38–42), John may allude to the spice imagery in the Song (Song 1:12–14, 4:10–14). Note how many of these intertexts focus on Jesus and his *female* disciples.

While any Christian allegorical reading of the Song must connect Old Testament to New, what makes these illuminations such unique exegesis is their subtlety. Any viewer unfamiliar with *Crucifixion*, *Resurrection*, and the butterfly in Mark can still derive great meaning from the Song of Songs illuminations. As I have written elsewhere in regards to the *Saint John's Bible*'s treatment of Old Testament texts frequently read christologically, the typology is implied, but the Old Testament illuminations also stand on their own.[67] Further, the specifics of the medium of an illuminated manuscript mean that the art never covers up or replaces the text with image. But of course, there is no division between text and image in calligraphy—what Jeffrey Hamburger might call *iconic script*.[68] It is to the words, both as interpretive text and shaped letterforms, we turn next.

## The Body of the Text:
## Materiality and the Vineyard of the Text

Spiritual or allegorical readings of the Song are often deemed *disembodied*, distorting the Song by erasing its eros.[69] Yet this artistic, spiritual reading of the Song is also *highly* embodied—not only in how the viewer's body is engaged in the inseparable acts of reading and viewing but also in the materiality of the letters and the vellum itself. In the *Saint John's Bible*, the text becomes word made flesh, an image drawing both on John and on medieval images of *lectio divina*.

---

York: Oxford University Press, 2005), 163–67; Bobbi Dykema Katsanis, "Meeting in the Garden: Intertextuality with the Song of Songs in Holbein's *Noli Me Tangere*," *Int* 61 (2007): 402–16.

67. See my comments on *Suffering Servant* (Isa 52–53) in Homrighausen, *Illuminating Justice*, 40–43.

68. Jeffrey F. Hamburger, *Script as Image* (Leuven: Peeters, 2014).

69. Matter, *Voice of My Beloved*, 139–42.

Reading, in the early medieval European conception and in the *Saint John's Bible*, is always embodied. Bernard of Clairvaux likens the practice of *lectio divina* to a cow ruminating on its food for hours. Gregory the Great likens reading Scripture to eating honey: the text is slowly digested, much as the prophet Ezekiel swallows the scroll given him by the angel in Ezek 3.[70] Reading, even when done in solitude, was also oral, creating what Ivan Illich calls "communities of mumblers."[71] The significance of communal reading for the Benedictine monks who sponsored this Bible is reflected in the use of oscillographs on every page of the *Saint John's Bible* Psalter, visual representations of the sound waves created by the monks of Saint John's Abbey chanting the daily office, reminding the reader that the Psalms were and are not meant to be read silently and privately but communally and aloud.[72] In another monastic metaphor, the text ruminated on becomes like a vineyard, the reader a harvester who continues to find spiritual fruit while ruminating around the garden. Even the Latin term *pagina* can also refer to a row of vines joined together, because of the physical shape of lines of text on a page.[73] Thus the pages of the *Saint John's Bible* itself become a vineyard in which the reader plucks exegetical and spiritual fruit through her *lectio*. Not only is the garden a symbol on the page, the red circle with its square border and two gates, but all four of its bifolia become gardens. Beautifully shaped marginalia grow like plants within their architectural frame of the letters, like grapevines growing on the tresses of a vineyard.

From this perspective, the delicately shaped letterforms—the rows of the vineyard—are not merely signifiers of meaning but images in themselves. Jackson wrote the italic script for the Song himself, attempting to capture its emotive qualities in his lines and letters.[74] We might notice the feeling of the letters, the elegance of the flourishes in ascenders, descenders, and at the ends of the words; the rhythm of the poetic indentation the words are shaped into; the slight variations in letterforms that make them come alive, as in the varied majuscule T's in 2:13 and 2:14. The personality of these letters is graceful, even a bit playful, much like the dance of love within the

---

70. Ivan Illich, *In the Vineyard of the Text: A Commentary to Hugh's Didascalicon* (Chicago: University of Chicago Press, 1996), 57–58.
71. Illich, *In the Vineyard*, 54.
72. Sink, *Art of the Saint John's Bible*, 154–56.
73. Illich, *In the Vineyard*, 57–58.
74. Calderhead, *Illuminating the Word*, 232.

Song itself, in a way that reflects well Grabar's notion of calligraphy, or ornamented letterforms, as mediator conveying "emotions and stances" toward its semantic content.[75]

The iconicity of Jackson's script is best captured in his text treatment of Song 8:6–7, often described as the theological thesis statement of the Song (fig. 3.10).[76] The colors of these letters match the "flashes of fire," in various shades of red; their strong contrast between thin and thick lines gives the piece the energy and life of a flickering flame. Instead of the quills used to write the *Saint John's Bible*, Jackson used a reed pen for this piece to create a soft-edged effect—what Sink describes as an "earthly, primitive feel."[77]

Jackson's emphasis on the physicality of the letterform, and his use of the medieval technology of hand-scribing a Bible, closely links with the incarnational theology of the *Saint John's Bible*. This theology of Christ as Word made flesh is most celebrated in the *Saint John's Bible* by *Word Made Flesh*, a full-page illumination of John 1 depicting the presence of the Word becoming golden flesh. Jackson comments that in this illumination, he hoped "to remember the Patristic focus of 'Word' as a template for the universe and the origins of creation."[78] Words, whether they are physical letters on a page or Christ, the Word made flesh, are *physical*. They are eaten, they are heard, they are touched—and, depending on the ink, while wet they may be smelled. In crafting the words of the Song as iconic script worth paying attention to in itself, Jackson follows medieval techniques and theologies of the incarnational element of calligraphy—the word made flesh.[79] And just as calligraphed letters take on their own physical presence on the page, Jackson often speaks of the physicality of *making* calligraphy, a full-body experience that, he says, "brings into play all the senses and

---

75. Grabar, *Mediation of Ornament*, 230.
76. Davis, *Proverbs, Ecclesiastes*, 296–98.
77. Calderhead, *Illuminating the Word*, 234; Sink, *Art of the Saint John's Bible*, 126.
78. Quoted in Peter Halliday, ed., *Holy Writ: Modern Jewish, Christian, and Islamic Calligraphy* (Lichfield: Lichfield Cathedral, 2014), 41.
79. For more on this, see Homrighausen, "Words Made Flesh"; Hamburger, *Script as Image*; Laura Kendrick, *Animating the Letter: The Figurative Embodiment of Writing from Late Antiquity to the Renaissance* (Columbus: Ohio State University Press, 1999); Ben C. Tilghman, "The Shape of the Word: Extralinguistic Meaning in Insular Display Lettering," *WI* 27 (2011): 292–308.

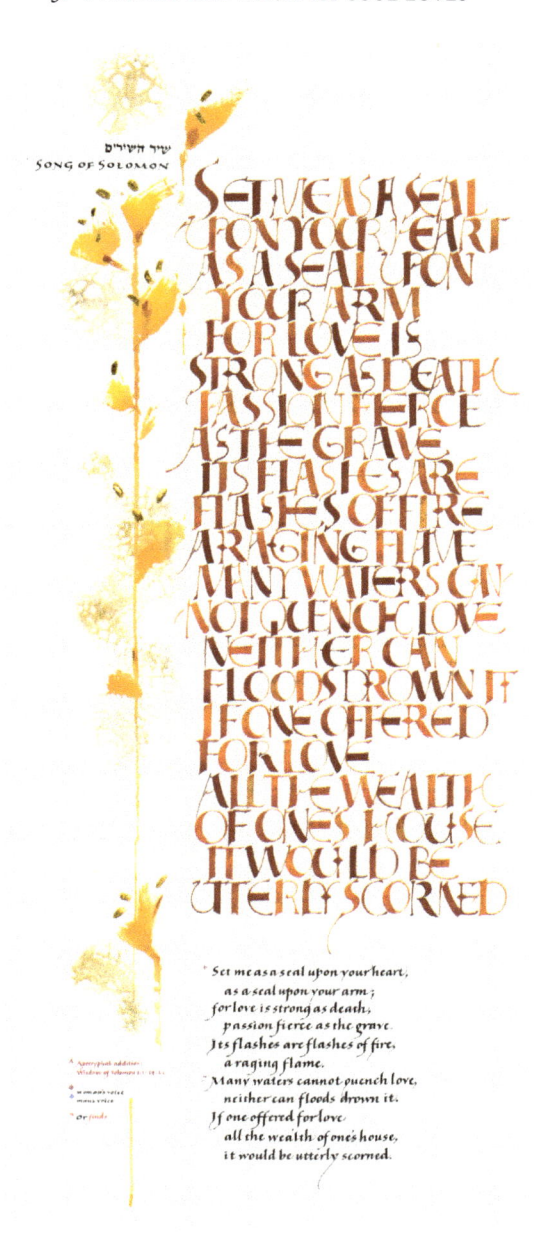

Fig. 3.10. Donald Jackson, detail from *Set Me As a Seal* (Song 8:6–7), Donald Jackson, *Set Me as a Seal*, Scribe: Sally Mae Joseph; Hebrew Script: Izzy Pludwinski. 2006. From *The Saint John's Bible*. Gouache and ink on vellum, page measures 15¾ x 23½". Saint John's University, Collegeville, Minnesota.

allows a total involvement."[80] Letters are physical, embodied, both in their viewing and their creation.

The embodiment of letters takes place within the embodiment of the book. In our print-saturated Protestant culture, we often overlook the specificity and materiality of the book when engaging sacred text. The *Saint John's Bible* reclaims a medieval sensibility that the book is not a mere vehicle for a message but a significant object in its own right—and indeed, in a manuscript world there is no such thing as identical books. This visual, spiritual reading of the Song points to the *book itself* as the embodiment of the word and draws the reader into a physical relationship with the book. This book is itself made of mammal flesh and written on with bird feathers—literally, the Word made flesh of John 1. Just as ornament is inseparable from meaning, so is material. Far from being disembodied, this visual (and material) exegesis of the Song brings the viewer-reader's body into their engagement with the incarnated words.

## Conclusions

This essay shows how Jackson intertwines symbol, ornament, materiality, and a deep understanding of how calligraphic treatment mediates the experience of sacred text, all to deliver a powerful aesthetic and meditative experience of the Song for the reader-viewer. By encouraging the reader to ponder the Song imaginatively, to free associate with its symbols in *lectio divina*, he opens the door to the kind of canonical, typological, allegorical readings of the Song most prevalent for the medieval Christian forebears of his manuscript art. Form and content, ornament and structure, materiality and theology intertwine and are ultimately inseparable from exegesis and spirituality.

For scholars of art, Jackson's work raises questions about *how calligraphy means* as an art form—an art form that, in its twentieth-century Roman script revival, remains relatively understudied and underappreciated for its exegetical nuances and possibilities. For scholars of the Song, the *Saint John's Bible* is the visual counterpart to other Christian interpreters, both medieval and contemporary, who claim a spiritual, christological, and/or allegorical reading of the Song. The Song's reception in the arts,

---

80. Jackson, quoted in David Harris, *Calligraphy: Modern Masters; Art, Inspiration and Technique* (New York: Crescent, 1991), 54.

both Jewish and Christian, can enrich the contemporary discussion over the hermeneutics of the Song, providing here a reading of the Song that is both literal *and* allegorical, spiritual *and* embodied.

## Works Cited

Baker, Jack R., Jeffrey Bilbro, and Daniel Train, eds. *The Saint John's Bible and Its Tradition: Illuminating Beauty in the Twenty-First Century*. Eugene, OR: Pickwick, 2018.

Bartal, Ruth. "Medieval Images of 'Sacred Love': Jewish and Christian Perceptions." *ASAH* 2 (1996): 93–110.

———. "'Where Has Your Beloved Gone?': The Staging of the *Quaerere Deum* on the Murals of the Cistercian Convent at Chełmno." *WI* 16 (2000): 270–89.

Bucher, Christina. "The Song of Songs and the 'Enclosed Garden' in Paintings and Illustrations of the Virgin Mary." Pages 96–116 in *Between the Text and the Canvas: The Bible and Art in Dialogue*. Edited by J. Cheryl Exum. Sheffield: Sheffield Phoenix, 2007.

Calderhead, Christopher. *Illuminating the Word: The Making of the Saint John's Bible*. 2nd ed. Collegeville, MN: Liturgical Press, 2015.

Calkins, Robert G. "Liturgical Sequence and Decorative Crescendo in the Drogo Sacramentary." *Gesta* 25 (1986): 17–23.

Carr, David M. *The Erotic Word: Sexuality, Spirituality, and the Bible*. New York: Oxford University Press, 2005.

Cavallo, Adolfo Salvatore. *The Unicorn Tapestries in the Metropolitan Museum of Art*. New York: Metropolitan Museum of Art, 2005.

Cowell, Norman D. "Cyrenaican Church Floor Mosaics of the Justinianic Period: Decoration or Meaning?" *LS* 45 (2014): 85–96.

Daley, Brian E. "The 'Closed Garden' and the 'Sealed Fountain': Song of Songs 4:12 in the Late Medieval Iconography of Mary." Pages 254–78 in *Medieval Gardens*. Edited by Elisabeth B. MacDougall. Washington, DC: Dumbarton Oaks Research Library, 1986.

Davis, Ellen F. *Proverbs, Ecclesiastes, and the Song of Songs*. WestBC. Louisville, KY: Westminster John Knox, 2000.

Dykema Katsanis, Bobbi. "Meeting in the Garden: Intertextuality with the Song of Songs in Holbein's *Noli Me Tangere*." *Int* 61 (2007): 402–16.

Exum, J. Cheryl. "Seeing the Song of Songs: Some Artistic Visions of the Bible's Love Lyrics." Pages 91–127 in *Das Alte Testament Und Die*

*Kunst*. Edited by John Barton, J. Cheryl Exum, and Manfred Oeming. Münster: LIT, 2005.

———. *Song of Songs*. OTL. Richmond: Westminster John Knox, 2005.

———. "Toward a Genuine Dialogue between the Bible and Art." Pages 473–504 in *Congress Volume Helsinki 2010*. Edited by Martti Nissinen. VTSup 148. Leiden: Brill, 2012.

Fanucci, Laura Kelly. "Variation on a Theme: Intertextuality in the Illuminations of the Gospel of Luke." *Obsculta* 2 (2009): 21–30.

Finney, Paul Corby, ed. "Pomegranate." Pages 346–47 in vol. 2 of *The Eerdmans Encyclopedia of Early Christian Art and Archaeology*. Grand Rapids: Eerdmans, 2017.

Freeman, Margaret B. *The Unicorn Tapestries*. New York: Metropolitan Museum of Art, 1976.

Germer, Renate. "Ancient Egyptian Pharmaceutical Plants and the Eastern Mediterranean." Pages 69–80 in *The Healing Past: Pharmaceuticals in the Biblical and Rabbinic World*. Edited by Irène Jacob and Walter Jacob. StAM 7. Leiden: Brill, 1993.

Gillow, John, and Nicholas Barnard. *Traditional Indian Textiles*. London: Thames & Hudson, 1991.

Gombrich, Ernst H. *The Sense of Order: A Study in the Psychology of Decorative Art*. Ithaca, NY: Cornell University Press, 1979.

Grabar, Oleg. *The Mediation of Ornament*. Princeton: Princeton University Press, 1992.

Halliday, Peter, ed. *Holy Writ: Modern Jewish, Christian, and Islamic Calligraphy*. Lichfield: Lichfield Cathedral, 2014.

Hamburger, Jeffrey F. *Script as Image*. Leuven: Peeters, 2014.

Harris, David. *Calligraphy: Modern Masters; Art, Inspiration and Technique*. New York: Crescent, 1991.

Hartt, Frederick, and David G. Wilkins. *History of Italian Renaissance Art: Painting, Sculpture, Architecture*. 7th ed. Upper Saddle River, NJ: Prentice Hall, 2011.

Homrighausen, Jonathan. *Illuminating Justice: The Ethical Imagination of the Saint John's Bible*. Collegeville, MN: Liturgical Press, 2018.

———. "Words Made Flesh: Incarnational, Multisensory Exegesis in Donald Jackson's Biblical Art." *RelArts*, forthcoming.

Illich, Ivan. *In the Vineyard of the Text: A Commentary to Hugh's Didascalicon*. Chicago: University of Chicago Press, 1996.

Impelluso, Lucia. *Nature and Its Symbols*. Los Angeles: Getty, 2004.

Jackson, Donald. "Gilding." Pages 177–98 in *The Calligrapher's Handbook*. 2nd ed. Edited by Heather Child. New York: Taplinger, 1986.

Jackson, Donald, and Saint John's University. *The Saint John's Bible: Gospels and Acts*. Collegeville, MN: Liturgical Press, 2005.

———. *The Saint John's Bible: Historical Books*. Collegeville, MN: Liturgical Press, 2011.

———. *The Saint John's Bible: Letters and Revelation*. Collegeville, MN: Liturgical Press, 2012.

———. *The Saint John's Bible: Prophets*. Collegeville, MN: Liturgical Press, 2006.

———. *The Saint John's Bible: Psalms*. Collegeville, MN: Liturgical Press, 2005.

John of the Cross. *The Collected Works of St. John of the Cross*. Rev. ed. Translated by Kieran Kavanaugh and Otilio Rodriguez. Washington, DC: ICS, 2010.

Keel, Othmar. *The Song of Songs*. Translated by Frederick J. Gaiser. CC. Minneapolis: Fortress, 1994.

Kendrick, Laura. *Animating the Letter: The Figurative Embodiment of Writing from Late Antiquity to the Renaissance*. Columbus: Ohio State University Press, 1999.

Kingsmill, Edmée. *The Song of Songs and the Eros of God: A Study in Biblical Intertextuality*. OTM. Oxford: Oxford University Press, 2009.

Koops, Robert. *Each according to Its Kinds: Plants and Trees in the Bible*. UTH. New York: United Bible Societies, 2012.

Leclercq, Jean. *The Love of Learning and the Desire for God: A Study of Monastic Culture*. Translated by Catherine Mizrahi. New York: Fordham University Press, 1982.

Longman, Tremper, III. *Song of Songs*. New International Commentary on the Old Testament. Grand Rapids: Eerdmans, 2001.

Marquand, Eleanor C. "Plant Symbolism in the Unicorn Tapestries." *Parnassus* 10.5 (1938): 3–40.

Matter, E. Ann. *The Voice of My Beloved: The Song of Songs in Western Medieval Christianity*. Philadelphia: University of Pennsylvania Press, 1992.

Meyers, Carol L. "Temple, Jerusalem." *ABD* 6:350–69.

Moore-Jumonville, Robert. "Beauty Cannot Be Rushed: An Invitation to Contemplation from the *Saint John's Bible*." Pages 43–58 in *The Saint John's Bible and Its Tradition: Illuminating Beauty in the Twenty-First*

*Century*. Edited by Jack R. Baker, Jeffrey Bilbro, and Daniel Train. Eugene, OR: Pickwick, 2018.

Moser, Matthew A. Rothaus. "Should Bibles Be Beautiful? How Beauty Teaches Us to Pray." Pages 26–42 in *The Saint John's Bible and Its Tradition: Illuminating Beauty in the Twenty-First Century*. Edited by Jack R. Baker, Jeffrey Bilbro, and Daniel Train. Eugene, OR: Pickwick, 2018.

Muller, Marion. "The Scribe Who Renounced the Pen." *ULC* 15.4 (November 1988): 26–29.

Munro, Jill M. *Spikenard and Saffron: The Imagery of the Song of Songs*. JSOTSup 203. Sheffield: Sheffield Academic, 1995.

Murphy, Roland E. *The Song of Songs*. Hermeneia. Minneapolis: Fortress, 1990.

Murray, Peter, and Linda Murray. *A Dictionary of Christian Art*. Oxford: Oxford University Press, 2004.

Musselman, Lytton John. *A Dictionary of Bible Plants*. New York: Cambridge University Press, 2012.

Nazari, Vazrick. "Chasing Butterflies in Medieval Europe." *JLS* 68 (2014): 223–31.

Nunn, John F. *Ancient Egyptian Medicine*. Norman: University of Oklahoma Press, 2002.

Patella, Michael. *Word and Image: The Hermeneutics of the Saint John's Bible*. Collegeville, MN: Liturgical Press, 2013.

Pearce, Susan. "The Hinton St. Mary Mosaic Pavement: Christ or Emperor?" *Britannia* 39 (2008): 193–218.

Pirotte, Emmanuelle. "Hidden Order, Order Revealed: New Light on Carpet Pages." Pages 203–8 in *Pattern and Purpose in Insular Art: Proceedings of the Fourth International Conference on Insular Art Held at the National Museum and Gallery, Cardiff 3–6 September 1998*. Edited by Mark Redknap, Nancy Edwards, Alan Lane, and Susan Youngs. Oxford: Oxbow Books, 2002.

Ripa, Cesare. *Iconologia, or, Moral Emblems*. London: Motte, 1709.

Robertson, Duncan. *Lectio Divina: The Medieval Experience of Reading*. Trappist, KY: Cistercian Publications, 2011.

Sink, Susan. *The Art of the Saint John's Bible: The Complete Reader's Guide*. Collegeville, MN: Liturgical Press, 2013.

Stokstad, Marilyn. "Gardens in Medieval Art." Pages 18–35 in *Gardens of the Middle Ages*. Edited by Jerry Stannard and Marilyn Stokstad. Lawrence: Spencer Museum of Art, University of Kansas, Lawrence, 1983.

Tilghman, Benjamin C. "Ornament and Incarnation in Insular Art." *Gesta* 55 (2016): 157–77.

———. "Pattern, Process, and the Creation of Meaning in the Lindisfarne Gospels." *West 86th* 24 (2017): 3–28.

———. "The Shape of the Word: Extralinguistic Meaning in Insular Display Lettering." *WI* 27 (2011): 292–308.

Toynbee, J. M. C. "A New Roman Mosaic Pavement Found in Dorset." *JRS* 54 (1964): 7–14.

Weinryb, Ittai. "Living Matter: Materiality, Maker, and Ornament in the Middle Ages." *Gesta* 52 (2013): 113–32.

Wechsler, Judith Glatzer. "A Change in the Iconography of the Song of Songs in Twelfth and Thirteenth Century Latin Bibles." Pages 73–93 in *Texts and Responses: Studies Presented to Nahum N. Glatzer on the Occasion of His Seventieth Birthday by His Students*. Edited by Michael A. Fishbane and Paul R. Flohr. Leiden: Brill, 1975.

Yanoviak, Eileen. "More than Marginal: Insects in the Hours of Mary of Burgundy." *Antennae* 26 (2013): 86–102.

Young, Victoria M. *Saint John's Abbey Church: Marcel Breuer and the Creation of a Modern Sacred Space*. Minneapolis: University of Minnesota Press, 2014.

# 4
# Touch Me, Don't Touch Me—Peter, Jesus, and Mary: Painted by Scarsellino and Portrayed by Cornelius à Lapide

HEIDI J. HORNIK

Peter and Mary Magdalene have significant encounters with Jesus that involve the strength of their faith. Peter loses his faith when he loses focus on Christ while walking on water in Matt 14. This results in Peter falling into the Sea of Galilee, Jesus touching his hand, and restoring his faith/focus, as painted by Ippolito Scarsellino (1550–1620) in figure 4.1. Mary Magdalene is the first disciple to see Jesus after the resurrection but mistakes him for the gardener. Scarsellino captures the moment (fig. 4.2) when Mary realizes who he is and Jesus tells her, "Don't touch me!" (John 20:17).

Ippolito Scarsella, commonly known by his contemporaries and friends as Scarsellino, was a Ferrarese artist, heavily influenced by his Venetian training, who produced post-Trent religious paintings in the mannerist style. Considered among the Reformers in late sixteenth-century Italy, his theological iconography anticipates the Baroque style of the next century. This study suggests that the writings of theological writer Cornelius à Lapide (1567–1637) were a source whose commentary on earlier writers may have value for an interpretation of Scarsellino's *Christ*

---

This study began during a 2017 visiting scholar fellowship in residence at Harvard University and a Baylor University research leave for the spring 2017 semester. I thank Deans Lee Nordt, Robin Driskell, Kimberly Kellison, and Professor and Chair Mark Anderson for their continued support of my work through research travel and financial support. I express my appreciation to Heather Linton, Division of European and American Art, for making it possible for me to review the curatorial files of the *Christ and Saint Peter at the Sea of Galilee* at the Harvard Art Museums.

Fig. 4.1. Scarsellino (Ippolito Scarsella). *Christ and Saint Peter at the Sea of Galilee.* ca. 1585–1590. Oil on canvas. 27¼ x 45¾". Credit Line: Harvard Art Museums/ Fogg Museum, Bequest of Grenville L. Winthrop.

Fig. 4.2. Scarsellino. *Noli Me Tangere.* ca. 1586. Oil on canvas, 74.5 x 93.5 cm. 1938E477. Photo: Franck Raux. Musee Magnin, Dijon, France. Photo Credit: © RMN-Grand Palais / Art Resource, NY.

*and Saint Peter at the Sea of Galilee* (Harvard Art Museums) and *Noli Me Tangere* (Musée Magnin, Dijon).[1] Cornelius à Lapide was born in Bocholt, Belgium, and studied humanities and philosophy at Jesuit colleges in Maastricht and Cologne. His theological studies included the University of Douai and Louvain. He entered the Society of Jesus on 11 June 1592 and was ordained a priest on 24 December 1595. Lapide became professor of Scripture at Louvain in 1596 and, a year later, was also named professor of Hebrew. In 1616, he was called to Rome by his Jesuit superiors to assume the same positions there. Lapide's *Great Commentary* incorporates the writings of the patristic church fathers from the second to the fourth centuries. Although his commentary was published posthumously, in 1681, it encapsulates the spirt of its age, while being a reliable treasure of the most popularly heeded, tradition-sanctioned opinions of the church fathers and the influential medieval *magistri*.[2]

Through an analysis of these paintings and the corresponding commentary by Lapide, a better understanding of why Peter and Mary Magdalene were two of the most important Counter-Reformation penitential saints at this time in history can be achieved. I will briefly discuss the connoisseurship issues of the *Christ and Saint Peter at the Sea of Galilee* painting, including its attribution to Scarsellino, and the dating of the painting. Eight gestural types that artists employed when depicting the *Noli Me Tangere* narrative will offer additional insight into the Scarsellino picture. I will use art-historical methodology, with a theological bent, to study both the *Christ and Saint Peter at the Sea of Galilee* and the *Noli Me Tangere*. This is among the first publications to discuss either painting as a Scarsellino work.[3]

---

1. Cornelius à Lapide, *The Great Commentary of Cornelius à Lapide: The Holy Gospel according to Saint Matthew*, trans. Thomas W. Mossman, rev. and completed by Michael J. Miller (Fitzwilliam, NH: Loreto, 2008).

2. Franco Mormando, "Teaching the Faithful to Fly: Mary Magdalene and Peter in Baroque Italy," in *Saints and Sinners: Caravaggio and the Baroque Image*, ed. Franco Mormando (Chestnut Hill, MA: McMullen Museum of Art, Boston College; Chicago: University of Chicago Press, 1999), 108.

3. For a comparison of the Scarsellino's *Christ and Saint Peter on the Sea of Galilee* with other scenes of walking on water, see an earlier version of this paper: Heidi J. Hornik, "St. Peter's Crisis of Faith at Harvard: The Scarsellino Picture and Matthew 14," in *"A Temple Not Made with Hands": Essays in Honor of Naymond H. Keathley*, ed. Mikeal C. Parsons and Richard Walsh (Eugene, OR: Wipf & Stock, 2018), 28–42.

## The Artist

The year of Scarsella's birth is estimated to be circa 1550, and he died on 27 October 1620.[4] We do know that he was born in Ferrara and his father, a "painter of architecture," was Sigismondo Scarsella (1530–1614).[5] Ippolito's initial training was with his father, probably between the ages of fifteen and seventeen. The main primary source for this artist is Girolamo Baruffaldi's *The Lives of the Ferrarese Painters and Sculptors*, written between 1697 and 1722.[6] Baruffaldi suggests that Ippolito went to Bologna "to study the famous works of that school and especially the miracles by the Carracci."[7] Baruffaldi also claims this occurred before Ippolito turned seventeen, so sometime between 1565 and 1570. This would have been impossible, as the Carracci were not yet active. If Baruffaldi is correct about Ippolito going to Bologna to study (which is very likely, as still today Ferrara is along the main travel passage between Bologna and Venice), then he would have encountered the work of later Mannerist painters Orazio Samacchini, Lorenzo Sabatini, and Prospero Fontana.[8] After this Bolognese period, Ippolito went to Venice and trained with Paolo Veronese for four years, beginning in 1570.[9] His earliest paintings find inspiration from Veronese and a richness of color reminiscent of Titian. Scholars also find stylistic echoes of earlier Ferrarese painters such as Sebastiano Filippi and Giuseppe Mazzuoli.[10]

## Christ and Saint Peter at the Sea of Galilee: Style, Connoisseurship, Attribution, and Dating

Formerly attributed to Jacopo Tintoretto, *Christ and Saint Peter at the Sea of Galilee* bears many of the hallmarks of sixteenth-century Venetian

---

4. Maria Angela Novelli, *Scarsellino* (Milan: Skira, 2008), 9. See also Ugo Ruggeri, "Scarsellino," Grove Art Online (2003), https://doi.org/10.1093/gao/9781884446054.article.T076347.

5. Novelli, *Scarsellino*, 9.

6. Girolamo Baruffaldi, *Vite de' pittori e scultori ferraresi* (Ferrara, 1697–1722), 2:65–107.

7. Novelli, *Scarsellino*, 9.

8. Novelli, *Scarsellino*, 9.

9. Ruggeri, "Scarsellino."

10. Ruggeri, "Scarsellino."

painting: a rustic outdoor setting, dramatic contrasts of light and dark, rich color, and a loose, gestural style of depicting drapery with "lightning bolt" strokes that index the rapid movements of the brush.[11] The work is oil on canvas and measures 27 1/4 inches by 45 3/4 inches. It depicts the moment that Peter loses faith in his ability to walk on water because he loses focus on Christ. Matthew alone among the gospels inserts this episode of Peter walking on water (Matt 14:28–31) into the story of Christ walking on the sea. The Sea of Galilee is calm after the storm that raged through the night has ended. In the Scarsellino picture, the disciples are in a boat having just endured a storm for most of the previous night, and they see Christ walking on water. Peter asks Jesus to allow him to walk on the water to prove that it is really him. Jesus says "Come," and Peter walks on water until he loses faith, becomes fearful of what is happening to him, loses his focus on Christ, and starts to fall in the water. Jesus reaches out to him and saves him. Three other disciples react to the event while still in the boat. As dawn breaks on the horizon, light surrounds Christ's head like an aureole. The expressive gestures and luminous seascape lend the scene an urgent, ecstatic quality.

The unpublished curatorial files of the Harvard Art Museums (combining the Fogg, the Sackler, and Busch-Reisinger Museums, now in one building designed by Renzo Piano) include secondary sources that attribute the painting to Tintoretto, a follower of Tintoretto, and, most recently (and most convincingly) to Scarsellino.[12] Connoisseurship plays a major role in the attribution to Scarsellino and the dating, circa

---

11. "*Christ and Peter at the Sea of Galilee* by Ippolito Scarsellino," Harvard Art Museums, http://www.harvardartmuseums.org/collections/object/230293?position=0.

12. On Tintoretto (in chronological order), see Erich von der Bercken and August L. Mayer, *Jacopo Tintoretto*, (Munich: Piper, 1923), 1, 6, 141, 197; Hans Tietze, ed., *Masterpieces of European Painting in America* (New York: Oxford University Press, 1939), 98, 314, cat. no. 85, repr. 98; Rodolfo Pallucchini, *La Giovinezza del Tintoretto* (Milan: Edizioni Daria Guarnati, 1950), 153; Carlo Bernari, *L'opera completa del Tintoretto* (Milan: Rizzoli Editore, 1970), 134, no. C1, repr.; Rodolfo Pallucchini and Paola Rossi, *Tintoretto: Le opere sacre e profane* (Venice and Milan: Alfieri/Gruppo Editoriale Electa, 1982), 242, no. A19. As follower of Tintoretto and as Scarsellino, see Burton B. Fredericksen and Federico Zeri, *Census of Pre-nineteenth-century Italian Paintings in North American Public Collections* (Cambridge: Harvard University Press, 1972), 184, 199; Edgar Peters Bowron, *European Paintings before 1900 in the Fogg Art Museum: A Summary Catalogue including Paintings in the Busch-Reisinger Museum* (Cambridge: Harvard University Art Museums, 1990), 129, repr. 692.

1585–1590. As is the case with connoisseurship, a painting's provenance (history of ownership/location) and study of who is giving the attribution, or change of attribution, in this case, is critical. The bill of sale lists the painting as by Jacopo Tintoretto when it was purchased in 1929 by Grenville Winthrop, New York. It was bequeathed to the Fogg Art Museum at Harvard in 1943 and carried the attribution as "Tintoretto (?)". In 1958, the attribution was changed to the sixteenth-century Venetian School by art historian Millard Meiss.

The painting currently maintains the (re)attribution to Scarsellino made in 1968 by Everett Fahy. He was working at the Fogg Art Museum at Harvard in Cambridge from 1968–1970 while completing his PhD there. Fahy received a letter of evaluation from Philip Pouncey of Sotheby's (London) dated 8 March 1968, suggesting an attribution to Scarsellino.[13] After the Fogg, Fahy became the curator-in-chief of the Metropolitan Museum of Art's European Paintings department, in 1970. In 1973, Fahy moved to the Frick Collection, where he served as its director for thirteen years. He returned to the Met as the first John Pope-Hennessy Chairman of European Paintings, a position he held until in 2009. Fahy, born in 1941, began serving as a consultant for Christie's in 2010.[14] Phillip Pouncey (1910–1990) was another distinguished art historian who worked at the Fitzwilliam, National Gallery in London, the British Museum and became the director of Sotheby's London in 1966. His reattribution of works was so renowned and respected that an exhibition of solely reattributed paintings was held on his seventy-fifth birthday at the British Museum.[15]

Most art historians and connoisseurs consider an attribution agreed on by Fahy and Pouncey to be a respected and secure attribution. Yet, the only monograph on Scarsellino, written in Italian by Maria Angela Novelli and published in 2008, does not discuss the Harvard picture. Novelli's book functions as a *catalogue raisonné* (evaluating the attributions of all of the known paintings attributed to a painter).[16] The Harvard painting is not listed in the 301 attributions or 28 former attributions.

---

13. Philip Pouncey to Everett Fahy, 8 March 1968, Curatorial File, Harvard Art Museums, object 1943.124.

14. "The Personal Collection of Dr. Everett Fahy," Christies, 3 October 2016, https://tinyurl.com/SBL6703g.

15. Lee Sorenson, "Pouncey, Phillip," Dictionary of Art Historians, https://tinyurl.com/SBL6703h.

16. Novelli, *Scarsellino*, 9.

Jonathan Bober, former curator of the Blanton Museum and now curator of prints and drawings at the National Gallery in Washington, DC, proposed the circa 1575–1580 dating and identified Scarsellino's period in Venice as about that time. The Ferrarese school is the current listing for Scarsellino.[17] The painting underwent treatment in February 2014 to correct discolored retouchings and glaze back braded areas in the distant landscape. The frame was conserved at the same time. Digital photographs before and after treatment in normal and ultraviolet light were taken.[18]

### Interpretation of Matthew 14: Visual Precedents and Lapide's Commentary

The story of Jesus walking on water appears in Matt 14:22–33; Mark 6:45–52; and John 6:15–21, but Peter walking on water is unique to Matt 14:28–31. Matthew 14 begins with the beheading of John the Baptist by Herod. After hearing this, Jesus flees Herod and goes to the desert, where he feeds five thousand people with five loaves and two fish.

> Immediately he made the disciples get into the boat and go on ahead to the other side, while he dismissed the crowds. And after he had dismissed the crowds, he went up the mountain by himself to pray. When evening came, he was there alone, but by this time the boat, battered by the waves, was far from the land, for the wind was against them. And earlier in the morning he came walking toward them on the sea. But when the disciples saw him walking on the sea, they were terrified, saying, "It is a ghost!" And they cried out in fear. But immediately Jesus spoke to them and said, "Take heart, it is I; do not be afraid." Peter answered him, "Lord, if it is you, command me to come to you on the water." He said, "Come." So Peter got out of the boat, started walking on the water, and came toward Jesus. But when he noticed the strong wind, he became frightened, and beginning to sink, he cried out, "Lord, save me!" Jesus immediately reached out his hand and caught him, saying to him, "You of little faith, why did you doubt?" When they got into the boat, the wind ceased. And those in the boat worshipped him, saying, "Truly you are the Son of God." (Matt 14:22–33 NEB)

---

17. Pouncey to Fahy, 8 March 1968.
18. "Painting Laboratory Treatment Reports," February 13, 2014, Curatorial File, Harvard Art Museums, object 1943.124.

The visual tradition begins with the lost mosaic, known as the *Navicella* (little ship), located above the entrance arcade that faced the main façade of Old Saint Peter's Basilica. It is attributed to Giotto di Bondone circa 1305–1308.[19] The scene of Matt 14:24–32 was almost completely destroyed when Saint Peter's was rebuilt in the seventeenth century, but original fragments were incorporated into a new design in 1675, installed in the center of the portico. The story of Christ's walking on water that includes Peter has been associated with a propapal context since this fourteenth-century mosaic in the first church of Christendom.

Another very early visual example of the *navicella* theme was by a contemporary of Giotto, Andrea da Firenze (di Bonaiuto) (1346–1349). His scene of *Christ and Peter on the Sea of Galilee* is in the frescoed dome of the Spanish chapel in the Florentine Dominican church of Santa Maria Novella (fig. 4.3). The fresco is part of a larger program in the chapel. It is one of four scenes (resurrection, *navicella*, ascension, and Pentecost) frescoed in the dome vault. A gold coin depicting *Christ Walking on the Water* (fig. 4.4) from the Papal States from the time of Pope Alexander VI (1492–1503) will be discussed below as an example of when Christ does not physically touch Peter and as an example of the propapal apologetic used by the Catholics.[20]

Scarsellino was painting just after the conclusion of the Council of Trent. Post-Tridentine art is largely a product of the decrees made in the twenty-fifth and final session, held on 3–4 December 1563. The decree "On Invocation, Veneration, and Relics of Saints, and on Sacred Images" directed bishops to see to the proper preaching on these subjects. Trent dealt with the veneration of sacred images, a subject that first received solemn church ratification at the Second Council of Nicaea, 787, in reaction to the violent outburst of iconoclasm in the Eastern empire.[21] Nicaea had declared that sacred images were legitimate and helpful for

---

19. Lionello Venturi, "La 'Navicella' di Giotto," *L'arte* 25 (1922): 50, fig. 2. For a more recent study, see Eston Dillon Adams, "The History and Significance of the Navicella Mosaic at Saint Peter's Basilica, Rome" (PhD diss., University of Louisville, 2018). I thank Dr. Adams for presenting a portion of his work at the 2019 Midwest Art History Society conference in Cincinnati and generously providing his comments regarding this study.

20. See "Kirchenstaat: Alexander VI," 1492–1503, Münzkabinett der Staatlichen Museen zu Berlin, https://tinyurl.com/SBL6703i.

21. John W. O'Malley, *Trent: What Happened at the Council* (Cambridge: Belknap Press of Harvard University Press, 2013), 244.

4. TOUCH ME, DON'T TOUCH ME     111

Fig. 4.3. Andrea di Bonaiuto. Vault. *Pendentive with Saint Peter's Boat*. Fresco (postrestoration 2003–2004). Spanish Chapel, S. Maria Novella, Florence, Italy. Photo Credit: Scala / Art Resource, NY.

Fig. 4.4. *Christ Walking on the Water*. Gold coin of the Papal States with a value of 5 ducats (verso). Time of Pope Alexander VI (1492–1503). Gold, diam. 41 mm, weight 16,75 g. Inv. 18232173. Muenzkabinett, Staatliche Museen, Berlin, Germany. Photo Credit: bpk Bildagentur / (Muenzkabinett, Staatliche Museen, Berlin, Germany) / (Lutz Jürgen Lübke) / Art Resource, NY.

instruction and devotion. Trent went further by saying they should be free of all "sensual appeal" (*lascivia*), false doctrine, and superstition.[22]

The Council of Trent declared that sacred images must be instructive and decorous.[23] It is critical for this study to ask whose written works and commentaries would have been of importance to Scarsellino and to his patrons. The commentary of earlier writers by seventeenth-century theological writer Cornelius à Lapide (1567–1637) may have value for this interpretation.

Lapide's *Great Commentary* commented on the works of Jerome, Origen, Tertullian, Hilary, Augustine, Ambrose, and John Chrysostom.[24] The relevant commentary includes Lapide's discussion of verses 28–31.

"Verse 28. And Peter making answer; said: Lord, if it be thou, bid me come to thee upon the waters." Lapide states that John Calvin accuses Peter of rashness and folly but that the fathers and commentators give a twofold answer. Lapide explains, "1. Peter recognised by his voice, gesture, dress and much more by an interior prompting that this was not an apparition, but Christ indeed. When, therefore, Peter says, if it be Thou, it is not the voice of doubt, but of one exulting with joy, desiring, furthermore, to come quickly to Christ, that he might be near to Him who was approaching miraculously on the sea and whom he loved above all things."[25] Scarsellino's interpretation echoes this sentiment when we study the disciples in the boat, who seem oblivious to what is happening. They did not get out of the boat and are distant from Jesus. The disciple in the center of the boat is actually pointing in a different direction, indicating that his attention is focused on something else. Lapide reminds us that Saint Hilary comments, "In Peter, consider how he goes before the others in faith." The painting reaffirms a positive reading of Peter's action as a leader and is an appropriate propapal message for Scarsellino's audience, contemporary Catholics in the 1570s. Further evidence of this story reinforcing the primacy of Peter at this time, and by extension the papacy, is the papal coin of

---

22. O'Malley, *Trent*, 244.

23. For the Decree of the Council of Trent Concerning Images, see Martin Chemnitz, *Examination of the Council of Trent* (Saint Louis: Concordia, 1986), 4:53–54, and exact date cited by James Waterworth, ed., *The Council of Trent: Canons and Decrees* (Chicago: Christian Symbolic, 1848).

24. For biographical information, see Charles A. Coulombe, foreword to Lapide, *Great Commentary*, vii–xv.

25. Lapide, *Great Commentary: Matthew*, 62.

Alexander VI (1492–1503) depicting *Christ Walking on the Water* (fig. 4.4). The coin depicts Christ and Peter in the lower right corner of the composition, while the boat dominates the field. Christ's body is placed on the edge of the coin and acts as a bridge in the inscription between "MODICE" and "FIDEI." The inscription continues "QVARE DUBI TASTI." It translates, "O you of little faith, why did you doubt." The disciples in the boat (on the coin and in the da Firenze) are actively watching, and reacting, to the event, while they seem unaware of what is happening in the Scarsellino.

Lapide explains the second answer given by the church fathers and commentators:

> 2. If you insist that the words, *if it be Thou*, are spoken in doubt, then it must be said that by the expression *bid me come to Thee upon the waters*, Peter asked that this command should not merely be given him, but that it should be given with power, in such manner, indeed, that Christ should command him, not only externally but also internally, and that by this command He should infuse such boldness, confidence and security, that he should not doubt that he would walk safely upon the waves, since Christ bade him.[26]

Peter is given the confidence to walk toward Christ, and in the Scarsellino Jesus welcomes him with open arms.

Verse 29: "And he said: Come. And Peter going down out of the boat walked upon the water to come to Jesus." Painters very rarely portrayed this verse. Perhaps they felt the drama of the moment was his sinking or that the walking on water should be reserved for Jesus. Lapide offers several explanations as to how it physically could have happened.

> This was done in one of three ways. Either Christ, by His divine power, held Peter fast, that he should not sink, as the angel held Habakkuk fast by the hair of his head, and carried him to Babylon (Daniel 14:35). Or else He did not allow Peter's body to be sufficiently heavy to weigh him down and sink him in the waves. Or else He did not concur with the yielding action of the water, but rather made the waters to be firm and solid beneath Peter's feet, like ice or crystal.[27]

---

26. Lapide, *Great Commentary: Matthew*, 63.
27. Lapide, *Great Commentary: Matthew*, 64.

Verse 30: "But seeing the wind strong, he was afraid: and when he began to sink, he cried out, saying: Lord, save me." Lapide comments, "The strength of the wind caused Peter to fear: fear caused doubt: doubt gave rise to danger. For the one whom faith bore upon the wave, doubt sank. The cause was Peter's little faith." Lapide's explanation is that Peter had not yet received the power of the Holy Spirit at Pentecost. He believes that Christ permitted this so that Peter could recognize his own weakness and his little faith, and might humble himself and ask Christ to increase his faith, that he might become the rock of the faith, according to the words, "Thou are Peter, and upon this rock I will build My church" (Matt 16:18).[28] Augustine says, "in Peter walking upon the waters are symbolized those who are strong in faith, but in Peter doubting, those who are weak in faith."[29] Peter, then, becomes an example of strength with a completely human character who becomes stronger after making a mistake.

"Lord save me" is the final statement of Peter in verse 30. Lapide recalls Augustine saying, "That shaking, brethren, was as it were the death of faith. But when he cried out, faith rose again. He could not have walked unless he believed, neither would he have begun to sink unless he had doubted. In Peter, therefore, we must regard the common condition of us all, that if in any temptation the wind is about to capsize and sink us in the waves, we should cry aloud to Christ."[30] Scarsellino choses to depict the Sea of Galilee as calm so as not to distract from the central focus of Peter falling into the water. Most visual examples of this scene include rough waters.[31]

In the Scarsellino and the Andrea da Firenze, the moment that is portrayed is when Christ saves Peter and raises him out of the water by the hand. In the Andrea, Peter holds onto Christ's hand with his two hands. The papal coin depicts Peter not yet touching Christ. In all of these visual renditions, Peter looks to be kneeling before Christ.

Verse 31: "And immediately Jesus stretching forth his hand took hold of him, and said to him: O thou of little faith, why didst thou doubt?" Lapide concludes,

---

28. Lapide, *Great Commentary: Matthew*, 64.
29. Lapide, *Great Commentary: Matthew*, 64.
30. Lapide, *Great Commentary: Matthew*, 65.
31. For a comparative study with another Italian mannerist, Alessandro Allori, see Hornik, "St. Peter's Crisis," 35–40.

For two things were here presented to Peter, that is to say, the strength of the wind making him afraid of being drowned, and the voice of Christ instilling confidence and security. But the strength of the wind was more obvious, and, therefore, more powerful than the voice of Christ. For it drew Peter's mind to itself, so that intent on that alone, and not thinking of Christ's promise, He wavered and feared drowning, when he ought to have listened with his full attention to Christ's voice reassuring him, and thus have resisted temptation.... Strictly speaking there is a lack of confidence in Peter here, originating however in a lack of faith. The same applies to anyone who is tempted by any temptation.[32]

Chrysostom parallels how Christ deals with Peter in the same way a mother cares for its young before they are old enough to fly. He says, "Like as a young bird which, before it is able to fly, falls out of its nest upon the ground, whose mother quickly restores it to the nest, so also at this time did Christ deal with Peter."

### *Noli Me Tangere*: Visual Types and Figural Gestures

The story of Mary and Jesus in the *Noli Me Tangere* is unique to the Gospel of John (John 20:1–17).[33] The other gospel writers have multiple women who appear with Mary Magdalene at the tomb (Matt 28:1–10; Mark 16:1–8; Luke 24:1–12) the morning of the resurrection, while John telescopes to a single individual, as he does with Nicodemus (John 3:11–15), Lazarus (11:1–44), and Thomas (20:21–29). This creates dramatic effect and establishes a relatable association between the reader and a specific character.

Although artists painted the narrative of Peter walking on water in one of two ways (Christ touches Peter or he does not), the painted versions

---

32. Lapide, *Great Commentary: Matthew*, 65.
33. Relevant and recent studies include Lisa M. Rafanelli, "The Ambiguity of Touch: Saint Mary Magdalene and the *Noli Me Tangere* in Early Modern Italy" (PhD diss., New York University, 2004); Lisa M. Rafanelli, "Sense and Sensibilities: A Feminist Reading of Titian's *Noli Me Tangere* (1509–1515)," *CA* 70.35–36 (2008): 28–47; Erin E. Benay and Lisa M. Rafanelli, *Faith, Gender and the Senses in Italian Renaissance and Baroque Art: Interpreting the Noli Me Tangere and Doubting Thomas* (Burlington, VT: Ashgate, 2015). Additional resources can be found in Susan Haskins, *Mary Magdalen: Myth and Metaphor* (New York: Harcourt Brace, 1993); Ingrid Maisch, *Mary Magdalene: The Image of a Woman through the Centuries* (Collegeville, MN: Liturgical Press, 1996).

of *Noli Me Tangere* have at least eight visual types for depicting the body positions and gestures of Jesus and Mary Magdalene throughout the history of art. The visual depictions are varied, but I will discuss and illustrate several repeated examples.[34] By outlining the types and providing links to illustrations of the paintings, it becomes apparent that Scarsellino's *Noli Me Tangere* (fig. 4.2) had many visual sources and precedents from which to choose, but Scarsellino very deliberately selected the gesture most closely aligned with his *Christ and St. Peter at the Sea of Galilee*.[35]

Christ's body position is determined by the gestures of his hands and arms. The eight types are as follows:

1. Christ with a blessing gesture with his right hand is especially popular among artists north of the Alps such as Albrecht Dürer (fig. 4.5) and Albrecht Altdorfer.[36]
2. The open palm with a "full stop" gesture of Christ's hand, often very close to touching Mary to prevent her from lunging at him, is popular in pictures painted by Benvenuto Tisi da Garofalo (fig. 4.6), Fra Bartolomeo, and Paolo Veronese.[37]
3. Perugino and Pietro Cavallini raise Christ's arm to a forty-five-degree angle with hand extended, revealing the stigmata.[38]

---

34. In cases where the works are not illustrated, links to high-resolution images are provided in the footnotes.

35. I thank Hélène Isnard and Sophie Harent at the Musèe Magnin, Dijon, for providing me with information from the curatorial files regarding their Scarsellino picture.

36. The more popular print of this subject by Dürer also depicts Christ about to touch the forehead of Mary Magdalene (type 6 discussed in the text). See Albrecht Dürer (1471–1528), *Passion: Noli Me Tangere*, 1510, Brooklyn Museum of Art. For a discussion of this work, see Bobbi Dykema Katsanis, "Meeting in the Garden: Intertextuality with the Song of Songs in Holbein's *Noli Me tangere*," *Int* 61 (2007): 402–16. Albrecht Altdorfer (1480–1538), *Noli Me Tangere*, ca. 1513, woodcut, Metropolitan Museum of Art, https://tinyurl.com/SBL6703j.

37. Benvenuto Tisi da Garofalo (1481–1559), *Noli me tangere*, ca. 1525, Kunsthistorisches Museum Wien; Fra Bartolomeo (1472–1517), *Noli me Tangere*, Musée du Louvre; Paolo Veronese, *Noli Me Tangere*, ca. 1576–1588, oil on canvas, 67 x 95 cm, Museum of Grenoble, https://tinyurl.com/SBL6703k.

38. Perugino (1445–1523), *Noli Me Tangere*, 1500–1505, tempera on panel, 27.3 x 46.3 cm, transferred to canvas, Art Institute of Chicago, https://tinyurl.com/SBL6703l; School of Pietro Cavallini, follower of Giotto, *Noli Me Tangere*, ca. 1310, fresco, San Domenico Maggiore, Naples.

Fig. 4.5. Albrecht Dürer. *Noli Me Tangere*. From the *Illustrated Bartsch*. Photo Credit: ARTSTOR. https://library-artstor-org.ezproxy.baylor.edu/asset/BARTSCH_6160090.

Fig. 4.6. Benvenuto Tisi da Garofalo. *Noli Me Tangere*. ca. 1525. Oil on Canvas. Kunsthistorisches Museum Wien. Photo Credit: ARTSTOR https://library-artstor-org.ezproxy.baylor.edu/asset/ARTSTOR_103_41822000570380.

4. Leaving Christ's arm by his side with his hand only slightly extended toward Mary Magdalene is popular with Fra Angelico, Pontormo, and Correggio (fig. 4.7).[39]
5. Jesus stands with his arm by his side and his hand flat and completely parallel to his body in Duccio's version.[40]
6. An interesting development in the visual tradition, discussed by Lapide below, occurs when Jesus places his hand on the head of Mary Magdalene, as painted by Alonso Cano (fig. 4.8) and Lavinia Fontana.[41]
7. In some paintings Jesus dramatically recoils from Mary. This was popular with Italian artists Titian (fig. 4.9) and Pietro da Cortona.[42]
8. Less frequently, but used by Caracciolo, Jesus raises both hands and extends his arms outward in a welcoming gesture.[43]

Interestingly, this final type (open hands and separated arms in a welcoming manner) is used by Scarsellino in *Christ and Saint Peter at the Sea of Galilee* (fig. 4.1). Mary Magdalene, although leaning forward, also has both hands open and arms extended to welcome Christ in Scarsellino's *Noli Me Tangere* (fig. 4.2). Mary Magdalene's gestures are far less varied in the *Noli Me Tangere* depictions. She is either contemplative (receiving the blessing, rebuke, placement of hand on her head) or active (lunging toward Christ).

---

39. Fra Angelico (1438–1445), Convent of San Marco, *Noli Me Tangere*, fresco, cell 1, Museo di San Marco, Florence; attributed to Pontormo or Agnolo Bronzino, *Noli Me Tangere*, ca. 1532, Casa Buonarroti, Florence, Inv. Gallerie 1890, no. 6307.

40. Duccio di Buoninsegna (d. 1319), *Noli Me Tangere*, 1308–1311, tempera on panel, Museo dell'Opera del Duomo, Siena.

41. Alonso Cano (1601–1667), *Noli Me Tangere*, ca. 1640, oil on canvas, 109.5 x 141.5 cm, Museum of Fine Arts, Budapest; Lavinia Fontana (1552–1614), *Noli Me Tangere*, Galleria degli Uffizi, Florence. See Franco Mormando, "Christ in the Garden: An Easter Reflection on Fontana's *Noli Me Tangere*," *America*, April 20, 2009, 27–28.

42. Titian (1490–1576), *Noli Me Tangere*, ca. 1514, oil on canvas, 110.5 x 91.9 cm, National Gallery, London. See also Sonia Waters, "Desired, Repeated, Replaced: Power and Loss in Titian's *Noli Me Tangere*," *PP* 60 (2011): 409–20. Pietro da Cortona (1596–1669), *Noli Me Tangere*, seventeenth century, oil on canvas, 74 x 61 cm, Oldenburg State Museum for Art and Cultural History, https://tinyurl.com/SBL6703m.

43. Giovanni Battista Caracciolo (Battistello) (1578–1635), *Noli Me Tangere*, ca. 1620, oil on canvas, 209 x 131 cm, Galleria Comunale, Prato, Italy, https://tinyurl.com/SBL6703m2b.

Fig. 4.7. Correggio. *Noli Me Tangere*. ca. 1525. 130 x 103 cm. Oil on panel transferred to canvas. Museo del Prado. Public Domain: https://www.wikiart.org/en/correggio/noli-me-tangere-1.

Fig. 4.8. Alonso Cano. *Noli Me Tangere*. ca. 1640. 109.5 x 141.5 cm. Oil on canvas. Museum of Fine Arts, Budapest, Hungary. Public Domain: https://www.wikiart.org/en/alonzo-cano/noli-me-tangere

Fig. 4.9. Titian. *Noli Me Tangere*. ca. 1514. 110.5 x 91.9 cm. Oil on canvas. National Gallery, London. Public Domain: https://www.wikiart.org/en/titian/do-not-touch-me-1512.

Mary Magdalene's life has often been associated with the active and the contemplative life. Lapide recalls Origen's statements, discussed below.

The inclusion of the gardener's hoe in Christ's other hand is not unique to any particular gestural type outlined above. Scarsellino does place a hoe in Christ's left hand and positions it over his shoulder. Scarsellino also uses the fourth gestural type (arm by his side with open hand extended slightly). This is not a rebuke but rather an acknowledgment of Mary's coming toward him. His drapery blows to the right, which is the direction he will probably move to avoid her touch. The drapery also echoes the transitory nature of the precise moment.

## Interpretation of John 20: Lapide's Commentary

> But Mary stood weeping outside the tomb, and as she wept she stooped to look into the tomb. And she saw two angels in white, sitting where the body of Jesus had lain, one at the head and one at the feet. They said to her, "Woman, why are you weeping?" She said to them, "They have taken away my Lord, and I do not know where they have laid him." Having said this, she turned around and saw Jesus standing, but she did not know that it was Jesus. Jesus said to her, "Woman, why are you weeping? Whom are you seeking?" Supposing him to be the gardener, she said to him, "Sir, if you have carried him away, tell me where you have laid him, and I will take him away." Jesus said to her, "Mary." She turned and said to him in Aramaic, "Rabboni!" (which means Teacher). Jesus said to her, "Do not cling to me, for I have not yet ascended to the Father; but go to my brothers and say to them, 'I am ascending to my Father and your Father, to my God and your God.'" Mary Magdalene went and announced to the disciples, "I have seen the Lord"—and that he had said these things to her. (John 20:11–18 NEB)

John 20:1–10 tells of Mary Magdalene arriving at the tomb on the morning of the Sabbath. As stated above, John only mentions Mary, and Lapide comments on this, "Verse 1. *Mary Magdalene cometh* with the other women, whom Matthew, Mark, and Luke mention; but she only is mentioned here, because she was leader of the others, and more fervent and industrious than the rest."[44] She sees the stone has been taken away and the tomb is empty. Lapide comments, "Verse 2. *She ran therefore, and cometh to Simon Peter,* (as the first of the Apostles, and already designated by Christ to be His vicar and successor, Matth. 16) *and to the other disciple whom Jesus loved.* To John, who, as she knew, was loved by Christ more than the others, and would therefore be more diligent in searching for the body of Christ."[45]

John gets there before Peter and sees the linen clothes but waits for Peter to enter the tomb. They enter together, and Lapide explains,

> Verse 8 *And he saw and believed.* Both of them, that is, Peter and John, believed—not that Christ had risen, but what Mary Magdalene said was true, namely, that the body of Christ had been removed from the

---

44. Cornelius à Lapide, *The Great Commentary of Cornelius à Lapide: The Holy Gospel according to Saint John*, trans. Thomas W. Mossman, rev. and completed by Michael J. Miller (Fitzwilliam, NH: Loreto, 2008), 750.

45. Lapide, *Great Commentary: John*, 751.

tomb, say Augustine, Theophylact, and Jansen. Cyril, Chrysostom, Euthymius, and Nyssen add that both believed that Christ had risen. But these words more clearly and correctly apply only to John, not to Peter. As if to say that John, seeing the linen cloths and the napkin folded by itself, remembered that Christ had predicted that He would rise on the third day; and so, comparing Christ's prediction with these signs, he believed that He was risen. But Peter, on account of the strangeness of a resurrection, and from His earnest desire to see Him alive again, was more slow to believe that Christ had risen. Whence the Angel significantly said to the women, "Go, tell His disciples and Peter." (Mark 16:7)

So, once again, the strength of Peter's faith is questionable. Yet, Lapide explains, "Ver. 9.—*For as yet they knew not the scriptures, that He must rise again from the dead.* For although He had solemnly assured them that He would rise, yet on account of its strange and wonderful nature they did not comprehend it, but thought that He spoke in a figure and parable, as He was wont to do."[46]

This brings us to the point in the narrative where Peter and John return to their home but Mary remains alone at the tomb weeping. "Verse 11 *Now as she was weeping, she stooped down and looked into the sepulcher.* Though she had looked in before and seen that the sepulcher was empty. For, as says S. Gregory, 'A single look suffices not one who loves, because the power of love increases the earnestness of the inquiry: she persevered in seeking, hence it came about that she found. And so it happened that her desires expanded and increased, and could thus take in that which they found.'"[47] Mary then sees two angels in the tomb. Lapide explains,

> Verse 12. *And saw two angels in white sitting, the one at the head, and the other at the feet, where the body of Jesus had been laid.* All these things ... were symbols of Christ's glorious resurrection, and prepared the mind of the Magdalen to believe it. Moreover, one sat at Christ's head and the other at the feet, to signify that the whole body of Christ had risen; and the angels' clothing that, in putting on immortality and glory through the resurrection, He had entered into the company pf the angels, and therefore had left these two angels, as guardians of the tomb, to announce the

---

46. Lapide, *Great Commentary: John*, 752.
47. Lapide, *Great Commentary: John*, 753.

fact to the Magdalen. Origen says that, mystically, the angel at the feet represented the active life, the angel at the head the contemplative life. For they are both of them from Jesus, about Jesus, through Jesus, and on account of Jesus.[48]

This statement by Origen applies to the two gestural types of Mary Magdalene in the *Noli Me Tangere* paintings discussed above. In the *vita contemplativa*, she sits calmly while receiving the blessing (or touch on her head) by Christ. Her lunging toward Christ and trying desperately to touch or hug him represent the *vita activa*.[49]

In verse 13, the angels ask her why she is weeping (when in fact she should be rejoicing and being glad), and Lapide gives reasons for us to understand,

> *She saith to them, Because they have taken away my Lord: and I know not where they have laid him.* I weep for three reasons. 1. Because of the ignominious death of my Lord. 2. Because His body has been removed from the tomb, for if I saw it, I should kiss it, lament over it, and anoint it, and so would assuage my grief somewhat. 3. Because I do not know where they carried it; I know not where to look for it. For if I knew, I would hasten to the spot, embrace it, and cover it with kisses. See here how Jesus allows the souls of those that love Him to remain in ignorance for a while, in order to sharpen and enkindle their desire for Him; and when it is thus sharpened and enkindled, to console and gladden them with the full revelation of Himself.[50]

Lapide explains why we must suffer in ignorance for a time until Jesus reveals himself completely to us.

Jesus appears first to Mary in verse 14, and she turns around but does not recognize him. Lapide comments,

> *When she had thus said, she turned herself back and saw Jesus standing; and knew not that it was Jesus.* Christ appeared behind the Magdalen, so that the angels who beheld Him rose up and bowed their heads, and showed Him other tokens of reverence and adoration. And this was why Mary Magdalen turned around: to see who it was whom the angels saluted so reverently.... Some think that Christ made a noise with His

---

48. Lapide, *Great Commentary: John*, 753.
49. Lapide, *Great Commentary: John*, 753.
50. Lapide, *Great Commentary: John*, 753–54.

feet behind Mary Magdalen's back to attract her attention, so that she would turn to Him.[51]

Not only does Lapide pass along explanations from Chrysostom and Pseudo-Athanasius, but he even offers that maybe Christ stepped on something to make her notice him.

Lapide, citing Gregory, explains that Jesus's appearing in the form of a gardener was not strange because he had appeared in other forms. He states,

> Just as He appeared in the form of a traveler at Emmaus. For glorified bodies can appear in any guise and form that they please, and they do this, not by changing their own appearance, but by preventing the form of their countenance from casting its species in their entirety upon the eye of the beholder, and allowing only refracted, diminished and fragmentary species to be perceived. Christ did this so as not to startle her at the first glance, says Chrysostom. Again, because she loved Jesus fervently He appeared to her; because she did not believe that Jesus was alive, as the angels had told her. He concealed Himself somewhat from her, and presented Himself to her outward sight as the person she fancied Him to be. So, S. Gregory (*Hom.* 23), speaking of the disciples at Emmaus.[52]

The gardener asks Mary why she weeps, and Lapide reminds us of the explanation given in a homily by Origen, "Love made her stand there, and sorrow caused her to weep. She stood and looked around, if perchance she could see Him whom she loved. She wept, as thinking that He whom she was looking for, had been taken away. Her grief was renewed, because at first she sorrowed for Him as dead, and now she was sorrowing for Him as having been taken away. And this last sorrow was the greater because she had no consolation."[53] Origen continues,

> And then he proceeds to lay open the sources of her sorrow, saying, "Peter and John were afraid, and therefore did not remain. But Mary feared not, because she felt that there was nothing left for her to fear. She had lost her Master, whom she loved with such singular affection, that she could not love or set her hopes on anything but Him. She had lost the life of her soul, and now she thought it would be better for her to die

---

51. Lapide, *Great Commentary: John*, 754.
52. Lapide, *Great Commentary: John*, 754.
53. Lapide, *Great Commentary: John*, 755.

than to live, for she might perchance thus find Him when dead, whom she could not find while she lived.[54]

The strength of Mary Magdalene's convictions evidenced here are a model for those who have lost people they love as well as those unable to see Christ in a bodily form.

Mary Magdalene, in her grief-induced stupor, initially thinks that this gardener has taken the body of Christ, and Lapide explains what may be going through her mind by citing Theophylact and Euthymius, who say, "'He was meanly dressed, and because He was in a garden, she thought he was the gardener.' She knew that Joseph of Arimathaea, the owner of the garden, did not live there, and therefore supposed that He was the person left in charge of the garden."[55] Mary speaks to him, "Sir, if you have carried him away, tell me where you have laid him, and I will take him away" (John 20:15). Mary wants to have the body returned and prevent further robbery. Jesus calls her by name, and Mary recognizes his voice. Lapide explains, "Verse 16. *Jesus saith to her, Mary. She turning, saith to Him, Rabboni (which is to say, Master).* He called her not merely by her own name, but with that tone of voice, that sweetness, grace, and efficacy, with which He used to speak to her during His life [on earth]; and she at once recognised Him."[56] It seems just prior to Jesus's calling her name, she was turned away from him. Lapide offers an explanation:

> *She turning.* For when Jesus was slow in answering, she had looked away from Him towards the angels, as if to ask them who was this gardener who was talking with her, and why they stood up and greeted Him with such reverence? But when she heard Jesus addressing her by name, *Mary*, and recognized Jesus' voice, she was enraptured with joy, and immediately turned back to face Him. The voice of the Shepherd, therefore, entering into the ears and the soul of the lamb, at once opened her eyes, and soothed all her senses with its secret power and wonted sweetness; and so carried her away out of herself, that she at once was carried away with unhoped for and inexplicable joy, and cried out *"Rabboni,"* my Master.... And accordingly, she fell down at His knees, and wished,

---

54. Lapide, *Great Commentary: John*, 755.
55. Lapide, *Great Commentary: John*, 756.
56. Lapide, *Great Commentary: John*, 757.

as she was wont, reverently to touch not His head but His feet, and cover them with kisses.[57]

This leads to the section of Lapide's commentary most relevant for the Scarsellino picture, "Verse 17. *Jesus saith to her: Do not touch me; for I am not yet ascended to My Father.*"[58] Lapide begins with the statement, "This is a difficult passage and the logical connection is even more difficult."[59] We now know that the traditional Vulgate translation of Jesus's words (*Noli me Tangere*, "Do not touch me") is incorrect; the original Greek in fact represents "a present imperative with a particular form of the negative ... [that] indicates that an action already in progress is to be stopped."[60] A precise translation would be "Cease from clinging to me" or "Stop holding me."[61]

Lapide turns to Augustine's comments, "Touch Me not, for as yet thou art not worthy to touch Me; for in thy thoughts regarding Me, I have not as yet ascended to My Father, for as yet thou dost not perfectly believe that I am the Son of God, and that I ascend to My Father."[62] Jerome has the same mystical understanding.

Searching for a more literal explanation, Lapide turns to Leontius, "I do not wish you to approach Me bodily, or recognise Me with thy bodily senses. I reserve thee for higher things. I am preparing for thee greater things. When I shall have ascended to My Father, then wilt thou touch Me more perfectly and truly, for thou wilt comprehend that which thou touchest not, and believe that which thou seest not."[63] Cyril continues this literal "not touching of the body" and associates it with the Eucharist and the Holy Spirit: "He forbade her to touch Him, to signify that no one ought to approach His glorified Body, which was now to be touched and received in the sacrament of the Eucharist as well, unless he had previously received the Holy Spirit."[64] Lapide is somewhat unsettled about the logic of either Leontius or Cyril and states, "But by this reasoning neither would

---

57. Lapide, *Great Commentary: John*, 758.
58. Lapide, *Great Commentary: John*, 758.
59. Lapide, *Great Commentary: John*, 758.
60. Mormando, "Teaching the Faithful," n. 57.
61. Mormando, "Teaching the Faithful," 115.
62. Lapide, *Great Commentary: John*, 758.
63. Lapide, *Great Commentary: John*, 758–59.
64. Lapide, *Great Commentary: John*, 759.

the other women, or Thomas, or the rest have been able to touch Christ after the resurrection: which yet they did, however."[65]

Lapide also presents commentary by Chrysostom, Theophylact, and Euthymius that indicates Christ wanted to be touched with greater reverence now. Lapide rejects those because "it is not apparent how the Magdalen failed in reverence; she belonged entirely to Christ, but as immortal and glorious."[66] Lapide is also unsatisfied with [Pseudo]-Justin, and after him Toletus and others who "explain it thus: Do not touch Me: for I am now heavenly, not earthly; although I have not yet ascended to heaven, I shall shortly ascend to it. For I wish to withdraw thee and others gradually from My accustomed presence and converse."[67]

Lapide insists that the best explanation is supplied by contemporary Jesuit theologian Francisco Suarez (d. 1617), who paraphrases Jesus's imperative thus: "Therefore do not delay, but go, so that My Apostles may share in the same joy that thou hast. Nor is it right that thou alone shouldst have this supreme joy in My resurrection, while My Apostles are wasting away with grief."[68] Christ afterward allowed himself to be touched by her and the other women, because they were then on their way to tell the apostles that he had risen (Matt 28:9).

As stated above and illustrated in Alonso Cano's *Noli Me Tangere* (fig. 8), one gestural type depicts Christ touching the forehead of Mary Magdalene. Lapide addresses this and recounts,

> Moreover when Christ said, Do not touch Me, He touched the forehead of the Magdalen with His fingers and left the marks of them imprinted upon it. Listen to Sylvester Prieras in his Life of S. Mary Magdalen in Surios. "In the year of Our Lord 1497 when I made a pilgrimage to the cave in which Blessed Mary Magdalen did penance, and visited her sacred relics in the church of S. Maximinus, her sacred and venerable head was shown to me several times; it was quite large, and entirely devoid of flesh everywhere except at that part of the forehead which the Saviour of all is said to have touched; for there some skin appears, resembling that of the Ethiopian woman, and in the skin the impressions of two fingerprints,

---

65. Lapide, *Great Commentary: John*, 759.
66. Lapide, *Great Commentary: John*, 759.
67. Lapide, *Great Commentary: John*, 759.
68. Lapide, *Great Commentary: John*, 760.

one of which is much more evident and deeper that the other, so that the flesh under the skin there turned white."[69]

In 1581, Lavinia Fontana (1552–1614) painted the moment just prior to Christ placing his hand on Mary Magdalene's forehead.[70] These artists, one male and one female, share an interest in having Christ actually touch Mary despite the words of Scripture. The physical contact and reverence of Mary Magdalene in being not only the first to see the resurrected Christ but also the first to be touched by Christ after his resurrection solidifies her importance as a disciple.

Lapide concludes the *Noli Me Tangere* section of the commentary by summarizing two additional points:

> 1. S. Epiphanius gives a moral reason, that Christ, in order to give us an example of the purest and most perfect chastity, did not wish to allow the Magdalen to touch Him on this occasion, since He was alone with a woman; but a little later in the presence of other women He permitted it. This example followed by SS. Augustine and Ambrose, S. Martin, S. Chrysostom, S. Charles Borromeo, and others. 2. Rupertus gives an allegorical reason. Mary, he says, here symbolized the Church which was called and gathered from the gentiles, not by corporeal contact, as in the case of the Jews, but rather by spiritual contact, that is, by faith, and which would come to Christ after His Ascension. come to Christ, not by corporal but by spiritual contact, after His Ascension.[71]

The remaining sections of Lapide's commentary on John (20:17–18) are not relevant to the painted narrative of the *Noli Me Tangere* scene.

## Peter, Jesus and Mary Magdalene: Penitential Figures of the Counter-Reformation

Mary Magdalene was the first witness of the resurrection, and Jesus's mandate to her to announce the good news to the apostles represents a privilege and an honor bestowed on no other female disciple.[72] In so bestowing,

---

69. Lapide, *Great Commentary: John*, 760–61.
70. For Lavinia Fontana's *Noli me tangere*, see https://tinyurl.com/SBL6703n.
71. Lapide, *Great Commentary: John*, 761.
72. Mormando, "Teaching the Faithful," 115.

Jesus rewarded Mary's great love and perseverance, and in effect made her "the apostle of the apostles," a traditional title of the Magdalene first documented in the writings of Bishop Hippolytus of Rome (ca. 170–ca. 235).[73] The Mary Magdalene known to the Renaissance and Mannerist artist was the composite Mary that scholars trace to a homily Gregory the Great delivered in 592. Gregory (540–604) combined three different figures from Scripture. The first was Mary of Magdala or Mary Magdalene, who is described in all four gospels. She was present at the crucifixion in John's Gospel (John 19:25), and she was the first to see Christ after the resurrection (John 20:11–18). The second is Mary, linked with Bethany on the basis of John 11:1, sister of Martha and Lazarus (Luke 10:38–42). The third is Luke's unnamed "woman in the city who was a sinner" (Luke 7:37). According to Gregory, she is also "whom John calls Mary, [and] we believe [her] to be the Mary from whom seven devils were ejected according to Mark."[74] Later, in another sermon, Gregory declared: "Mary Magdalene, who had been in the city a sinner, came to the sepulcher."[75] The composite picture of Mary Magdalen, Mary of Bethany, and the sinful woman who anointed Jesus as one person was now complete.

In the late medieval period, this composite Mary was at one and the same time a symbol for the penitent sinner in need of conversion (based on Luke 7), the exemplar of asceticism (based on later, extrabiblical legends of Mary's thirty-year period of self-imposed solitude in France), and the paradigm for the importance of the contemplative life (based on Luke 10:38–42).[76]

The Council of Trent (1554–1563) reaffirmed the traditional composite picture and assigned Mary Magdalene (along with Peter and the prodigal son) especially the role of penitent sinner par excellence.[77] Later a Roman missal was issued in 1570 affirming the Council of Trent's position. Esther de Boer writes: "Here the missal was not just taking up the image of Mary Magdalene which had been disseminated by Gregory the Great and

---

73. Haskins, *Mary Magdalen*, 63.
74. Gregory the Great, *Homily 33*, *PL* 76:1239, cited in Haskins, *Mary Magdalen*, 96.
75. Gregory the Great, *Homily 25*, *PL* 74:1180, cited in Haskins, *Mary Magdalen*, 96.
76. Heidi J. Hornik and Mikeal C. Parsons, *Illuminating Luke: The Public Ministry of Christ in Italian Renaissance and Baroque Painting* (New York: T&T Clark International, 2005), 2:115.
77. See John B. Knipping, *Iconography of the Counter Reformation in the Netherlands: Heaven on Earth* (Leiden: Sijthoff, 1974), 314–20.

others. This image emerged from the Counter-Reformation church. Over against the Reformation with its doctrine of grace, the Counter-Reformation emphasized the doctrine of penance and merits."[78] Consequently, Mary Magdalene "remained a favorite saint of Catholics throughout the Counter-Reformation."[79] This trend can be substantiated particularly in Counter-Reformation artwork. During this time period "the iconography of the Magdalene flourished anew in Southern Baroque art as she became a symbol for the defense of and devotion to the sacraments, especially the sacrament of penance, against the Reformers."[80] By the time of the Counter-Reformation, she was identified as a penitent and a saint. She simultaneously symbolized conversion, contemplation, and asceticism.

Franco Mormando explains that the popularity of Mary Magdalene and Peter was due not only to their privileged role in the New Testament salvation drama of Jesus's life, death, and resurrection but also to their appealing accessibility as role models.[81] They were recognizable, fallible humans who continually made mistakes and lost faith in the words spoken by Jesus. Mormando continues,

> In addition to their status as exemplars relevant to all Christians, male and female, Mary and Peter also served more specific functions: the former as role model for women, the latter as symbol of the papacy.... In addition to early modern Italians hearing about them in Sunday, Lenten, and other public sermons: they read of them in their chapbooks, catechisms, and other devotional didactic literature and, above all, they saw

---

78. Esther de Boer, *Mary Magdalene: Beyond the Myth* (London: SCM, 1996), 14–15. De Boer further notes that the Roman Catholic church did not change its official position on Mary Magdalene until 1970 (15).

79. Margaret Hannay, "Mary Magdalene," in *A Dictionary of Biblical Tradition in English Literature*, ed. David Lyle Jeffrey (Grand Rapids: Eerdmans, 1992), 487. Legend holds that Mary Magdalene was put on a ship and landed at Marseilles, France. There she evangelized the people and performed many miracles. She died after spending thirty years in solitude while not eating, only depending on the nourishment she received from the angels while communing with Christ. See Jacobus de Voragine, *The Golden Legend*, 1:376–381. Her relics were housed in the basilica of Vezelay in France. The Giovanni da Milano fresco cycle in S. Croce, Florence, shows the final fresco scene of the deceased Mary Magdalene in the foreground and a ship on the water in the background.

80. Diane Apostolos-Cappadona, "Saint Mary Magdalene," in *Dictionary of Christian Art* (New York: Continuum, 1994), 236.

81. Mormando, "Teaching the Faithful," 117.

images of Mary Magdalen and Peter in ecclesiastical and civil, public and private, institutional and domestic settings.[82]

Like the Magdalene, Peter too was a "saint who sinned" and as such was a compelling mirror of the laity's struggles against "the world, the flesh and the devil."[83] Peter appears in many roles, but perhaps the most characteristic representation of Peter in this period is the weeping penitent. Peter weeps after denying Christ three times (Luke 22:62). As art historian Pamela Jones points out, the immediacy and sensual realism of such devout compositions during the Counter-Reformation were intended to emphasize "the direct, intimate connection between saints and sinners," to remove the otherwise "formidable psychological barrier between saint and sinner" and to bluntly confront the viewer with a saintly exemplar to be imitated.[84]

The primacy of Peter as the first bishop of Rome had to be maintained. Peter was the first in apostolic succession (Matt 16:18–19), but he was still human. Peter lost focus on Jesus, and that was the moment Scarsellino painted. He removes the wind as a contributing element to the falling in the water. Instead, we are to conclude that Peter's mind wandered, and he became fearful with the realization that he was walking on water and could sink. Jesus, positioned close to shore, grabs Peter with his right hand, while his left guides him towards land. Jesus's lower body is positioned toward the shore and is in close proximity. Jesus raises Peter out of the water. This swift elevation is echoed in Peter's cape, extended behind him. Jesus does not rebuke Peter but rather teaches him to trust and have faith in him. The viewer understands that both Jesus and Peter will soon be safely on land.

Lapide cites Clement of Alexandria and reminds us of Heb 11:1: "Faith is the substance of things to be hoped for." The papal coin of Pope Alexander VI further emphasizes the power of this story. The inscription "(God) Save Us" is in the center of the coin. As stated above, "O you of little faith why did you doubt?" circles the outer portion of the coin, with Christ's body along the edge and continuing the inscription as it moves around the coin. The papacy is reaffirming the necessity of faith and associating it with

---

82. Mormando, "Teaching the Faithful," 107.
83. Mormando, "Teaching the Faithful," 120.
84. Mormando, "Teaching the Faithful," 123, quoting Pamela Jones, "The Power of Images: Paintings and Viewers in Caravaggio's Italy," in Mormando, *Saints and Sinners*, 28–29.

hope. Scarsellino's *Christ and Saint Peter at the Sea of Galilee* turns one of Peter's lowest moments into one of his highest. He is closer to Christ for coming to him and now touches Christ as Christ saves him.

Mary is not allowed to touch Christ in Scarsellino's *Noli Me Tangere*. That picture could be a companion piece to *Christ and Saint Peter at the Sea of Galilee*. Mary, like Peter, reaches out for Christ's assistance and the ability to restore their faith in him in a physical way. These two penitents are imperfect and yet leaders in the church because of their humanity. In both pictures, Christ turns toward the figure who implores him. The draperies emphatically emphasize the sense of the momentary and temporality of the act and the activity. Mary Magdalene and Peter are both desperate to return to Christ. Counter-Reformation Catholics were allowed to be in emotional distress and confused because Jesus would be present regardless of his ability to touch them or not touch them. This remains a relevant and potent message for believers still today.

## Works Cited

Adams, Eston Dillon. "The History and Significance of the *Navicella* Mosaic at Saint Peter's Basilica, Rome." PhD diss., University of Louisville, 2018.

Apostolos-Cappadona, Diane. *Dictionary of Christian Art*. New York: Continuum, 1994.

Baruffaldi, Girolamo. *Vite de' pittori e scultori ferraresi*. Vol. 2. Ferrara, 1697–1722.

Benay, Erin E., and Lisa M. Rafanelli. *Faith, Gender and the Senses in Italian Renaissance and Baroque Art: Interpreting the Noli Me Tangere and Doubting Thomas*. Burlington, VT: Ashgate, 2015.

Bercken, Erich von der, and August L. Mayer. *Jacopo Tintoretto*. Munich: Piper, 1923.

Bernari, Carlo. *L'opera completa del Tintoretto*. Milan: Rizzoli Editore, 1970.

Boer, Esther de. *Mary Magdalene: Beyond the Myth*. London: SCM, 1996.

Bowron, Edgar Peters. *European Paintings before 1900 in the Fogg Art Museum: A Summary Catalogue including Paintings in the Busch-Reisinger Museum*. Cambridge: Harvard University Art Museums, 1990.

Chemnitz, Martin. *Examination of the Council of Trent*. Vol. 4. Saint Louis: Concordia, 1986.

Coulombe, Charles A. "Foreword." Pages vii–xv in vol. 1 of *The Great Commentary of Cornelius à Lapide: The Holy Gospel according to Saint Matthew*. Translated by Thomas W. Mossman. Revised and completed by Michael J. Miller. Fitzwilliam, NH: Loreto, 2008.

Dykema Katsanis, Bobbi. "Meeting in the Garden: Intertextuality with the Song of Songs in Holbein's *Noli Me tangere*." *Int* 61 (2007): 402–16.

Fredericksen, Burton B., and Federico Zeri. *Census of Pre-nineteenth-century Italian Paintings in North American Public Collections*. Cambridge: Harvard University Press, 1972.

Hannay, Margaret. "Mary Magdalene." Pages 486–89 in *A Dictionary of Biblical Tradition in English Literature*. Edited by David Lyle Jeffrey. Grand Rapids: Eerdmans, 1992.

Haskins, Susan. *Mary Magdalen: Myth and Metaphor*. New York: Harcourt, Brace, 1993.

Hornik, Heidi J. "St. Peter's Crisis of Faith at Harvard: The Scarsellino Picture and Matthew 14." Pages 28–42 in *"A Temple Not Made with Hands": Essays in Honor of Naymond H. Keathley*." Edited by Mikeal C. Parsons and Richard Walsh. Eugene, OR: Wipf & Stock, 2018.

Hornik, Heidi J., and Mikeal C. Parsons. *Illuminating Luke: The Public Ministry of Christ in Italian Renaissance and Baroque Painting*. New York: T&T Clark International, 2005.

Jones, Pamela. "The Power of Images: Paintings and Viewers in Caravaggio's Italy." Pages 28–48 in *Saints and Sinners: Caravaggio and the Baroque Image*. Edited by Franco Mormando. Chestnut Hill, MA: McMullen Museum of Art, Boston College; Chicago: University of Chicago Press, 1999.

"Kirchenstaat: Alexander VI." Münzkabinett der Staatlichen Museen zu Berlin. https://tinyurl.com/SBL6703i.

Knipping, John B. *Iconography of the Counter Reformation in the Netherlands: Heaven on Earth*. Leiden: Sijthoff, 1974.

Lapide, Cornelius à. *The Great Commentary of Cornelius à Lapide: The Holy Gospel according to Saint John*. Translated by Thomas W. Mossman. Revised and completed by Michael J. Miller. Fitzwilliam, NH: Loreto, 2008.

———. *The Great Commentary of Cornelius à Lapide: The Holy Gospel according to Saint Matthew*. Translated by Thomas W. Mossman. Revised and completed by Michael J. Miller. Fitzwilliam, NH: Loreto, 2008.

Maisch, Ingrid. *Mary Magdalene: The Image of a Woman through the Centuries*. Collegeville, MN: Liturgical Press, 1996.
Mormando, Franco. "Christ in the Garden: An Easter Reflection on Fontana's '*Noli Me Tangere*.'" *America*, April 21, 2009, 27–28.
———. "Teaching the Faithful to Fly: Mary Magdalene and Peter in Baroque Italy." Pages 107–36 in *Saints and Sinners: Caravaggio and the Baroque Image*. Edited by Franco Mormando. Chestnut Hill, MA: McMullen Museum of Art, Boston College; Chicago: University of Chicago Press, 1999.
Novelli, Maria Angela. *Scarsellino*. Milan: Skira, 2008.
O'Malley, John W. *Trent: What Happened at the Council*. Cambridge: Belknap Press of Harvard University Press, 2013.
"Painting Laboratory Treatment Reports." February 13, 2014 (painting); March 26, 2014, and July 17, 2014 (frame). Curatorial File, Harvard Art Museums, object 1943.124.
Pallucchini, Rodolfo. *La Giovinezza del Tintoretto*. Milan: Edizioni Daria Guarnati, 1950.
Pallucchini, Rodolfo, and Paola Rossi. *Tintoretto: Le opere sacre e profane*. Venice and Milan: Alfieri/Gruppo Editoriale Electa, 1982.
"The Personal Collection of Dr. Everett Fahy." Christies, 3 October 2016. https://tinyurl.com/SBL6703g.
Rafanelli, Lisa M. "The Ambiguity of Touch: Saint Mary Magdalene and the *Noli Me Tangere* in Early Modern Italy." PhD diss., New York University, 2004.
———. "Sense and Sensibilities: A Feminist Reading of Titian's *Noli Me Tangere* (1509–1515)." *CA* 70.35–36 (2008): 28–47.
Ruggeri, Ugo. "Scarsellino." Grove Art Online. 2003. https://doi.org/10.1093/gao/9781884446054.article.T076347.
Sorenson, Lee. "Pouncey, Phillip." Dictionary of Art Historians. https://tinyurl.com/SBL6703h.
Tietze, Hans, ed. *Masterpieces of European Painting in America*. New York: Oxford University Press, 1939.
Venturi, Lionello. "La 'Navicella' di Giotto." *L'arte* 25 (1922): 49–69.
Waters, Sonia. "Desired, Repeated, Replaced: Power and Loss in Titian's *Noli Me Tangere*." *PP* 60 (2011): 409–20.
Waterworth, James, ed. *The Council of Trent: Canons and Decrees*. Chicago: Christian Symbolic, 1848.

# 5
# THE VACANT GIRL: BERNARDINO LUINI'S SALOME

## ELA NUŢU

Neither St Matthew, nor St Mark ... nor any of the sacred writers had enlarged on the maddening charm and potent depravity of the dancer. [Salome] had always remained ... beyond the reach of punctilious, pedestrian minds, and accessible only to brains shaken and sharpened and rendered almost clairvoyant by neurosis.... She had become, as it were, the symbolic incarnation of undying Lust, the Goddess of immortal Hysteria, the accursed Beauty exalted above all other beauties ... the monstrous Beast, indifferent, irresponsible, insensible, poisoning.
— Joris-Karl Huysmans, *Against Nature*

The issue with Salome is that of lack. In the short biblical narratives that mention her, the nameless daughter of Herodias has no identity, no agency, and no defense. She is seen to bring about a prophet's death, yet it is she who falls.

Jewish historian Flavius Josephus introduces Salome by name in his *Antiquitates judaicae* (18.136) as the daughter of Herodias by her first husband, also called Herod (descendant of Herod the Great and half-brother to Herod Antipas, who is Herodias's husband in the gospels). Salome only appears in Matt 14 and Mark 6 (Matt 14:1–12; Mark 6:14–29), both describing the death of John the Baptist. The gospel narratives assign guilt and intent for the prophet's death to either Herod or Herodias, not Salome. Mark includes an editorial note that Herodias "had a grudge against [John] and wanted to kill him. But she could not, for Herod feared John, knowing that he was a righteous and holy man, and he protected him" (Mark 6:19–20).[1] Matthew records that it was Herod who wanted "to put [John]

---

1. Unless otherwise indicated, all biblical quotations are from the NRSV.

to death but feared the crowd, because they regarded him as a prophet" (Matt 14:5). Josephus's later version of the story mentions neither Herodias nor Salome and her dance; Herod has the Baptist killed because of his popularity (*A.J.* 18.118). If Josephus's version is true,[2] Matthew's take on Herod's character is more plausible than Mark's.

True or not, the story of the Baptist's death is little more than a brief note in the Gospels of Matthew and Mark and left out altogether in the gospels according to Luke and John. Nicole Wilkinson Duran calls the story "frankly lurid and gory ... a brutal anecdote that leads nowhere" and cites Rudolf Bultmann's judgement that it is merely "a legend exhibiting no Christian characteristics."[3] However, Regina Janes argues that the story has theological value, inasmuch as establishing that "Mark's Baptist is the secret Elijah to Jesus' Messiah.... The Scriptures are littered with slaughtered, suffering prophets. Identifying John as Elijah, Mark narrows the field and simultaneously identifies Jesus as Lord. As the living John identifies Jesus as Christ so a dying Elijah enables a dying Messiah."[4] As the story goes, it seems that during one of Herod's birthday banquets, the daughter of the tetrarch's second wife, Herodias, dances and pleases Herod and those reclining with him (Matt 14:6 // Mark 6:22). Herod then promises to give the little girl whatsoever "she should ask" (Matt 14:7), even "up to half of [his] kingdom" (Mark 6:23). Salome seeks her mother's advice, "What shall I ask?," and Herodias responds, "The head of John the Baptist" (Mark 6:24; implied in Matt 14:8: "having been urged by the mother"). The little girl returns to Herod with her request, "I desire that at once you give to me upon a platter the head of John the Baptist" (Matt 14:8 // Mark 6:25). Herod has already imprisoned John, and he orders the prophet's execution, because, the tetrarch simply has to keep the promise he made openly in front of those "reclining with him" (Matt 14:9 // Mark 6:26). When presented with John's severed head brought to her on a platter, the

---

2. The whole episode may have been a rewriting of a different story, namely, that of Roman senator Lucius Quinctius Flaminius, who lost his position in the Senate in 184 BCE due to his ordering the beheading of a condemned man at the request of a courtesan during a banquet. See further John Dominic Crossan, *Jesus: A Revolutionary Biography* (San Francisco: HarperSanFrancisco, 1994).

3. Nicole Wilkinson Duran, "Return of the Disembodied or How John the Baptist Lost His Head," in *Reading Communities, Reading Scripture*, ed. Gary Phillips and Nicole Wilkinson Duran (Harrisburg, PA: Trinity Press International, 2002), 278.

4. Regina Janes, "Why the Daughter of Herodias Must Dance (Mark 6.14–29)," *JSNT* 28 (2006): 444.

girl gives it to her mother. The disciples then take the decapitated body of John and bury him in a tomb (Matt 14:12 // Mark 6:29).

I use the term *girl* deliberately, because the daughter of Herodias is probably of prepubescent age in the narrative. The term used to describe her by both Matthew and Mark is "little girl," κοράσιον (diminutive of κορη; ταλιθα in Aramaic, as used in Mark 5:41), and this is the same term used for Jairus's daughter, who is said to be twelve years old in Mark 5:42 (see Matt 9 // Mark 5). Justin Martyr also understood Salome to be a child, and he uses the term *child*, παῖς, when describing her in his *Dialogue with Trypho* (49.4–5). Jairus's daughter is also described by the gender-neutral term, παιδίον, in Mark 5:40. In the biblical narrative, the daughter of Herodias is κοράσιον, or little κορη, a little maiden; a παιδίον by association, a prepubescent child of neutral gender. And yet, despite all this, and indeed despite the clear distribution of guilt to either Herod or Herodias in the biblical text, the little girl has become the epitome of the femme fatale, both irresistible and deadly. As I have argued elsewhere,[5] thanks in part to fin de siècle Decadent art, the daughter of Herodias is sutured to her identity as Salomé and survives still as the "symbolic incarnation of undying Lust, the Goddess of immortal Hysteria, the accursed Beauty … the monstrous Beast, indifferent, irresponsible, insensible, poisoning."[6] This metamorphosis is fascinating; many have focused on her dance as its catalyst. Even ancient and medieval readers may have found the dance challenging. In his *Catena aurea*, Thomas Aquinas supports Theophylact's earlier assessment that "Satan danced in the person of the damsel."[7] It may be interesting, therefore, to consider works of art that depict Salome away from the dance, and this is what I would like to explore here, specifically the work of early sixteenth-century Lombard painter Bernardino Luini.

Luini was born around 1480, in Dumenza, in Lombardy—northern Italy—and he seems to have lived until 1533. There is relatively little known about him. Giorgio Vasari himself makes only a few remarks about Luini (whom he calls Bernardino del Lupino), all of "no biographical value at all" in James Mason's opinion.[8] Vasari does, however, record:

---

5. Ela Nuțu, "How Salomé Fell for the Baptist, or John the Baptist as *L'Homme Fatal*: Artistic Interpretations of a Biblical Narrative," *BRec* 5 (2018): 99–126.

6. Joris-Karl Huysmans, *Against Nature*, trans. Robert Baldick (Harmondsworth, UK: Penguin, 1959), 65–66.

7. Thomas Aquinas, *Catena aurea* (Oxford, 1841–1845), 2:116.

8. James Mason, *Bernardino Luini* (London: Jack & Jack, ca. 1910), 18.

Bernardino del Lupino, who was also a Milanese; this artist was an exceedingly delicate and pleasing painter ... most perfectly painted in fresco ... worked extremely well in oil also, he was a most obliging person, friendly and liberal in all his actions. To him therefore is deservedly due all the praise which belongs by right to those artists who do themselves no less honour by the courtesy of their manners and the excellence of their lives, than by the distinction to which they attain in their art.[9]

The lack of detail on Luini is deplored by nineteenth-century art critic Alexis-François Rio as "the most unforgiving and incomprehensible" of all of Vasari's gaps.[10] Rio's contemporary art historian George Williamson, editor of the 1899 series *The Great Masters in Painting and Sculpture*, declares that Vasari's "praise is either withheld or bestowed with a grudging hand, in terms very inadequate to the merits of the master's poorest work. There must be some reason for this curious circumstance."[11] Mason also speculates, "There seems to be some reason for the silence. Perhaps it was an intimate and personal one, some unrecorded bitterness between the painter and one of Vasari's friends, or between Vasari himself and Luini or one of his brothers or children."[12] However one interprets what appears to be a lacuna in Vasari's work, what is clear is that it is perceived as undeserved, possibly as a result of a tendency in Vasari to disregard northern, particularly Lombard, painters. In his 1625 guidebook on his collection of Italian Renaissance art, *Musaeum*, Federico Borromeo suggests that Vasari was "unduly biased in favour of Central Italy."[13] Borromeo was a seventeenth-century archbishop of Milan, who founded in 1620 the Ambrosian Accademia del Disegno in order to "teach aspiring artists how to create effective sacred art."[14] Borromeo's collection included works by Bernardino Luini, which he listed among "originals

---

9. Giorgio Vasari, *Le Vite dei Pittori Italiani* (Florence, 1550), 156, as quoted in George C. Williamson, *Bernardino Luini* (London: Bell & Sons, 1899), 2.
10. Alexis-François Rio, *De l'Art Chrétien* (Paris: Hachette, 1847), 3:193. The full quote is: "De toutes les lacunes, qu'on sginalée dans l'ouvrage incomplete de Vasari, celle-ci est à la fois de plus impardonable et la plus incompréhensible."
11. Williamson, *Bernardino Luini*, 3.
12. Mason, *Bernardino Luini*, 18.
13. In the opinion of Pamela M. Jones, "Defining the Canonical Status of Milanese Renaissance Art: Bernardino Luini's Paintings for the Ambrosian Accademia del Disegno," *AL*, n.s. 100 (1992): 89.
14. Jones, "Defining the Canonical Status," 89.

by major artists."[15] The quality of Luini's work is further demonstrated by the fact that a number of his works had been attributed first to Leonardo da Vinci, most notably Luini's *St Catherine*, the two versions of which are now in the collections of the National Gallery in London and the Hermitage in Saint Petersburg, and his *Vanity and Modesty*, now in a private collection, which was attributed to Leonardo while in the Sciarra Colonna Palace in Rome.[16]

There seems to be indeed a connection between Bernardino Luini and Leonardo da Vinci (1454–1519), for Luini is believed to have studied under the great Leonardo for a while. Luini is known to have trained under Ambrogio Bergognone (1470s–1524) of the Milanese school of painting; Luini himself produced several works in the city of Milan (frescoes and oil paintings).[17] However, it is also said that Luini trained under Bergognone's more prominent contemporary, Leonardo, who was known to have worked in Milan between 1482 and 1500 when he was in the service of the duke of Milan, Ludovico Sforza (known also as Il Moro). It was in Milan that Leonardo painted his famous *Last Supper* fresco, after all, in the refectory of the Convent of Santa Maria delle Grazie. There is strong evidence to suggest that Leonardo had apprentices while in Milan (it is likely that it was for these Milanese apprentices that Leonardo wrote the texts that were later compiled into his *Treatise on Painting* in 1651). It seems that Leonardo's patron, Ludovico Sforza, asked Leonardo to open an academy, which is likely to have indeed been founded around 1485–1486. Luini is thought to have been associated with the Academia Leonardo Vinci, alongside Giovanni Antonio Boltraffio (1466–1516), Cesare da Sesto

---

15. Pamela M. Jones, "Bernardino Luini's Magdalene from the Collection of Federico Borromeo: Religious Contemplation and Iconographic Sources," *SHA* 24 (1990): 68.

16. Williamson, *Bernardino Luini*, 89. See in particular the notes on *St Catherine* by Williamson, who writes that the Hermitage St Catherine "inaccurately bears the name of Leonardo da Vinci" (69).

17. Most of his documented work was for the Old Monastery, Saint Maurice of Milan, commissioned by the Count Giovanni Bentivoglio. His frescoes in the Villa Pelucca in Sesto San Giovanni and in the church of Santa Maria dei Miracoli in Saronno are also notable. He was well known for his fresco work in chapels and city buildings through Milan but also completed several noteworthy oil paintings. These include *Madonna of the Rose Hedge*, which show Madonna's gaze in Luini's classic Luinesque, or squinted eyes, for which his female figures were known. See "Bernardo Luini," Virtual Uffizi Gallery, https://tinyurl.com/SBL670o.

(1477–1523), Francesco de Melzi (ca. 1491–1568), and Giovanni Paolo Lomazzo (1538–1600).[18] However, Leonardo himself is likely to have left Milan in 1499, when Il Moro had to flee Milan due to political unrest and was later imprisoned by Louis XII.

Since Luini is said to have arrived in Milan a year later, in 1500, it is unlikely that Luini met Leonardo in person, although the dates may be incorrect (certainly the time margin is rather small).[19] While the influence or inspiration of Leonardo is clear, Luini may have been merely an imitator, a follower of the great Florentine painter rather than directly his pupil. Either way, some of the works completed by Luini and others from Leonardo's Milanese academy—Luini may have worked there for some years, before establishing his own reputation as a master before 1507—would have been signed in Leonardo's name.[20] Interestingly, when comparing the two artists, John Ruskin prefers Luini:

> Luini is ten times greater than Leonardo;—a mighty colourist, while Leonardo was only a fine draughtsman in black, staining the chiaroscuro drawing like a coloured print; [Luini] perceived and rendered the delicatest types of human beauty that have been painted since the days of the Greeks, while Leonardo depraved his finer instincts by caricature and remained to the end of his days the slave of an archaic smile; and [Luini] is a designer as frank, instinctive and exhaustless as Tintoret, while Leonardo's design is only an agony of science, admired chiefly because it is painful and capable of analysis in its best accomplishment. Luini has left nothing behind him that is not lovely.[21]

As the leading Victorian art critic influenced by the evangelical revival and the English Romantics, Ruskin may indeed have preferred Luini also because of his perceived Christian modesty and piety, his "lofty religious creed," as expressed through his art, which is almost in its entirety biblical or religious.[22] In Ruskin's eyes, Luini was idealized as "the only man who

---

18. Williamson, *Bernardino Luini*, 9.
19. Williamson, *Bernardino Luini*, 9.
20. See "Bernardino Luini," Virtual Uffizi Gallery.
21. John Ruskin, *The Queen of the Air: Being A Study of the Greek Myths of Cloud and Storm* (New York: Maynard, Merrill, 1893), 211–12.
22. Ruskin, *Queen of the Air*, 212.

entirely united the religious temper which was the spirit-life of art, with the physical power which was its bodily life."[23]

By the seventeenth century, art had been firmly identified as an expression of divine creativity. Da Vinci himself had declared that "the knowledge of the painter transforms his mind into the likeness of the divine mind."[24] Thus critics used divine standards when distinguishing between "good" and merely "mediocre" art. Giovambattista Armenini made the distinction clear in his 1587 *De'veri precetti della pittura*: "Even an artist of mediocre talent can master [portraiture] as long as he is experienced in colours."[25] Armenini further implies that a truly good artist, a virtuoso, moves beyond the act of copying nature, the "*ritrare*," for he cannot "endure" the "awkwardness and weakness" of natural faces. Therefore, a true virtuoso should invent and indeed *perfect* a face. Vincenzo Danti also remarks, "By the term *ritrare* I mean to make something exactly as another thing is seen to be; and by the terms *imitare* I similarly understand that it is to make a thing not only as another has seen the thing to be, but to make it as it would have to be in order to be of complete perfection."[26] "Le arie del bel viso," or the art of idealized, perfected face, came to represent the beauty of the art of painting itself.[27]

Whether Luini was a pupil or a follower of Leonardo who "sweetened Leonardo's face with [his] own instinct," as Williamson himself postulates,[28] can only be a matter of opinion, since facts are so scarce. Leonardo's influence on Luini is clear. When one considers, for example, two other significant works from Leonardo's period in Milan, his two versions of the *Virgin of the Rocks* (sometimes *Madonna of the Rocks*) currently at the Louvre in Paris and at the National Gallery in London, respectively, and Luini's own *Madonna of the Rose Bush* in the Brera Pinacoteca in Milan and *Madonna and Child with Saints Catherine and Barbara*

---

23. Ruskin, *Queen of the Air*, 211.

24. Jean Paul Richter, *The Literary Works of Leonardo da Vinci* (London, 1939); Martin Kemp, "From Mimesis to 'Fantasia': The Quattrocento Vocabulary of Creation, Inspiration, and Genius in the Visual Arts," *Viator* 8 (1977): 347–98.

25. Quoted in Fredrika H. Jacobs, *Defining the Renaissance Virtuosa: Women Artists and the Language of Art History and Criticism* (Cambridge: Cambridge University Press, 1997), 44.

26. Vincenzo Danti, "Il primo libro del trattato delle perfette proporzioni," in *Scritti d'arte del cinquecento*, ed. Paola Barocchi (Milan: Ricciardi, 1960), 1:241.

27. Jacobs, *Defining the Renaissance Virtuosa*, 46.

28. Williamson, *Bernardino Luini*, 27.

at the Museum of Fine Arts in Budapest, the resemblance is evident. The women in Leonardo's Louvre *Virgin* and London *Madonna* and Luini's two *Madonna* paintings (and indeed other Luini works, most notably *Herodias/Salome*, now at the Uffizi in Florence, and the contested *St Catherine* mentioned above) have the same face: same features; same hair; same eyes, nose, mouth; same inclination of the head; same gaze. One could venture: same (Milanese) model. Same hand would be perhaps going too far, although there is some debate whether the London version came straight from Leonardo's hand.[29]

Turning to the subject of this brief study, let us explore Luini's Salome paintings, starting with his Uffizi *Herodias/Salome* (fig. 5.1).[30] Painted between 1527 and 1531, this Salome was also originally thought to be one of Leonardo's works, then "rightfully" (the Uffizi would insist) attributed to Luini in 1793.[31] This Salome appears to be very different from the hot and deadly women of Wilde, Strauss, and their fin de siècle Decadent contemporaries. She is, at first glance, rather sweet and demure ... a good girl. Perhaps apt, since Luini himself is described by the curators at the Uffizi as being "not an intellectual painter, but ... a sweet, light hearted man of high religious ideals."[32]

Modestly (yet not cheaply) dressed, Salome casts a sideway glance that falls outside the frame. Her head is slightly tilted to one side—her right—gracefully; her hair is up, in an elaborate net of plaits, with only a few strands allowed to fall loosely around her face; a small jeweled pin

---

29. The speculation is that the Louvre version, dated between 1483 and 1486, did not meet with Leonardo's client's full satisfaction, which enabled Louis XII to acquire it around 1500–1503. The second, replacement picture (now in London) may have been painted by Ambrogio de Predis under Leonardo's supervision between 1495 and 1508. See Séverine Laborie, "The Virgin of the Rocks," Louvre, https://tinyurl.com/SBL6703p. This possibility may explain the different tones and stronger lines in the Louvre version, which certainly more closely resembles Leonardo's sketches.

30. Some ancient Greek translations of Mark read "Herod's daughter Herodias" (rather than "daughter of the said Herodias"). To scholars using these ancient texts, both mother and daughter had the same name. However, scholars using the Latin Vulgate Bible did not confuse the two; thus, Western church fathers tended to refer to Salome as "Herodias' daughter" or just "the girl." Nevertheless, because she is otherwise unnamed in the Bible, the idea that both mother and daughter were named Herodias gained some currency in early modern Europe.

31. See "Bernardino Luini," Virtual Uffizi Gallery.

32. See "Bernardino Luini," Virtual Uffizi Gallery.

5. THE VACANT GIRL: BERNARDINO LUINI'S SALOME        143

Fig. 5.1. Bernardino Luini, *The Executioner Presenting Herodias with the Head of John the Baptist*, 1527, oil on panel, 51 x 58 cm, Galleria degli Uffizi, Florence / Bridgeman Images. © 2019 Ministero dei Beni e delle AMinistero dei Beni e delle Attività Culturali e del Turismo—Gallerie degli Uffizi.

adorns her coiffure. This girl's face is beautiful, without blemish; youthful, with pink cheeks; and peaceful. Her delicate red mouth is closed, its ends curling up slightly, in something that is not quite a smile. Some might interpret this feature as mysterious. I see it as betraying a rather submissive, deferential attitude in the young woman. Luini presents us not merely with a portrait of Salome, however, but rather with the narrative scene of her receiving the decapitated head of John the Baptist. Presented by the executioner, who still holds it in his fingers by the hair, John's head hovers over the dish, which stands on a solid surface (the top of a table perhaps), Salome's left hand resting on it while her right points to it. The dish here resembles more closely a chalice (on the altar?) rather than a platter. Salome looks serenely away from the head, which it is not at all gruesome—in fact, it is rather Jesus-like: peaceful, as if sleeping. The only signs of death are John's black mouth (perhaps denoting the kiss of death) and the few blood drops falling and captured in the dish. John's features are not unlike Salome's: their faces have similar shape and angle; similar hair texture, coloring, and parting. By contrast, John's executioner, who still grips the head by the hair, appears brutal, unfeeling, beastly, with a bulbous, furrowed brow hanging over sunken eyes fixed on John's head, and a large, grimacing mouth, opened to show irregular lower teeth. This depiction seems a deliberate choice on Luini's part, as much as introducing the old woman on the left, perhaps, who is peering curiously over Salome's shoulder to get a closer look at John's head. Who is she? Is she a maid, as her modest attire suggests? Or is she Herodias? There is, of course, the train of thought that Herodias is indeed rather old and unappealing when the death of the Baptist occurs—hence Herod's quick infatuation with Salome, the young and attractive princess. Yet, this woman is not altogether convincing as the tetrarch's wife.

This composition is not unique to Luini. Most notably, two of Caravaggio's later depictions of *Salome with the Head of John the Baptist* (1607–1610), in the National Gallery in London and the Palacio Real in Madrid, respectively, place her in a very similar context, between maid and executioner. As I have argued elsewhere,[33] the executioner and the maid may be introduced in order to confuse the balance of guilt in the composition, for artists themselves can be ambivalent about Salome's role in the Baptist's death: Is she innocently subservient to her mother's wishes (like a maid), or is she willingly complicit in the violent act of decapitation itself (like the executioner, though he would not have had much choice), which is implied in Caravaggio's more nuanced Madrid version? Williamson's own 1899 reading of Luini's Uffizi *Salome* assigns guilt to the young girl rather clearly:

> She is a beautiful, sensuous and voluptuous woman, devoid of sympathy or tenderness, self-satisfied and indifferent to the sufferings of others, and these characteristics are marked not only in her face, but in her form and her hands. The executioner is a hard, rough, hideous man, strong in physical power, and wanting entirely in tenderness, and he stands out of the background in brutal contrast to the lascivious and careless woman who bears the dish, and who is so proud of her own beauty and skill.[34]

---

33. Ela Nuţu, "Reading Salomé: Caravaggio and the Gospel Narratives," in *From the Margins II: Women of the New Testament and Their Afterlives*, ed. Christopher C. Rowland and Christine E. Joynes (Sheffield: Sheffield Phoenix, 2009), 210–26.

34. Williamson, *Bernardino Luini*, 66.

What skill? Seduction, one infers. Yet, this does not strike me as a reading of Luini's depiction but rather of the biblical narrative behind it. I am not convinced that Williamson's description of Salome reflects Luini's work at all. I see very little sentiment in this Salome's face, yes, so she may indeed be said to be "indifferent" (though my argument is that Salome is devoid of individual identity), yet, she does not appear to me to be "lascivious" and "proud of her own beauty and skill." Her face is the same face as Luini's Madonnas, after all (as above); would Williamson, I wonder, offer the same reading of the mother of Christ? Perhaps not.

What of Luini's own take on Herod's stepdaughter? In order to attempt to answer that question, let us consider other Salome depictions by Luini, starting with three others, found at the Louvre in Paris (fig. 5.2), the Prado in Madrid (fig. 5.3), and the Museum of Fine Arts in Boston (fig. 5.4). In all of the four depictions, including the Uffizi version, Salome is quite similar, bearing a similar stance and expression: she looks away as she holds what is clearly a platter to her left ready for the executioner (reduced to a disembodied arm in the Louvre and Boston versions and bearing softer, somewhat reverential, if not remorseful, features in the Prado version) to place John's decapitated head on it. The head bears almost identical features and is held upright by the hair in all versions. The platter, too, has similar features and proportions, though in the Louvre version the small amount of blood dripping from John's severed neck threatens to spill over the edge of the platter. The old woman is absent from all other versions. She only appears in the Uffizi depiction.

In all four versions Salome's head is tilted at a similar angle, her gaze falling outside the frame to the left, at a slightly higher angle in the Uffizi and Boston versions, and higher still—though not enough to threaten the overall effect—in the Louvre version. Salome also bears similar features in all four depictions, though she is slightly more voluptuous in the Prado version. She wears similar clothing and adornments, with some differences, namely, the addition of a pearl hair band in the Prado and a pearl-and-ruby one in the Boston version, while in the Louvre version she appears to wear some hair net or covering of some kind, the result being a more modest demeanor (possibly balancing Salome's slightly loftier gaze in that version). In the Prado and Boston versions, Salome's clothing is slightly more appealing, her décolletage lower and thus more revealing; and she wears the same cameo pendant in both paintings: a standing male

Fig. 5.2. Bernardino Luini, *Salome with the Head of St. John the Baptist*, oil on canvas, 62 x 55 cm, Musée du Louvre, Paris / Peter Willi / Bridgeman Images. © Musée du Louvre.

archer, whose suggested identity is Cupid,[35] though in my opinion he is more likely a young Pythian Apollo. The Cupid theory is found in a short entry on Luini's *Salome* in a 1921 volume of Boston's *Museum of Fine Arts Bulletin* and has since found significant tracking. Among others, Christopher Nygren develops the association between Luini's Salome and Cupid

---

35. Identified as Cupid in G., "Salome with the Head of John the Baptist," *MFAB* 19.116 (December 1921): 72.

Fig. 5.3. Bernardino Luini, *Salome Receiving the Head of the Baptist*, 1501–1515, oil on canvas, 62 x 78 cm, Museo Nacional del Prado, Madrid. © Photographic Archive Museo Nacional del Prado.

further by arguing that "Salome's adornment with the arrows of Cupid establishes her as the unattainable object of erotic desire."[36] That may be so, for it reflects some of the traditions cultivating the motif of Herod's potential infatuation with his young stepdaughter.

However, in my opinion, the cameo worn by Salome in both the Boston (fig. 5.5) and the Madrid (fig. 5.6) versions depicts Apollo, in a rather Belvedere pose. Admired for a considerable time as one of the most beautiful examples of art from classical antiquity,[37] the *Apollo Belvedere*,

---

36. Christopher J. Nygren, "Stylizing Eros: Narrative Ambiguity and the Discourse of Desire in Titian's So-Called *Salome*," in *Renaissance Love: Eros, Passion, and Friendship in Italian Art around 1500*, ed. Jeanette Kohl, Marianne Koos, and Adrian W. B. Randolph (Berlin: Deutcher Kunstverlag, 2014), 38.

37. In particular by German art historian Johann Joachim Winckelmann, but also by the likes of Goethe, Schiller, and Byron, who all admired the *Apollo Belvedere*. Artists such as Michelangelo and Dürer used it as inspiration, as have neo-classical

Fig. 5.4. Bernardino Luini, *Salome with the Head of Saint John the Baptist*, 1515–1525, oil on panel, 62.23 x 51.43 cm, Museum of Fine Arts, Boston. Gift of Mrs. W. Scott Fitz. 21.2287. Photograph © 2019 Museum of Fine Arts, Boston.

or *Pythian Apollo*, is "considered the sculptural embodiment of the ideal male nude and one of the most perfect expressions of classical art."[38] At 224 centimeters in height, it depicts the Greek god Apollo standing tall and naked, but for a loose short *chlamys* draped around his shoulders and

---

sculptors such as Antonio Conova, who used the *Apollo Belvedere* as a model for his *Perseus with the Head of Medusa*. Apollo Belvedere was also used by NASA as its official emblem for the Apollo 17 lunar mission in 1972, designed by Robert T. McCall. See "Apollo Imagery," NASA, https://tinyurl.com/SBL6703q.

38. Valeria Cafà, "Ancient Sources for Tullio Lombardo's Adam," *MMJ* 49 (January 2014): 39.

5. THE VACANT GIRL: BERNARDINO LUINI'S SALOME        149

his left arm, sandals, and a quiver for his arrows. His right arm rests on a tree trunk, around which climbs a serpent—a sign for the Delphic Python, whom Apollo kills in retaliation for the serpent tormenting his mother, Leto, while pregnant with him and his twin sister, Artemis. Apollo's head is turned to his left, beautiful curls falling down his strong neck. His gaze follows the trajectory set by his left arm, which leads the viewer to imagine the flight of the arrow that may have just escaped his bow, a fragment of which remains in Apollo's left hand. This imagining is further supported by the fact that his left leg is set back for balance, toes on the ground and heel in the air. Found in 1489 in Antium and initially part of the art collection of Cardinal Giuliano della Rovere, who became Pope Julius II in 1503, the surviving white marble statue is now at the Vatican Museums. Owing its name to the Belvedere Court in the Vatican Museums and dated 120–140, this marble version is thought to be a copy of a much earlier bronze statue from circa 330–320 BCE attributed to Athenian sculptor Leochares. The *Apollo Belvedere* came to be in vogue and indeed revered very quickly, and it is very likely that Luini was at least familiar with the work.

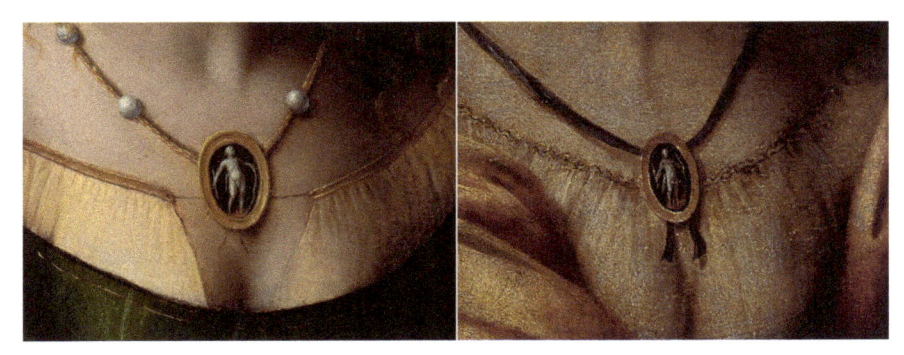

Fig. 5.5. Bernardino Luini, *Salome with the Head of Saint John the Baptist*, 1515–1525, oil on panel, 62.23 x 51.43 cm. Museum of Fine Arts, Boston. Gift of Mrs. W. Scott Fitz. 21.2287. Photograph © 2019 Museum of Fine Arts, Boston. Detail.

Fig. 5.6. Bernardino Luini, *Salome Receiving the Head of the Baptist*, 1501–1515, oil on canvas, 62 x 78 cm, Museo Nacional del Prado, Madrid. © Photographic Archive Museo Nacional del Prado. Detail.

The pose of the *Apollo Belvedere* is very similar if not identical to the figure on Salome's cameo pendant, but it is not the only thing that persuades me that it is indeed Apollo whom Luini invokes. In Greek mythology, twin brother to Artemis, the chaste goddess of hunting, Apollo emerges as the god of fertility, patron to the Muses and protector of the young. He leads the Muses and his sister's nymphs into song and dance, and he is invited to play his lyre at the marriages of other gods, among them Eros and Psyche and Peleus and Thetis. As the ideal male youth, *kouros*, Apollo also takes the role of *kourotrophos*:[39] guardian and teacher, nurturer and healer to boys and girls, *kouroi* and *korai*. Luini places Salome, the little *kore* who dances like a nymph, under Apollo's auspices. Why? Wouldn't Luini's admired Christian "lofty religious creed" limit his accessing classical Greek mythology?

Perhaps what we have here is an indication that Bernardino Luini is aware of the potential or perceived allure of the biblical character, which he frames, however, as vulnerability rather than skill. His Salome is the innocent—or rather unaware—girl placed in a rather perilous circumstance when dancing in a way that her lascivious stepfather finds pleasing, and used for nefarious purposes by her self-serving mother. It is thought that Luini used his own sister as a model for his Madonna and Salome (and indeed Christ, for example, in his *Christ in the Attitude of Benediction* in the Ambrosian Library in Milan and *Christ among the Doctors* in the National Gallery in London), for she was said to have "an ideal face, with pensive eyes, sensitive lips, not without sadness, but ready to sweeten into a smile, and an ample expanse of forehead, serene and calm."[40] By introducing the *Apollo Belvedere*—known to his audiences—perhaps Luini invokes the protection of Apollo for the young woman in his paintings even from the gaze of viewers who would readily interpret Salome as a fully grown femme fatale, a "lascivious [woman] ... proud of her own beauty and skill."[41] Luini uses the same model, possibly his young sister, in *The Virgin on a Throne with Saints* at the Brera Pinacoteca in Milan, though not for the Madonna herself but rather for St. Barbara, who stands to the right of the painting (and the left of the Madonna and the Christ child) holding a chalice and a palm leaf. On the left of the composition stands Luini himself, fashioned as Saint Anthony. He stands holding a crozier and a clasped book. Luini depicts himself as rather old, with white hair under a cap and a long white beard. The interesting thing is that at his feet

---

39. See more on the concept of male *kourothropoi* in François de Polignac, *Cults, Territory, and the Origin of the Greek City-State* (Chicago: University of Chicago Press, 1995), 44.
40. Williamson, *Bernardino Luini*, 85.
41. Williamson, *Bernardino Luini*, 66.

Luini places a pig, known as an "emblem of unclean desire."[42] Luini also appears in his *Susanna* now in the Princely Collection in Liechtenstein, in which he depicts himself as one of the scheming and predatory elders, hidden behind a tree in background, while Susanna, bearing Salome's features, looks out of the frame in the same fashion as Salome. Since the story of Susanna speaks of the virtue of young women and the depravity of old men, Luini may wish to protect the innocence of young Salome by invoking Apollo's protection and thus reminding his viewers of Salome's youthful naivete if not purity. It is perhaps for this reason that Luini does his utmost to limit the horror and violence of the narrative in his depictions of Salome.

Luini's attitude toward Salome's innocence can be further explored in one other of his Salome paintings, now in the Kunsthistorisches Museum in Vienna (fig. 5.7). This is the Salome of the Bible, in my opinion. The composition is different: Salome is no longer holding an empty dish, for the Baptist's beautiful head is already resting (peacefully) on it; his curly hair (close in color and appearance to Salome's) is clean, and neat, and carefully arranged within the boundaries of the platter; nothing is spilling over at all, not even the little blood underneath John's beard. The violence of the decapitation is again displaced; discarded as *abject*,[43] signified only by the presence of the executioner. The man stands behind Salome, on her right, and his features are dark and common but for one flourish: the curl at the end of his mustache. He and Salome form a striking pair, more akin to a satyr and a nymph.

In her essay on abjection, *Pouvoirs de l'horreur*, or *Powers of Horror*, Julia Kristeva describes abjection as the psychoanalytical amplification of universal horror, which creates a link between the subject and what the subject recognizes as times of desolate crisis. It is easily understood that, because of the horror element, the abject is all the more powerful while it remains hidden, unknown. Analytically, however, while that happens, what also remains hidden is the "other side of religious, moral, and ideological codes on which rest the sleep of individuals and the respites of societies. Such codes are abjection's purification and repression."[44] Ana-

---

42. Williamson, *Bernardino Luini*, 29.
43. Apropos Kristeva.
44. Julia Kristeva, *Powers of Horror: An Essay on Abjection*, trans. Leon S. Roudiez (New York: Columbia University Press, 1982), 209; translation modified by John Lechte, "Horror, Love, Melancholy," in *Julia Kristeva* (London: Routledge, 1990), 158.

Fig. 5.7. Bernardino Luini, *Salome with the Head of John the Baptist*, ca. 1525–1530, oil on panel, 55.7 x 42.5 cm, Kunsthistorisches Museum, Vienna / Bridgeman Images. © KHM-Museumsverband.

lytically, the abject is the ambiguous element that disrupts the confines of the ego, that which resists unity and disturbs the formation of identity on a unified premise, that which resists system and order. Examples of the abject number not only material filth and waste (corpses, too) but also elements of moral and political hypocrisy, such as "the traitor, the liar, the criminal with a good conscience, the shameless rapist, the killer who claims he is a saviour," where corruption is the most conventional "socialized aspect of the abject."[45] In contrast to this, the sacred is formed, in Kristeva's opinion, as a "two-sided sacred,"[46] on the premise of the subject-object dyad and the resulting subjects and social codes, which are constructed on the division between murder (the murder of the father) and incest (engaging the mother). This theory corresponds to Freud's own take on totem and taboo, which sees the existence of the sacred predicated on murder and incest, more precisely on its difference *from* murder and incest. As the separation from the mother is a feared moment—the same moment when unified identity is exposed as illusory—it is associated with other elements that threaten the unity of the "I," elements that exist on the border of identities, namely, filth and defilement.[47]

Kristeva maintains that the symbolic is not strong enough to cause or impose the separation from the mother on its own, however. Thus, before the child's entrance into the symbolic order, there exists the experience of certain impulses and drives toward rejecting, or expelling, the

---

45. Kristeva, *Powers of Horror*, 4, 16.
46. Kristeva, *Powers of Horror*, 57–58.
47. See on this the work of Mary Douglas, *Purity and Danger* (London: Routledge & Kegan Paul, 1979).

mother, toward making the mother into the abjected object. "The abject would thus be the 'object' of primal repression."[48] It is possible, Kristeva explains, that through toilet training and other cleanliness-related habits the mother becomes associated, at the presymbolic level, with that which is expelled. Thus, abjection could be understood as an undesirable part of ourselves, something that we do not wish to face, "the mud of Narcissus' pool," as John Lechte puts it, "the moment of narcissistic perturbation."[49] Elements such as bodily waste, nail clippings, menstrual blood, and so on, which create a hazy contour for the body, ambiguous and undefined, become subject to ritualistic habits, so that the abjection linked to them is warded off. Corpses undergo similar treatment for the same reasons. These rituals, however, while intending to affirm identities, emphasize the existence of, and separation between, subject and object. This is similar to the removal of the mother (and the threat that she brings to identity contours), which only establishes the mother as the Other. The mother, as the expelled element, becomes associated with the abject. For Kristeva, defilement marks the separation between the semiotic authority and the symbolic law, between the realm of the mother and that of the father.[50]

In all the other of Luini's interpretations, Salome is rather a nonentity, sweet and compliant, vacant. As much as she is in the biblical text, one could argue: an unnamed girl whose unshaped, vacant self—what Jacques Lacan would call her *manque-à-être*—allows Herodias to project her powers and manipulate her *Other* flesh. Lacan names *manque-à-être*, our initial lack-of-being, the experience of rupture from the imaginary fullness of being, from the mother, from the object of desire. The identity that we take on is given to us from outside, produced by the "Symbolic Order of our culture, the social languages that identify us and lend us identities, all of which exceed consciousness and never assume the form of knowable or conscious identity (which, for Lacan, is always phantasmatic). Our identity is given to us from outside, and we are constitutively alienated."[51] The inception of subjectivity, of the "I," comes through seeing, in the mirror, a reflection of the embodied self that has boundar-

---

48. Kristeva, *Powers of Horror*, 12.
49. Lechte, "Horror, Love, Melancholy," 160; Kristeva, *Powers of Horror*, 15.
50. Kristeva, *Powers of Horror*, 73.
51. Julie Rivkin and Michael Ryan, "Strangers to Ourselves: Psychoanalysis," in *Literary Theory: An Anthology*, ed. Julie Rivkin and Michael Ryan (Oxford: Blackwell, 1998), 124.

ies, which becomes the model for all future identifications; the subject acquires an identity by virtue of that "I" being reflected *by* the other and from the *location* of the other, back to the subject. As Lacan has it, "this development is lived like a temporal dialectic that decisively projects the formation of the individual in history."[52] Jane Gallop sees this as the crux of the "high tragedy" that she considers Lacan's mirror stage to be. She associates it with the story of Genesis and the expelling of Adam and Eve from paradise. Thus, just as the first man and woman cannot enter the human condition before they are expelled from Eden, so with the child, who, already born, cannot become an individual self until experiencing the mirror stage. Both developments are like dual birth processes: once born into nature, and the second time into history. While Adam and Eve anticipate mastery when eating the forbidden fruit, only to acquire sight of their nakedness, the child anticipates a totalized, mastered body, only to recognize their inadequacy.[53]

Lacan associates the dawn of individuality in the infant with the acquisition of language. Rather than a Cartesian *res cogitans*, or thinking being, Lacan's subject is a speaking subject, the subject of speech, *parle-être*, not only in the sense that the subject speaks but also in the sense that the subject is "spoken through by language." It is language that makes the subject, meaning that when one learns to say the name of an object one has to accept separation from it; the object is sacrificed, because the presence of the sign/word represents the absence of the signified thing itself. The entrance into the symbolic and the breaking of the imaginary thus consists of the "installation of a combined linguistic/psychological separation of the child both from its initial object, the mother, and from the undifferentiated matter of natural existence."[54] From that moment on, the mother becomes the Other, symbolic of all forbidden desires and lost objects, the absence of which will leave a gap that we try to fill but never succeed in filling. Lacan suggests that throughout life, we try to come to terms with this separation, the gaps in our existence, our *manque-à-être*. Thus, we slide along a chain of signifiers, a play of metonymy, parts rather than a whole. Drives such as scopophilia, or the pleasure of the gaze, voyeurism,

---

52. Jacques Lacan, *Ecrits: A Selection*, trans. Alan Sheridan (London: Tavistock, 1977), 97.

53. Jane Gallop, *Reading Lacan* (Ithaca, NY: Cornell University Press, 1985), 82–85.

54. Rivkin and Ryan, "Strangers to Ourselves," 124.

are rooted in the our *manque-à-être*, our lack of being, which we forever try to fill and heal.

In his Vienna work (fig. 5.7), Luini allows Salome a spark of individuality, of self. Her sideway glance is no longer graceful and subservient here; it is instead furtive and impish, playful and amused (while perhaps attempting to achieve the required degree of decorum under the rather odd circumstances). It betrays the tainted innocence of a child who is on the precipice of knowledge, of self-identity, of adulthood. This is indeed the Salome who asks for the platter—her one explicit choice different from her mother's, her individual identity as expressed through language, the one detail Herodias's daughter adds to her mother's instructions in the biblical text, the detail that proved such a catalyst for Salome's metamorphosis into the stylized icon of fin de siècle, Decadent Europe. Her own speech separates her from the mother and gains her an individual identity. As Julie Rivkin and Michael Ryan explain, "Before language assigns us an 'I,' we possess no sense of self. It is language that gives us identity."[55] René Girard would argue, however, that Salome's identity is in fact a *mimesis*, a copy, of her mother's.[56] Girard bases his argument on the fact that Salome appropriates the desire expressed by Herodias as her own. He also suggests that perhaps the platter may have been the result of a child's naive, literal interpretation of an adult's words:

> When Herodias, in answer to Salome, says, "the head of John the Baptist," she probably does not allude to decapitation. In Greek, as in English, to demand someone's head is to demand his death. Period. The head is a figure of speech that consists in taking the part of the whole. Rhetoricians call this "metonymy."... Even in countries where beheading is practiced, to demand someone's head must be taken rhetorically, and Salome takes her mother literally. She does not do so intentionally—she has not yet learned to distinguished words from things. She does not recognise the metonymy.... She seems perverse and sadistic, and perhaps she is, but it is the same as being merely childish.[57]

I am not convinced that Salome appropriates the identity of her mother; in fact, Salome may act out of the desire for a self of her own, different from Hero-

---

55. Rivkin and Ryan, "Strangers to Ourselves," 123.
56. See René Girard, "Scandal and the Dance: Salome in the Gospel of Mark," *NLT* 15 (Winter 1984): 311–24.
57. Girard, "Scandal and the Dance," 318.

dias—hence the platter. Yet, I cannot help but wonder whether Salome, in her desire for self-identity, does indeed add the monstrous—a literal bloody head on a platter—into a story that may have otherwise proved rather pedestrian.

Salome's subjectivity is further threatened by what Lacan and Claude Lévi-Strauss would call a "bad grammar" of kinship, ill-defined family nomenclature. Salome is stepdaughter to her uncle, niece to her stepfather, daughter to her stepuncle, stepniece to her father, daughter to a woman who is wife to her brother-in-law, and sister-in-law to her husband. As Girard states, "incestuous propagation leads to formless duplications, sinister repetitions, a dark mixture of unnameable things: 'a monstrous commingling of fathers, brothers, sons; of brides, wives and mothers!'"[58] In Lacan's view,

> The primordial law is therefore that which in regulating marriage ties superimposes the kingdom of culture on that of a nature abandoned to the law of mating. The prohibition of incest is merely its subjective pivot.... This law, then, is revealed clearly enough as identical with an order of language. For without kinship nominations, no power is capable of instituting the order of preferences and taboos that bind and weave the yarn of lineage through succeeding generations. And it is indeed the confusion of generations which, in the Bible as in all traditional laws, is accused as being the abomination of the Word (*verbe*) and the desolation of the sinner.[59]

Having been accused publicly by John the Baptist as having engaged in irregular marriage practices by taking Herodias as his second wife while her husband, his brother, was still alive, is Herod acting out in the Gospels a sinner's desolation? Or does the story fulfill its role in cementing a link between John and Elijah, as Janes suggests, which puts Herod in the role of Ahab, who threatens Elijah's life only when Ahab's wife, Jezebel, become involved?[60] Janes puts forward the theory that the men "meet with hostility, but respect"—the kings' attitude "fundamentally sympathetic and respectful" toward the men of God—before the kings' women get involved, and

---

58. René Girard, *Violence and the Sacred* (Baltimore: Johns Hopkins University Press, 1979), 75.

59. Jacques Lacan, "The Symbolic Order," in Rivkin and Ryan, *Literary Theory*, 185. See also Claude Lévi-Strauss, *The Elementary Structures of Kinship*, trans. James Harle Bell, John Richard von Sturmer, and Rodney Needham (Boston: Beacon, 1969).

60. Janes, "Why the Daughter," 449.

only then are the prophets in peril.[61] I do not find this argument particularly convincing. Herod had already imprisoned John, and, as Janes herself acknowledges, all other sources, including Josephus, reject this picture of the gentleman tetrarch. While one could indeed connect Jairus's daughter with Herodias's, Janes's proposal that "the resurrection of Jairus' daughter is the act by Jesus that heralds his own resurrection … as the Baptist's death and tomb are those that Jesus overcomes"[62] makes little theological room for Salome. The daughter of Herodias has dramatic value instead. It strikes me that Janes has a theory, and her reading of the text is rather subservient to it. The binary assertion that Jairus's daughter is Salome's "good twin"[63]—the corollary being that the daughter of Herodias is the "bad twin"—I find injudicious.

The value of self-identity and the gaze can be further explored in Luini's *The Conversion of the Magdalene* or *Allegory of Modesty and Vanity* at the San Diego Museum of Art (fig. 5.8). The alternative title comes from Luini's *Modesty and Vanity* painting that was originally attributed to Leonardo da Vinci (as mentioned above) now in a private collection, which depicts Martha and Mary but is similar in composition. The viewer is presented with two contrasting young women in the *Conversion*. The one on the left is in profile, focused on the other, as if ready to engage her in conversation—no doubt concerning spiritual matters, for her right hand points up to heaven, while her left rests empty on the table between the two characters, pointing perhaps to the other woman's possessions. In stark contrast to her plain, humble persona, the woman on the right is clearly a woman of the world. She is dressed in rich fabrics similar in color and style to those of the Vienna Salome (a gown of a beautiful, lush green). Her hair is curled and loose (also in a similar style to the Vienna Salome). The Magdalene's right hand vainly directs attention to her beauty, while her left rests possessively on a porcelain jar that identifies her (incorrectly, yet within an established artistic tradition[64]) as Mary Magdalene. She smiles alluringly

---

61. Janes, "Why the Daughter," 449.
62. Janes, "Why the Daughter," 452.
63. Janes, "Why the Daughter," 455.
64. Mary Magdalene is often, at least in the Western tradition, connected with the "sinful woman" of Luke 7:36–50. Though she is not named in these verses, Luke immediately follows the sinful woman's conversion story with a list of the women who accompanied the Lord. Among these women is "Mary, called Magdalene, from whom seven demons came out" (Luke 8:2).

Fig. 5.8. Bernardino Luini, *The Conversion of the Magdalene*, ca. 1520, oil on panel, 64.7 x 82.5 cm, San Diego Museum of Art, San Diego. Gift of Anne R. and Amy Putnam in memory of their sister, Irene / Bridgeman Images. © 2019 The San Diego Museum of Art.

while holding the viewer's gaze with confidence. It is not the rich, colorful clothes on their own that make this Magdalene vain, for Luini styles his holy women in a similar fashion, most notably Mary, the mother of Jesus. A few examples are *The Holy Family* at the Louvre; the *Infant Jesus Sleeping* also at the Louvre; and the *Holy Family with the Infant Saint John* at the Prado in Madrid. These Virgins share the grace—and, in my opinion, vacuity—that comes with the tilted head, sideway glance, and subservient smile of Luini's earlier Salomes. Luini's Magdalene is not dissimilar to his Vienna Salome (fig. 5.7)—indeed, their shared features may indicate that he used the same model for both (his sister?). However, what distinguishes the two biblical women is the gaze: while Salome appears to have shifted her gaze at the last moment, avoiding thus the viewer's scrutiny, the Magdalene meets that challenge head-on; she looks directly at the viewer.

Does the confidence betrayed by the direct gaze convey vanity, indeed knowledge of sin and evil, however, or simply knowledge? Luini's Jesus, too, meets the viewer's gaze directly—for example, in his *Christ in the Attitude of Benediction* in the Ambrosian Library in Milan and *Christ among the Doctors* in the National Gallery in London—as does his Saint Catherine—most notably in Luini's *Madonna and Child with Saints Catherine and Barbara* at the Museum of Fine Arts in Budapest. Both are depicted as scholars—Christ is engaged in a debate in the temple, while Catherine holds a book and a quill, which is in keeping with her established hagiography. The direct gaze, therefore, is meant to reveal knowledge, but knowledge of the divine. If in Luini's *Conversion* the young woman on the right is meant to represent an allegory of Vanity, the painting's didactic function (discouraging vanity in female viewers, presumably) is undermined by the association with Mary, the sister of Martha; its message is a little too facile and thus not altogether convincing. She is likely the Magdalene, and her direct gaze betrays *self*-awareness and *self*-possession. This young woman owns her individual and independent "I"—she is Mary of Magdala, her name proving that her identity was her own and not dependent on a man, either father or husband—and she is very much aware of that fact. Furthermore, the Magdalene can safely inhabit her identity as a newly converted and thus "clean" woman.

Luini's *The Magdalene*, now at the National Gallery of Art in Washington, DC, features the same model, the same green gown, and the same porcelain dish. Alone in the frame, the Washington Magdalene arrests the viewer's gaze as directly as the Magdalene in the San Diego work. There are no allusions to vanity in this work, and thus one is free to interpret the gaze not as a sign of pride (a pride in her "skill"?), but rather as knowledge—of self and of God. The direct gaze was also important for Borromeo, who included *The Magdalene* in his *Biblioteca Ambrosiana*, "for post-Tridentine reformers felt that emotional appeal enhance a picture's suitability for contemplation."[65] In his sermons, published as *I Ragionamenti Spirituali* in 1632, Borromeo encourages Christians to engage their imagination when praying, conjuring up images of biblical stories, even looking at a suitable painting of a given narrative. Borromeo is said to have had a number of Magdalenes in his collection, including some of Luini's and indeed Titian's work on the subject. It seems that Borromeo valued the story of the Magdalene's repentance as well as Christ's passion as "efficacious topics for prayer," and Pamela Jones declares that the Magdalene's "idealised face presented the transcendent state that she

---

65. Jones, "Bernardino Luini's Magdalene," 69.

had achieved through prayer and pure love of Christ."[66] The Magdalene can look directly at the viewer because she is a convert, redeemed, saved, protected by Christ himself.

By contrast, Salome is read as the vilified seductress, an object of lascivious desire, and also of hatred and loathing. Girard argues, "The metamorphosis of desire into hatred results from its mimetic nature. The more mimetic it becomes, the more it incites imitation, and the more rapidly it is transmitted from one individual to another."[67] In Peter Conrad's words, "Salome flourishes in the atmosphere of perverted spirituality, where religious ardour merges into sexual desire and all the senses are synesthetically exploited and deranged."[68] Depictions of the daughter of Herodias may serve the purpose of image, condensed simulacrum aiding the pious in their imaginings. Yet, as Fredrika Jacobs remarks, the beauty of the perfected face, the idealized *bel viso*, "had the power to propel the beholder up the Platonic *scala amoris*, or ladder of love. But it could do so only after the painted or sculpted image had acquired the immediacy of a psychological presence."[69] Unlike fin de siècle artists, Luini attempts to guard Salome's acquiring a psychological presence, and to limit, curtail, indeed, direct the subjugating power of the viewer's gaze away from the little *kore* he exhibits, by offering empty images and protective signs from classical myth. Luini's vacant girl looks away, her gaze falling outside the frame. Luini's message is "Look; but do not linger.... Look away now."

## Works Cited

"Apollo Imagery." NASA. https://tinyurl.com/SBL6703q.
"Bernardino Luini." Virtual Uffizi Gallery. https://tinyurl.com/SBL670o.
Cafà, Valeria. "Ancient Sources for Tullio Lombardo's Adam." *MMJ* 49 (January 2014): 32–47.
Conrad, Peter. "Opera, Dance and Painting." Pages 144–78 in *Romantic Opera and Literary Form*. London: University of California Press, 1977.

---

66. Jones, "Defining the Canonical Status," 92–93.
67. Girard, "Scandal and the Dance," 313 .
68. Peter Conrad, "Opera, Dance and Painting," in *Romantic Opera and Literary Form* (London: University of California Press, 1977), 159.
69. Jacobs, *Defining the Renaissance Virtuosa*, 46.

Crossan, John Dominic. *Jesus: A Revolutionary Biography.* San Francisco: HarperSanFrancisco, 1994.

Danti, Vincenzo. "Il primo libro del trattato delle perfette proporzioni." Pages 207–69 in vol. 1 of *Scritti d'arte del cinquecento.* Edited by Paola Barocchi. Milan: Ricciardi, 1960.

Douglas, Mary. *Purity and Danger.* London: Routledge & Kegan Paul, 1979.

Duran, Nicole Wilkinson. "Return of the Disembodied or How John the Baptist Lost His Head." Pages 277–91 in *Reading Communities, Reading Scripture.* Edited by Gary Phillips and Nicole Wilkinson Duran. Harrisburg, PA: Trinity Press International, 2002.

G. "Salome with the Head of John the Baptist." *MFAB* 19.116 (December 1921): 72.

Gallop, Jane. *Reading Lacan.* Ithaca, NY: Cornell University Press, 1985.

Girard, René. "Scandal and the Dance: Salome in the Gospel of Mark." *NLT* 15 (Winter 1984): 311–24.

⸻. *Violence and the Sacred.* Baltimore: Johns Hopkins University Press, 1979.

Huysmans, Joris-Karl. *Against Nature.* Translated by Robert Baldick. Harmondsworth, UK: Penguin, 1959.

Jacobs, Fredrika H. *Defining the Renaissance Virtuosa: Women Artists and the Language of Art History and Criticism.* Cambridge: Cambridge University Press, 1997.

Janes, Regina. "Why the Daughter of Herodias Must Dance (Mark 6.14–29)." *JSNT* 28 (2006): 443–67.

Jones, Pamela M. "Bernardino Luini's Magdalene from the Collection of Federico Borromeo: Religious Contemplation and Iconographic Sources." *SHA* 24 (1990): 67–72.

⸻. "Defining the Canonical Status of Milanese Renaissance Art: Bernardino Luini's Paintings for the Ambrosian Accademia del Disegno." *AL*, n.s. 100 (1992): 89–94.

Kemp, Martin. "From Mimesis to 'Fantasia': The Quattrocento Vocabulary of Creation, Inspiration, and Genius in the Visual Arts." *Viator* 8 (1977): 347–98.

Kristeva, Julia. *Powers of Horror: An Essay on Abjection.* Translated by Leon S. Roudiez; New York: Columbia University Press, 1982.

Laborie, Séverine. "The Virgin of the Rocks." Louvre. https://tinyurl.com/SBL6703p.

Lacan, Jacques. *Ecrits: A Selection*. Translated by Alan Sheridan. London: Tavistock, 1977.

———. "The Symbolic Order." Pages 184–89 in *Literary Theory: An Anthology*. Edited by Julie Rivkin and Michael Ryan. Oxford: Blackwell, 1998.

Lechte, John. "Horror, Love, Melancholy." Pages 157–98 in *Julia Kristeva*. London: Routledge, 1990.

Lévi-Strauss, Claude. *The Elementary Structures of Kinship*. Translated by James Harle Bell, John Richard von Sturmer, and Rodney Needham. Boston: Beacon, 1969.

Mason, James. *Bernardino Luini*. London: Jack & Jack, ca. 1910.

Nuțu, Ela. "How Salomé Fell for the Baptist, or John the Baptist as *L'Homme Fatal*: Artistic Interpretations of a Biblical Narrative." *BRec* 5 (2018): 99–126.

———. "Reading Salomé: Caravaggio and the Gospel Narratives." Pages 210–26 in *From the Margins II: Women of the New Testament and Their Afterlives*. Edited by Christopher C. Rowland and Christine E. Joynes. Sheffield: Sheffield Phoenix, 2009.

Nygren, Christopher J. "Stylizing Eros: Narrative Ambiguity and the Discourse of the Desire in Titian's So-Called *Salome*." Pages 23–44 in *Renaissance Love: Eros, Passion, and Friendship in Italian Art around 1500*. Edited by Jeanette Kohl, Marianne Koos, and Adrian W. B. Randolph. Berlin: Deutcher Kunstverlag, 2014.

Polignac, François de. *Cults, Territory, and the Origin of the Greek City-State*. Chicago: University of Chicago Press, 1995.

Richter, Jean Paul. *The Literary Works of Leonardo da Vinci*. London, 1939.

Rio, Alexis-François. *De l'Art Chrétien*. Paris: Hachette, 1847.

Rivkin, Julie, and Michael Ryan. "Strangers to Ourselves: Psychoanalysis." Pages 119–27 in *Literary Theory: An Anthology*. Edited by Julie Rivkin and Michael Ryan. Oxford: Blackwell, 1998.

Ruskin, John. *The Queen of the Air: Being a Study of the Greek Myths of Cloud and Storm*. New York: Maynard, Merrill, 1893.

Thomas Aquinas. *Catena aurea*. 4 vols. Oxford, 1841–1845.

Vasari, Giorgio. *Le Vite dei Pittori Italiani*. 3 vols. in 1. Florence, 1550.

Williamson, George C. *Bernardino Luini*. London: Bell & Sons, 1899.

# 6

## Picturing the Parable of the Sower

### CHRISTINE E. JOYNES

Although the storytelling techniques of gospel parables have been widely discussed, little work has been done on visual depictions of the parables in art.[1] Focusing on the parable of the sower (Matt 13:1–23; Mark 4:1–20; Luke 8:4–15), my essay will explore four different nineteenth-century depictions of this parable. I will suggest (developing here the work of Paolo Berdini) that despite superficial appearances, the sower is sometimes shown as sloppy or incompetent, indicating that the images are often not intended to show the actual practice of sowing. This can be contrasted with Jure Mikuž's suggestion that, in portraying the sower, artists "attempted to elevate peasant work to the level of a symbol, signifying eternal glorification of human work on earth."[2] As will become apparent through the parabolic pictures explored below, the political and social implications of the sower image are particularly significant and may explain the popularity of this figure in nineteenth-century Europe. Furthermore, images of the sower also prompt the viewer to ask what role an artist's intention and context play in the act of interpretation.

---

1. David Gowler's recent volume *The Parables after Jesus: Their Imaginative Receptions across Two Millennia* (Grand Rapids: Baker, 2017) has begun to redress this situation. On storytelling techniques of gospel parables, see for example Ruben Zimmermann, *Puzzling the Parables of Jesus: Methods and Interpretation* (Minneapolis: Fortress, 2015).

2. Jure Mikuž, "Ivan Grohar," Oxford Art Online, 2003, https://doi.org/10.1093/gao/9781884446054.article.T035021.

## How to Identify the Sower

From coins to canvas, stained-glass windows to sacred-book illuminations, images of the sower have served a variety of functions. It is important, though, not to overstate the popularity of picturing the parables. As Doug Adams points out, the parables rarely featured in the first thousand years of Christian art.[3] Indeed, they are notably omitted from Gertrud Schiller's compendium of early Christian art.[4] Similarly Louis Réau points only to a twelfth-century miniature in the *Hortus deliciarum* and the thirteenth-century stained glass in Canterbury Cathedral in his entry under "La parabole du semeur."[5] Adams proposes that the tendency of earliest Christian art to focus on the divinity of Christ led to the miracles proving more popular than parables as subjects for artistic representation.[6] In contrast, the parables illustrate Jesus's role as a teacher. Indeed, some images, such as Erhard Schön's 1525 woodcut (now in the British Museum), include Jesus teaching a crowd juxtaposed with the sower in the same frame to highlight this feature.

The parable of the sower (Matt 13:1–23; Mark 4:1–20; Luke 8:4–15) occurs in all three Synoptic Gospels, as well as the Gospel of Thomas, with some notable differences of presentation. While it is beyond the scope of this essay to discuss the similarities and differences between these narratives, it is worth mentioning Mark's particular emphasis on the surprising yield at the conclusion of his parable, with the harvest of good seed increasing thirtyfold, sixtyfold, and one hundredfold. In summary, then, Mark's reading of the parable highlights that, despite outward appearances to the contrary, there will be an abundant harvest. I follow Markan priority in determining synoptic relations and therefore maintain that Mark was the source that influenced the subsequent accounts. However, as I have argued elsewhere, artistic representations more usually *harmonize* elements from different gospel accounts.[7]

---

3. Doug Adams, "Changing Patterns and Interpretations of Parables in Art," *ARTS* 19 (2007): 5; similarly, Claus M. Kauffmann, "The Sainte-Chapelle Lectionaries and Illustrations of the Parables in the Middle Ages," *JWCI* 67 (2004): 2.

4. Gertrud Schiller, *Iconography of Christian Art* (Gütersloh: Gütersloher Verlag, 1971).

5. Louis Réau, *Iconographie de l'art chretien* (Paris: Presses universitaires de France, 1957), 2:341.

6. Adams, "Changing Patterns and Interpretations," 5.

7. Christine E. Joynes, "Wombs and Tombs: The Reception History of Mark 16.1–20," in *From the Margins II: Women of the New Testament and Their Afterlives*, ed. Christine E. Joynes and Christopher C. Rowland (Sheffield: Sheffield Phoenix, 2009), 226–43.

Not only are there difficulties in establishing which gospel the images of the sower parable are based on, but there is a more fundamental problem one encounters when dealing with the parable of the sower in art: namely, when is *a* sower not *the* sower? After all, the very fact that Jesus used images drawn from the agrarian culture around him itself highlights that many sower images may simply be rural pictures bearing no relation to the biblical text.[8] Furthermore, artists frequently omitted giving titles to their work, leaving their images open to broader interpretation. Paolo Berdini, in his analysis of Jacopo Bassano's painting (*The Parable of the Sower*, ca. 1560), has rightly drawn attention to the contentious issue of how to identify when an image of a sower is a conscious allusion to the biblical narrative. Berdini defines a parable as "a literary form in which language and images derived from ordinary life become the metaphorizing agents of religious discourse."[9]

Bassano's *The Parable of the Sower* (fig. 6.1) has widely been regarded by art critics as "a pastoral."[10] Rejecting this conclusion, however, Berdini argues that the painter "*puts in motion a set of responses that eventually lead the viewer to reconsider what he or she sees in light of what he or she knows or suspects. This involves the ability to activate the metaphor, and thereby rescue religious discourse from literal obliviousness.*"[11] Or as he writes elsewhere, "There are incongruities in Bassano's picture that resist surrender to literal description."[12]

Commenting on Bassano's picture, Berdini observes:

> The farmer is sowing with peculiar randomness and seeds are cast onto portions of the ground that are ill-disposed to fertilization.... The presence of parabolic discourse becomes evident as soon as the figures in the image are seen to contradict rather than fulfil the roles that realism assigns to them.... What ultimately makes the parable in Bassano's

---

8. See, e.g., the image of E. Wood Perry, which the reviewer distinctly states is "not based on the scriptural type." See "Our Illustrations," *AU* 1.6–7 (1884): 117.

9. Paolo Berdini, "Jacopo Bassano: A Case for Painting as Visual Exegesis," in *Interpreting Christian Art*, ed. Heidi J. Hornik and Mikeal C. Parsons (Macon, GA: Mercer University Press, 2004), 173.

10. Berdini, "Jacopo Bassano," 172. See for example the attempt to de-Christianize the image by R. W. Rearick, cited and refuted by Berdini.

11. Berdini, "Jacopo Bassano," 175, emphasis added. It is beyond the scope of the present essay to explore other strategies used by artists to make the link to the biblical text clear, such as by inserting a banner referencing the gospel narrative.

12. Berdini, "Jacopo Bassano," 176.

Fig. 6.1. Jacopo Bassano (Jacopo da Ponte), *The Parable of the Sower*, ca. 1560. Oil on canvas. 139 x 129 cm. Museo Nacional Thyssen-Bornemisza, Madrid. Photo © Museo Nacional Thyssen-Bornemisza, Madrid.

> picture recognizable is the tension between the representation of the ordinary vis-à-vis an insufficient compliance with those modalities of customary behaviour that would make that reality characterizable as ordinary. And if the parable fulfils its mimetic requirements, it is only as a function of a metaphorical reality, so that ultimately the beholder can only make sense of the image by engaging a metaphorical register.[13]

Interestingly, a metaphorical approach to reading the parable of the sower is used by Bernard Aikema to account for what he perceives to be the lack of popularity of Bassano's image. He interprets it as an anti-Erasmian defense of virginity and celibacy, suggesting that Bassano here follows the approach of sixteenth-century polemicists, who regarded the seed "falling into good ground" as those practicing virginity, the seed "falling on stony

---

13. Berdini, "Jacopo Bassano," 176.

places with not much earth" as those adopting celibacy, and the "seed falling by the wayside" as those who chose marriage.[14] Aikema concludes, "No wonder Jacopo's renderings of the *Parable of the Sower* were copied less often than *The Annunciation to the Shepherds*: after all, celibacy has never been terribly popular."[15] The contrasting interpretations of Bassano's *Parable of the Sower* by Berdini and Aikema highlight the ambiguity of the image, even though both scholars acknowledge a connection between the painting and the gospel texts.

## Peasant Power:
### Situating the Sower in Nineteenth-Century Europe

The analysis above outlined some of the difficulties in interpreting sowers. I turn now to examine images of the sower in nineteenth-century Europe, reflecting further on the importance of context. Contrary to Stefano Zuffi's assertion that the parable of the sower was popular *only* in the sixteenth and seventeenth centuries,[16] a cursory glance at the output of some nineteenth-century European artists demonstrates that this biblical passage continued to have appeal. When we juxtapose the images from this period, we find contrasting foci: thus, some artists emphasize the actions of the sower (Millet, Tissot), while others draw attention to the fate of the seed (Millais), suggesting a moralizing or didactic purpose. I have chosen four contrasting sower pictures to focus on by way of case studies: images produced by Jean-François Millet, John Everett Millais, Vincent van Gogh, and Oscar Roty.[17]

---

14. Bernard Aikema, *Jacopo Bassano and His Public* (Princeton: Princeton University Press, 1996), 76-77. Aikema suggests this reading is derived from Jerome. His interpretation of it as an anti-Erasmian defence of virginity and celibacy is contrary to Berdini's reading of the image as a reference to hearing and responding to "the word" represented by the seed.

15. Aikema, *Jacopo Bassano*, 79–80.

16. Stefano Zuffi, *Gospel Figures in Art*, trans. Thomas Hartmann (Los Angeles: J. Paul Getty Museum, 2003), 231. He suggests that the episode is "little shown in art because of the complexity of portraying the four different types of earth on which the seeds are thrown in a single, figuratively plausible painting." See the anonymous reviewer of Millais's *Parables*, who regards the parables as "a subject not well suited, on the whole, to pictorial illustration." See "Millais' Parables," *NP* 1 (March 1864): 146.

17. I have selected Roty's sower in this small case-study sample not only because it is a different kind of art (coinage) but also because it presents a female sower, raising interesting gender issues that deserve further exploration.

## 1. Jean-François Millet (1814–1875)

The first example comes from France, where Millet's *Sower* made a significant impact.[18] It was shown in the Paris Salon in 1850 and is completely dominated by the sower figure (fig. 6.2).[19] With a purposeful, commanding stride, the sower scatters the seed with his right hand in a sweeping gesture that is barely contained by the canvas, while his left hand clutches the cloth wrapped around him to form a seed bag. According to Horst Janson and Anthony Janson, "This 'hero of the soil' is a timeless symbol of the unending labor that the artist viewed as the peasant's inescapable lot."[20] Or, as Hugh Brigstocke puts it, Millet had an ability to "elevate the mundane to the heroic and the specific to the general."[21] This resulted, however, in the artist being accused of romanticizing the grinding harshness of rural poverty.[22]

The date of the painting (1850) is important. As the painting appeared shortly after the 1848 revolution, Millet's decision to focus on a rural laborer was seen as highly political. While Millet himself was not socially radical, nevertheless his painting of *The Sower* was "championed by liberal critics because it was the very opposite of the Neoclassical history paintings endorsed by the establishment."[23] As Alexandra Murphy argues, "A peasant who moved resolutely across a darkened plain wearing a red shirt, with his face hidden and unreadable in shadow, was unquestionably a challenging if not threatening image."[24] This is clearly highlighted when we compare our

---

18. As an aside, it is worth noting that the Salon catalogue records the image as "un semeur," which would be more accurately translated as "*A* Sower" rather than "*The* Sower."

19. It is beyond the scope of the present essay to examine the debate about which version of *The Sower* was exhibited in the Salon. I follow the persuasive arguments of Alexandra Murphy in this respect, who proposes that the Boston Sower was the one exhibited. See Murphy, *Jean-François Millet* (Boston: Little, Brown, 1984), 32. For the alternative position in favour of the Philadelphia version, see Griselda Pollock, *Millet* (London: Oresko Books, 1977), 40.

20. Horst W. Janson and Anthony F. Janson, *History of Art*, 6th ed. (London: Thames & Hudson, 2001), 672.

21. Hugh Brigstocke, *The Oxford Companion to Western Art* (Oxford: Oxford University Press, 2001), 479.

22. Brigstocke, *Oxford Companion*, 479.

23. Janson and Janson, *History of Art*, 672.

24. Murphy, *Jean-François Millet*, 32. However, Pollock points out that Millet's paintings were displayed in the homes of industrialists and were therefore not necessarily regarded as threatening by these figures (*Millet*, 8).

Fig. 6.2. Jean-François Millet, *The Sower*, 1850. Oil on canvas. 101.6 x 82.6 cm. Gift of Quincy Adams Shaw through Quincy Adams Shaw Jr. and Mrs Marian Shaw Haughton. Museum of Fine Arts, Boston. Photograph © 2021. Museum of Fine Arts, Boston.

version of *The Sower* with an earlier version Millet painted (1847–1848).[25] However, Millet's attraction to a rural laborer in his work *The Sower* was by no means unusual for this artist, as he regularly chose to feature such figures in his paintings. By way of comparison, and dating from the same period, one might note *The Winnower* (1847–1848).[26] It is no surprise,

---

25. Found in the National Museum of Wales, Cardiff.
26. Now in the National Gallery, London.

then, that he came to be referred to as the "peasant painter," a title he himself appears to have promoted.[27]

The extent to which Millet's *Sower* alludes to our gospel parable is contested by critics. Despite describing Millet as a "close student of the Bible," Robert Herbert suggests that finding religious connotations in *The Sower* is problematic, though he does not explain the reasons behind this conclusion.[28] In contrast, Griselda Pollock, in her analysis of Millet's *Sower*, proposes that it "may have originated in the biblical parable."[29] A biblical influence can certainly be found in other works Millet produced, such as his painting *Harvesters Resting* (1850–1853), which he originally titled *Ruth and Boaz*, or his *Flight to Egypt* (1864).[30]

Further evidence of Millet's biblical interests can be found in a diary entry by Eugène Delacroix regarding a visit by Millet (16 April 1853). He notes that Millet "talked of Michelangelo and the Bible, *the only book, more or less, which he reads*. That explains the slightly pretentious appearance of his peasants. Indeed he himself is a peasant and boasts of it."[31] The same interest is reflected in a letter from Camille Pissarro to his son Lucien (dated 2 May 1887). Responding to Millet's disavowal of socialist intentions, Pissarro writes, "He was a bit too biblical. Another of those blind men, leaders or followers who, unconscious of the march of modern ideas, defend the ideas without knowing it, despite themselves."[32]

Of particular interest for our analysis of Millet's *Sower* is the way in which it was interpreted autobiographically.[33] As Judy Sund puts it, "Millet's earthy and pious peasant themes were linked to his own beleaguered but devout existence."[34] The romanticizing of the artist's own peasant

---

27. Robert L. Herbert argues that Millet himself was responsible for perpetuating this identification. See Herbert, "Millet Reconsidered," *AICMS* 1 (1966): 33.

28. Herbert, "Millet Reconsidered," 35.

29. Pollock, *Millet*, 40.

30. The former is now in the Museum of Fine Arts, Boston. The latter can be found in the Art Institute of Chicago.

31. Pollock, *Millet*, 10, emphasis added.

32. Cited in Pollock, *Millet*, 5.

33. In a bid to align himself with his subjects and deflect criticism, the artist himself proclaimed, "I was born a peasant and a peasant I will die" (cited in Pollock, *Millet*, 10).

34. Judy Sund, "The Sower and the Sheaf: Biblical Metaphor in the Art of Vincent van Gogh," *ArtB* 70 (1988): 663. The devout nature of Millet's existence is challenged by Herbert ("Millet Reconsidered," 35).

origins continued after his death, as indicated in the memorial article published in the *Gazette des beaux-arts* in 1875. Its author writes:

> How did he free himself from the social fatalities that crushed his cradle? How was he able to get out of this environment? How did he scale the barriers that forbade him access to art? How did this child, condemned to servitude even in his mother's womb, break his chain? It is possible then that the parable of the sower doesn't always hold true, that the seed that falls among the weeds having grown among weeds may succeed in choking the weeds instead of being choked by them.[35]

Here, then, the parable of the sower is directly cited, though applied to the artist himself, rather than to his work. The impact of Millet's *Sower*, with its enlarged figure dominating the canvas, can be found in subsequent sowers, more clearly based on the gospel parable, such as James Tissot's "Semeur" (1886–1894), which forms part of his series *La Vie de Notre Seigneur Jesus Christ*.[36] Although Millet's *Sower* is not identifiably "sloppy," nevertheless the viewer's focus is clearly directed toward the symbolism of the sower figure, rather than the fate of the seeds.

2. John Everett Millais (1829–1896)

Our second example of a nineteenth-century sower (fig. 6.3), by English artist John Everett Millais, is indisputably based on the biblical parable of the sower and was specifically commissioned by the Dalziel brothers for their volume *The Parables of Our Lord and Saviour Jesus Christ* (1864). In contrast to Millet's oil-on-canvas painting, this image is a wood engraving on paper.[37]

Millais played a significant role as a founding member of the Pre-Raphaelite Brotherhood, a group of artists who sought to challenge the prevailing artistic mode of "idealization" by producing, rather, a "truthful mode of painting that was natural and sincere."[38] This feature was picked

---

35. Ernest Chesneau, "Jean-François Millet," *GBA* 11 (1875): 426.
36. Found in the Brooklyn Museum, New York.
37. Note that Holman Hunt, also of the Pre-Raphaelite Brotherhood, studied under Millet and purchased *The Sower*.
38. Gowler, *Parables after Jesus*, citing Adams, "Changing Patterns and Interpretations." John Ruskin defended the Pre-Raphaelite Brotherhood in his 1851 pamphlet of that name, where he describes their work as "going to nature and carrying out the faithful representation of real objects just as he had exhorted them to do at the end of *Modern Painters*."

up by a reviewer of the Dalziel volume in the March 1864 edition of *The New Path*, who expresses appreciation for *The Sower* precisely because of

Fig. 6.3. Sir John Everett Millais (1829–1896), *The Sower* from illustrations to *The Parables of Our Lord*, engraved by the Dalziel Brothers (London: Routledge, Warne, & Routledge, 1864). Wood engraving on paper. 140 x 108 mm. Tate, London. Photo © Tate.

the strongly pre-Raphaelite element of gradient texture in the landscape and the resulting "*truthfulness* of the stony foreground on which the unprofitable seeds are falling, to be choked by thorns, withered by heat and devoured by the fowls of the air."[39]

Nevertheless, this same reviewer concludes overall that the image is a disappointment and challenges the artist for the symbolical and clumsy representation of the birds and for dressing the farmer in "inaccurate Eastern attire" rather than in English garb. He writes: "Why should the artist have tried to guess how an Eastern farmer was dressed when he knew very well how an English farmer looks. Why run the risk of telling an untruth, as he possibly has done, when by going into the next field for his model he might have told a truth with which everyone about him would have been familiar."[40] Furthermore, Millais is accused of distorting the biblical narrative by focusing on the negative fate of the seed, rather than including the optimistic dimension of the parable. According to the reviewer, Millais's illustration juxtaposes a threatening and unproductive obtrusion of stony ground "to the ungracious exclusion of the good ground."[41]

The image received a warmer response from American author James Jackson Jarves, whose review in his volume *Art Thoughts* (1869) describes Millais's *Sower* as "an impressive composition of profound aesthetic as well as moral meaning, a serious thought put into serious colouring and suggestive design of prodigious force."[42]

The mixed responses to Millais's image of the sower parable highlight important questions about artists as biblical interpreters. In particular, Millais's image was challenged by critics both for its apparent lack of faithfulness to the biblical narrative and for its attempt to portray the sower in contextually plausible clothing. However, both these criticisms contain questionable assumptions about the task of an artist and how artists are expected to interact with the biblical text.

---

39. "Millais' Parables," 149, emphasis added.
40. "Millais' Parables," 150.
41. "Millais' Parables," 150. The reviewer also criticizes the artwork because he regards the parable images to be only intelligible to those with prior knowledge of the narratives (147).
42. James Jackson Jarves, *Art Thoughts: The Experiences and Observations of an American Amateur in Europe* (New York: Hurd & Houghton, 1869), 212.

## 3. Vincent van Gogh (1853–1890)

Our third sower image (fig. 6.4) was produced by Dutch artist Vincent van Gogh, whose voluminous correspondence with his family and friends provides an abundant source of information about his aesthetic aims. As has been widely noted, Millet's *Sower* had a profound influence on van Gogh's work.[43] As early as 1877 van Gogh spoke of reading the parable of the sower with his friend Gladwell (1:139).[44] By May 1881 he had made a sketch from Millet's *Sower* (1:232), and the following September he made sketches of sowers from real life (1:239). Van Gogh produced many studies of sowers prior to attempting his own distillation of the theme.

In contrast to Millet's *Sower*, which he describes as a "colourless gray," van Gogh's correspondence with his brother Theo about progress on his sower image concentrates heavily on the importance of color in his composition.[45] Writing to his friend Émile Bernard about his composition, van Gogh admits to "taking great liberties with the truthfulness of the colours" and explains that he has a "great longing for the infinite, which for him the sower and the sheaf symbolized" (3:491–493). According to Sund, van Gogh "heightened the suggestiveness of *The Sower* by infusing it with Delacrucian colour, but at the same time," she writes, "he avoided the overt religiosity of Delacroix's theme [*Christ in the Boat*] by *subsuming its Christian message in the portrayal of rural labor*."[46] Sund goes on to suggest that "this *Sower* is not so much a figural piece as a landscape." The first Van Gogh *Sower* to appear in paint was completed in Arles in June 1888.[47] This familiar image was the finished product.[48]

Again the relationship of the image to the biblical text is somewhat ambiguous. Helen Dow notes the *symbolic* function of the sun, "referring

---

43. See, for example, Sund, "Sower and the Sheaf," 663.
44. References from *The Complete Letters of Vincent van Gogh*, 2nd ed., 3 vols. (Greenwich, CT: New York Graphic Society, 1959), cited by volume and page.
45. It is notable that, despite being influenced by Millet, his own image is here very different in emphasis.
46. Sund, "Sower and the Sheaf," 667, emphasis added.
47. A later *Sower* image, painted in Arles in October 1888, has a different focus, with the sower featuring much more prominently, alongside a gnarled tree. See Vincent van Gogh, *The Sower* (1888), Rijksmuseum Amsterdam.
48. Van Gogh has an ongoing interest in the sower, producing many different paintings on this theme.

6. PICTURING THE PARABLE OF THE SOWER 175

Fig. 6.4. Vincent van Gogh (1853-1890), *The Sower*, 1888. Oil on canvas. 64.2 x 80.3 cm. Kröller-Müller Museum, Otterlo, the Netherlands. Photograph © Kröller-Müller Museum, Otterlo, the Netherlands.

to the presence of the infinite ... [and also] lending to the sower himself an eternal aspect." Dow links this to the Matthean version of the sower parable, where the sower is seen to represent Christ, "and we must remember," she cautions, "that it was in this religious context the subject first aroused Van Gogh's interest."[49]

Just as Millet was likened to the image of the sower he produced, van Gogh himself made this connection in his own correspondence, where he equates the artist and sower (2:421).[50] Dow notes the biblical significance of this equation and comments: "The painting of a sower is actually a

---

49. Helen J. Dow, "Van Gogh Both Prometheus and Jupiter," *JAAC* 22 (Spring 1964): 269–88.

50. A similar equation is made in a letter to van Gogh from Gauguin, who comments: "Having prepared the earth, man casts the seed, and by defending himself daily against the chance of bad weather he manages to reap. But we poor artists, where does

painting of an artist ... yet even here the reference is again to the biblical image, since van Gogh regarded Christ as the perfect artist (3:496)."[51]

### 4. Oscar Roty (1846–1911)

Our final example of a nineteenth-century sower (fig. 6.5) is a familiar one in France, for until 2001 she featured on the fifty-centimes coin and on the one-, two-, and five-franc coins; she was then subsequently reproduced on the ten-, twenty-, and fifty-centime Euro coins. Debora Silverman humorously notes, "Millet's raggedy giant was replaced by Roty's miniature image of a sprightly female light of foot."[52]

Oscar Roty was one of three medal engravers commissioned to produce a design for the French coinage in 1895. Roty's presentation of a slim Marianne as a sower, wearing the Phrygian cap of Liberty, provoked an outcry, as witnessed by the responses of the newspapers at the time: "What is she sowing, this woman, with the fancy Phrygian cap? She is sowing disorder, anarchy, rye grass, hatred born of lies and immorality."[53] "These seeds that she generously sows are the innumerable ideas that will germinate one day when we are no longer here," responded *La Liberté*.[54] In contrast, the Museé d'Orsay curator suggests, "The gesture is in fact more symbolic than realistic, because one does not broadcast seeds into the wind."[55] Here then, in Roty's image, we again encounter a

Fig. 6.5. Oscar Roty, Five francs. Copper-Nickel. 29 x 2.09 mm. Private collection. Photograph © Christine Joynes.

---

the grain we plant go, and when will the harvest come?" (cited in Sund, "Sower and the Sheaf," 675).

51. Dow, "Van Gogh," 279.

52. Debora L. Silverman, *Art Nouveau in Fin-de-siècle France: Politics, Psychology and Style* (Berkeley: University of California Press, 1989), 178.

53. *Le Moniteur*, 28 February 1897, cited at "Oscar Roty, The Sower," Musée d'Orsay, https://tinyurl.com/SBL6703r.

54. *La Liberté,* 8 October 1897, cited at "Oscar Roty, The Sower."

55. "Oscar Roty, The Sower."

"sloppy sower," but one functioning in a significantly different way from Bassano's sower.

As an aside at this point, the appearance of Roty's *Sower* on coins and subsequently stamps highlights a different kind of art from the other images considered so far. The significant impact of art circulated in this way is not to be underestimated.[56] One might note here, though from a later period, another sower figure (fig. 6.6), identified with Thomas Davis, leader of the Young Ireland movement.

Davis poignantly asserted that liberal nationalism can sow the seeds of freedom (Saoirse, as inscribed on the sower's apron in this stamp). The editor of the *New Hibernia Review* confidently asserts, "As every Irish person—Catholic or Protestant—would have recognised in 1945, this icon *alludes directly to the parable of the Sower in Matthew, Mark and Luke*."[57] This returns us to the question with which we began, namely, when is *a* sower identifiable as *the* sower from the gospel parable? Roty's depiction of a *female* sower raises particularly interesting gender issues worth further exploration in this regard.

Fig. 6.6. Irish commemorative stamps. Centenary of the death of Thomas Davis. 1945. Ink on paper. 20 x 23 mm. Private collection. Photograph © Christine Joynes.

## Concluding Reflections

The visual arts played a significant part in the wider debates about faith and reason taking place during the nineteenth century, while also reflecting the widespread social protest of the time. So for example, naturalistic depictions of the parable of sower were sometimes used to defend the Bible's historicity, as well as portraying Jesus in human terms. It is also important to remember other events taking place in nineteenth-century Europe, such as the publication of Ernst Renan's *Vie de Jésus* in 1863, which led to him being branded as the antichrist.

---

56. Note Silverman's reference to the aim of creating "beauty" through the coinage.
57. "Clúdach: Cover," *NHR* 10 (2006): 157, emphasis added.

With reference to Millet's *Sower*, the Jansons point out, "Ironically, the painting monumentalizes a rural way of life that was rapidly disappearing as a result of the industrial revolution, For that very reason, however, the peasant was seen as the chief victim of the evils arising from the machine age."[58]

It is my contention that the parable of sower was popular during the nineteenth century precisely because of its apparent relevance to events taking place in Europe at that time.[59] This particular gospel narrative was open to broad interpretation due to the nature of parabolic discourse and could therefore readily be applied to contemporary debates.

## Reading the Gospels through Art

This essay has brought some well-known images of the sower into dialogue with other less frequently discussed representations, but what impact does it have to read the gospel texts through these visual images? Perhaps the most notable feature is the ongoing allegorization of the parable of the sower through art. Despite biblical scholars' attempts to separate the parable from its allegorical interpretation, artistic representations show how the two are inextricably intertwined. Thus the question is asked: "What seed does Roty's sower sow?" with various allegorical interpretations of the seed supplied.

The political dimensions of the gospel parables are also vividly illustrated through the various representations of the sower. Whilst biblical scholars have been quick to categorize Jesus's parabolic teaching as simply illustration from his daily context, the examples I have considered all demonstrate that selecting a *sower* as one's subject carried political implications.

My investigation has also raised three broader issues worth further reflection in the ongoing debate about the relationship between the Bible and visual art. First, what is the place of the artist's intentions? The abundant correspondence of many of the nineteenth-century artists considered above highlights the question of how much weight should be assigned to the artist's intentions when discussing the meaning of a painting. Second,

---

58. Janson and Janson, *History of Art*, 672.
59. Note for example, Pollock's suggestion that Millet loved the Bible "because it was full of poetry of the land and its cultivation" (*Millet*, 8).

what is the significance of labels and titles? The ambiguity concerning the relationship of various images to the biblical text (notably those of Millet, van Gogh, and Roty) again highlights the important role of titles in the interpretation of images. Third, what is the significance of context? Placing Millet's *Sower* in the context of the popular unrest in France during the mid-nineteenth century inevitably casts a different light on the image. This then raises the question of to what extent a painting's context determines its meaning.

This brief survey of the sower parable in some select examples of nineteenth-century European art has highlighted the complexities that frequently arise when assessing the images' relationship to the biblical narrative. But, I would argue, this is no more problematic than the prevailing ambiguity that surrounds parabolic discourse more widely.

## Works Cited

Adams, Doug. "Changing Patterns and Interpretations of Parables in Art." *ARTS* 19 (2007): 5–13.

Aikema, Bernard. *Jacopo Bassano and His Public*. Princeton: Princeton University Press, 1996.

Berdini, Paolo. "Jacopo Bassano: A Case for Painting as Visual Exegesis." Pages 169–86 in *Interpreting Christian Art*. Edited by Heidi J. Hornik and Mikeal C. Parsons. Macon, GA: Mercer University Press, 2004.

Brigstocke, Hugh. *The Oxford Companion to Western Art*. Oxford: Oxford University Press, 2001.

Chesneau, Ernest. "Jean-François Millet." *GBA* 11 (1875): 426–41.

"Clúdach: Cover." *NHR* 10 (2006): 157.

Dow, Helen J. "Van Gogh Both Prometheus and Jupiter." *JAAC* 22 (Spring 1964): 269–88.

Gogh, Vincent van. *The Complete Letters of Vincent van Gogh*. 3 vols. 2nd ed. Greenwich, CT: New York Graphic Society, 1959.

Gowler, David. *The Parables after Jesus: Their Imaginative Receptions across Two Millennia*. Grand Rapids: Baker, 2017.

Herbert, Robert L. "Millet Reconsidered." *AICMS* 1 (1966): 28–65.

Janson, Horst W., and Anthony F. Janson. *History of Art*. 6th ed. London: Thames & Hudson, 2001.

Jarves, James Jackson. *Art Thoughts: The Experiences and Observations of an American Amateur in Europe*. New York: Hurd & Houghton, 1869.

Joynes, Christine E. "Wombs and Tombs: The Reception History of Mark 16.1–20." Pages 226–43 in *From the Margins II: Women of the New Testament and Their Afterlives*. Edited by Christine E. Joynes and Christopher C. Rowland. Sheffield: Sheffield Phoenix, 2009.

Kauffmann, Claus M. "The Sainte-Chapelle Lectionaries and Illustrations of the Parables in the Middle Ages." *JWCI* 67 (2004): 1–22.

"Millais' Parables." *NP* 1 (March 1864): 145–52.

Mikuž, Jure. "Ivan Grohar." Oxford Art Online. 2003. https://doi.org/10.1093/gao/9781884446054.article.T035021.

Murphy, Alexandra. *Jean-François Millet*. Boston: Little, Brown, 1984.

"Oscar Roty, *The Sower*." Musée d'Orsay. https://tinyurl.com/SBL6703r.

"Our Illustrations." *AU* 1.6–7 (1884): 117.

Pollock, Griselda. *Millet*. London: Oresko Books, 1977.

Réau, Louis. *Iconographie de l'art chretien*. Vol. 2. Paris: Presses universitaires de France, 1957.

Schiller, Gertrud. *Iconography of Christian Art*. Gütersloh: Gütersloher Verlag, 1971.

Silverman, Debora L. *Art Nouveau in Fin-de-siècle France: Politics, Psychology and Style*. Berkeley: University of California Press, 1989.

Sund, Judy. "The Sower and the Sheaf: Biblical Metaphor in the Art of Vincent van Gogh." *ArtB* 70 (1988): 660–76.

Zimmermann, Ruben. *Puzzling the Parables of Jesus: Methods and Interpretation*. Minneapolis: Fortress, 2015.

Zuffi, Stefano. *Gospel Figures in Art*. Translated by Thomas Hartmann. Los Angeles: J. Paul Getty Museum, 2003.

# 7
## "The Belated Return of the 'Son'":
## Thomas Hart Benton's *Prodigal Son*

DAVID B. GOWLER

Introduction

Jesus's parable about the prodigal son, his father, and his brother (Luke 15:11–32) has intrigued interpreters over the centuries not just because of its greater length and complexity compared to other parables of Jesus, but also because of its more developed characters, with which interpreters tend to identify.[1] In addition, the story evokes a number of compelling themes about the human condition, such as generational conflicts, sibling rivalry, disrespectful children, the loss and restoration of community, and the relationship between justice and mercy.[2] It is no surprise, then, that the story of the prodigal son is the parable most frequently illustrated in Western art.[3]

---

Sections of this paper were revised extensively and published in David B. Gowler, *The Parables after Jesus* (Waco, TX: Baylor University Press, 2020), 209–13.

1. See Mikeal C. Parsons, "The Prodigal's Elder Brother: The History and Ethics of Reading Luke 15:25–32," *PRSt* 23 (1996): 147–74; see also David B. Gowler, "The Characterization of the Two Brothers in the Parable of the Prodigal Son (Luke 15:11–32): Their Function and Afterlives," in *Characterization in Luke-Acts*, ed. Frank Dicken and Julia Snyder (London: Bloomsbury, 2016), 55–72. As Lischer notes, the parable includes several scene changes, a more extensive plot, a greater amount of conflicts, three major characters, and more developed characterization than in other parables. See Richard Lischer, *Reading the Parables* (Louisville: Westminster John Knox, 2014), 97.

2. Darryl Tippens, "Shakespeare and the Prodigal Son Tradition," *ERC* 14 (1988): 60.

3. The other most frequently illustrated parables include the good Samaritan (Luke 10:25–37), the rich man and Lazarus (Luke 16:19–31), and the wise and foolish

The parable depicts a father with two sons, the younger of whom requests his inheritance. The father acquiesces and divides his property between his two sons, and the younger son leaves home, travels to a distant country, and squanders his entire inheritance in "dissolute living" (Luke 15:13). After a famine arises, the younger son hires himself out as a keeper of pigs. He becomes so hungry that he desires to eat the pigs' food, but no one gives him anything. He then finally "comes to himself" and devises a plan to return to his father and ask to be treated as one of his father's hired hands. Upon his return, however, his father joyfully welcomes him home as a beloved son; gives him the best robe, a ring, and sandals; and throws a party to welcome him home, with music, dancing, and feasting on a fatted calf.

When the older son learns about the celebration for his younger brother's return, he becomes angry and refuses to enter the house. His father goes outside and pleads with him to join the celebration, and the older son complains that his father had never rewarded him for his faithfulness with such a celebration. The father assures him, "All that is mine is yours," but declares that the family has to celebrate because the older son's brother "was lost and has been found." The parable ends without revealing the older son's response.

## Characterization of the Father and the Two Sons in Luke

Jesus tells this parable—the third and final of the "lost" parables in Luke 15—immediately after the parables of the lost sheep (15:4–7) and the lost coin (15:8–10).[4] The Lukan Jesus directs all three parables to the Pharisees and scribes, who are complaining that he "welcomes sinners and eats with them" (Luke 15:2). Therefore, in the context of the Gospel of Luke, the parable of the prodigal son is the culmination of the three lost parables that

---

virgins (Matt 25:1–13). See Ellen D'Oench, *Prodigal Son Narratives, 1480–1980* (New Haven: Yale University Art Gallery, 1995), 3.

4. For more extended analyses, see David B. Gowler, "Characterization in Luke: A Socio-narratological Approach," *BTB* 19 (1989): 54–62; Gowler, *Host, Guest, Enemy and Friend: Portraits of the Pharisees in Luke and Acts* (New York: Lang, 1991), 250–56; Gowler, "Characterization of the Two Brothers," 55–72; Gowler, "Sit and Listen; Go and Do: The Parables of the Good Samaritan and Prodigal Son in Howard Thurman's Life and Thought," in *Anatomies of the Gospels and beyond the Gospels*, ed. Elizabeth Struthers Malbon, Mikeal C. Parsons, and Paul N. Anderson, BibInt (Leiden: Brill, 2018), 440. The following is developed from those discussions.

defend Jesus's ministry to these tax collectors and sinners and challenge the Lukan Pharisees and scribes to joyfully celebrate these lost sinners being found, returning home, and being restored to community—and, of course, implicitly criticizing those who do not join the celebration.

In the Gospel of Luke, then, the three main characters in the parable symbolize characters in the larger narrative (as well as others who share similar traits). Thus, the parable almost functions as a *mise en abyme* that serves to characterize (through indirect presentation) characters in the larger narrative.

Luke clearly intends the younger son to reflect the tax collectors and sinners in Luke 15:1, and the older son to symbolize the Pharisees and scribes in 15:2. The narrative has prepared readers for these characterizations since the five controversy stories in Luke 5:17–6:11, with the most explicit comparison in 7:29–30: the authoritative narrator declares that tax collectors were among those people who acknowledged God's justice, but that the Pharisees and scribes had "rejected God's purpose for themselves." That declaration specifically prepares readers for the contrast in the next story (7:36–50) between the sinful woman who anoints Jesus in the house of Simon the Pharisee (the woman's "many" sins were forgiven), but a similar dynamic is found in the prodigal son:

> The function of the two brothers in Luke's narrative is clear: the Pharisees and scribes object to Jesus joyfully welcoming sinners into the family of God, and Jesus urges them to join the celebration over the lost being found. God's blessings are still all theirs (15:31), but they must rejoice over the tax collectors and sinners drawing near to Jesus. The open-ended parable—does the older son join the celebration?—reflects the still-unanswered question of whether the Pharisees and scribes will respond positively to Jesus' invitation.[5]

In Luke, the father symbolizes how God welcomes back the prodigal (e.g., tax collectors and sinners) with joy, compassion, forgiveness, and love, restoring them to favored status in the family of God. The father also shows love, compassion, and forgiveness to the older son (e.g., Pharisees and scribes). He pleads with him to join the celebration and, after the older son dishonors him (e.g., by refusing to address his father with a title, 15:29), he addresses his son with an affectionate title (τέκνον: "my son"),

---

5. Gowler, "Characterization of the Two Brothers," 58.

assures him "all that is mine is yours," and (gently) reminds him that the celebration is for his brother in an effort to reestablish full kinship relations (15:31–32).

## Representations of the Prodigal Son Parable in Visual Art

Visual representations of the parable usually focus on one of three scenes.[6] First, some artists choose to portray the dissolute living of the prodigal son in a tavern, usually with a prostitute or two, or gambling, or both. For example, the prodigal son stained-glass window in Chartres Cathedral, created around 1210 CE, elaborates extensively on the "dissolute living" of the prodigal. Seven out of the thirty scenes that depict the parable focus on the son's decadent activities, six of which depict the older son's (unsubstantiated) claim to his father that the younger son "devoured your property with prostitutes" (Luke 15:30) by showing the younger son cavorting and carousing with two prostitutes. The seventh scene portrays the younger son gambling. His opponent holds three dice in his hand, and the prodigal already has literally lost his shirt.

Another interesting example of this genre is James Tissot's 1880 painting *Suite de l'enfant prodigue: En pays étranger*. In this image, the "far country" is envisioned as Japan, where the prodigal's debauchery includes sitting to watch geishas dancing, holding a cup of sake, with one geisha

---

6. Some interpreters, however, choose other aspects of the parable to portray, such as the prodigal son leaving home, but the following three scenes dominate visual art. Other works include aspects or themes of the prodigal son parable, even if they do not directly portray the parable itself. Hieronymus Bosch's painting *The Pedlar* (or *The Vagabond*) is an intriguing example (currently housed in the Museum Boijmans Van Beuningen in Rotterdam). It depicts a moral decision similar to that made by the prodigal, including elements of numerous visual representations of the parable. Some scholars argue, in fact, that it depicts the prodigal son. The man with oddly mismatched shoes and a wounded leg has a knife tucked in at his waist and uses a walking stick, the latter two items being common in portrayals of the prodigal in visual art. The man looks backward at aspects of his dissolute life (including seven pigs, an amorous couple in the doorway of an inn, a man urinating on the side of the inn, etc.) and heads toward what appears to be a more stable and prosperous future (represented by the sturdy gate on the right side of the painting, with a cow behind it). See William Fraenger, *Hieronymus Bosch* (New York: Dorset House 1983), 260. As Fraenger notes, Bosch himself may also be identifying with the man/prodigal son in this image (258).

Fig. 7.1. James Tissot, *The Parable of the Prodigal Son, No. II: In Foreign Climes. L'enfant prodigue: En pays étranger.* The Parable of the Prodigal Son series, 1882. Etching on laid paper; second state of two. The Metropolitan Museum of Art, New York, NY. Photo Credit: The Elisha Whittelsey Collection, The Elisha Whittelsey Fund, 1968.

sitting beside him, leaning her head on his shoulder. An 1881 etching by Tissot, *In Foreign Climes* (fig. 7.1), captures the same scene:[7]

A further elaboration in visual art of the dissolute living of the prodigal son is the artist's self-identification with the prodigal. For example, Rembrandt's 1634–1636 *Self-Portrait with Saskia in the Guise of the Prodigal Son*, the largest of Rembrandt's multitude of self-portraits, portrays him as

---

7. *In Foreign Climes* is inscribed by Tissot and dated 1881. Tissot's etching rendition of the prodigal-son parable, after an opening image of a dog-eared Bible turned to the parable of the prodigal son, consists of four other images. The first, third, and fourth images all take place along the Thames River: (1) *The Departure*, (3) *The Return*, and (4) *The Fatted Calf*.

the prodigal son celebrating extravagantly in a tavern with a prostitute on his lap. The model for the prostitute is Rembrandt's wife, Saskia.[8]

Second, other artists, most notably Albrecht Dürer, choose to portray the moment when the prodigal comes to himself while kneeling in destitution and in penance among the pigs. In fact, depictions of this scene are rare in visual art before Dürer,[9] but his motif in this image of the son kneeling among the pigs not only established a trend; it also influenced later images of the son returning home to his father and kneeling before him.

In Dürer's 1496 engraving *The Prodigal Son amongst the Pigs* (fig. 7.2), the urgency of the pigs aggressively seeking to obtain food is matched by the physical and spiritual hunger of the prodigal, who, like all the buildings around him, is also in a wretched physical state of disrepair.

Dürer captures the moment when the prodigal repents while kneeling among the pigs—allegedly repenting, since the parable itself, apart from its context, is ambiguous in that regard[10]—decides to go home, ask his father's forgiveness, and request to be treated as a servant. Another distinctive element in this engraving is that it appears that Dürer portrays himself as the repentant prodigal.[11]

The third moment from the parable, and that most commonly depicted by visual interpreters, is the reception of the prodigal son by his father, often with the older brother looking on, such as Rembrandt's 1667–1669 paint-

---

8. The slate board at the top left (to keep track of drinks ordered) and the peacock pie on the table are standard elements in representations of the prodigal son's dissolute life in a tavern. See Ernst van de Wetering, *Rembrandt: A Life in 180 Paintings* (Amsterdam: Local World BV, 2008), 91; Gowler, "Characterization of the Two Brothers," 63. Rembrandt obviously had great affinity with the prodigal-son parable, since he depicted it many times over his long career, beginning with his 1632/3 drawing *The Departure of the Prodigal Son* (which includes the prodigal's mother) and ending with his masterpiece 1667–1669 painting *The Return of the Prodigal Son*. See Gowler "Characterization of the Two Brothers," 63–65; and Ingrid Cartwright's discussion of artists identifying with the dissolute living of the prodigal son in seventeenth-century Dutch and Flemish art. See Cartwright, "Hoe schilder hoe wilder: Dissolute Self-Portraiture in Seventeenth-Century Dutch and Flemish Art" (PhD diss., University of Maryland, College Park, 2007).

9. D'Oench, *Prodigal Son Narratives*, 4.

10. It can be seen merely as a plan of action to ensure that he did not starve. Levine, for example, sees more evidence of "conniving" than "contrition." See Amy-Jill Levine, *Short Stories by Jesus* (New York: HarperOne, 2014), 53–54.

11. D'Oench, *Prodigal Son Narratives*, 7; Gowler, *Parables after Jesus*, 110–13.

Fig. 7.2. Albrecht Dürer, *The Prodigal Son amongst the Pigs*, 1496. Engraving, 9 3/4 x 3 15/16 in. National Gallery of Art, Washington, DC.

ing *The Return of the Prodigal Son*, or with the older brother on his way home from the field, such as in Rembrandt's 1636 etching *The Return of the Prodigal Son* (fig. 7.3). In that 1636 etching, the prodigal kneels before his father in abject supplication, hands clasped before him, in what D'Oench calls "one of [Rembrandt's] most intense expressions of human anguish."[12] The prodigal's appearance clearly depicts his desolation: an emaciated body, ragged clothes, and disconsolate face. His meager possessions consist of clothes around his waist, a knife, and the walking stick that lies on the steps beside him. The returning son's father bends over him and tenderly touches his son's back with his right hand (fig. 7.4). Two servants rush out the door, bringing the robe and sandals, and another servant watches the reunion from a window; all three avert their eyes from the pathos-filled reunion. The older brother is in the background, still out in the fields, and not aware of his brother's return and their father's forgiveness.[13]

There are occasional variations of the reception of the prodigal son by his father in visual art. Some works, for example, provide an answer to the unresolved question at the end of the parable by providing the obviously desired answer that the older brother listens to his father's pleas, becomes reconciled with his errant younger brother, and agrees to join the celebration. The stained-glass window of the prodigal son in Chartres Cathedral, for example, depicts this celebration in six scenes, In the final of those six scenes, the father sits at a banquet table together with his two sons as a servant brings food for their mutual reconciliation and celebration.[14]

Thomas Hart Benton, though, provides a strikingly distinctive visual representation of the prodigal son's return home. His 1939 lithograph *Prodigal Son* (fig. 7.5) is an idiosyncratic depiction of a prodigal like Benton (and others) who waited far too long to return home. This haunting image includes no joyful reconciliation of any kind, in a surprising subversion of the parable.

---

12. D'Oench, *Prodigal Son Narratives*, 7.

13. See Gowler, *Parables after Jesus*, 152–53.

14. Although such portrayals of the reconciliation of the two brothers are uncommon in receptions of the parable, they are found in numerous media such as, for example, a *kontakion* (chanted sermon) by Romanos the Melodist (sixth century); Antonia Pulci's *The Play of the Prodigal Son* (fifteenth century); the blues song "The Prodigal Son," by Robert Wilkins (ca. 1964); the play/film *Godspell* (film: 1973). Some works of visual art portray the father and his two sons together as the father attempts to reconcile the brothers, but they do not include evidence as to whether that attempt is successful (e.g., the final scene [panel 20] of the prodigal-son stained-glass window in Bourges Cathedral, and a twelfth-century illuminated manuscript perhaps a century later in Florence; see Parsons, "Prodigal's Elder Brother," 153).

7. "THE BELATED RETURN OF THE 'SON'" 189

Fig. 7.3. Rembrandt, *The Return of the Prodigal Son*, 1636. Etching, 6 1/4 x 5 1/2 in. Rembrandt House Museum, Amsterdam. Photograph by David B. Gowler.

Fig. 7.4. Rembrandt, *The Return of the Prodigal Son* (detail), 1636. Etching, 6 1/4 x 5 1/2 in. Rembrandt House Museum, Amsterdam. Photograph by David B. Gowler.

## Thomas Hart Benton (1889–1975)

Thomas Hart Benton was born in Missouri in 1889. He studied at the Art Institute of Chicago and then spent three years at the Fine Arts Academy in Paris, from 1908 to 1911. Benton eventually settled in New York City, where he continued to struggle both to survive and to find his artistic voice. After a stint in the Navy, Benton began teaching at the Art Students League in New York City, where he taught, among others, Jackson Pollock, who later became a leader in abstract expressionism. In 1935, Benton moved to Kansas City, Missouri, to chair the painting department at the Kansas City Art Institute. Although he was fired in 1941, he lived in Kansas City until his death in 1975.

As Benton's success grew in the 1920s, so did criticism of his work. Some critiques were aimed at the content of his images. His 1933 mural for the state of Indiana, which was two hundred feet long and twelve feet high, was controversial, for example, because it portrayed members of the Ku Klux Klan in full regalia in its depiction of the historical development of Indiana. Likewise, Benton's 1936 mural for the Missouri State Capitol building, *A Social History of Missouri*, generated controversy because it included Huckleberry Finn with Jim the slave, a lynched slave, the outlaws Frank and Jesse James, and Tom Pendergast, a corrupt political boss from Kansas City.

Benton was also criticized because he had difficulty getting along with people; he participated in disputes that ranged from artistic to political to personal quarrels. He attacked individuals and groups in harsh and distasteful ways, and he was described, often to his delight, as nasty, belligerent, crotchety, and pugnacious, among other things.[15] The dedication of his autobiography, *An Artist in America*, to his son T. P. thus is appropriate: "To T. P. Who said when Rita corrected his manners, *I don't want to be a gentleman when I grow up. I want to be like my Dad.*"

But it just was not his choice of topics to paint, or his acerbic personality, or his prejudices, or his politics that generated controversy. It was also his style of painting. In the early 1920s, Benton began to abandon the abstract styles with which he had experimented (impressionism, cubism, pointillism, and synchronism) for a dynamic and realistic style that was called, initially by critics, *regionalism*, and Benton was one of the

---

15. A significant amount of Benton's rejection by many in the art community stemmed from his virulent antigay rhetoric.

"regionalist triumvirate": Benton, John Steuart Curry, and Grant Wood.[16] Benton began to develop this alternative approach to art in 1918, when he served in the US Navy in Norfolk, Virginia, and came into contact with a number of people from the South, people with whom he felt more at home because of his own family context and history.[17]

In his autobiography, *An Artist in America*, Benton writes that he "was moved by a great desire to know more of the America" that he had glimpsed back home in Missouri in 1924, while visiting his father before his father's death. Benton describes this development as:

> I started going places, but I sought out those which would present best the background out of which my people and I had come and I left the main traveled roads, the highways, and plowed around in the back counties of our country where old manners persisted and old prejudices were sustained. Having no beliefs as to what was good for man, no moral convictions as to conduct, and no squeamish bodily reluctances, I was able to enter intimately into much that was automatically closed to social investigators with uplift psychologies.... I traveled without interests beyond those of getting material for my pictures.[18]

Benton began traveling throughout the United States as "he began to search for signs of distinctly American elements in the environments he discovered."[19] His work also emphasized the importance and experience of place—influenced by the pragmatist philosophy of John Dewey and the writings of historian Lewis Mumford—which connect the validity of ideas with their practical utility. He created a distinctive style that stresses that art should represent life as it is experienced in a specific time and place, as it is "known and felt" by people he called "ordinary Americans,"[20] serv-

---

16. See Wood's iconic *American Gothic* (Art Institute of Chicago) and Curry's *Tragic Prelude—John Brown* in the murals Curry created for the Kansas state capitol.

17. Thomas Hart Benton, *An Artist in America* (Columbia: University of Missouri Press, 1983), 45. Benton's mother, Elizabeth Wise Benton, was raised in Texas, and Benton's father, Maecenas Eason Benton, was originally from Tennessee, served in the Confederate army under Nathan Bedford Forrest, and was a member of the US House of Representatives (from Missouri) from 1897 to 1905.

18. Benton, *Artist in America*, 77. Just a few pages later Benton withdraws "all claims to objectivity" but still declares that he tries to stay as close to the truth "as possible" (79).

19. J. Richard Gruber, *Thomas Hart Benton and the American South* (Augusta, GA: Morris Museum of Art, 1998), 18.

20. Benton, *Artist in America*, 9.

ing practical, not intellectual, purposes. Early in his career Benton also became convinced that historically all great art was inspired by religion or culture, and its meaning emerged from the way in which people lived.[21] So much of Benton's art included an interest in the history, culture, and lives of the people he sought to represent, especially those experiences not usually documented by artists.[22]

Although a 1934 issue of *Time* magazine celebrated Benton and his work as an example of "new American art," his style of art was attacked as provincial by many art critics and other artists. Some critics thought his works were sentimental caricatures or cartoon-like.[23] Benton himself also cites criticisms of his work that called it "tabloid art," "cheap nationalism," or asserted that it was "degrading America."[24] Marilyn Stokstad, however, notes that Benton had a "life-long fascination with the Old Masters," including El Greco, and she favorably compares this "Ozark hillbilly" to El Greco, saying that Benton "transplanted El Greco's visionary style to the Ozarks" and "reformed the Mannerist style to tell the story" of the United States.[25]

For many people in the United States, especially in the late 1920s and 1930s, Benton "spoke their language, painted their lives, and believed wholeheartedly in the significance of their experiences," as Justin Wolff puts it.[26] President Harry Truman, for example, called his fellow Missourian not only "the best damned painter in America" but also "the greatest artist of this century."[27]

## Religious Elements in Thomas Hart Benton's Visual Art

Religion did not play a dominant role in Benton's work—Benton himself had little use for religion—but he believed that its role in the United

---

21. Polly Burroughs, *Thomas Hart Benton: A Portrait* (Garden City, NY: Doubleday, 1981), 49.

22. Benton, *Artist in America*, 74–80.

23. Justin P. Wolff, *Thomas Hart Benton: A Life* (New York: Farrar, Straus & Giroux, 2012), 197.

24. Benton, *Artist in America*, 248.

25. Elizabeth Broun, Douglas Hyland, and Marilyn Stokstad, *Benton's Bentons* (Lawrence, KS: Spencer Museum of Art, 1980), 34.

26. Wolff, *Thomas Hart Benton*, 4–11.

27. Wolff, *Thomas Hart Benton*, 13.

States could not be ignored, and many of his works, especially his larger murals, include religious elements. Benton argued that in "any authentically painted epic that purported to represent a social history of ordinary Americans, religion would have to occupy an important place."[28]

Religion also is a central element in what Benton says was his first regionalist painting on Martha's Vineyard, *The Lord Is My Shepherd* (1926). This work depicts George and Sabrina West sitting at the kitchen table in their farmhouse. The saying "The Lord is My Shepherd" (Ps 23:1), although partially obscured, is framed and hanging on the wall behind them. The Wests lived in Martha's Vineyard and farmed and fished to make a modest living—the painting portrays them with misshapen hands weathered by hard work. These New England Yankees symbolize for Benton not only reliance on God but also self-reliance, frugality, perseverance, strength, and independence—qualities Benton valued.[29]

In his book, *An Artist in America*, Benton writes about some of his experiences with various aspects of American religious life and practice while on his numerous journeys around the United States. He spends several pages on "the Holy Roller Faith," an ecstatic form of religion in the South that he describes as a "wild mixture of sex, exhibitionism, and hysteria" that he says "had its origin in that home of extravagant idiocy."[30]

This ecstatic form of Christianity is portrayed in Benton's painting *Holy Roller Camp Meeting* (1926), a work that reflects aspects of a worship service he attended in the mountains of western Virginia. One of Benton's more popular paintings, *Lord Heal the Child* (1934), helps illustrate what Benton saw in these Holy Roller churches. This painting stems from a healing service that Benton attended in Greenville, South Carolina, whose participants served as models for the painting.[31] The preacher was a North Carolina woman who had a reputation as a healer. She had felt the call of God to leave her job in a textile mill, and she had a large following of what Benton calls "perfectly steady, though somewhat moronic, mill people." The service included both times of great quiet, with the preacher praying over a sick child, and times of great tumult—shouting, singing, and

---

28. Robert L. Gambone, "Religious Motifs in the Work of Thomas Hart Benton," in *Thomas Hart Benton: Artist, Writer, and Intellectual*, ed. R. Douglas Hurt and Mary K. Dains (Columbia: State Historical Society of Missouri, 1989), 71.
29. See Gambone, "Religious Motifs," 73.
30. Benton, *Artist in America*, 97.
31. Benton, *Artist in America*, 101–8.

Fig. 7.5. Thomas Hart Benton, *Prodigal Son*, 1939. Lithograph, 10 1/8 x 13 1/4 in. Ackland Art Museum, The University of North Carolina at Chapel Hill. © 2019 T.H. and R.P. Benton Testamentary Trusts / UMB Bank Trustee / Licensed by VAGA at Artists Rights Society (ARS), NY.

"roaring calls for God's mercy" (and a boy who was knifed just outside the service because of jealousy over a girl with whom he was sitting in church).

In some ways Benton was sympathetic to such Holy Rollers and other fundamentalist Christians, although in a condescending way. Benton writes that there was "poetic justification" for their projection into the "void" of a Being who embodies all the attributes to which human beings aspire, in his words, "an old whiskered man who sits eternally in infinite space, whose power is all-embracing, who does what he likes and who sometimes unbends and comes down to talk matters over with his weak, erring, and suffering children."[32] So Benton responded to this Holy Roller faith with mixed feelings, as he notes in his autobiography: "I saw a good deal of God's work off and on in further expeditions along the edges of

---

32. Gambone, "Religious Motifs," 79.

the hills. There were times when its Dionysiac madness moved me deeply. There were others when my sides would split with suppressed laughter."[33]

Benton also discusses how people living in such circumstances would be attracted to these Holy Roller churches: "Poor, beaten people rising to testify find themselves, for the moment, the center of attention and thereby get some compensation for the miseries of their unnoticed lives."[34] He also laments, however, that such Holy Rollers were "increasing mental irregularity" in the United States, were "developing hysteria in much the same way that a war spirit is developed," and were "cultivating a weed patch of aberrant psychologies which will be very difficult to clear out of the fields of our future social plantings."[35]

Before he moved to Kansas City, Benton started what became a fifteen-year project: a series of lithographs on "The American Scene" that captured many of Benton's experiences on his travels around the United States, especially to rural areas. Some of these lithographs chronicle the religious lives and practices of Americans, such as a pastor preaching to his small white congregation in the mountains of West Virginia (*The Meeting*, 1941, from a 1928 drawing). In his autobiography, Benton speaks appreciatively of a man who spends all day "cradling wheat"—very physically demanding work—who then spends three hours in the evening working to get the music of the church choir "right." A similar view of work and religion could be reflected in two other lithographs: African Americans headed to their small country church in southern Arkansas (*Sunday Morning*, 1939), and people headed to an evening prayer meeting in a small country church in the Bible belt, a scene that Benton says could be "anywhere south of the Mason-Dixon line" (*Prayer Meeting* or *Wednesday Evening*, 1949).[36]

## Thomas Hart Benton's *Prodigal Son* Lithograph (1939)

In 1939, Benton produced a lithograph, *Prodigal Son* (fig. 7.5), that was a study for his later painting of the same name (the painting is now found in the Dallas Museum of Fine Arts). Benton's own description of the lithograph is: "Study for a painting—owned by Dallas Museum.

---

33. Benton, *Artist in America*, 100–101.
34. Benton, *Artist in America*, 109.
35. Benton, *Artist in America*, 109–10.
36. Benton, *Artist in America*, 111.

Picture of the belated return of the 'son.' The house was at the foot of the Boston hill in Chilmark, Martha's Vinyard (sic). It has long since hit the ground."[37]

Benton first painted the house in 1921 (*The Flanders' House*),[38] but in the intervening years the abandoned house had collapsed and was a suitable site to depict the desolation awaiting the return of this aging prodigal son. The 1939 lithograph is very similar to the later painting (ca. 1941), although, due to the lithographing process, the painting's image is the reverse of the lithograph. The evocative black-and-white lithograph only hints at the warm, subtle hues of the painting, and some aspects of the painting are less clear in the lithograph, such as the howling-dog-shaped cloud over the dilapidated house. Overall, however, the stark image of the lithograph remains more powerful than does the painting:

> The lithograph presents an idiosyncratic and haunting view of a prodigal son who has waited far too long to "come to himself" and return home. His hair has turned white, and his left hand touches his white/gray beard as he ponders what had been and what was now. His old truck is off in the distance, and his suitcase—tied together with ropes—sits on the ground just behind him. There is no longer any father to run out, throw his arms around him, and kiss him. No best robe, ring, or sandals are forthcoming either, and, as the bottom right of the lithograph makes clear, there will be no feast with a fatted calf: the sun-bleached bones of a cow are all that's left of what could once have been a fatted calf, if only the prodigal had returned earlier. The dead tree branch at the man's feet also reflects the death and devastation that had come upon his home in his absence. The house stands as only a ramshackle shell of its former self, completely deserted and dilapidated—not only with no father inside to greet the prodigal, but also no servants to attend to him, and no elder brother to complain about him. The sun sets in the sky behind him as well, another indication that he had waited too late; all he loved was gone.[39]

---

37. Thomas Hart Benton, *The Lithographs of Thomas Hart Benton*, ed. and compiled by Creekmore Faith (Austin: University of Texas Press, 1979), 78.

38. See Burroughs, *Thomas Hart Benton*, 69.

39. Gowler, *Parables after Jesus*, 210–11; some sections below were revised for the book.

## Benton's *Prodigal Son* as Provocation?

How should this image be interpreted? Perhaps some people in the churches that Benton visited on his travels would have interpreted this image as a sermon of warning, one that says: "Do not wait too long to return to the father. Someday it will be too late." These cautionary words, like some of the parables of Jesus, urgently warn prodigal sons and daughters to return home to their father while there is still time. Such an interpretation, for many Christian interpreters, might be attractive, although it does not follow the story line of the parable. In reality, though, Benton's *Prodigal Son* should have been shocking to those Christians, since this image subverts and undermines the parable of Jesus: the loving, forgiving, compassionate God is not there to welcome the repentant sinner home.

Benton certainly had a penchant for provocative images; he delighted in shocking people in the name of what he believed to be artistic honesty and integrity. His provocative works include not just his historical murals; they also include one of his best-known religious paintings: his 1938 *Susanna and the Elders* shocked audiences by its rather graphic nude portrayal of the heroine of a story found in the Apocrypha (or Dan 13 in the Catholic Bible). The painting became infamous in 1939, when the director of the City Art Museum in Saint Louis (renamed Saint Louis Art Museum in 1972) threatened to ban the painting. He eventually allowed it to be displayed in the museum but roped off the area in front of the painting so the audience could not get a prurient view of Susanna, who, in his words, was "much too nude." A local pastor, Mary Ellis, described the painting this way: "The nude is stark naked. It's lewd, immoral, obscene, lascivious, degrading, an insult to womanhood, and the lowest expression of pure filth." When Benton heard about her remarks, he replied, "That's funny as hell." He was irritated by some criticism of the painting, however; when a former student called the painting not as good as a "bar-room nude," Benton called him a "flea-bitten red rock coyote."[40]

The painting, *Susanna and the Elders*, interprets the biblical/deuterocanonical story in a contemporary way, something that Rembrandt, Tintoretto, Veronese, and others had previously done. In Benton's case, he portrays Susanna as a Midwestern woman with red hair and fingernails—wearing a wedding ring—who has taken off her clothes and is dipping her

---

40. Gambone, "Thomas Hart Benton," 83–85.

left foot into the water as she holds onto a branch of an oak tree with her right hand. Two men sneak up behind her—one looks suspiciously like Benton—and the church in the background implies that they are elders (or deacons) of the church who have come up for a closer look. The painting was shocking to many people because of its portrayal of a naked Susanna, but not, apparently, because of its misogynistic voyeurism or the way in which it interpreted the story of Susanna.

The lithograph of the prodigal son, however, should also have been provocative and shocking for many Christians, since it disrupts, subverts, and even undermines the biblical story.

Benton's *Prodigal Son* as Autobiographical?

Benton's own interpretation of the *Prodigal Son* lithograph is unclear, but some scholars postulate that the prodigal son in this work portrays Benton himself at this stage of his life, as he reflects on what seemed to be the downward trajectory of his career and his contentious return home to Missouri. The choice of the Chilmark farm on Martha's Vineyard supports the interpretation that Benton is implying that he, like the prodigal, had squandered his career—that had started in earnest at Martha's Vineyard—and was, at that time, depressingly devoid of hope.[41] Benton's homecoming to Missouri after years in New York City was not as welcoming as he had expected: a campaign led by Howard Huselton had already begun in 1938 to oust Benton from his position at the Kansas City Art Institute, and he felt estranged from many of his artistic contemporaries, such as his former student Jackson Pollock and others. Regionalism itself was often discussed already in the past tense. As D'Oench argues, "For Benton, like his prodigal son, going home to find resolution was an aspiration without hope."[42]

Benton's *Prodigal Son* as Social, Political, and Economic Critique?

Thus it is likely, because of his personal circumstances at the time he created the image, that Benton's lithograph of the prodigal son returning

---

41. Gambone, "Thomas Hart Benton," 83–88.
42. D'Oench, *Prodigal Son Narratives*, 26. Benton's possible self-identification with the prodigal son in this lithograph parallels earlier artists who, as noted above, likely identified with the prodigal son in their works (e.g., Dürer, Bosch, Rembrandt).

home is partly autobiographical. Yet there are clearly other contexts that help explain why, for Benton, returning home does not guarantee a joyful reconciliation. In the context of the 1930s, the lithograph portrays an understanding of labor, economic exploitation by the elite, and migration of the exploited poor that is similar to the one envisioned in John Steinbeck's *The Grapes of Wrath*.

In fact, in 1939, the same year he created the lithograph *Prodigal Son*, Benton was commissioned to create a series of drawings of the characters of Steinbeck's *The Grapes of Wrath* for the 1940 Twentieth Century Fox film adaptation of the novel, which, in spite of its controversial subject matter, won the 1940 Pulitzer Prize for the Novel.[43] Benton's *The Departure of the Joads*, 1939 (fig. 7.6), which depicts the Joads loading their beat-up Hudson truck for their journey down Highway 66, evokes the same feelings of loss and barrenness as does the lithograph of Benton's *Prodigal Son*. Both images depict dispossessed refugees: one where people leave their ravaged home; the other where the prodigal returns to his ravaged home. The parallels become even clearer in another episode from the novel. In chapter 6, when Tom Joad first returns to his childhood farm home, he finds it deserted, because the banks had evicted all the farmers from their land, a scene eerily similar to Benton's *Prodigal Son* lithograph.[44]

J. Richard Gruber claims that the spirit of the Depression era was not only oriented toward a blue-collar ideological point of view; it was also antiurban, because the economic collapse was blamed on the evil ways of New York, especially Wall Street and the banks.[45] Benton himself thought that the "American character was formed by hard-working non-intellectual people who were sometimes victimized by their circumstances." Benton also could be described as a populist, as envisioned during the 1930s: someone whose art was sympathetic to the plight of "common" human beings, critical of special interests, and supporting moderate reforms.[46] Beginning in the 1930s, for example, Benton pilloried urban politicians, big business, big industry, and their effects on the "common person,"

---

43. In 1947, the award was renamed Pulitzer Prize for Fiction, first won in 1948 by James Michener's *Tales of the South Pacific*.
44. John Steinbeck, *The Grapes of Wrath, and Other Writings, 1936–1941* (New York: Library of America, 1996), 251–73.
45. Gruber, *Thomas Hart Benton*, 16.
46. Wolff, *Thomas Hart Benton*, 4–11.

Fig. 7.6. Thomas Hart Benton, *The Departure of the Joads*, 1939. Lithograph, 12 7/8 in x 18 1/2 in. San Diego Museum of Art. © 2019 T.H. and R.P. Benton Testamentary Trusts / UMB Bank Trustee / Licensed by VAGA at Artists Rights Society (ARS), NY.

including the "moral, self-sufficient, self-supporting rural individual."[47] One of his major concerns was that the exploitative business practices of modern industries "would ravage the land and destroy the culture he was trying so hard to record and preserve."[48]

Another example of Benton's concern about exploitation of land may be symbolized in his controversial work *Persephone*, which was also completed in 1939. One contemporary review of that painting in *Art Digest* argues that it symbolized "the despoliation of the land by the American farmer.... Benton is scoring the greed of those who cultivate the land to exhaustion, to the point of droughts, erosion, and dust storms."[49]

---

47. Matthew Baigell, "Recovering America for American Art: Benton in the Early Twenties," in *Thomas Hart Benton: Chronicler of America's Folk Heritage*, ed. Linda Weintraub (Annandale-on-Hudson, NY: Edith C. Blum Art Institute, 1984), 23, 27.

48. Karal Ann Marling, *Tom Benton and His Drawings* (Columbia: University of Missouri Press, 1985), 67.

49. Henry Adams, *Thomas Hart Benton: An American Original* (New York: Knopf, 1989), 287. That assessment may be too generous. *Persephone*, like *Susanna and the*

As Erika Doss points out, when Benton created the lithograph of the prodigal son, he was undergoing "a profound lack of faith in the tradition he had celebrated throughout the [1930s]."[50] Benton also writes of the political and economic divisions that President Roosevelt was struggling to overcome. The reforms of the New Deal were faltering within the United States, and clouds of war were gathering. Benton himself notes that, as early as 1936, "there came over me now and then a sense of uneasiness. I could feel the winds from Europe blowing with accelerating force toward world conflict."[51] Perhaps his strongest words about his situation are these: "When the time for America's entrance into the World War arrived, I was in the most confused and, secretly, depressed state of mind I had even been in. Chicago, Paris, and New York had left me finally in a purposeless void. The great cities and the 'life of art' had failed me."[52] Aspects of this failure seem to be both reflected and foreshadowed in Benton's *Prodigal Son*.

## Conclusion

Benton's lithograph *Prodigal Son* rightly could be interpreted as an autobiographical expression of Benton's self-identification as a prodigal son with no one to celebrate his return home. In addition, the image engages larger,

---

*Elders*, is an example of the male gaze that involves Benton (as depicted in the paintings) and a nude, unsuspecting female. In this instance "Persephone" lies naked beside a stream, and a man dressed as a farmer (greatly resembling Benton, playing the role of Hades) stares at her body from his hiding place. Robert Hughes, an art critic, denigrated it as being "fit for a Moscow subway," and art historian Karal Ann Marling described it as "one of the great works of American pornography" (Wolff, *Thomas Hart Benton*, 265–66). The work was originally titled *The Rape of Persephone*, and the image goes disturbingly beyond voyeurism, which no amount of allegorizing can hide. The painting is housed at the Nelson-Atkins Museum in Kansas City, but Benton originally allowed it to be displayed at the Diamond Horseshoe nightclub in New York City.

50. Erika Doss, *Benton, Pollock, and the Politics of Modernism: From Regionalism to Abstract Expressionism* (Chicago: University of Chicago Press, 1991), 264.

51. Benton, *Artist in America*, 296–97.

52. Benton, *Artist in America*, 42. See Benton's hyperbolic reaction to the beginning of World War II in his *Year of Peril* series, in which a painting titled *Again* contains a disturbing use of Jesus on the cross being stabbed by a spear (held by German, Japanese, and Italian soldiers) and strafed by a German warplane. Benton himself calls these works "deliberate propaganda pictures" (*Artist in America*, 298).

contemporary issues such as labor and compensation, economic exploitation by the elite, and migration of the economically oppressed. In light of this work appearing in the era of the Great Depression and the Dust Bowl—specifically in comparison with Benton's images for the film *The Grapes of Wrath*—the lithograph of the prodigal son can speak volumes about the utter despair of those people in the rural areas of the United States who were not able to survive on their desolated farms, suffering foreclosures and evictions, and thereby becoming dispossessed refugees.

In an analogous way, the issues of poverty, (im)migration, and the expectations of hospitality echo throughout the stories of Jesus in the gospels. In the Gospel of Matthew, for example, Joseph, Mary, and Jesus travel as immigrants to Egypt, receive hospitality, and then return to Israel after Herod the Great dies (Matt 2:13–23). Matthew's Gospel also includes Jesus's parable of the sheep and goats (Matt 25:31–46), which declares that giving hospitality to those in need, such as strangers/immigrants like Jesus and his family were in Egypt, is the same as giving hospitality to Jesus himself. This parable also teaches that God will judge human beings on their hospitality, how they treat the "least of these," the hungry, thirsty, stranger/immigrant, sick, ill-clothed, and imprisoned. The critical importance of these acts of hospitality is found throughout the teachings of Jesus—such as extending hospitality to "the poor, the crippled, the lame, and the blind" (Luke 14:12–24).

Ultimately, the response to Benton's *Prodigal Son* lithograph is, of course, up to each interpreter, but in my view this image can stimulate additional interpretations and responses—what Mikhail Bakhtin calls "Answerability"[53]—in light of our contemporary social and economic issues, including those of labor and a living wage, economic exploitation by the elite, and (im)migration—welcoming the stranger. In other words, in addition to deliberating over what message this parable/image seeks to convey and how it communicates that message, interpreters should also realize that this parable/image challenges us to respond. In other words, what does this parable/image *want* if not *demand* from us?[54]

---

53. "I have to answer with my own life for what I have experienced and understood in art, so that everything I have experienced and understood would not remain ineffectual in my life." See Mikhail Bakhtin, *Art and Answerability: Early Philosophical Essays by M. M. Bakhtin* (Austin: University of Texas Press, 1990), 1.

54. As William J. T. Mitchell notes: "The question to ask of pictures from the standpoint of poetics is not just what they mean or what they do but what they *want*—what

Benton's *Prodigal Son* acknowledges that in the world in which we live, there is no guarantee of a joyful reconciliation or positive outcome. Life simply does not work that way. In this case, Benton decides to identify with the prodigal son, a stance that echoes the decisions of many interpreters over the years; whether Benton's prodigal has repented, as the Lukan context of the parable suggests is a prerequisite, is not addressed. No one is there to welcome him home. Benton, like most interpreters before him, chooses not to identify with an older brother who, as the Lukan parable "wants" the older brother to do, joins the celebration of his brother's return. And, of course, Benton also obviously does not choose to identify with the father, a stance adopted by almost no interpreters over the centuries—including the Lukan context of the parable, since it uses the father to reflect God. Interpreters instead envision a God/father who welcomes prodigals home.

We also live in an era in which joyful reconciliations or positive outcomes are difficult to envision. The Trump administration, for example, advocated building a "wall" across the US southern border, separated refugee children from their parents, detained approximately fifteen thousand migrant children, illegally closed of ports of entry for asylum seekers, and radically limited the number of people who could apply for asylum each day, including unaccompanied children. These and other actions resulted in the deaths of at least 260 people in 2018, including two young children in US custody: Jakelin Caal Maquin, a seven-year old girl, and Felipe Gómez Alonzo, an eight-year-old boy, both of whom who fled Guatemala with their fathers.

In light of these atrocities, perhaps it is time to identify not with the younger son or the older son; instead, both the Lukan parable and Benton's bleak representation of it should encourage us to identify with the father, the one who joyfully, lovingly, and compassionately initiates reconciliation and restoration and who welcomes the prodigals/immigrants/strangers home.[55] Benton's dystopian vision of prodigals/immigrants/strangers

---

claim they make upon us, and how we are to respond." See Mitchell, *What Do Pictures Want?* (Chicago: University of Chicago Press, 2005), xv. The same is true for parables: parables are meant to challenge us to do things, not just to think things. Jesus spoke them with one ear already listening for our responses. See David B. Gowler, *What Are They Saying about the Parables?* (New York: Paulist, 2000), 103.

55. A similar argument is found in Henri Nouwen, *The Return of the Prodigal Son* (New York: Doubleday, 1992), 119. "The challenge now, yes the call, is to become the

returning home—or escaping their devastated homes—is a problem that all of us can work to help prevent.

## Works Cited

Adams, Henry. *Thomas Hart Benton: An American Original*. New York: Knopf, 1989.

Baigell, Matthew. "Recovering America for American Art: Benton in the Early Twenties." Pages 13–31 in *Thomas Hart Benton: Chronicler of America's Folk Heritage*. Edited by Linda Weintraub. Annandale-on-Hudson, NY: Edith C. Blum Art Institute, 1984.

Bakhtin, Mikhail. *Art and Answerability: Early Philosophical Essays by M. M. Bakhtin*. Austin: University of Texas Press, 1990.

Benton, Thomas Hart. *An Artist in America*. Columbia: University of Missouri Press, 1983.

———. *The Lithographs of Thomas Hart Benton*. Edited and compiled by Creekmore Faith. Austin: University of Texas Press, 1979.

Broun, Elizabeth, Douglas Hyland, and Marilyn Stokstad. *Benton's Bentons*. Lawrence, KS: Spencer Museum of Art, 1980.

Burroughs, Polly. *Thomas Hart Benton: A Portrait*. Garden City, NY: Doubleday, 1981.

Cartwright, Ingrid. "Hoe schilder hoe wilder: Dissolute Self-Portraiture in Seventeenth-Century Dutch and Flemish Art." PhD diss., University of Maryland (College Park), 2007.

D'Oench, Ellen. *Prodigal Son Narratives, 1480–1980*. New Haven: Yale University Art Gallery, 1995.

Doss, Erika. *Benton, Pollock, and the Politics of Modernism: From Regionalism to Abstract Expressionism*. Chicago: University of Chicago Press, 1991.

Fraenger, William. *Hieronymus Bosch*. New York: Dorset House, 1983.

Gambone, Robert L. "Religious Motifs in the Work of Thomas Hart Benton." Pages 65–93 in *Thomas Hart Benton: Artist, Writer, and Intellectual*. Edited by R. Douglas Hurt and Mary K. Dains. Columbia: State Historical Society of Missouri, 1989.

---

Father myself." See also David B. Gowler, "White Evangelical Christians Need Jesus—Not Donald Trump—If Their Movement Is Going to Survive," *Salon*, 25 December 2018, https://tinyurl.com/SBL6703s.

Gowler, David B. "Characterization in Luke: A Socio-narratological Approach." *BTB* 19 (1989): 54–62.

———. "The Characterization of the Two Brothers in the Parable of the of the Prodigal Son (Luke 15:11–32): Their Function and Afterlives." Pages 55–72 in *Characterization in Luke-Acts*. Edited by Frank Dicken and Julia Snyder. London: Bloomsbury, 2016.

———. *Host, Guest, Enemy and Friend: Portraits of the Pharisees in Luke and Acts*. New York: Lang, 1991.

———. *The Parables after Jesus*. Waco, TX: Baylor University Press, 2020.

———. "Sit and Listen; Go and Do: The Parables of the Good Samaritan and Prodigal Son in Howard Thurman's Life and Thought." Pages 434–51 in *Anatomies of the Gospels and beyond the Gospels*. Edited by Elizabeth Struthers Malbon, Mikeal C. Parsons, and Paul N. Anderson. BibInt. Leiden: Brill, 2018.

———. *What Are They Saying about the Parables?* New York: Paulist, 2000.

———. "White Evangelical Christians Need Jesus—Not Donald Trump—If Their Movement Is Going to Survive." *Salon*, December 25, 2018. https://tinyurl.com/SBL6703s.

Gruber, J. Richard. *Thomas Hart Benton and the American South*. Augusta, GA: Morris Museum of Art, 1998.

Levine, Amy-Jill. *Short Stories by Jesus*. New York: HarperOne, 2014.

Lischer, Richard. *Reading the Parables*. Louisville: Westminster John Knox, 2014.

Marling, Karal Ann. *Tom Benton and His Drawings*. Columbia: University of Missouri Press, 1985.

Mitchell, William J. T. *What Do Pictures Want?* Chicago: University of Chicago Press, 2005.

Nouwen, Henri. *The Return of the Prodigal Son*. New York: Doubleday, 1992.

Parsons, Mikeal C. "The Prodigal's Elder Brother: The History and Ethics of Reading Luke 15:25–32." *PRSt* 23 (1996): 147–74.

Steinbeck, John. *The Grapes of Wrath, and Other Writings, 1936–1941*. New York: Library of America, 1996.

Tippens, Darryl. "Shakespeare and the Prodigal Son Tradition." *ERC* 14 (1988): 57–77.

Wetering, Ernst van de. *Rembrandt: A Life in 180 Paintings*. Amsterdam: Local World BV, 2008.

Wolff, Justin P. *Thomas Hart Benton: A Life*. New York: Farrar, Straus & Giroux, 2012.

# 8
## Visualizing the Beloved Disciple in the Art of the Reclining Banquet

JEFF JAY

Over the last fifteen years, scholars have started to interpret early Christian texts with renewed interest in the crucial epistemological and rhetorical precept that reading or hearing words incites the creation of mental images.[1] Some instructively ground this principle in cognitive scientific accounts about the role image and visualization play in thought and understanding, and underline the radically constructive function of cognitive blending in communication.[2] Many at the same time recognize that this new insight into the interrelation of word and image is, rather, quite

---

1. For recent volumes of collected essays, see Vernon K. Robbins, Walter S. Melion, and Roy R. Jeal, eds., *The Art of Visual Exegesis: Rhetoric, Texts, Images*, ESEC 19 (Atlanta: SBL Press, 2017); Annette Weissenrieder and Robert B. Coote, eds., *The Interface of Orality and Writing: Speaking, Seeing, Writing in the Shaping of New Genres*, BPCS (Eugene, OR: Cascade, 2015), 205–82; also Annette Weissenrieder, Friederike Wendt, and Petra von Gemünden, eds., *Picturing the New Testament: Studies in Ancient Visual Images*, WUNT 2/193 (Tübingen: Mohr Siebeck, 2005). For an overview of important monographs and individual approaches, see Vernon K. Robbins, "New Testament Texts, Visual Material Culture, and Earliest Christian Art," in Robbins, Melion, and Jeal, *Art of Visual Exegesis*, 13–54.

2. L. Gregory Bloomquist, "Methodology Underlying the Presentation of Visual Texture in the Gospel of John," in Robbins, Melion, and Jeal, *Art of Visual Exegesis*, 89–120; Bloomquist, "Eyes Wide Open, Seeing Nothing: The Challenge of the Gospel of John's Nonvisualizable Texture for Readings Using Visual Texture," in Robbins, Melion, and Jeal, *Art of Visual Exegesis*, 121–67; also, for a summary, see Annette Weissenrieder and Friederike Wendt, "Images as Communication: The Methods of Iconography," in Weissenrieder, Wendt, and von Gemünden, *Picturing the New Testament*, 3–49, esp. 38–44.

old. In ancient rhetorical theory, effective speech requires orators to craft their language in order that hearers might see what the orators describe. Painting scenes for the mind's eye with words endows narratives with clarity and credibility, engenders within an audience emotions favorable to persuasion, and adds weight, grandeur, and urgency to what one says (Quintilian, *Inst.* 4.2.63–65; 6.2.29–36; 8.3.62–72; 9.1.27; 9.2.40; Aristotle, *Rhet.* 3.11.2–4 [1411b–1412a]; 3.1.6 [1404a]; also Longinus, *Subl.* 15.1–11).[3] Quintilian cites the Greek term ἐνάργεια, which means "lucidity" or "vividness," as the ideal aim of orators, who should exhibit with words rather than merely speak them. He instructs speakers to induce audiences to form φαντασίαι, again using the Greek for the mental images present to the mind. Quintilian emphasizes that it is by embellishing minor details and incidental features that speakers create such vivid and lively scenes. In this regard, he cites Cicero as exemplary for his relishing in the little items of a vividly described banquet: "I seemed to see some entering, others exiting, some staggering from wine, others sluggish from yesterday's drinking. The ground was filthy, muddied with wine, buried with wilted garlands and fishbones" (*Inst.* 8.3.66).[4] Quintilian applauds Cicero's ability to capture everything one would see upon entering the room, and this enhances what is likely Cicero's aim, that is, to malign an opponent's character for participating in such carousing.

In the Gospel according to John, we often encounter rich little details like these. Scholars have thus rightly started to inquire into what role the visual plays in understanding the scenes this gospel, as it were, paints with words.[5] This raises the question that I shall address here as I narrow my

---

3. See Roy R. Jeal, "Visual Interpretation: Blending Rhetorical Arts in Colossians 2:6–3:4," in Robbins, Melion, and Jeal, *Art of Visual Exegesis*, 59–63; also, Harry O. Maier, "Paul, Imperial Situation, and Visualization in the Epistle to the Colossians," in Robbins, Melion, and Jeal, *Art of Visual Exegesis*, 176–79; see also Harry O. Maier, *Picturing Paul in Empire: Imperial Image, Text, and Persuasion in Colossians, Ephesians and the Pastoral Epistles* (London: Bloomsbury T&T Clark, 2013).

4. All translations are by the author.

5. See Petra von Gemünden, "Weisheitliche Bilderkonstellationen im Johannesevangelium? Einige strukturell Überlegungen," in Weissenrieder, Wendt, and von Gemünden, *Picturing the New Testament*, 159–82; von Gemünden, "Die Palmzweige in der johanneischen Einzugsgeschichte (Joh 12, 13): Ein Hinweis auf eine symbolische Uminterpretation im Johannesevangelium?," in Weissenrieder, Wendt, and von Gemünden, *Picturing the New Testament*, 207–22; Gabriele Elsen-Novák and Mirko Novák, "'Ich bin der wahre Weinstock und mein Vater ist der Weingärtner':

focus to one little vivid narrative nugget in John 13:23, 25; and 21:20, where the Beloved Disciple during dinner reclines "in the lap" (ἐν τῷ κόλπῳ) and "on the chest" (ἐπὶ τὸ στῆθος) of Jesus. What mental image does this provoke? What visual context would have influenced the reception of these verses and their broader thematic significance? Ancient art has proved a valuable source for answering such questions. Paintings, sculptures, mosaics, and the visual grammars of their intricate iconographic languages form, as it were, the visual landscape of both public and domestic spheres. They can reasonably be taken to condition the visual aspects of communication as well as textual interpretation and understanding.[6] Visual images taken from material artifacts outside the text can thus be helpful in understanding this lap-holding pose, and this evidence has not yet been mined for interpreting this posture in John and the more comprehensive semantics with which it connects.

Reclining together, lap holding, and couch sharing are typical not only at a symposium but also at other banquets and reclining dinners throughout the Greco-Roman world. Two people reclining in the lap on a couch during dinner persists as one communicative item in the iconography of the reclining banquet, which appears, with various local adaptations, over a wide chronological and geographical spectrum of ancient Mediterranean cultures. Two reclining on a couch with one nestled in the lap of the other consistently connects with other thematic constellations, associated as it is with erotic love, the vine and the drinking of wine, warnings against excessive drinking, and the ideals of community and sociability. This iconography portrays luxurious dining even as it sometimes fosters distancing and ironic attitudes toward such opulence.[7] Images that feature two reclining figures with one in the lap

---

Zur Semiotik des Weinstocks in Joh 15, 1–8 aus Sicht der Altorientalistik," in Weissenrieder, Wendt, and von Gemünden, *Picturing the New Testament*, 183–206. Also see Bloomquist, "Methodology"; Bloomquist, "Eyes Wide Open," 89–167.

6. See David L. Balch, whose work focusing on the relevance of wall paintings in domestic spaces for the interpretation of early Christian texts has been groundbreaking. He has now collected his previously published essays in *Roman Domestic Art and Early House Churches*, WUNT 228 (Tübingen: Mohr Siebeck, 2008). More recently, see Balch, "Women Prophets/Maenads Visually Represented in Two Roman Colonies: Pompeii and Corinth," in Weissenrieder and Coote, *Interface of Orality and Writing*, 236–59.

7. Helpful methodologically here has been Elsen-Novák and Novák, who emphasize how the vine in images from the ancient Near East commonly belongs to a "Kon-

in connection with these other themes thus can be shown to perform a visual semiotics of dining and banqueting. To take a cue from Erwin Panofsky's iconology, this art furthermore reveals basic underlying cultural sensibilities and patterns, and is expressive of deeper cultural logics, trends, and attitudes.[8] Indeed, my argument, which at this stage remains suggestive and probative, depends on the plausibility of these two claims: (1) that the iconography of the reclining banquet reaches far over time and place throughout ancient Mediterranean cultures and (2) that it brings to visualization an underlying cultural semiotics of dining and reclining. One can thus reasonably posit that iconography of the kind I will examine and/or the cultural semiotics operative within it would have conditioned the visual imagination as it shaped the reception of the beloved reclining in the lap of Jesus. I shall argue that their lap holding might be taken to imply mutual romantic devotion that distinguishes their love from other love relationships. I will also demonstrate how such lap holding during dinner connects with the broader context of these verses, which are part of Jesus's Farewell Discourses in John 13–17, where discussion turns significantly to the vine as well as to ideals of love and community. Moreover, standards of sacrificial service and the shadow of Jesus's impending death upend the affluence normally characterizing reclining banquets. We will, in effect, become tuned to how John might be read, or seen, as a kind of textual image by looking attentively at several specimens of this splendid art. This, in turn, clarifies how reclining in the lap connects more extensively with other prominent motifs of the reclining banquet as they appear

---

notationskette," which weaves together themes of the vine-branch, paradise and pleasure garden, and fertility as linked to power, civilization, and order ("'Ich bin der wahre Weinstock,'" 195–202). For the methodological importance of analyzing thematic patterns and constellations, see Weissenrieder and Wendt, "Images as Communication," 21–27.

8. Erwin Panofsky, "Iconography and Iconology: An Introduction to the Study of Renaissance Art," in *Meaning in the Visual Arts* (Chicago: University of Chicago Press, 1955), 26–41; for the continued relevance of Panofsky in art history and the visual exegesis of the New Testament, see Weissenrieder and Wendt, "Images as Communication," 5–13; also Brigitte Kahl, "The Galatian Suicide and the Transbinary Semiotics of Christ Crucified (Galatians 3:1): Exercises in Visual Exegesis and Critical Reimagination," in Robbins, Melion, and Jeal, *Art of Visual Exegesis*, 195–240; also Kahl, *Galatians Re-imagined: Reading with the Eyes of the Vanquished*, PCC (Minneapolis: Fortress, 2010).

throughout John 13–17. My argument also thus contributes to the growing realization that these chapters cohere around the fact that they evoke in several ways the material and literary culture of dining and reclining in the Greco-Roman world.[9]

## 1. Reclining in the Lap in the Visual Culture of the Ancient Mediterranean World

The image of a person reclining to dine or drink persists in the visual culture of the ancient Mediterranean world for well over one thousand years. From the late seventh century BCE to the fifth century CE, it appears over an astonishing geographical range, including Greece, Etruria, archaic Italy, and Rome, as well as many regions of the empire. It decorates an array of artifacts, including drinking cups and other vessels used for dining, and the walls of tombs and the walls and floors of dining rooms, as well as other carved grave monuments and temple friezes. The image, to be sure, underwent adaptation to local dining practices, which were always developing and subject to change, as these peoples interacted through trade, settlement, and conquest.[10] As Katherine Dunbabin writes, "the image of the reclining banqueter is one of amazing and enduring potency, and among the most characteristic of Graeco-Roman art."[11] The more specific portrayal of two recliners sharing a couch, with the inner recliner posed intimately in the lap of the outer, regularly surfaces as part of this widespread banqueting imagery. Since the motif of one reclining in the lap

---

9. Already in this direction, see George L. Parsenios, *Departure and Consolation: The Johannine Farewell Discourses in Light of Greco-Roman Literature*, NovTSup 117 (Leiden: Brill, 2005), 111–50; also Esther Kobel, *Dining with John: Communal Meals and Identity Formation in the Fourth Gospel and Its Historical and Cultural Context*, BibInt 109 (Leiden: Brill, 2011), 69–110, 173–214, 251–300. She treats both the literary and sociocultural issues and helpfully analyzes John's other meal scenes.

10. The scholarly literature is accordingly vast, and I shall cite specific studies as they become relevant for the interpretation of the examples discussed below. For helpful and important surveys, see Jean-Marie Dentzer, *Le motif du banquet couché dans le proche-orient et le monde grec du VIIe au IVe siècle avant J.-C.*, BEFAR (Rome: Palais Farnèse, 1982); Katherine M. D. Dunbabin, *The Roman Banquet: Images of Conviviality* (Cambridge: Cambridge University Press, 2003); François Lissarrague, *The Aesthetics of the Greek Banquet*, trans. Andrew Szegedy-Maszak (Princeton: Princeton University Press, 1990).

11. Dunbabin, *Roman Banquet*, 14.

of another is most conducive to visualizing our pair of recliners in John 13:23–25 and 21:20, I shall examine several select examples and highlight how and what this motif communicates in connection with other recurring banqueting themes.

In order to visualize lap holding at dinner in accordance with its depiction in ancient art, let us travel first in our mind's eye to Pompeii and for a point of departure view three paintings in the triclinium of the so-called House or Bakery of the Chaste Lovers. Walking northeast along the Via dell' Abbondanza toward Pompeii's amphitheater, through a corridor of the city once bustling with commerce, past shops and houses peppered with electoral inscriptions promoting political candidates, our building appears on the left at door 6 in *insula* 12 of region 9 (IX.12.6). As is now clear from the excavation that has been ongoing since 1987, this address is the location of a business complex, which includes a mill, bakery, and storefront bake shop as well as possibly catering services and rental access to the sizable triclinium.[12] This once-two-story structure, with a balcony over the street, may also have housed the proprietor, his family, and servants, and nothing rules out that the baker himself used the triclinium. But its size and decorative scheme, which is more upscale and elaborate than in the other rooms, suggests the possibility that it was for rent and thus provided a supplementary source of income.[13] From the street, anyone about to use the dining room enters a vestibule, then passes a large oven, behind which stand four flour mills. The triclinium has a window on its south wall providing natural light from an open court with a raised garden. Though large

---

12. For the initial reports of the excavation and its progress, see Antonio Varone, "Scavi recenti a Pompei lungo la via dell' Abbondanza (*regio* IX, *ins*. 12, 6–7)," in *Ercolano 1738–1988: 250 anni di ricerca archeologica*, ed. Luisa Franchi dell' Orto (Rome: L' Erma di Bretschneider, 1993), 617–40; Varone, "New Finds in Pompeii: The Excavation of Two Buildings in Via dell' Abbondanza," *Apollo* 138 (July 1993): 8–12; Varone, "Pompeii. Attività dell' Ufficio Scavi: 1990," *RSP* 4 (1990): 201–11; Varone, "Pompeii. Attività dell' Ufficio Scavi: 1989," *RSP* 3 (1989): 225–38. For descriptions and interpretations of this building and the paintings in the triclinium, see Mary Beard, *The Fires of Vesuvius: Pompeii Lost and Found* (Cambridge: Harvard University Press, 2008), 170–77; John R. Clarke, *Art in the Lives of Ordinary Romans: Visual Representation and Non-elite Viewers in Italy, 100 B.C.–A.D. 315* (Berkeley: University of California Press, 2003), 227–33; Dunbabin, *Roman Banquet*, 52–56; Matthew B. Roller, *Dining Posture in Ancient Rome: Bodies, Values, and Status* (Princeton: Princeton University Press, 2006), 139–45.

13. Beard, *Fires of Vesuvius*, 176.

and lavishly painted, the triclinium would have offered modest accommodations for nonelite patrons.[14] After all, a would-be diner would have not only accessed the room by walking through an active mill, thus encountering workers and flour dust, and feeling the heat wafting from the oven, but also would have reclined in close proximity to the stables that housed the animals that powered the mills. Excavators uncovered the remains of two animals in the kneading room, where they may have run during the eruption for safety or escape from their stable, which is located two doors down from the triclinium. The eastern wall of the triclinium separates it from another stable, where excavators located five more equine skeletons.[15]

Reclining in this dining room, with the smells and sounds of the bakeshop and stables in the air, the would-be diners would have viewed and possibly discussed among themselves the room's decorative scheme. Red and black panels alternate, and the overall design is suggestive of the late Third Style, circa 35–45 CE.[16] Antonio Varone, the lead excavator, reports that the east wall had been later restored using the same scheme after suffering damage from the earthquake in 62.[17] In the red panels to each side, little winged figures appear holding baskets with fruit, game, *thyrsi*, flowers, lances, jugs, and cornucopias. But the main attractions

---

14. For the modesty of these accommodations and the nonelite status of its users, see Beard, *Fires of Vesuvius*, 176; Clarke, *Art in the Lives*, 230; also Dunbabin, *Roman Banquet*, 54–56.

15. For details, see Beard, *Fires of Vesuvius*, 174–75; also Angelo Genovese and Tiziana Cocca, "Internal Organization of an Equine Stable at Pompeii," *Anth* 31 (2000): 119–23. For the DNA analysis of the remains, see Maria Sica et al., "Analysis of Five Ancient Equine Skeletons by Mitochondrial DNA Sequencing," *AncBio* 4 (2002): 179–84.

16. For a summary of the characteristics of painting in the Third Style, see Joanne Berry, *The Complete Pompeii* (London: Thames & Hudson, 2007), 170–71; for a detailed account, with helpful references and figures, see John R. Clarke, *The Houses of Roman Italy: 100 B.C.–A.D. 50; Ritual Space and Decoration* (Berkeley: University of California Press, 1991), 30–77.

17. For details, see Varone, "Scavi recenti," 623; Varone, "New Finds," 9; also Dunbabin, *Roman Banquet*, 53. In addition to the restored east wall of the triclinium, other evidence suggests that this building required renovations due to the earthquake in 62, though they remained unfinished during the time of the eruption: cracks appear in the oven, one of which had been plastered over; three of the four mills were not operational, with two of them holding lime for the ongoing repairs; lime was piled in the triclinium, suggesting that it was not in use at the time of the eruption (Beard, *Fires of Vesuvius*, 172–76).

are the three banqueting scenes that stand at the center of each main wall and thus lure viewers to fix their attention on them and decipher their details.[18] They portray an abundance, luxury, and indulgence that quite outdo the establishment's own lack of pretension and feature a total of six couples reclining two to a couch, with the woman lying directly in the lap of the man.

The painting on the west wall (fig. 8.1) shows two couples wearing wreaths thus reclining in reach of two tripod tables set with drinking vessels. Three of them raise their right arms gesturing toward a woman, also wreathed, whose visage appears unsteady and perhaps somewhat pained as she holds a cup loosely in her hand and finds much-needed support from the servant behind her. Visible between the couples, another man reclines sunken in sleep, with his right hand behind his head and elbow in the air. The scene suggests the end of a drinking party whose excesses have caused the tottering woman to be led away or even dismissed now that her partner lies there passed out. The woman on the right may be pouring out her cup in reaction to the drunk-sick pair, whom she takes to be a warning against the consequences of having one too many. This is not far from the scene of the banquet Cicero paints with words previously cited. This painting reproduces a prototype, as is clear from the fact that another version appeared elsewhere in Pompeii. Though now lost, it is known from two nineteenth-century drawings and shows only the couple on the left couch with the tottering drunk behind them. This version adds a servant on the right, who holds a ladle and represents the object of the man's gaze, as he perhaps orders the boy to help the unsteady woman.[19] Judging from the behavior of the women, their intimate in-the-lap repose and their prodigal drinking, they are hetaerae.[20] The scene thus presents a convivial travesty and even a humorous portrayal of decadent dining's denouement. At least some recliners renting this bakeshop triclinium would have viewed this image with bemused irony, and perhaps others as a fantasy of the luxury that, as Dunbabin writes, they could only hope to find "in their dreams or in their cups."[21]

---

18. For the way Third Style wall paintings draw viewers' attention to a "bit-by-bit examination" of the "miniaturistic details" of the central frame, see Clarke, *Houses of Roman Italy*, 63–64.

19. For plates of the drawings and details, see Varone, "Scavi recenti," 636.

20. Clarke, *Art in the Lives*, 231–33.

21. Dunbabin, *Roman Banquet*, 56.

Fig. 8.1. Fresco from the House of Chaste Lovers (IX.12.6), triclinium, west wall, ca. 35–45 CE, 63.5 x 74 cm. Pompeii. Photo: © Scala/ Art Resource, NY.

The painting on the north wall similarly invites viewers to adopt an ironic attitude and weaves together these same motifs, opulence, eroticism, and inebriation.[22] Set outside under an awning, this banquet features two couples reclining, with the women in the men's laps. The behavior of the woman on the left confirms her status as an intoxicated hetaera, for she has lost her sandal from her left foot and her right arm hangs loosely. She leans into her partner for the kiss that has given this building its name, the Chaste Lovers, which is ironic, to be sure, since nothing appears to be chaste about these lap-holding couples unless they are compared to the overtly pornographic paintings in the hallway of the Lupanar (VII.12.18) or the apodyterium of the Suburban Baths. The hetaera on the right is

---

22. For color plates of the fresco, see Clarke, *Art in the Lives*, pl. 18; also Varone, "Scavi recenti," 639, pl. CLIX.

lightly clothed, holds a *kantharos*, and looks toward a servant pouring wine from an amphora into a luxury apparatus designed for cooling wine for the affluent. She reclines in the embrace of a man who looks left and gestures toward the two women on the left. The one who sits is a musician holding a double oboe but refrains from entertaining the diners and ignores the request of one of the men who hired her because she is too busy drinking. Finally, scholars are unsure how to interpret the badly worn and enigmatic figure standing behind the banqueters who is holding a stick, wearing a long tunic, and wreathed, which suggests his participation in the banquet.[23] Like its counterpart on the west wall, moreover, the craftsperson has executed this painting according to a model, as is evident from the fact that another version once appeared in Pompeii, though its precise provenance there is uncertain (fig. 8.2). Currently located in the Museo Archeologico Nazionale in Naples, this painting presents one major variant in that the servant pouring the wine is absent.[24]

The third painting on the restored east wall of the triclinium, painted by a different artist, who executed a less complex subject, presents a final set of not-so-chaste, lap-holding, drunken lovers, who recline wearing wreaths on extravagant draperies and cushions.[25] The hetaera on the left, who is nude from her waist, supports her couch-companion's head with her left hand as she pours a stream of wine into his mouth from a *rhyton* in her right hand. Her partner holds still more wine in a cup in his left hand. Next to them reclines a man who has not been so successful in holding his drink. Out cold on the couch, he dangles his left arm and precariously balances an empty cup on his fingertips. He thus evokes the man on the east wall, directly opposite this painting, who also lies comatose and likewise represents the repercussions of too much booze. A servant stands fanning him, and his hetaera, who is in his lap and wears a light,

---

23. For options, see Clarke, *Art in the Lives*, 231. For the appearance of a figure like this in outside dining scenes in other paintings, see Antonio Varone, "Pompei: il quadro Helbig 1445, 'Kasperl in Kindertheater,' una nuova replica e il problema delle copie e delle varianti," in *I Temi figurativi nella pittura parietale antica (IV sec. a.C.–IV sec. d.C.): Atti del VI Convegno Internazionale sulla Pittura Parietale Antica (Bologna, 20–23 settembre 1995)*, ed. Daniela Scagliarini Corlàita (Bologna: University Press Bologna, 1997), 149–52, 351–52, figs. 1–6.

24. For a color plate of the fresco, see Varone, "Scavi recenti," 639, pl. CLIX.

25. Varone, "Scavi recenti," 623; also Clarke, *Art in the Lives*, 230. For color plates of the fresco, see Varone, "Scavi recenti," 640, pl. CLX, 1; also Clarke, *Art in the Lives*, pl. 17.

Fig. 8.2. Fresco from Pompeii, mid-first century C.E., 44 x 48 cm. Naples, Museo Archeologico Nazionale 9015. Photo: © Erich Lessing/ Art Resource, NY.

almost diaphanous, dress, supports his head with her left hand and points toward the other couple with her right. John Clarke suggests that this scene portrays the outcome of a drinking contest. With his hetaera's help, the man on the left has gained victory over the other, whose own hetaera, since her partner has lost, protests the outcome.[26]

Couch sharing and lap holding thus appear in these paintings to be motifs anchored in the rather specific iconographic language of the banquet and to link up with broader cultural patterns and dining themes. Lap holding here constitutes one communicative item in a visual context that highlights wine's humorous effects and parodies its wrecking power as well

---

26. Clarke, *Art in the Lives*, 228–30.

as other forms of opulence and luxury. Another important and abiding undertone in these convivial dynamics, and one with which lap holding is especially conducive, is the eroticism. The hetaerae recline in the men's embrace, one of them is nude from the waist, another kisses her partner, others are lightly clothed, and all of them are intimately poised in their partners' laps.

Both Dunbabin and Clarke argue that these paintings, and their constellation of themes, summon the world of Greek dining and sympotic culture.[27] As is undeniable for the paintings on the west and north walls, because other versions of these scenes are attested elsewhere, they belong to a standard repertoire, possibly derived by the artists from pattern books, which were developed from the Hellenistic iconographic prototypes that the artists of this period often utilized. Typically Greek, for example, is that the couples share individual couches. This differs from the layout of the Roman triclinium, where it is usual for three recliners to share three couches for a total of three per couch. It also departs from the Roman *stibadium*, or S-shaped couch, usually shared by seven or eight recliners.[28] Also typically Greek is the character of these scenes, which feature a female musical performer drinking wine as well as men with hetaerae whose actions are less than matronly.[29] It would have been a serious breach of decorum for respectable Roman women, who did have a place at the *convivium* and may have reclined in this triclinium, to bare their breasts, to depart drunkenly, or to help her partner win a drinking contest. Though these types of behavior surely occurred in the Roman world at more indulgent banquets, these scenes cohere, as Dunbabin argues, much more readily with the atmosphere of drinking, sexual indulgence, and luxury as it is portrayed throughout, for example, the Greek erotic epigrams and in Greek vase painting.[30] The focus on drinking together, the literal meaning of *symposium*, is also characteristically Greek, whereas the variety and richness of food played a much more important role in the *convivium*, as Dunbabin argues.[31] In this way distance opens up between the banquet, as

---

27. Clarke, *Art in the Lives*, 227–33; Dunbabin, *Roman Banquet*, 52–56.
28. Dunbabin, *Roman Banquet*, 36–71.
29. Clarke, *Art in the Lives*, 230.
30. Dunbabin, *Roman Banquet*, 56, 67–68. See especially the sympotic epigrams collected in book 11 of the Greek Anthology as well as the many erotic epigrams collected in books 5 and 12, which are often set in a sympotic context.
31. Dunbabin, *Roman Banquet*, 20–22.

it would have unfolded in this triclinium, and the conduct that these paintings show. As Clarke argues, at least some Pompeiian recliners plausibly could have viewed these to be depictions of people from a faraway place and time dramatizing the ups and downs of this brand of dining.[32] Much of this coheres with Third Style painting in general. When artists designed walls so as to draw attention to a central panel, as in this triclinium, houses become veritable picture galleries, which were supposed to attest to the owner's taste as a person of culture and epicure of Greek art.[33]

Only a small amount of material depicting banquets survives from the Hellenistic period, and so time has ravaged the Hellenistic prototypes on which the artists in Campania based images such as these.[34] However, earlier Attic vase paintings provide a trove of artifacts frequently showing two people reclining per couch in the lap while drinking. Similarly, they connect this with the motifs of luxury, inebriation, and eroticism. Attic vase painting thus highlights how traditional and widespread this concatenation of themes was throughout the convivial visual culture of the ancient Mediterranean world. One example dramatizing the persistence and longevity of this iconographic grammar is a red-figure *kylix* currently in the Metropolitan Museum of Art in New York (figs. 8.3–4).[35] Originally produced in Attica circa 480 BCE and then exported to Etruria, which is this artifact's provenance, possibly from Vulci, the cup displays a symposium.[36] The content of the cup's decoration thus matches its function. As a would-be drinker drains wine from this cup, he or she is invited to participate in the festivities as they are portrayed and to mimic four of the figures shown on the cup, who also drink from a *kylix*. Six couples, men and their hetaerae, share six couches. Three of them recline two per couch with the hetaera in the lap. The middle couple in figure 8.3 have become

---

32. Clarke, *Art in the Lives*, 230–33.
33. Clarke, *Houses of Roman Italy*, 64–65.
34. For a review of the meager remains of dining imagery from the Hellenistic period, including funerary reliefs, see Dunbabin, *Roman Banquet*, 17–18.
35. Metropolitan Museum of Art, New York, 20.246; for a description and color plates with close-ups of individual figures, see Joan R. Mertens, *How to Read Greek Vases* (New Haven: Yale University Press, 2010), 116–20.
36. J. D. Beazley, *Attic Red-Figure Vase-Painters*, 2nd ed. (Oxford: Clarendon, 1963), 467.118, who attributes the cup to Makron as painter. Also see Thomas H. Carpenter, Thomas Mannack, and Melanie Mendonça, *Beazley Addenda*, 2nd ed. (Oxford: Oxford University Press, 1989), 245; and see the publication record listed in the database of the Classical Art Research Center (http://www.beazley.ox.ac.uk).

220                                JEFF JAY

especially cozy. Lap holding in their case has led, conducive as it is, to their embracing, as they stare lovingly and longingly into each other's eyes, their legs under cover and their chests bare. To one side of them, there reclines a man holding a *skyphos*. He invites a naked hetaera to share his couch, as she undoes her hair and hangs her clothing behind her. To the other side, another hetaera lies naked in the lap of a man who wraps his arm around her shoulder and his leg around her waist. They both look in the direction of the slave boy under the handle, who holds a strainer and an *oinochoē*, possibly asking him for a refill, for the woman dangles her empty cup from her fingertips, and the man appears to be without one entirely. In figure 8.4 there reclines another couple in the lap, both naked from the waist and turning to gaze at the female flute player who stands before a man who reclines and throws his head back, thus opening his chest, in order to maximize the beauty and power of his voice as he sings.[37]

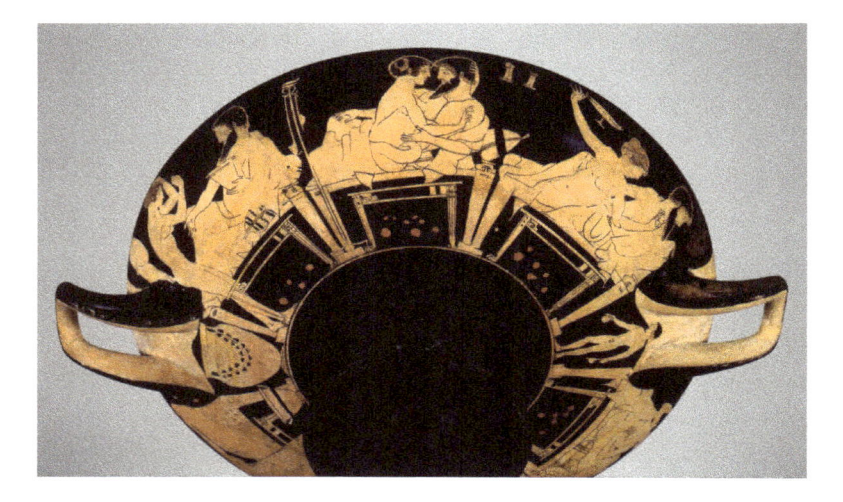

Fig. 8.3. Terracotta red-figure kylix, ca. 480 BCE, signed by Hieron, attributed to Makron, height 13.8 cm., diameter 33.2 cm. Metropolitan Museum of Art, New York.

However, just as wine can lead to love and song, so can it lead in excess to disgust and pain. The next couple, though badly damaged, dramatizes this potential hazard of the symposium. The hetaera, this time fully

---

37. For analogies, see Lissarrague, *Aesthetics of the Greek Banquet*, 129–34.

Fig. 8.4. Terracotta red-figure kylix, ca. 480 BCE, signed by Hieron, attributed to Makron, height 13.8 cm., diameter 33.2 cm. Metropolitan Museum of Art, New York.

clothed, disdainfully turns away as she holds the head of her partner, who vomits into a container on the ground. Immoderation thus thwarts the carnal joys of love, sex, and song, which hang in precarious balance. Under the handle stands the krater. As François Lissarrague argues, this vessel appears to symbolize the party's ideals. All the participants drink from it, underlining their community and sociability as a group. Also in the krater the pure wine has been mixed with water, thus diluting its power and ideally at least promoting moderation and balance, though, as the vomiting recliner shows, this is not always so easy for everyone to achieve.[38] This exquisitely decorated cup thus promotes all the pleasures of drinking wine together even as it warns of the consequences for one who contravenes delicate harmonies.

Let us travel, finally, in our mind's eye this time to Antioch on the Orontes, for a stunning floor mosaic (fig. 8.5) from the early third century CE showing two reclining per couch and further demonstrating the reach and impact of the Hellenistic artistic tradition in this city of the later Eastern empire.[39] During excavations starting in the 1930s, archeologists

---

38. Lissarrague, *Aesthetics of the Greek Banquet*, 19–46.
39. For a review of the mosaics, see Christine Kondoleon, "Mosaics of Antioch," in *Antioch: The Lost Ancient City*, ed. Christine Kondoleon (Princeton: Princeton University Press, 2000), 63–77. She emphasizes the "remarkable continuity with the Hellenistic artistic tradition" (63). For detailed descriptions and published plates of the

uncovered numerous mosaics covering the floors of domestic rooms and triclinia, which patrons had put there at great expense, funding artists who painstakingly placed tiny *tesserae* of limestone, marble, and glass into wet plaster with extraordinary technical aptitude. One mosaic of concern for our purposes comes from the House of the Boat of Psyches, whose partially excavated rooms center on a triclinium that looks out into a colonnaded portico and fountain with five semicircular niches. Guests reclining here would have gazed on the central mosaic, depicting Europa on the bull.[40] The surrounding rooms possibly also functioned to receive visitors, who may have been invited into another room, directly east of the central triclinium and also decorated with mosaic panels in the *T*-shape pattern usual for triclinia. There guests may have rested on couches around the central panel, which shows a picture that is unique in the remains of ancient art and gives this house its name. A winged Eros stands on the back of two Psyches with butterfly wings steering them as they swim through the ocean as though they were his boat. In the panel immediately below this, Lycurgus struggles in the vine's tendrils. As punishment for persecuting Dionysus, this Thracian king goes mad and attempts to kill a maenad, Ambrosia, whom Earth transforms into a vine and thus delivers. On either side of this panel are other Dionysiac figures. A satyr leads a lion by the leash on the left, while on the right, though the image is fragmentary, a satyr likely pursues a bacchante holding a tambourine.[41] This room's decorative program thus inscribes now-familiar banqueting motifs, connecting Dionysus, the vine, and wine with Eros, who steers a boat of Psyches through the wine-dark sea. As both Lissarrague and Christine Kondoleon show, the ocean frequently appears as a metaphor for drinking parties in both literature and art.[42] Dionysus steers, and the drinkers serve as his sailors.

The vine, wine, and love—these motifs persist throughout these rooms' decorative scheme, as we learn upon entering the room to the northeast of the central triclinium next to the narrow vestibule, where our mosaic resides (fig. 8.5). In the central mosaic a woman naked from the waist

---

finds, see Doro Levi, *Antioch Mosaic Pavements*, 2 vols. (Princeton: Princeton University Press, 1947). For the mosaics portraying banquet scenes in particular, see Dunbabin, *Roman Banquet*, 69–70.

40. Levi, *Antioch Mosaic Pavements*, 1:167–70; 2:XXVa–b.

41. Levi, *Antioch Mosaic Pavements*, 1:175–83; 2:XXXVIIa–b, XXXVIIIa–d.

42. Kondoleon, "Mosaics of Antioch," 74; Lissarrague, *Aesthetics of the Greek Banquet*, 107–22.

Fig. 8.5. Opōra, Agros, and Oinos at Dinner, Syria (present-day Turkey), third century, Stone, glass, and lime mortar, 94½ x 124½ x 2½ in (240 x 316.2 x 6.4 cm). The Baltimore Museum of Art: Antioch Subscription Fund, BMA 1937.127. Photograph by Mitro Hood.

reclines in the lap of the man whose torso is also bare. He wraps his arm around her and rests his right hand on her shoulder. They look at each other, and the woman rests her foot on a stool and holds fruit in the folds of her mantle. The wine, moreover, flows abundantly in the cups on the table, while the man holds his cup, and a Silenus, attendant of Dionysus, carrying a thyrsus and dressed in the white garment of the stage costume with buskins on his feet, serves another cup from a large krater filled with red wine.[43] These motifs of wine and intimate love as well as luxury and abundance are clear enough, but the mosaic yields another delightful surprise. Inscriptions identify the figures as characters from mythology. The woman is Ὀπώρα, a goddess of the harvest, especially of the vintage, and

---

43. For interpretations and plates, see Levi, *Antioch Mosaic Pavements*, 1:186–90; 2:XLIIa–b; Kondoleon, "Mosaics of Antioch," 71–74; Dunbabin, *Roman Banquet*, 69–70.

thus a personification of the autumn. In some myths she couples with Trygaeus (from τρύγη, meaning "vintage"), with whom she gives birth to the grape cluster. In this image, however, her partner is identified as Ἀγρός, a personification of the field, who thus functions as a close stand-in for Trygaeus and also can be related to Dionysus, one of whose epithets is Ἄγριος, as the deity who resides over the fields.[44] The Silenus who serves them fittingly bears the name Οἶνος, signaling his function in the picture as the conveyer of wine to the couple from the krater, which itself underlines the vine's power to create sociability and intimate bonding. The inventive mosaicist who designed this perhaps found inspiration, as Kondoleon suggests, from Antioch's own fertile location or from the function of this larger complex of rooms. Though the room is not designed in the *T*-shape of the triclinium, space for a couch appears on the northwest side of the room, and Kondoleon posits that it may have served as a more cozied and private space for dining.[45] Here, then, would-be diners would have reclined while viewing a couple intimately poised in the lap on a couch. Again, this is predicated to themes of abundant food and drink, luxury, tender love, the vintage, and ample wine.

The few examples analyzed here, selected from many others, demonstrate the persistence of this motif picturing couples sharing a couch poised in the lap across spans of time and geography, belonging as it does to the enduring iconographic semiotics of the banquet in the ancient Mediterranean world. As Doro Levi writes as he traces the history of this visual pattern in his commentary on Opōra reclining in the lap of Agros, "We have in this intimate scene a very early motif of Greek art, whose details could be alternated at will, according to the artist's caprice or to the requirements of the representation."[46] Indeed, whether we are drinking from the Attic red-figure *kylix* or reclining in the Bakery of the Chaste Lovers in Pompeii or the House of the Boat of Psyches in Antioch, a couple reclining in the lap during dinner or drinking functions as one communicative item in an iconographic language that regularly weaves together themes of corporeal intimacy and love, sociability and community, luxury, wealth, and bounty, as well as the vine, wine, and intoxication. All of these images, moreover, invite viewers, who are themselves potentially reclining

---

44. For the background of these figures in iconography and myth, see Levi, *Antioch Mosaic Pavements*, 1:187–88.

45. Kondoleon, "Mosaics of Antioch," 71.

46. Levi, *Antioch Mosaic Pavements*, 1:109.

banqueters, to embrace these scenes as ideals or fantasies and also often as humorous, moralistic warnings against the excesses that might tear such banquets awry. In terms of Panofsky's iconological analysis, this art thus brings to view a cultural semiotics of reclining and dining. It remains to analyze how the Beloved Disciple in John 13:23, 25; and 21:20 might have been visualized by those embedded in the cultural dynamics to which these images give visual expression. What thematic linkages surface when this text is read in terms of the banqueting motifs and semantics brought to visualization in this rich iconography?

## 2. The Beloved in the Lap of Jesus: A Visual Exegesis

With such a visual context in view, it is time to take another look at the Gospel according to John, where the disciple "whom Jesus loved" (ὃν ἠγάπα ὁ Ἰησοῦς) reclines "in the lap" (ἐν τῷ κόλπῳ) and "on the chest" (ἐπὶ τὸ στῆθος) during dinner (13:23, 25; 21:20). It is important to clarify up front that it is the demonstrable context of John's text that is in view and not that of the historical Jesus in early first-century Palestine. The exact location of the composition remains unknown, but scholars reasonably posit an urban hellenized center somewhere in the Eastern empire. There are strong arguments for Ephesus, where the earliest testimonies place this text's composition; Antioch, due in part to evocations of Johannine traditions and language in the early second-century writer Ignatius of Antioch; or Alexandria, where this text gained popularity in the second century.[47]

Also relevant is the author's knowledge of the literary symposium. George Parsenios underlines several features present in John 13–17 that typify this genre.[48] Jesus, for example, turns eventually to discuss love and friendship (13:34–35; 15:9–17), thus emphasizing the sociability of the dinner, a theme that is heighted by the contrast with enmity (15:18–16:4). Moreover, the discourses can only get under way after the stock figure of the offended guest, that is, Judas, departs (13:18, 27–30), which allows sociable concourse to blossom. In keeping with the philosophical symposia, this is also a feast of words, as Jesus and his disciples hold discussions that stretch over the course of several chapters. While this is not enough

---

47. For a recent review of the scholarship, see Kobel, *Dining with John*, 18–20.
48. Paresenios, *Departure and Consolation*, 111–50.

to constitute a literary symposium proper, Parsenios argues, the "loose but discernable connections" with this genre are abundant.[49]

Parsenios does not discuss lap holding and couch sharing in this regard, but it should be taken to be among the other sympotic motifs he highlights. In his analysis of this genre Josef Martin includes among the *stehende Figuren* of these texts the *Liebespaar*, which is a role that Jesus and the disciple "whom Jesus loved" (ὃν ἠγάπα ὁ Ἰησοῦς) clearly assume (13:23).[50] When it features the *Liebespaar* reclining in the lap, moreover, the iconography examined here portrays their love to be erotic or romantic. To be sure, the physical closeness of the pairs who are portrayed varies. The eroticism ranges from overt to subtle. For example, Opōra very modestly reclines in the lap of Agros, and his torso does not touch her back. Still, both are naked from the waist. Agros wraps his arm around her and cups her bare shoulder with his right hand. The two share a loving glance. Romantic love thus lurks in this image, especially when it is read in light of the broader iconographic program of the complex of rooms of which it is a part. But it is subtle, especially when compared with the middle couple on the red-figure *kylix*. The woman reclining in the lap turns to look at her partner. With torsos bare and legs enwrapped under a cover, they tightly envelop each other and hungrily stare into each other's eyes. This more overtly erotic love also colors the woman, for example, who leans back to kiss her partner on the north wall of the House of the Chaste Lovers, where all the paintings feature couples in various degrees of intimacy and undress. Reclining in the lap facilitates physical closeness and sets the couch-sharing pair up for whatever degree of coziness or coquettish conduct they happen to prefer. Jesus and the beloved in John thus assume a posture at the very least conducive to physical expressions of romantic love, but how far romantic love can be taken to go in their case and how subtle or overt it may be remain open to question.

The romantic lap-holding pairs in the art of the reclining banquet nonetheless warrant precisely this kind of inquiry. What kind of love is this between Jesus and the beloved? That a closer, more physical intimacy between Jesus and the beloved is in view becomes clear as the story unfolds. Peter gestures to the beloved provoking him to ask Jesus about the identity of the betrayer Jesus has foretold in 13:21. This suggests that Peter

---

49. Parsenios, *Departure and Consolation*, 113.

50. Josef Martin, *Symposion: Die Geschichte einer literarischen Form* (Paderborn: Ferdinand Schöningh, 1931), 33–115.

perceives the beloved to be enmeshed with Jesus at least to the degree that he is positioned to demand Jesus's attention in a way that Peter cannot. In 13:25 the beloved "leans back" (ἀναπεσών) even closer "on the chest" of Jesus, bringing his torso and head still more intimately into proximity with Jesus's own. Evidently, they are close enough now on the couch for Jesus to whisper the identity of the betrayer into the beloved's ear (13:26). As the scene unfolds, none of the disciples seem to have heard Jesus's rather clear answer or to have understood the symbolic act revealing the betrayer's identity in 13:26. They cannot comprehend what Jesus asks Judas to do or why Judas leaves the dinner in 13:27–30. Lap holding thus appears here to be elastic and dynamic. Poised in the lap in intimate contact, the beloved leans still closer into Jesus, draws more cozily into his torso, and bends his head warmly toward Jesus's own as the scene progresses. But in place of a kiss, like the kiss the beloved in the lap gives to her lover in the House of the Chaste Lovers, he whispers a question and quietly receives an answer.

All the couples thus far examined picture women reclining in the laps of men. But the beloved in the lap of Jesus more closely matches the male pairs who likewise thus recline in this iconography. Earlier examples abound in Attic red-figure vase painting, which provided the prototypes for one remarkable depiction of several reclining male pairs painted in fresco on the walls of the Tomb of the Diver circa 470 BCE in Paestum, a Greek colony in southern Italy.[51] So called from the unique image of

---

51. For recent documentation of the tomb with color plates, see R. Ross Holloway, "The Tomb of the Diver," *AJA* 110 (2006): 365–88. He catalogues prototypes for each of the tomb's figures in Attic vase painting (376–81). The first to publish the tomb was Mario Napoli, *La tomba del tuffatore* (Bari: De Donato, 1970). Recently, see Bernard Andreae, "Das Grab des Turmspringers," in *Malerei für die Ewigkeit: Die Gräber von Paestum*, ed. Ortrud Westheider and Michael Philipp (Hamburg: Hirmer Verlag, 2007), 24–27; Walter Duvall Penrose Jr., "Before Queerness? Visions of a Homoerotic Heaven in Ancient Greco-Italic Tomb Paintings," in *Sex in Antiquity: Exploring Gender and Sexuality in the Ancient World*, ed. Mark Masterson, Nancy Sorkin Rabinowitz, and James Robson (London: Routledge, 2015), 137–56; Angela Pontrandolfo, Agnès Rouveret, and Marina Cipriani, *La tomba del tuffatore e le altre tombe dipinte di Paestum* (Paestum: Pandemos, 2015), 27–36, with large, high-resolution color reproductions; also Dentzer, *Motif du banquet couché*, 245–48. For treatments of earlier examples abounding in Attic red-figure vase painting and related evidence, see Kenneth Dover, *Greek Homosexuality*, 2nd ed. (Cambridge: Harvard University Press, 1989), 86, 94, R200, R283; Martin F. Kilmer, *Greek Erotica* (London: Duckworth, 1993), 11–26, 67–72, 103–7, 177–78, 182, R223, R283, R495; also Andrew Lear and

Fig. 8.6. Fresco on the north wall of the Tomb of the Diver. Ancient Greek, ca. 480–470 BCE, 195.5 x 79.5 cm. Museo Archeologico Nazionale, Paestum, Italy. Photo: © Vanni Archive/ Art Resource, NY.

the diver on the inside of its lid, this oldest known example of Greek wall painting shows a symposium. On the long northern (fig. 8.6) and southern (fig. 8.7) walls ten males recline, four of whom are bearded men, in whose laps lie four beardless youths. Erotic overtones prevail especially for the couple on the right on the northern wall. The man slips his arm around the youth in his lap and grabs the youth's head with his right hand. But the youth, who holds a lyre, rejects his advance and gestures for him to go no further. The youth of the middle couple on the north wall holds his *kylix* for a throw of *kottabos*. This drinking game consists of flinging the lees of wine at a target, while the player devotes his throw to his lover.[52] The two sharing the middle couch on the southern wall look intently into each other's eyes, while the youth lying on the couch on the right on the southern wall plays the flute as his partner sings along. The tomb thus portrays a symposium with strong undercurrents of male erotic love in various forms and stages of intimacy. This imagery, moreover, coheres with the art examined above insofar as here too erotic love links up with the consumption of wine, for the krater appears on the east wall, with a small servant alongside, thus symbolizing the banqueters' drinking and comradery.

This tomb's walls, therefore, highlight by way of one example how lap holding between male couples belongs squarely within the iconography of the reclining banquet. The presence of these paintings on the walls of a tomb and the resulting association between the reclining symposium and death show the influence of the Etruscans, who also decorated their tombs

---

Eva Cantarella, *Images of Ancient Greek Pederasty: Boys Were Their Gods* (Routledge: London, 2008), 57–59, 159–61, 178–79.

52. Lissarrague, *Aesthetics of the Greek Banquet*, 80–86.

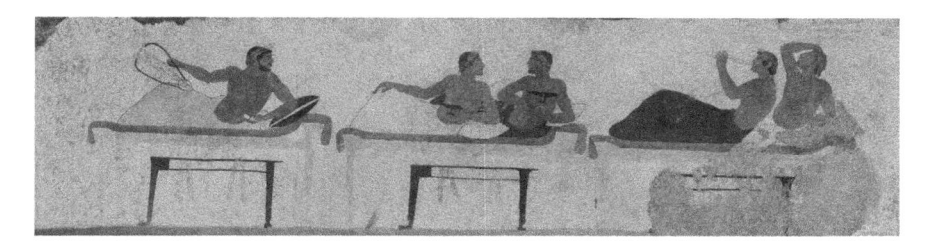

Fig. 8.7. Fresco on the south wall of the Tomb of the Diver. Ancient Greek, ca. 480–470 BCE, 193 x 79.2 cm. Museo Archeologico Nazionale, Paestum, Italy. Photo: © Vanni Archive/ Art Resource, NY.

with banqueting scenes depicting men reclining with women in the lap.[53] But the Diver paintings, with their depiction of youths reclining in the laps of smitten men, dramatize Greek pederasty and what Walter Duvall Penrose Jr. calls the Greek "homonormative paradigm."[54] Indeed, the symposium provided one of the primary locales for men to court the youths they desired, and one can see in this art how reclining in the lap opens the door for caresses, hugs, flirtation, or sexual advance.[55]

To be sure, this tomb and the Attic red-figure vases on which the artists modeled its male couples date rather early from the fifth century BCE and are far removed from the reception of John's Gospel in the eastern Roman empire at the end of the first or beginning of the second century CE. Nonetheless, these couples help to visualize a form of male intimacy that endured into later antiquity. The literature of the later empire amply attests to the persistence of male love and romance, as many scholars have documented and analyzed.[56] Male couples reclining specifically "in the

---

53. For the Etruscan paintings, see Dunbabin, *Roman Banquet*, 25–34. On the relationship between the Diver paintings and Etruscan art, see Holloway, "Tomb of the Diver," 373–76; Penrose, "Before Queerness," 142–47; also Angela Pontrandolfo, "Wall-Painting in Magna Graecia," in *The Western Greeks: Classical Civilization in Western Mediterranean*, ed. Giovanni Pugliese Carratelli (London: Thames & Hudson, 1996), 458–59. The eschatology of the paintings, which I cannot address in this context, has been described as Pythagorean, Orphic, Hesiodic, and Etruscan. For these options and good bibliographies, see Holloway, "Tomb of the Diver," 373–85; Penrose, "Before Queerness," 143–48; Pontrandolfo, "Wall-Painting in Magna Graecia," 459.

54. Penrose, "Before Queerness," 139, 149.

55. Dover, *Greek Homosexuality*, 94.

56. Amy Richlin, *The Garden of Priapus: Sexuality and Aggression in Roman Humor* (Oxford: Oxford University Press, 1983); Amy Richlin, *Marcus Aurelius in Love* (Chicago: University of Chicago Press, 2006); also Craig A. Williams, *Roman*

lap" (ἐν τῷ κόλπῳ) and "on the chest" (ἐπὶ τὸ στῆθος) during dinner in a few cases appear in the later antique literature of dining and reclining. In every example that I have found, this more intimate in-the-lap posture, which appears more rarely than friendly or familial couch sharing more generally, characterizes pairs who are unambiguously portrayed as lovers.[57] Male lap holding during dinner thus comes directly into the cultural world of the reception of the Johannine text at least in this literature. That Jesus and the beloved may have been visualized on the model of the lap-holding lovers who appear in the iconography examined above thus remains suggestive, even if further research into the imagery of male lap-holding pairs in later antiquity will be required to establish this with greater certainty.

As one reads on in the Johannine text, the beloved's other appearances underline that his relationship with Jesus is one that is set apart from Jesus's relationships with other disciples. It is also this disciple to whom Jesus entrusts his mother's care before dying on the cross in 19:25–27. If he is the "other disciple" in 18:15, he is the only one initially to enter with Jesus into the courtyard of the high priest to witness his teacher's trial. Outrunning Peter, he is also the first to see the empty tomb in 20:3–5 and first recognizes Jesus after the large catch of fish in 21:7. It is also plausible that the beloved is to be identified with the unnamed disciple who stays

---

*Homosexuality*, 2nd ed. (Oxford: Oxford University Press, 2010); Thomas K. Hubbard, ed., *Homosexuality in Greece and Rome: A Sourcebook of Basic Documents* (Berkeley: University of California Press, 2003), 383–532.

57. See Jeff Jay, "In the Lap of Jesus: The Hermeneutics of Sex and Eros in John's Portrayal of the Beloved Disciple," *JHistSex* 28 (2019): 483–513; Dio Cassius, *Hist. rom.* 79.16.5; Juvenal, *Sat.* 2.117–120; Aulus Gellius, *Noct. att.* 6.12.14–15; Cicero, *Cat.* 2.22–24; Greek Anthology 5.17, 25, 107, 116, 136, 165, 173, 275; 12.34; Plutarch, *Amat.* 751A. See Encolpius, who is the pederastic antihero of the vulgarly sexed mock-epic *Satyricon* by Petronius; also Encolpus, who is the slave of his master the pederast Aulus Pudens (Martial, *Epigr.* 1.31; 5.48). For an earlier but now-outdated account also suggestive of pederasty, see Sjef van Tilborg, *Imaginative Love in John* (Leiden: Brill, 1993), 59–110. It is not insignificant that the largest body of examples comes from the Greek erotic epigrams collected in the Greek Anthology, many of which were circulating as part of collections in the first century CE. For details about the date and the complex history of compilation that lies behind the Greek Anthology, see Peter Bing and Jon Steffen Bruss, "Introduction," in *Brill's Companion to Hellenistic Epigram*, ed. Peter Bing and Jon Steffen Bruss (Leiden: Brill, 2017), 20–26; Alan Cameron, *The Greek Anthology: From Meleager to Planudes* (Oxford: Clarendon, 1993); also W. R. Paton, trans., *The Greek Anthology, Books 1–5*, rev. Michael A. Tueller (Cambridge: Harvard University Press, 2014), xvi–xx.

with Jesus in 1:38–39, where his anonymity, which contrasts with all of the other named disciples in 1:35–51, is consistent with his anonymity throughout the gospel. This would imply that he has spent a long time with Jesus, and this, together with his presence at the trial, crucifixion, empty tomb, and resurrection appearance, uniquely positions him to serve as the authority behind this gospel; as 21:24 makes clear, it is the beloved who is credited for writing the text. This privileging of the beloved as one well-positioned to convey the teacher's way of life to subsequent epochs also coheres with male love as it functions in philosophical schools, where numerous teacher-student lovers appear. The lover passes on his teaching and way of life to a beloved, who is singularly equipped for this task from the life the two lovingly share.[58]

As in almost all of the examples above, where beloveds are seen to be held in the lap of lovers, there is a dimension of eros inflecting John's statement that the disciple in the lap is "the one whom Jesus loved" (ὃν ἠγάπα ὁ Ἰησοῦς; 13:23). The use of the verb ἀγαπᾶν here is consistent with the terminology for love throughout the gospel, where the term ἔρως or cognates never appear. John also employs the verb φιλεῖν without any discernible difference between ἀγαπᾶν and φιλεῖν, which alternate throughout the text (5:20; 11:3, 11; 15:13–15; 16:27; 21:15–21). The use of ἀγαπᾶν cannot predetermine that eros should be excluded. Robert Joly has refuted the argument that Christian writers chose ἀγαπᾶν and cognates in order to remove erotic feeling from what they took to be authentic, that is, nonerotic, Christian love. Joly successfully demonstrates these terms' context-dependent meanings.[59] The precise inflection of the love that

---

58. See, e.g., Richlin, who argues that it is evident from the correspondence between Marcus and his teacher Fronto that their relationship is best described as comprising mutual romantic devotion (*Marcus Aurelius in Love*). For teacher-student couples in the philosophical schools, see Diogenes Laertius, *Vit. phil.* 2.19, 23, 49; 3.29–30, 31; 4.19, 21, 22, 29, 41; 5.3, 39; 7.17; 8.86. Also see Persius, who writes lovingly of his teacher Cornutus, to whom the poet recalls entrusting himself as into the "Socratic lap" (*Socraticus sinus*), and emphasizes their intimacy, long days together, and the evenings they spent in leisure (*Sat.* 5).

59. Robert Joly, *Le vocabulaire chrétien de l'amour est-il original? Philein et agapan dans le grec antique* (Brussels: Presses universitaires de Bruxelles, 1968). Joly successfully dismantles the earlier and now-outdated view of Ceslaus Spicq that the Christian usage of ἀγαπᾶν necessarily precludes irrational eros. Spicq's four volumes on love in the New Testament otherwise still have extraordinary value. See Spicq, *Agapè dans le Nouveau Testament*, 3 vols. (Paris: Librairie Lecoffre, 1958); Spicq, *Agapè: prolé-*

ἀγαπᾶν expresses should be determined through contextual exegesis. In this regard, Greek authors readily employ ἀγαπᾶν in contexts where eros predominates.[60] One telling example for the present argument appears in the second-century writer Lucian of Samosata. Hera complains to Zeus that he has again found another Danae and, tormented "by love" (ὑπὸ τοῦ ἔρωτος), will assuredly turn into a shower of gold and fall "into the lap of the beloved" (εἰς τὸν κόλπον τῆς ἀγαπωμένης; *Jupp. trag.* 2).[61] When the author of John describes this disciple reclining in the lap during dinner as "the one whom Jesus loved" (ὃν ἠγάπα ὁ Ἰησοῦς), this would be a legitimate way to say "loved erotically" and can be taken to express romantic devotion in light of both the other textual clues in the Johannine text and the visual evidence of lap holding in the art of the reclining banquet.

This would mean that Jesus longs for and desires this disciple; the two forge a life together with a love that outstrips the love Jesus has for his other disciples.[62] This love, moreover, is expressed corporally in the very act of lap holding, which is a form of physical expression. This does not necessarily entail sexual contact, but then again nothing in the text of John rules it out, even as it is not explicitly portrayed. Their relationship might be

*gomènes à une étude de théologie néo-testamentaire* (Leuven: Nauwelaerts, 1955). Also influential especially in theology has been Anders Nygren, *Agape and Eros*, trans. Philip S. Watson (Chicago: University of Chicago Press, 1982). Spicq and Nygren still unduly shape what too often seems to be the default framework for interpreting ἀγαπᾶν in the New Testament. For a more properly nuanced approach, see Paul Victor Furnish, *The Love Command in the New Testament* (Nashville: Abingdon, 1972), 219–31; see also Oda Wischmeyer, *Liebe als Agape: Das frühchristliche Konzept und der moderne Diskurs* (Tübingen: Mohr Siebeck, 2015), esp. 58–72; also John Boswell, *Same-Sex Unions in Premodern Europe* (New York: Vintage, 1994), 3–10. Bowell has rightly discerned this.

60. Boswell collects an impressive number of examples demonstrating, in his words, the "relative fungibility of the terms" (*Same-Sex Unions*, 6 n. 4). For additional examples, see Sappho frag. 132; Plato, *Symp.* 180b; [Demosthenes], *Erot.* 6, 30 (Dover, *Greek Homosexuality*, 50); Greek Anthology 5.51; Plutarch, *Amat.* 765D; 766A; Pseudo-Lucian, *Erōtes* 54; and Eunapius, *Vit. soph.* 502–503.

61. See Lucian, *Tim.* 41, for a similar reference to the κόλποι of a virgin ready to receive her lover like Danae Zeus. Also see Lucian, *Dial. mar.* 319. There Danae receives Zeus as golden rain ἐς τὸν κόλπον and as a result becomes pregnant.

62. This author is perfectly capable of expressing reclining at dinner with friends without implying romance. In John 12:2 Lazarus, whom Jesus is also said to love in 11:3, reclines during dinner, but only "with" Jesus, not in his lap, which is the more intimate position reserved for the Beloved Disciple.

described as "affectionate" or "intimate" male love, or, to use the words of Amy Richlin as she characterizes the relationship between Marcus Aurelius and his teacher Fronto, it is a "sentimental friendship" that comprises "romantic mutual devotion but not necessarily" sexual consummation. For Richlin, this is sufficient for calling Marcus and Fronto "lovers," which in this precise sense at least might also be a viable way to characterize the relationship between Jesus and his beloved.[63]

In this iconography, reclining two per couch with the beloved in the lap appears also in conjunction with drinking, intoxication, wine, and the vine, which ideally promote harmony among the drinkers, who sociably partake from a common krater. The romantic love of particular lap-holding couples is one part of a broader sociability and companionship among all the parties and individuals in attendance. Dining and drinking together induce a friendly atmosphere. A new coherence can thus be seen to emerge between the reclining couple in John 13:23–25 and 21:20 and the value placed on the vine and communal love for one another in 15:1–17, which constitutes a literary subunit in the Farewell Discourse. In 15:1 Jesus declares himself to be the vine, and this metaphor remains in view throughout this unit. "The branch that bears fruit" in 15:2 mirrors 15:16, where the disciples are to bear fruit, thus providing an *inclusio* for the unit as a whole. Furthermore, what links the vine imagery with communal love is the emphasis placed throughout on abiding, expressed by the term μένειν in 15:4, 5, 7, 9, 10, and 16. If the disciples are to abide in Jesus's love (15:9), just as they are to abide in Jesus as the vine (15:4–5), then they must keep his command (15:10), which, he specifies in 15:12, consists of "loving one another," thus reiterating the instruction to love that he gave at the beginning of the Farewell Discourse in 13:34. The loving harmony of the disciples remains at issue also toward the end of the discourse, when Jesus prays that "they be one" (17:11, 21, 23).

Moreover, the image of the vine in 15:1–7 strongly evokes the role that wine consumption plays at the Eucharist. John nowhere relates the Eucharist narrative known from Paul (1 Cor 11:21–26) and the Synoptics (Mark 14:22–25). But the "vine" elicits the eucharistic cup in early Christian tradition: after distributing the wine in Mark's account, Jesus says he will no longer drink "from the fruit of the vine" (ἐκ τοῦ γενήματος τῆς ἀμπέλου); also, in Did. 9.2, as part of the words of institution thanks is given ὑπὲρ

---

63. Richlin, *Marcus Aurelius in Love*, 6.

ἀμπέλου Δαυίδ ("for the vine of David"), which is identified as Jesus. The death of Jesus, furthermore, looms over all accounts of the Eucharist and is in view here too, not only in the Farewell Discourses' placement before the passion but also explicitly in John 15:13, where Jesus cites the noblest act of love to be self-sacrifice for friends. Finally, the emphasis in the metaphor on abiding evokes a eucharistic theology that underlines the intimacy of union with Jesus (e.g., 1 Cor 10:16) and echoes the language of the expressly eucharistic statement in John 6:56, where the key term μένειν is used for one who "abides" in Jesus by drinking his blood.[64] The vine and the drinking of wine likewise coalesce with themes of communal love and friendly harmony in the iconography, which thus provides a visual parallel to the way these motifs interweave textually in 15:1–17. As in the iconography, where banqueters recline in the lap, the fruits of the vine and communal love closely and ideally follow.

The art portraying reclining banqueters, finally, always accentuates first-class luxuries and upscale amenities. Reclining to dine with servants in attendance signals prestige, privilege, and power. The examples examined above foster various attitudes toward the elite diners depicted. In a wealthy domicile such as the House of the Boat of Psyches in Antioch, the lavish setting that befits the mythic pair Opōra and Agros serves as an ideal to which one aspires and which even stands within the affluent householder's reach. In contrast, the nonelite viewers renting the bakehouse triclinium of the Chaste Lovers may have viewed the paintings there with bemused irony. Wine, love, and community flourish at these opulent banquets, to be sure, but they drolly dramatize the distasteful effects of surfeit with sauced drinkers out cold and paid entertainers boozing it rather than performing. Indeed, these paintings can grow a bit moralistic. Even the red-figure *kylix*, whose imagery invites the one who drains this cup to mimic the drinking, erotic love, and communal festivity it portrays, at the same time pictures the vomiting recliner as a warning against excess.

When interpreted alongside the more ironic and distancing versions of this iconography, it is possible to see how the portrayal in John 13:1–17 similarly upends the normal prestige ascribed to reclining. Jesus overturns convention when he rises, sets aside his clothes, and ties a towel around his waist in order to wash the disciples' feet. This is a shockingly humble

---

64. For these arguments, see Raymond E. Brown, *The Gospel according to John*, AB 19 (New York: Doubleday, 1970), 2:659–84.

task for a reclining banqueter to perform. Jesus most closely resembles the several servants who appear in the iconography, some small in stature, always ready to serve the elite recliners beside the krater with ladles, strainers, and wine-pouring vessels. Peter accordingly resists this gesture, but Jesus replies in 13:7 that this act means something other than what Peter understands it to mean, "What I do you do not understand now, but you will know after these things." To be sure, in 13:12, now that the washing is finished (i.e., "after these things"), Jesus, who is again reclining, gives the disciples to "know" the significance of this event, which serves as an ethical paradigm. They are to mimic the teacher and Lord by washing each other's feet as servants of one another (13:14–16).

However, the ethical interpretation does not exhaust the meaning of the foot washing. The retrospective understanding implied by "after these things" in 13:7 usually occurs after the resurrection in John (see 2:22; 12:16; 14:26). Hence, the true meaning of this action emerges after the passion and resurrection and may be taken at that time to symbolize the death of Jesus. The death is already in view in 13:1, where Jesus is said to love "to the end." In 13:3–4 there is a causal connection between Jesus's foreknowledge that "he is going to God" and his rising to perform this act of humility. Finally, the use of the verb τιθέναι in 13:4 for taking off clothes is not typical but appears in John several times for Jesus's giving of his life (see 10:11, 15, 17–18; 15:13). Similarly, λαμβάνειν does not usually express the putting on of clothes, as it does in 13:12; however, in John this term expresses Jesus's taking his life back up again (10:17–18). This would mean that this sequence, wherein Jesus disrobes to wash feet then reclothes, symbolizes and foreshadows his death and resurrection. This, furthermore, coheres with the baptismal language in 13:8–11, insofar as New Testament writers hold baptism and death to be closely related (e.g., Mark 10:38–39; Rom 6:1–11).[65]

Even if the foot washing is read simply as an example of humility, it does not lose its reference to death. John 15:12–15, for example, correlates with the command for service in 13:14–16. Service here might require sacrificial death, as it will for Jesus and possibly for his followers. All of this is, moreover, a commentary on what it means for Jesus to "love to the end" in 13:1, that is, he washed the disciples' feet as a humble servant and model for his followers, and he died sacrificially, which is itself a model for the

---

[65]. For these arguments, see Brown, *Gospel according to John*, 2:545–72.

kind of love with which disciples should love one another. The visual imagery examined here sometimes encourages viewers to ponder the ironies of upended banquets. It is possible for this to transfer into an interpretation of how this text, with these themes of death, humble servitude, and sacrificial love, likewise capsizes and dissociates itself from the opulence, luxury, and prestige normally characterizing reclining banquets.[66]

## 3. Conclusion

The art of the reclining banquet, so far-reaching over geography and time across ancient Mediterranean cultures, in many cases forefronts a couple intimately reclining on a single couch with one in the lap of another. Reclining in the lap is a motif that appears as one communicative item in the broader iconographic language of the banquet, which weaves together the recurring themes of erotic love, luxury and opulence, the vine, the consumption of wine, and ideals of sociability and community. At the level of iconology, this artistic program gives visual expression to deep-rooted cultural patterns and sensibilities underlying and shaping the practice of and attitudes toward dining and reclining. This artistic program and/or the cultural dynamics that come to visualization may have affected the visual imagination as it shaped the reception of the Gospel according to John. The words of John 13:23, 25; and 21:20 suggestively come to be seen for the ways they cohere with other banqueting tropes. The beloved reclining in the lap and on the chest of Jesus suggests romantic intimacy. As the text of John unfolds, this intimate lap holding is predicated to a broader relationship between Jesus and the beloved, who emerges as one well-poised to transfer to future generations his intimate knowledge of his lover's life and teaching. Lap holding and erotic love, moreover, appear in light of this art to be coherent with other themes that emerge in the course of the farewell dinner and discourses. Here, too, reclining in the lap is connected with the vine, the consumption of wine, and communal love, which belong

---

66. The way this text interweaves love, death, and the reclining banquet warrants further research, especially in comparison with the sculpted images of reclining and in some cases couch-sharing diners that appear with some regularity on marble ash-urns, grave altars, *loculus* covers, and *kline* monuments. For treatments of this evidence in relation to dining practice and reclining posture, see Dunbabin, *Roman Banquet*, 103–40; also Roller, *Dining Posture*, 22–45, 123–39. For its relevance to John, see Parsenios, *Departure and Consolation*, 134–41.

together as sympotic themes in John 15:1–17. Here, too, the normal prestige and luxury of reclining banqueters is upended, with John's emphasis on sacrificial death and humble servitude. John 13–17 thus finds deep coherence as a literary composition in light of the semiotics of reclining and dining in the Greco-Roman world. Above all, this exercise in visual exegesis, as probative as it remains, dramatizes the fruitful intersection between image and text, insofar as the latter can be read and seen anew in the effort to reinvest the central role word-provoked mental imaging plays in reception, interpretation, and understanding.

## Works Cited

Andreae, Bernard. "Das Grab des Turmspringers." Pages 24–27 in *Malerei für die Ewigkeit: Die Gräber von Paestum*. Edited by Ortrud Westheider and Michael Philipp. Hamburg: Hirmer, 2007.

Balch, David L. *Roman Domestic Art and Early House Churches*. WUNT 228. Tübingen: Mohr Siebeck, 2008.

———. "Women Prophets/Maenads Visually Represented in Two Roman Colonies: Pompeii and Corinth." Pages 236–59 in *The Interface of Orality and Writing: Speaking, Seeing, Writing in the Shaping of New Genres*. Edited by Annette Weissenrieder and Robert B. Coote. BPCS. Eugene, OR: Cascade, 2015.

Beard, Mary. *The Fires of Vesuvius: Pompeii Lost and Found*. Cambridge: Harvard University Press, 2008.

Beazley, John D. *Attic Red-Figure Vase-Painters*. 2nd ed. Oxford: Clarendon, 1963.

Berry, Joanne. *The Complete Pompeii*. London: Thames & Hudson, 2007.

Bing, Peter, and Jon Steffen Bruss. Introduction to *Brill's Companion to Hellenistic Epigram*. Edited by Peter Bing and Jon Steffen Bruss. Leiden: Brill, 2017.

Bloomquist, L. Gregory. "Eyes Wide Open, Seeing Nothing: The Challenge of the Gospel of John's Nonvisualizable Texture for Readings Using Visual Texture." Pages 121–67 in *The Art of Visual Exegesis: Rhetoric, Texts, Images*. Edited by Vernon K. Robbins, Walter S. Melion, and Roy R. Jeal. ESEC 19. Atlanta: SBL Press, 2017.

———. "Methodology Underlying the Presentation of Visual Texture in the Gospel of John." Pages 89–120 in *The Art of Visual Exegesis: Rheto-*

*ric, Texts, Images*. Edited by Vernon K. Robbins, Walter S. Melion, and Roy R. Jeal. ESEC 19. Atlanta: SBL Press, 2017.

Boswell, John. *Same-Sex Unions in Premodern Europe*. New York: Vintage, 1994.

Brown, Raymond E. *The Gospel according to John*. 2 vols. AB 19. New York: Doubleday, 1970.

Cameron, Alan. *The Greek Anthology: From Meleager to Planudes*. Oxford: Clarendon, 1993.

Carpenter, Thomas H., Thomas Mannack, and Melanie Mendonça. *Beazley Addenda*. 2nd ed. Oxford: Oxford University Press, 1989.

Clarke, John R. *Art in the Lives of Ordinary Romans: Visual Representation and Non-elite Viewers in Italy, 100 B.C.–A.D. 315*. Berkeley: University of California Press, 2003.

———. *The Houses of Roman Italy. 100 B.C.–A.D. 50: Ritual Space and Decoration*. Berkeley: University of California Press, 1991.

Dentzer, Jean-Marie. *Le motif du banquet couché dans le proche-orient et le monde grec du VIIe au IVe siècle avant J.-C.* BEFAR. Rome: Palais Farnese, 1982.

Dover, Kenneth. *Greek Homosexuality*. 2nd ed. Cambridge: Harvard University Press, 1989.

Dunbabin, Katherine M. D. *The Roman Banquet: Images of Conviviality*. Cambridge: Cambridge University Press, 2003.

Elsen-Novák, Gabriele, and Mirko Novák. "'Ich bin der wahre Weinstock und mein Vater ist der Weingärtner': Zur Semiotik des Weinstocks in Joh 15, 1–8 aus Sicht der Altorientalistik." Pages 183–206 in *Picturing the New Testament: Studies in Ancient Visual Images*. WUNT 2/193. Edited by Annette Weissenrieder, Friederike Wendt, and Petra von Gemünden. Tübingen: Mohr Siebeck, 2005.

Furnish, Paul Victor. *The Love Command in the New Testament*. Nashville: Abingdon, 1972.

Gemünden, Petra von. "Die Palmzweige in der johanneischen Einzugsgeschichte (Joh 12, 13): Ein Hinweis auf eine symbolische Uminterpretation im Johannesevangelium?" Pages 207–22 in *Picturing the New Testament: Studies in Ancient Visual Images*. WUNT 2/193. Edited by Annette Weissenrieder, Friederike Wendt, and Petra von Gemünden. Tübingen: Mohr Siebeck, 2005.

———. "Weisheitliche Bilderkonstellationen im Johannesevangelium? Einige strukturell Überlegungen." Pages 159–82 in *Picturing the New Testament: Studies in Ancient Visual Images*. WUNT 2/193. Edited by

Annette Weissenrieder, Friederike Wendt, and Petra von Gemünden. Tübingen: Mohr Siebeck, 2005.

Genovese, Angelo, and Tiziana Cocca. "Internal Organization of an Equine Stable at Pompeii." *Anth* 31 (2000): 119–23.

Holloway, R. Ross. "The Tomb of the Diver." *AJA* 110 (2006): 365–88.

Hubbard, Thomas K., ed. *Homosexuality in Greece and Rome: A Sourcebook of Basic Documents*. Berkeley: University of California Press, 2003.

Jay, Jeff. "In the Lap of Jesus: The Hermeneutics of Sex and Eros in John's Portrayal of the Beloved Disciple." *JHistSex* 28.3 (2019): 483–513.

Jeal, Roy R. "Visual Interpretation: Blending Rhetorical Arts in Colossians 2:6–3:4." Pages 55–88 in *The Art of Visual Exegesis: Rhetoric, Texts, Images*. Edited by Vernon K. Robbins, Walter S. Melion, and Roy R. Jeal. ESEC 19. Atlanta: SBL Press, 2017.

Joly, Robert. *Le vocabulaire chrétien de l'amour est-il original? Philein et agapan dans le grec Antique*. Brussels: Presses universitaires de Bruxelles, 1968.

Kahl, Brigitte. "The Galatian Suicide and the Transbinary Semiotics of Christ Crucified (Galatians 3:1): Exercises in Visual Exegesis and Critical Reimagination." Pages 195–240 in *The Art of Visual Exegesis: Rhetoric, Texts, Images*. Edited by Vernon K. Robbins, Walter S. Melion, and Roy R. Jeal. ESEC 19. Atlanta: SBL Press, 2017.

———. *Galatians Re-imagined: Reading with the Eyes of the Vanquished*. PCC. Minneapolis: Fortress, 2010.

Kilmer, Martin F. *Greek Erotica*. London: Duckworth, 1993.

Kobel, Esther. *Dining with John: Communal Meals and Identity Formation in the Fourth Gospel and Its Historical and Cultural Context*. BibInt 109. Leiden: Brill, 2011.

Kondoleon, Christine. "Mosaics of Antioch." Pages 63–77 in *Antioch: The Lost Ancient City*. Edited by Christine Kondoleon. Princeton: Princeton University Press, 2000.

Lear, Andrew, and Eva Cantarella. *Images of Ancient Greek Pederasty: Boys Were Their Gods*. London: Routledge, 2008.

Levi, Doro. *Antioch Mosaic Pavements*. 2 vols. Princeton: Princeton University Press, 1947.

Lissarrague, François. *The Aesthetics of the Greek Banquet*. Translated by Andrew Szegedy-Maszak. Princeton: Princeton University Press, 1990.

Maier, Harry O. "Paul, Imperial Situation, and Visualization in the Epistle to the Colossians." Pages 171–94 in *The Art of Visual Exegesis: Rhetoric, Texts, Images*. Edited by Vernon K. Robbins, Walter S. Melion, and Roy R. Jeal. ESEC 19. Atlanta: SBL Press, 2017.

———. *Picturing Paul in Empire: Imperial Image, Text, and Persuasion in Colossians, Ephesians and the Pastoral Epistles*. London: Bloomsbury T&T Clark, 2013.

Martin, Josef. *Symposion: Die Geschichte einer literarischen Form*. Paderborn: Ferdinand Schöningh, 1931.

Mertens, Joan R. *How to Read Greek Vases*. New Haven: Yale University Press, 2010.

Napoli, Mario. *La tomba del tuffatore*. Bari: De Donato, 1970.

Nygren, Anders. *Agape and Eros*. Translated by Philip S. Watson. Chicago: University of Chicago Press, 1982.

Panofsky, Erwin. "Iconography and Iconology: An Introduction to the Study of Renaissance Art." Pages 26–41 in *Meaning in the Visual Arts*. Chicago: University of Chicago Press, 1955.

Parsenios, George L. *Departure and Consolation: The Johannine Farewell Discourses in Light of Greco-Roman Literature*. NovTSup 117. Leiden: Brill, 2005.

Paton, William R., trans. *The Greek Anthology, Books 1–5*. Revised by Michael A. Tueller. Cambridge: Harvard University Press, 2014.

Penrose, Walter Duvall, Jr. "Before Queerness? Visions of a Homoerotic Heaven in Ancient Greco-Italic Tomb Paintings." Pages 137–56 in *Sex in Antiquity: Exploring Gender and Sexuality in the Ancient World*. Edited by Mark Masterson, Nancy Sorkin Rabinowitz, and James Robson. London: Routledge, 2015.

Pontrandolfo, Angela. "Wall-Painting in Magna Graecia." Pages 457–70 in *The Western Greeks: Classical Civilization in Western Mediterranean*. Edited by Giovanni Pugliese Carratelli. London: Thames & Hudson, 1996.

Pontrandolfo, Angela, Agnès Rouveret, and Marina Cipriani. *La tomba del tuffatore e le altre tombe dipinte di Paestum*. Paestum: Pandemos, 2015.

Richlin, Amy. *The Garden of Priapus: Sexuality and Aggression in Roman Humor*. Oxford: Oxford University Press, 1983.

———. *Marcus Aurelius in Love*. Chicago: University of Chicago Press, 2006.

Robbins, Vernon K. "New Testament Texts, Visual Material Culture, and Earliest Christian Art." Pages 13–54 in *The Art of Visual Exegesis: Rhet-*

*oric, Texts, Images.* Edited by Vernon K. Robbins, Walter S. Melion, and Roy R. Jeal. ESEC 19. Atlanta: SBL Press, 2017.

Robbins, Vernon K., Walter S. Melion, and Roy R. Jeal, eds. *The Art of Visual Exegesis: Rhetoric, Texts, Images.* ESEC 19. Atlanta: SBL Press, 2017.

Roller, Matthew B. *Dining Posture in Ancient Rome: Bodies, Values, and Status.* Princeton: Princeton University Press, 2006.

Sica, Maria, Serena Aceto, Alessia Genovese, and Luciano Gaudio. "Analysis of Five Ancient Equine Skeletons by Mitochondrial DNA Sequencing." *AncBio* 4 (2002): 179–84.

Spicq, Ceslaus. *Agapè dans le Nouveau Testament.* 3 vols. Paris: Librairie Lecoffre, 1958.

———. *Agapè: Prolégomènes à une étude de théologie néo-testamentaire.* Leuven: Nauwelaerts, 1955.

Tilborg, Sjef van. *Imaginative Love in John.* Leiden: Brill, 1993.

Varone, Antonio. "New Finds in Pompeii: The Excavation of Two Buildings in Via dell' Abbondanza." *Apollo* 138 (July 1993): 8–12.

———. "Pompeii. Attività dell' Ufficio Scavi: 1989." *RSP* 3 (1989): 225–38.

———. "Pompeii. Attività dell' Ufficio Scavi: 1990." *RSP* 4 (1990): 201–11.

———. "Pompei: il quadro Helbig 1445, 'Kasperl in Kindertheater,' una nuova replica e il problema delle copie e delle varianti." Pages 149–52, 351–52 in *I Temi figurativi nella pittura parietale antica (IV sec. a.C.–IV sec. d.C.): Atti del VI Convegno Internazionale sulla Pittura Parietale Antica (Bologne, 20–23 settembre 1995).* Edited by Daniela Scagliarini Corlàita. Bologna: University Press Bologna, 1997.

———. "Scavi recenti a Pompei lungo la via dell' Abbondanza (*Regio* IX, ins. 12, 6–7)." Pages 617–40 in *Ercolano 1738–1988: 250 anni di ricerca archeologica.* Edited by Luisa Franchi dell' Orto. Rome: L' Erma di Bretschneider, 1993.

Weissenrieder, Annette, and Robert B. Coote, eds. *The Interface of Orality and Writing: Speaking, Seeing, Writing in the Shaping of New Genres.* BPCS. Eugene, OR: Cascade, 2015.

Weissenrieder, Annette, and Friederike Wendt. "Images as Communication: The Methods of Iconography." Pages 3–49 in *Picturing the New Testament: Studies in Ancient Visual Images.* WUNT 2/193. Edited by Annette Weissenrieder, Friederike Wendt, and Petra von Gemünden. Tübingen: Mohr Siebeck, 2005.

Weissenrieder, Annette, Friederike Wendt, and Petra von Gemünden, eds. *Picturing the New Testament: Studies in Ancient Visual Images.* WUNT 2/193. Tübingen: Mohr Siebeck, 2005.

Williams, Craig A. *Roman Homosexuality.* 2nd ed. Oxford: Oxford University Press, 2010.

Wischmeyer, Oda. *Liebe als Agape: Das frühchristliche Konzept und der moderne Diskurs.* Tübingen: Mohr Siebeck, 2015.

# 9
## A Seat at the Table:
## Grant Wood's *Dinner for Threshers*

### MEREDITH MUNSON

Grant Wood's 1934 *Dinner for Threshers*, though not as well known perhaps as *American Gothic* (though what in Wood's oeuvre is?), enjoyed immense popularity in the eyes of the public and significant discussion by contemporary critics and amateur reporters alike (fig. 9.1).[1] It was voted the third-most popular painting at its debut at the Carnegie International exhibition in Pittsburgh in 1934.[2] The painting was also chosen for the International Exhibition of Art in Venice that year, and it was discussed in a number of national newspapers in columns punctuated with terse and fervent quotations by Wood himself about the production of art in his country.[3] Numerous critics deemed it necessary to discuss the painting, including figures no less than esteemed critics Edward Alden Jewell and Henry McBride. Jewell effusively lauded the painting, saying, "Here we have, noble alike in sentiment and in presentation, a portrait of rural America ... the spirit of honest labor, close to the soil."[4] McBride, how-

---

1. See, for example, Edward Alden Jewell, "GRANT WOOD, IOWA ARTIST; His Collected Work at Ferargil Reveals Development of Painter from Youth," *New York Times*, April 21, 1935; Penelope Redd, "American Painters Show Freshness of Viewpoint," *Pittsburgh Sunday Sun-Telegraph*, November 4, 1934.

2. Dorothy Grafly, "Strength of American Art Stressed at Carnegie International," *Philadelphia Record*, October 21, 1934.

3. Anonymous, "The Venice Biennial," *New York Times*, May 12, 1934; Anonymous, "Grant Wood Discusses Revolt against the City, Other Publications," *New York Times*, June 9, 1935.

4. Edward Alden Jewell, as quoted in James M. Dennis, *Grant Wood, a Study in American Art and Culture* (Columbia: University of Missouri Press, 1986), 135.

244                    MEREDITH MUNSON

Fig. 9.1. Grant Wood, *Dinner for Threshers,* 1934, oil on beaverboard, 20 x 80 in., Fine Arts Museums of San Francisco, © Figge Art Museum, successors to the Estate of Nan Wood Graham/Licensed by VAGA, New York, NY.

ever, showed considerably less appreciation, calling the work "repressed" and "monotonous."[5]

Wood himself asserted, "Dinner for Threshers is from my own life. It includes my family, our neighbors, our tablecloth, our chairs and our hens.... It is of me and by me."[6] Clearly, this painting is a carefully encoded visual text of this artist's personal memory of his childhood in Cedar Rapids, Iowa. At the same time, the painting became almost instantly emblematic of a broader cultural memory, representative of an earlier time in American history during the hardships of the Great Depression. Wood's panel, though seemingly quaint and benign, has a great deal to tell us about both America in the 1930s and his own personal history, both of these situated within the language of traditional religious iconography.

Often found hanging alongside Thomas Hart Benton's *Susanna and the Elders* in the de Young Museum of San Francisco, Wood's panel calls immediately to the museum patron's attention its religious tones. Other artists in Wood's time also created works with religious scenes but relied mainly on contemporary sources, such as John Steuart Curry's *Baptism in Kansas.* This contrasts with Wood's appropriation of religious compositional elements with his more secular subject matter. The *Dinner for Threshers* panel is squat and long, divided into thirds, much like the predella of a Gothic or Renaissance triptych altar panel. The compositional arrangement further underscores this visual association, with the men

---

5. Henry McBride, "Artistic Pulses of the Nations Stir Pittsburgh International," *New York Sun,* October 20, 1934.

6. As quoted in Darrell Garwood, *Artist in Iowa: A Life of Grant Wood* (New York: Norton, 1944), 192.

gathered around the table, mirroring the figure groupings traditionally pictured in biblical Last Supper depictions. However, scholars have not gone beyond the panel's traditional visage to explore the extremely provocative connotations that such a connection might actually suggest.

*Dinner for Threshers* generally receives a brief glossing in Wood monographs, but the work's composition and nostalgic subject matter provide the framework for rich exploration. Perhaps because of its subject matter, some scholars, such as Travis Nygard, characterize this painting as a "vehemently positive image," which I am not quite certain is the case.[7] The elements of sentimental nostalgia are present in this painting, to be sure, but the austere setting and tenuous familial relationships deserve a much more nuanced reading. Most make mention of the work's appropriation of traditional religious compositional elements, but few go to great lengths to explore the ramifications of the use of this imagery beyond Wood's celebration and sacralization of the regional rural American life and culture.

Wood's painting is oil and tempera on a panel support, encased in what is probably the original frame, made by the artist. Within the triptych-like composition, Wood portrays what initially appears to be a quaint depiction of farm life, with a house that has been bisected by the artist, rendering it open for us to see the life and events inside. On the left side of the panel, we see the yard spanning the distance between the porch and the big red barn, with the year 1892 legible in the shade of the roof. The sun is high, casting short shadows beneath the buildings, animals, and wagons, telling the viewers that we are witnessing a midday scene. A windmill, Wood's favorite of all rural constructions, peeks just beyond the left roofline of the barn. Horses leisurely eat while chickens stand at attention, watching the men wash and prepare for their meal. Reading the panel left to right, we step inside the house and approach a red-checkered table, where fourteen seated and suntanned men enjoy food, coffee, and their company.[8] One woman stands in conversation, while another

---

7. Travis E. Nygard, "Grant Wood and the Visual Culture of Agribusiness," *Athanor* 27 (2009): 80.

8. While I acknowledge that the subject matter of the Last Supper traditionally features thirteen men (Christ and the twelve disciples), I believe that Wood's inclusion of a fourteenth man has more to do with his own biography in this instance. When Wood was fourteen, he submitted a drawing to a national contest and won third place. By his own account, this was when he decided to become an artist. See Grant Wood, "Return from Bohemia," Archives of American Art, Smithsonian Institution, D24.

enters in from the kitchen bearing a heaping bowl of mashed potatoes, bedecked with a tiny slab of butter. Just beyond her lies the kitchen, where two other women benignly work over an iron stove, observed by a small cat. Another building, trees, and grass are visible through the screen door. The details are meticulous. The wallpaper's design is carefully etched to perfection (a detail noticeable in raking light), with even the minutiae of the house, the scrollwork on the stove, and the bead-board kitchen cabinets all rendered painstakingly. While the peaceful banality of rural farm life does lend itself easily to a pleasant composition, surely there must be something more at play.

In order to delve into the significance of the composition, let us first examine the sociohistorical significance of the painting's subject matter. *Dinner for Threshers* portrays a well-known event of farming life, the midday meal for hardworking farmers that took place annually during harvesting season. As the threshing machine came to each farm to process the crop, local men would join together to aid one another's farms with the work. The act of threshing itself was actually intense and dangerous, involving a boiler-powered steam thresher driven by vibrating belts (without safety guards), spewing splinters of straw into the air in all directions. Threshing days required multiple men to work simultaneously to operate the machinery.

At each farm, while the men harvested the fields outside, the women worked in the kitchen to cook dinner for their neighbors as a means of thanking them for helping to thresh the plentiful harvest. Threshing dinners were thus a celebration, first and foremost, of neighborly camaraderie and communal well-being. Furthermore, because of this communal aspect, the threshing dinners became one of the few designated arenas of social interaction for both genders in the Midwest, particularly for unmarried young people.[9] Men proved their worth through their assistance in the field, while women enacted their own brand of self-promotion through the cooking and production of the best meal possible.[10] In his unpublished biography, "Return from Bohemia," Wood himself recalls,

> Mother was working furiously now preparing for the great dinner she would have to serve the threshers. She cleaned the house from top to

---

9. J. Sanford Rikoon, *Threshing in the Midwest, 1820–1940* (Bloomington: Indiana University Press, 1988), 121.

10. Rikoon, *Threshing in the Midwest*, 121.

bottom until it fairly glistened. From the cellar she brought up quantities of jellies, preserves, and pickles and lined them up on the pantry shelves. She gathered all manner of garden vegetables and put them in baskets out in the summer kitchen.... The last two days, she did a baking such as I had never seen. Golden loaves of bread, pies, cakes, doughnuts, and big crocks of baked beans appeared in the pantry. She prepared chickens for frying and baked two great hams.[11]

In his account, interestingly, Wood describes his mother's preparations for threshing day in much greater detail than his father's work. I believe this verbal account directly coincides with Wood's impetus to depict this particular moment (as opposed to the much more dynamic and dangerous scene of the actual threshing). The event referred to in the title of course alludes to the threshing work of the males, but the spotlight arguably shines here on the women at work within the domestic sphere and the enjoyment of the fruits of their labor, highlighting the domestic side of American farm life; food was part and parcel of the farming family's existence.

Wood originally painted *Dinner for Threshers* with the intent to create a work accessible to a broader audience not only as a large-panel painting but also with the eventual goal to convert it into a mural.[12] The task for present-day viewers, then, is to discern: What is the message Wood is conveying through this quaint depiction of (traditionally patriarchal) rural America, and how does this intersection of the domestic sphere within the public arena affect the way in which we, as viewers, read the painting? And, more to the point, how would Wood and his contemporaries have viewed this painting?

In order to answer these questions, we must first examine the time period in which Wood set his scene. Certain scholars present a mixed chronology of the painting, first calling to attention the year "1892" on the barn as Wood's birth year (though this is a common misconception, as Wood himself referred to that as his birth year; he was actually born

---

11. Wood, "Return from Bohemia."

12. After his *Daughters of Revolution* elicited protests from Daughters of the American Revolution members and the Carnegie hung the painting behind a door, Wood responded, "That's fine, I'm painting *Dinner for Threshers* now, and it's so large that no one will be able to hide it behind any door." See Nan Wood Graham, John Zug, and Julie Jensen McDonald, *My Brother, Grant Wood* (Des Moines: State Historical Society of Iowa, 1993), 95; Edward Alden Jewell, "Quickenings; Visions That Stir the Mural Pulse," *New York Times*, May 27, 1934.

in 1891).[13] At the same time, however, these scholars also assert that the dresses are in 1930s style.[14] Though ostensibly removed from the more modern fashions of the 1930s, even rural farm women wore dresses with raised hems by that time. We know that Wood carefully studied historic dress, as evidenced by his collection of turn-of-the-century tintypes.[15] The desire to place the painting in Wood's contemporary day is a persuasive and easy designation, albeit an incorrect one.

When attempting to shape an art-historical canon for America in the twentieth century, scholarship has tended to create firm distinctions between the avant-garde and everyone else; often, due to the accessibility of his paintings and as an outspoken advocate of regionalist painting, for many highbrow critics, Grant Wood became the champion of kitschy pedestrian culture, Luddites, and outré fashion (therefore attributing the reason for the long-hemmed dresses to a simple matter of rural America's being merely behind the times). Life on the farm is posited as quaint and backward, as the opposite of industrial life. While this interpretation may not necessarily be entirely incorrect, it renders *Dinner for Threshers* a thin, one-note painting without much more to tell us. When we place the dresses as turn of the century, when they would have actually been fashionable, we immediately travel back to Wood's childhood and wade into the murkier waters of memory. Everything about this painting—from the tea-leaf dinnerware to the step-top stove—smacks of late nineteenth-century style, therefore leading us to a moment from the artist's own past. Even the black-and-white print on the wall was an object from Wood's memory; his sister recalls, "Many farm homes exhibited a reproduction of a painting of horses in a storm. [Grant] hunted everywhere for one of these, but they seemed to be a thing of the past."[16] Wood endeavored to

---

13. Nygard, "Grant Wood and the Visual Culture," 80.

14. Nygard, "Grant Wood and the Visual Culture," 80.

15. Wanda M. Corn and Grant Wood, "The Birth of a National Icon: Grant Wood's 'American Gothic,'" *AICMS* 10 (1983): 261.

16. The print was actually produced by Joseph Hoover & Sons, titled *Spirited Horses, No. 2*. Hoover & Sons was a prominent chromolithographic company, whose enterprise flourished from the 1880s through the turn of the century. Vintage editions of this print are still available for purchase from auction houses and galleries, but apparently Wood had some trouble tracking a copy down for his own study while preparing for this panel. The painting's version of the print resembles the actual print much more closely than that of the preparatory drawing. Nan Wood Graham goes on to say, "Dr. McKeeby remembered that the mother of his dental assistant's boyfriend

create a chronologically and geographically accurate portrayal of farm life from the era of his childhood.

The period in which Wood created this painting in the United States was full of unrest, and Iowa was no exception. During the Great Depression, farmers around the country struggled with crop inflation and failing banks. In the periodical titled *Social Forces* published in March 1934, James Babcock expressed the violence and unrest occurring within the agricultural industry in Iowa. Verbal protests on the part of Iowa farmers in reaction to compulsory tuberculin tests escalated to the point that they elicited a military response in 1931.[17] Babcock characterizes the Iowa farmer's enemies as "Governor," "Rockefeller," "That damned county agent," and "Hoover, Hyde, Hell and Hard Times," and says that in recent days "they were lumped into a great pile and called the 'city' or 'big business.' The 'city' then tended to emerge as a giant personality symbolizing the great foe to 'right' and 'justice.'"[18] Grant Wood's own invective rhetoric, then, did not emerge from a vacuum. His 1935 manifesto, "Revolt against the City," shares much of the same sentiment as Babcock's essay and is worth presenting here:

> In short, America has turned introspective.... It is certain that the Depression Era has stimulated us to a re-evaluation of our resources in both art and economics, and that this turning of our eyes inward upon ourselves has awakened us to values which were little known before the grand crash of 1929 and which are chiefly nonurban.... Central and dominant in our Midwestern scene is the farmer. The depression, with its farm strikes and the heroic attempts of the Government to find solutions for agrarian difficulties, has emphasized for us all the fact that the farmer is basic in the economics of the country—and, further, that he is a human being.[19]

Regionalism as an artistic movement emerged from a variety of factors, but mainly as an attempt to find what these artists deemed an authentically

---

had one hanging in the parlor of her farm home. Before the dental assistant got around to borrowing it, she quarreled with her boyfriend, and Grant had to play peacemaker to secure the picture." See Wood Graham, Zug, and Jensen McDonald, *My Brother, Grant Wood*, 113.

17. James O. Babcock, "The Farm Revolt in Iowa," *SF* 12 (March 1934): 370.

18. Babcock, "Farm Revolt in Iowa," 370–71.

19. Grant Wood, "Revolt against the City," pamphlet, Iowa City, Iowa, 1935, repr. in Dennis, *Grant Wood*, 231, 235.

American voice, one that could only be articulated away from the Euro-derivative culture of America's metropolitan centers. Wood's *Dinner for Threshers*, so seemingly benign, with its smiling farmers and bountiful harvest, becomes a visual accompaniment to this manifesto.

Noticeably absent in the painting are the machines of modern farming, underscoring the nostalgic theme of the painting. By 1930, the predecessor of the combine had already become commonplace, and there were 920,000 tractors on American farms.[20] However, the implementation of these agricultural apparatuses did not come to pass without heated debate regarding the efficacy of the machinery and the cost-benefit analysis regarding the availability of work for unemployed hands and the subsequent inevitable changes in social relationships. Similarly, in Wendell Berry's novel *Jayber Crow*, written about American rural life in the 1930s and 1940s, the advent of industrial farming and the economic crash serve to commoditize food. The protagonist asserts, "And so the farm came under the influence of a new pattern, and this was the pattern of a fundamental disagreement such as it had never seen before. It was a disagreement about time and money and the use of the world."[21]

In Wood's scene, there is as much to note here in what is absent as in what is present. In lieu of tractors, here an empty wagon and an unhitched team of horses stand in the barnyard, where we also are reminded of the presence of the antiquated way of life by the appearance of the windmill in the top left corner. Above the men in the dining room, a kerosene lamp hangs in the center of the composition; the house has no signs of electrification. In the kitchen (ironically or not, generally the one room of a house that speaks more to the current day than any other), a red hand-pump sits in the corner behind the wooden stove, complete with the match holder affixed to the wall. All of these elements hark back to a more prosperous and peaceful era of American farming and, undoubtedly, a more prosperous and peaceful era of Grant Wood's own life.

On closer inspection, however, we note the cleanliness of the attire of both the men and the women in this painting; aprons and shirts gleam with a pristine white that does not correspond with the presumed morning of work for which this meal rewards all involved. The simple pageantry of beauty and abundance as rendered in Wood's painting is perhaps better

---

20. Thomas Burnell Colbert, "Iowa Farmers and Mechanical Corn Pickers, 1900–1952," *AgHist* 74 (2000): 538.

21. Wendell Berry, *Jayber Crow* (Washington, DC: Counterpoint, 2000), 186.

understood through a lens of nostalgia than actual history. Nostalgia and memory, though both function as reconstructions of the past, differ in that nostalgia often occurs as an amplified reconstruction of something that never existed originally, or to put it more simply, as Marcel Proust says, "The only paradise is paradise lost."[22] In her study of the construction of public spaces in post–World War II America, Margaret Farrar connects nostalgia with embodied space and anxiety that emerges out of rootlessness. Certain landscapes, or "echoes of past places," act as triggers for nostalgia in this instance.[23] These ideas are certainly relevant to *Dinner for Threshers*. Each turn-of-the-century element would have taken viewers familiar with the aesthetic back to their own experiences, thereby comparing and contrasting the past with the present. In the days of the Great Depression, it is not hard to imagine which era emerged as the more palatable of that comparison. Of course, one of the main difficulties that arises with issues of nostalgia is the inability to return to that former Edenic state.

In this painting, by sparking a communal sense of nostalgia for the pre-Depression era, perhaps Wood is also commenting on the social fragmentation brought about by the modern farming methods and machinery. It is not well known today how much farmers understood of the ramifications of their treatment of the land during the years of the taming of the great American prairie (overplowing that led to the travesty now known as the Dust Bowl), but at the very least, people were beginning to sense the changes that would result from the new agriculture. This perhaps is the reasoning behind the presence of horses and wagons here, as opposed to motorized machines.

However, cultural critique is not the only element at play in this panel. What are we to do, then, with Wood's traditional religious treatment of a seemingly secular subject in this turn-of-the-century scene? Most scholars who work with this painting, such as Timothy Burgard, curator at San Francisco's de Young Museum, assert that Wood "does not focus on the religious beliefs of his farmers but instead suggests that his subjects are emblematic of Jeffersonian democracy—America's de facto religion."[24] This

---

22. Margaret E. Farrar, "Amnesia, Nostalgia, and the Politics of Place Memory," *PRQ* 64 (December 2011): 727.

23. Farrar, "Amnesia, Nostalgia," 728.

24. Timothy Burgard, "Grant Wood, *Dinner for Threshers*: The Regionalist Renaissance," in *Masterworks of American Painting at the de Young* (San Francisco: Fine Arts Museums of San Francisco, 2005), 341.

argument does have some merit, particularly in regard to the emphasis on Thomas Jefferson as a champion of the gentleman farmer in America, but the negation of the importance of traditional religion (in this case, Christianity) fails to give credit to Wood's own background and artistic creativity. In the more public interpretation of the painting, the subject matter both secularizes and is sanctified by the use of traditional sacred iconography, something of which the artist would have been acutely aware. Wood grew up in the household of two Quaker parents, and in "Return from Bohemia," young Grant recalls his father questioning the worth of drawing or even of reading *Grimm's Fairy Tales*, asserting, "We Quakers can read only true things."[25] His childhood was steeped in religion; therefore, religion should play at least a small role in how we interpret this scene.

Wood could have depicted any moment during the threshing, but the way in which he chose to portray this event plays on obvious art-historical referents. Wood's impetus to create this image based on traditional biblical models in the midst of the Great Depression may stem from both nostalgia and a personal sense of reckoning with his own complicated familial relationships. The influence of the northern Gothic and Renaissance painters emerges in his mature style, with its emphasis on everyday domesticity and realism as a vehicle for portraying sacred scenes. Clear visual correlations arise when we compare and contrast this image with other well-known religious table scenes such as the Last Supper, the supper at Emmaus, and the wedding at Cana. Arguably, the Gothic and Renaissance referents hold the key to this painting's interpretation, when taken into consideration with the artist's own acknowledged emphasis on personal memory and nostalgia. By probing the seemingly obvious connections with traditional depictions of these familiar narratives, we may understand why the artist appropriated these models for his painting of rural America. These three scenes that occur around the dinner table in the Scriptures occur at pivotal moments within Christ's life and ministry. First, the wedding at Cana, depicted in the Gospel of John (John 2:1–12), though not in the Synoptic Gospels, marks the beginning of Christ's ministry. At the wedding, Mary, mother of Christ, calls her son into action, directing him to intervene during the celebration of a wedding and remedy the fast depletion of celebratory wine. Christ does so by changing water into wine, thereby performing his first miracle and revealing his divinity. In Paolo

---

25. Wood, "Return from Bohemia."

Veronese's chaotic depiction, for example, Christ is seated at the center of the composition amid the joyous merriment and festivity, underscoring his enjoyment of celebrations among those in community together (fig. 9.2). The idea of communal celebration correlates easily to the annual threshing dinner depicted here.

Fig. 9.2. Johann Gottfried Saiter, after Paolo Caliari, called Veronese, *Marriage Feast at Cana*, seventeenth century, engraving, 21 3/4 x 21 7/8 in. Harvard Art Museums.

Second, the supper at Emmaus occurs in the Gospel of Luke after the resurrection as one of the last appearances of Christ on earth before his assumption into heaven. In the account (Luke 24:13–32), Christ joins two of his followers on the road (who fail to recognize him), and they recount the events of the week that culminated in the crucifixion. Jesus then unpacks these proceedings through an exegetical discussion of the prophetic Scriptures. However, it is not until Christ blesses the meal and breaks the bread that his followers finally recognize him. This is the moment depicted in Diego Velázquez's rendition of the narrative, in which a soft light simultaneously bathes and emanates from Christ, while marking his companions' own moment of illumination (fig. 9.3). This account helps both the characters and the readers of the story to understand the true nature of God and of Christ.

Fig. 9.3. Velázquez, *The Supper at Emmaus*, 1622–1623, oil on canvas, 48 1/2 x 52 1/4 in., Metropolitan Museum of Art.

Third, the Last Supper is presented in the Synoptic Gospels as a Passover Seder (also an annual celebration) held directly before Christ's crucifixion (Matt 26:20–30; Mark 14:17–26; Luke 22:14–38). As is well known, at this meal, Christ broke bread and drank wine with his disciples, foreshadowing his pending arrest and crucifixion. During this discussion, he revealed the true character of Judas Iscariot, who had betrayed him and sealed his fate. Biblically, the Last Supper cemented the relationships of the people around the table to one another (while highlighting one specific relationship that had resulted in negative consequences), while at the same time underscoring the relationship of the creator to his creation. In this way, then, the Eucharist is a Christian sacrament that is first and foremost about relationships. The story of the Last Supper underscores the relationship of God to the world through the revelation of Christ's character (and that of certain followers) around the table. Both spiritually and pragmatically speaking, I would argue that a similar dynamic is at play here in this panel. Wood, as this scene's creator, is creating a commentary on the members of his family present in this painting. So, what does Wood seem to say about his own relationships in light of character placement in traditional Last Supper paintings?

Wood's biographer R. Tripp Evans focuses much of his argument on the placement of Wood's father, Maryville. Though each man in the painting looks fairly generic in appearance, the one man with blond hair is set apart visually from the rest by sitting not in a more comfortable chair but on the piano stool. As he is marked by a bright, triangular red bandanna tucked into the back pocket of his overalls, most scholars (including Evans) agree that this figure is Wood's father. Evans says, "In its central and slightly elevated position, this figure mirrors Christ's location in traditional Last Supper imagery." [26] While it is tempting to underscore the father figure here, Grant had a complicated relationship with his Quaker father, who did not approve of his artistic interests as a child. Christ has, to my knowledge, *never* been portrayed within Last Supper imagery with his back to the viewer. In a perhaps juicier psychoanalytic reading, that position is almost always reserved for the figure of Judas, as evident in the famous Renaissance *Last Supper* renditions by Giotto, Ghirlandaio, Tintoretto, Lorenzo Monaco, or Andrea del Castagno. If we are to deal with this painting within the tradition of art history, the misapprehension of Judas for Jesus could be a slightly earth-shattering faux pas.

Three extant preparatory drawings vary only in the minutest degrees from the completed work, telling us that this composition was painstakingly planned (two of these drawings are owned by New York's Whitney Museum of American Art, and the other is in a private collection). As mentioned earlier, in raking light it is possible to see careful score marks for the patterning of the wallpaper. Each detail arguably holds some significance

---

26. R. Tripp Evans, *Grant Wood: A Life* (New York: Knopf, 2010), 174.

within the composition. Wood himself reacted to criticism of a seemingly insignificant aspect as the shadow of chickens by pulling out a ruler and explaining the astronomical exactitude of his calculations.[27] Investment in such seemingly inconsequential details would signify that the artist had carefully thought out such basic elements as the two-dimensional perspective, particularly regarding the architecture of the house, which has puzzled a number of scholars.

Wood's decision to depict a section drawing of the house, though rather unorthodox for his particular time period, was not a new artistic formal element. Artists dating back to Giotto have utilized this technique as a way to allow the viewer visibility into an interior setting, while still including certain exterior elements in the composition. The section drawing of the house seems to have the rather archaic lack of perspective that appears in the works of Giotto and his contemporaries. However, the problematic perspective employed by Wood actually underscores the importance of character placement when compared with the traditional Gothic and Renaissance positions of Judas and Jesus in these scenes. For instance, in Leonardo's *Last Supper*, Christ is the vanishing point and clearly the center of attention (fig. 9.4). If we follow the lines of the architecture down, we see that the vanishing point of *Dinner for Threshers* is not a person but the window in the dining room (fig. 9.5).

According to Grant's sister, Nan Wood Graham, the window depicted here in this scene is the window by which their father died. She recalls, "Father ate a hearty meal of ham and eggs, and after reading the mail, said he thought that he would drive into town. He stepped to the window to view the weather, Mother heard a crash. Father was lying on the floor. His summons from beyond had come."[28] Though this painting foreshadows the death of Wood's father, drawing a correlation between Maryville and Christ is problematized due to his position with his back to us in the composition. Instead, the focal point is the window, to which Wood's father directs his gaze.

The open architecture of this small farmhouse also denotes some level of theatricality on the part of the artist. The delineation of the floor line along the bottom of the panel visually acts as a stage, inviting viewers to take in the scene but precluding them from actually taking part in the

---

27. Garwood, *Artist in Iowa*, 168.
28. As quoted in Evans, *Grant Wood*, 175.

Fig. 9.4. Leonardo da Vinci, *Last Supper* [with perspective lines], ca. 1495–1498, and oil on plaster, 15 ft 1 in x 29 ft. Santa Maria della Grazie, Milan. Perspective added by author.

Fig. 9.5. Grant Wood, *Dinner for Threshers* [with perspective lines] (1934), oil on beaverboard, 20 x 80 in. Fine Arts Museums of San Francisco. Perspective added by author.

act. Theatricality in this instance is not to be taken lightly. The dramatic events that took place in Grant Wood's life directly following this joyous scene served to shape him for the rest of his life. Beyond that, however, the theatrical aspect of the scene could serve as a way for the artist, himself, to engage with the past; the pageantry of the scene becomes a sort of performative nostalgia. Though Wood never moved back to farm life after this early childhood period, he shaped his mythical public persona as a folksy agrarian. Almost every press photograph taken of the artist shows him to be wearing overalls, and in his most famous folkloric quote, he remarked, "All the really good ideas I've ever had came to me while I was milking a cow."[29] Perhaps through engaging with the agrarian lifestyle of his father and in portraying this secular-yet-sacred holiday in *Dinner for Threshers*, Wood is able to return to the past as it appears in his memory, pristine, triumphant, and entirely familial.

Maryville Wood died when Grant was ten years old. Shortly thereafter and because of his death, the Wood family was forced to leave their life on the farm for a more urban existence in Cedar Rapids, Iowa. As a single mother, Hattie Weaver Wood moved her family from place to place, scraping by whatever living she could manage to support her four children. Food could not be taken for granted, which most likely would have resonated in the painter's mind as he created this scene of peaceful abundance. Wood's scene, therefore, becomes a literal and figurative Last Supper, a depiction of perhaps the last threshing dinner that his family enjoyed before the economic hardship that they endured in later years without their primary breadwinner.

Perhaps, then, it is not surprising that Grant Wood chose a typically religious iconographical framework to present his own memory of a meal in his childhood home. His family's agrarian life had vanished, and the nature and structure of farming in his day had already begun to change dramatically. Wood's Midwestern landscape depicted America's farmland before the drought that had consumed the plains by the time of this painting and would be christened the Dust Bowl the next year. Environmentalists and ecologists now understand the Dust Bowl "as a result of the largest, long-running agricultural and environmental miscalculation in American history."[30] Today's viewers of the painting are even further removed, in both time and practice, from these preindustrialized methods of farming (and possibly from the neighborly affection demonstrated in Wood's panel). The family meal of Wood's memory becomes the vehicle to convey his personal values and desire to return to an Edenic, preindustrialized state of agricultural life.

While Grant Wood was undoubtedly utilizing nostalgia to make a point about the progression of industry and the changes occurring nationally within the agricultural way of life, by placing his father in the position

---

29. As quoted in Brady Roberts, *Grant Wood: An American Master Revealed* (Portland, OR: Pomegranate Communications, 2004), 32.

30. John Opie, "Moral Geography in High Plains History," *GR* 88 (1998): 244.

of Judas, Wood also attached a sense of culpability to his father that may otherwise be overlooked or misunderstood without a knowledge of traditional biblical and art-historical precedent. I believe that he was creating a highly personal visual text about the resentment, transformation, and loss that accompanied the death of his father and the tumultuous experience that ensued from this particular event. Moreover, this painting celebrates the role that his mother played in providing for the family before, during, and after his father's death. His mother is the silent, peaceful presence that permeates the panel, both inside the house and in the yard beyond. This panel is a good reminder, therefore, that in order to truly understand the personal dynamics at play in social relationships, we must always be careful to note where we sit at the table.

## Works Cited

Anonymous. "Grant Wood Discusses Revolt against the City, Other Publications." *New York Times*, June 9, 1935.

———. "The Venice Biennial." *New York Times*, May 12, 1934.

Babcock, James O. "The Farm Revolt in Iowa." *SF* 12 (March 1934): 369–73.

Berry, Wendell. *Jayber Crow*. Washington, DC: Counterpoint, 2000.

Burgard, Timothy. "Grant Wood, *Dinner for Threshers*: The Regionalist Renaissance." Pages 338–41 in *Masterworks of American Painting at the de Young*. San Francisco: Fine Arts Museums of San Francisco, 2005.

Colbert, Thomas Burnell. "Iowa Farmers and Mechanical Corn Pickers, 1900–1952." *AgHist* 74 (2000): 530–44.

Corn, Wanda M., and Grant Wood. "The Birth of a National Icon: Grant Wood's 'American Gothic.'" *AICMS* 10 (1983): 252–75.

Dennis, James M. *Grant Wood, a Study in American Art and Culture*. Columbia: University of Missouri Press, 1986.

Evans, R. Tripp. *Grant Wood: A Life*. New York: Knopf, 2010.

Farrar, Margaret E. "Amnesia, Nostalgia, and the Politics of Place Memory." *PRQ* 64 (December 2011): 723–35.

Garwood, Darrell. *Artist in Iowa: A Life of Grant Wood*. New York: Norton, 1944.

Grafly, Dorothy. "Strength of American Art Stressed at Carnegie International." *Philadelphia Record*, October 21, 1934.

Jewell, Edward Alden. "GRANT WOOD, IOWA ARTIST; His Collected Work at Ferargil Reveals Development of Painter from Youth." *New York Times*, April 21, 1935.

———. "Quickenings; Visions That Stir the Mural Pulse." *New York Times*, May 27, 1934.

McBride, Henry. "Artistic Pulses of the Nations Stir Pittsburgh International." *New York Sun*, October 20, 1934.

Nygard, Travis E. "Grant Wood and the Visual Culture of Agribusiness." *Athanor* 27 (2009): 79–85.

Opie, John. "Moral Geography in High Plains History." *GR* 88 (1998): 241–58.

Redd, Penelope. "American Painters Show Freshness of Viewpoint." *Pittsburgh Sunday Sun-Telegraph*, November 4, 1934.

Rikoon, J. Sanford. *Threshing in the Midwest, 1820–1940*. Bloomington: Indiana University Press, 1988.

Roberts, Brady. *Grant Wood: An American Master Revealed*. Portland, OR: Pomegranate Communications, 2004.

Wood, Grant. "Return from Bohemia." Archives of American Art, Smithsonian Institution, D24.

———. "Revolt against the City." Pamphlet. Iowa City, Iowa, 1935.

Wood Graham, Nan, John Zug, and Julie Jensen McDonald. *My Brother, Grant Wood*. Des Moines: State Historical Society of Iowa, 1993.

# 10
# Seeing Christ's Angel: Visual Exegesis of Revelation 10

## IAN BOXALL

## Albrecht Dürer and the Mighty Angel

Few visual artists have proved as influential in the visual reception of the book of Revelation as German painter and draftsman Albrecht Dürer (1471-1528).[1] Dürer's iconic series of fifteen woodcuts of the Apocalypse, published in 1498 as *Die heimliche Offenbarung Johannis* and in a Latin version as *Apocalypsis cum figuris*, manifest the artist's skill and exegetical sophistication (by way of comparison, the thirteenth-century Abingdon Apocalypse contains 156 half-page miniatures). Although the illustrated Bible published in Nuremberg in 1483 by his godfather Anton Koberger, which served as partial model for Dürer's work, contained even fewer images (eight in the block-book style, ultimately derived from the Cologne Bible of ca. 1478), what Erwin Panofsky calls Dürer's "dynamic calligraphy"[2] and his use of chiaroscuro have resulted in a compelling set of images. These combine a sense of the "breathless pace" in which Revelation's visions unfold with a convincing naturalism in the depiction of specific characters.[3]

The influence of Dürer's Apocalypse woodcuts has been enormous, due in no small part to their ease of production and relatively low cost.

---

1. On Dürer and the Apocalypse, see, e.g., Erwin Panofsky, *The Life and Art of Albrecht Dürer* (Princeton: Princeton University Press, 1955); Natasha F. H. O'Hear, *Contrasting Images of the Book of Revelation in Late Medieval and Early Modern Art: A Case Study in Visual Exegesis*, OTM (Oxford: Oxford University Press, 2011), 142–75.
2. Panofsky, *Life and Art*, 47–50.
3. O'Hear, *Contrasting Images*, 160–61.

Most subsequent Western artists show at least some indebtedness to them, whether by way of imitation or repudiation. Unlike earlier exemplars, where the images generally serve to illustrate the biblical text or to complement the accompanying commentary, with Dürer it is the images that now dominate.[4] Perhaps the most famous is Dürer's fourth woodcut, depicting the *Four Horsemen of the Apocalypse* (Rev 6:2–8), galloping energetically across the page and conveying a message of profound social critique (both rich and poor, including at least one bishop, being trampled underfoot).

Yet the scholarly assessment of the ninth of his Apocalypse images, illustrating Rev 10 (*St. John Devouring the Book*, fig. 10.1), has been mixed. In its favor, it has greater clarity than the Koberger model, which combined Rev 10 with the sixth trumpet plague (Rev 9:13–21). Two figures dominate: the angel at the center and John in the bottom right, while the heavenly altar in the top left represents the origin of the angel's authority. Compositionally, Dürer's image is in some ways closer to the Flemish Apocalypse (ca. 1400; Bibliothèque Nationale, Paris, BN Néerl. 3), which also focuses on the figures of John and the angel, than to the Koberger prototype.[5]

Moreover, Dürer's portrayal of the figure of John is compelling for the sheer energy with which it conveys John's devouring the angel's book, the source of the seer's prophetic inspiration (Rev 10:8–11; see Ezek 2:1–3:4). Indeed, a good case may be made for this being a self-portrait, a symbol of the artist's own prophetic, visionary inspiration, in "seeing again" what John once saw for the end of the fifteenth century, a time of turmoil and increased apocalyptic anxiety.[6] The title conventionally given to this woodcut prioritizes this dimension of the chapter, the depiction of John beneath a tree in the bottom right compositionally dependent on earlier visual representations of John on Patmos (e.g., Martin Schongauer, *St. John on Patmos*, ca. 1475/1480; National Gallery of Art, Washington, DC; Hieronymus Bosch, *St. John the Evangelist on Patmos*, ca. 1489; Staatlichen Museen, Berlin), a scene absent from Dürer's cycle.

---

4. This is evidenced, not least, by the carelessness in matching image with appropriate section of the biblical text on the facing page (O'Hear, *Contrasting Images*, 154–60).

5. O'Hear, *Contrasting Images*, 150.

6. O'Hear, *Contrasting Images*, 163–66. This would then be a potent example of the second-type actualization articulated by Judith Kovacs and Christopher Rowland. See Kovacs and Rowland, *Revelation: The Apocalypse of Jesus Christ*, BBC (Oxford: Blackwell, 2006), 9–10.

Fig. 10.1. Albrecht Dürer, *St. John Devouring the Book*, ca. 1498. Woodcut, 15 1/2 x 11 5/16 in. Metropolitan Museum of Art, New York, 40.139.6(10), Gift of Mrs. Felix M. Warburg, 1940.

By contrast, however, his central figure of the "mighty angel" disappoints. Falling back on established precedents (notably the angel in the Koberger Bible), Dürer has produced one of the most stilted and overly literal images of the mighty angel. The angel's torso is an actual cloud (Dürer's own addition to his Koberger model), precariously balanced on columns like stilts, their fiery character conveyed by flames emerging like leaves from their tops. The angel's head apparently hovers in midair, and his hands seem almost disembodied. Dürer has represented the angel's face like the sun by a circle of spike-like rays.[7] The choice of a cloudy formation

---

7. We also see here indications of the increasing literalism of the Renaissance emphasis on the grammatical-historical sense.

is arguably an improvement on the Koberger prototype. Still, the contrast with Dürer's depiction of John in the same woodcut is striking. One could make the argument that Revelation's description of the angel means that he will "always look faintly ridiculous" in visual art, even at the hands of a genius of Dürer's stature.[8] The remainder of this chapter will explore a select number of alternative renderings, both earlier and later than Albrecht Dürer, to discover whether this is necessarily the case. How have artists engaged the textual ambiguities surrounding Revelation's description of this angelic figure? What kind of issues have they sought to address through visual exegesis? How successful have their visualizations been?

## The Mighty Angel in Textual Exegesis

Dürer's image of *St. John Devouring the Book* (fig. 10.1) brings into sharp relief the challenges faced by the artist attempting to visualize Rev 10:1–7. Despite being one of the shortest chapters in the Apocalypse of John, it has more than its fair share of exegetical challenges. John witnesses another "mighty angel" (the second of three angels so described: 5:2; 18:21) descending from heaven holding a "little scroll" or "little book" (the Vulgate translates the Greek βιβλαρίδιον as *libellum*) in his hand. The angel straddles land and sea, and utters a loud cry, likened to a lion's roar. John then hears seven thunderclaps speak (i.e., the thunder communicates an intelligible message) but is told to seal them up and not write them down—the antithesis of a normal apocalypse, where the purpose of sealing is subsequent disclosure (e.g., Dan 12:4; 4 Ezra 14:26, 45–46)—so that the reader never discovers what they said. The angel raises his right hand and makes a solemn oath, declaring that χρόνος οὐκέτι ἔσται (literally "there will no longer be time"; Vulgate: *tempus amplius non erit*), a phrase that has confounded the best of Bible translators. English translations include "there should be time no longer" (KJV), "There will be no more delay" (NRSV, NIV), "The time of waiting is over" (NJB), and "The time is up" (CEB). The angel then announces the completion of "the mystery of God," good news that God proclaimed (εὐηγγέλισεν) to "his servants the prophets," though without clarification as to whether specific prophets are intended.

---

8. Natasha O'Hear and Anthony O'Hear, *Picturing the Apocalypse: The Book of Revelation in the Arts over Two Millennia* (Oxford: Oxford University Press, 2015), 45.

In the part of the chapter foregrounded in Dürer's woodcut (Rev 10:8–11), John is then invited to approach the angel and to take and eat up the little scroll in a command (Λάβε καὶ κατάφαγε αὐτό) that strikingly echoes Jesus's eucharistic words in Matthew's version of the Last Supper, to "take and eat" (Λάβετε φάγετε, Matt 26:26). Finally, John is commissioned as a prophet, to prophesy again either *about* or *to* "many peoples, nations, languages and kings" (the precise meaning of the preposition ἐπὶ here is disputed). The vision is thus a key turning point in the apocalyptic narrative.

To ground the discussion and explicate some of the challenges of visualization, a brief discussion of the textual exegesis of this passage is in order. Most modern scholars emphasize the angelic character of this figure, albeit a particularly exalted angel, as a mediator of divine revelation. This accounts both for the echoes of earlier descriptions of God and Christ (e.g., the feet like pillars of fire, the face like the sun, the rainbow encircling his head, the voice like a roaring lion: see Rev 1:12–16; 4:3; 5:5), and for the sharp distinction Revelation makes between the worship of angels and the worship of God and the Lamb (the former being strictly forbidden: Rev 19:10; 22:8–9).[9] This "mighty angel" is understood to be an angel of God put at Christ's disposal, functioning effectively as "an icon of the glorified Christ in his role of the heavenly messenger of God to his people on earth."[10] A variant scholarly position is that the mighty angel of Rev 10 is Christ's own angel,[11] who comes to deliver to John the revelation that God gave to Christ the Lamb in heaven. This solution finds its interpretative key in Rev 1:1 ("sending *his* angel to his servant John"). That is, if the Son of Man of Rev 1 is regularly described by scholars as *angelomorphic* (Christ appearing in angel-like form), this mighty angel might be called *christomorphic* (an angel who resembles Christ).[12]

---

9. For the arguments, see, e.g., Craig R. Koester, *Revelation: A New Translation with Introduction and Commentary*, AYB 38A (New Haven: Yale University Press, 2014), 474–94.

10. Louis Andrew Brighton, "The Angel of Revelation: An Angel of God and an Icon of Jesus Christ" (PhD diss., Saint Louis University, 1991), 219.

11. E.g., Ian Boxall, *The Revelation of St. John*, BNTC (Peabody, MA: Hendrickson, 2006), 152. For the notion that individuals have their own angel, see, e.g., Matt 18:10; Acts 12:15; the angel like Joseph in Jos. Asen. 14–17.

12. Charles Gieschen helpfully defines *angelomorphic* as "an inclusive term which means having some of the various forms and functions of an angel, even though the figure may not be explicitly called an 'angel' or considered to have the created nature of

By contrast, the almost universal view of the patristic period and Western medieval exegetes is that the mighty angel is Christ himself, that is, the vision, like that in Rev 1, presents an angelomorphic Christology (a view with only minority support among modern scholars).[13] It is an interpretation first attested in the earliest Latin commentary by Victorinus of Pettau (*In Apoc.* 10.1), developed in the fourth century by the influential exegete Tyconius of Carthage, and thence perpetuated by a string of important commentators: Primasius, Beatus, Bede, and many medieval and early modern commentators.[14] In the case of Tyconius, the christological interpretation is combined with an ecclesiological one, given Tyconius's rule "Concerning the Lord and His Body" (whereby what is said of Christ in Scripture can also be applied to the church, his body, and vice versa). Hence, the angel clothed in a cloud is the Lord clothed in the church, "constantly being born from the church by [the work of] God" (Tyconius, *Exp. Apoc.* 10.1).[15]

There are rare exceptions in the West to this christological interpretation of the mighty angel. In the thirteenth century, an emerging prophetic-historical approach read the Apocalypse as foreseeing the unfolding history of the church until the end, in chronological sequence, leading to the identification of John's visionary characters as specific historical characters. German Franciscan Alexander Minorita (or Alexander of Bremen), who finished the first edition of his Apocalypse commentary in 1235, made a distinction between the "mighty angel" in verse 1 and the angel straddling the earth and sea in verse 8. The first is staunchly orthodox Emperor Justin (518–527), the second his successor, Justinian (527–565), who "stands in the place of Justin." Alternatively, both angels symbolize the

---

an angel." See Gieschen, *Angelomorphic Christology: Antecedents and Early Evidence*, AGJU 42 (Leiden: Brill, 1998), 3 n. 2.

13. E.g., Robert H. Gundry, "Angelomorphic Christology in the Book of Revelation," in *1994 Seminar Papers: One Hundred Thirtieth Annual Meeting, November 19–22, 1994, the Chicago Hilton and Towers, Chicago, IL*, SBLSP 33 (Atlanta: Scholars Press, 1994), 662–78; Gieschen, *Angelomorphic Christology*, 256–60.

14. The eighth-century Hiberno-Latin Reference Bible extends this Christocentricity to almost every angel in Rev 10–20, including Michael in Rev 12. See Francis X. Gumerlock, ed., *Early Latin Commentaries on the Apocalypse* (Kalamazoo: Medieval Institute Publications, Western Michigan University, 2016), 10.

15. English quotation from Tyconius, *Exposition of the Apocalypse*, trans. Francis X. Gumerlock, FC 134 (Washington, DC: Catholic University of America Press, 2017), 103.

father of Western monasticism, St. Benedict.[16] However, this prophetic-historical interpretation appears not to have affected the visual reception. There is no trace of it in the illustration to Rev 10 in the illuminated version of Alexander's *Expositio in Apocalypsim* in Cambridge (MS UL Mm.5.31, p. 86), nor in the Apocalypse triptych by Master Bertram (ca. 1400; Victoria and Albert Museum, London), whose images are derived from the Alexander illustrations. This is particularly striking given that both visualize another aspect of Alexander's commentary, which identifies the "seven thunders" of Rev 10:3 as seven doctors of the church.[17] Another exception is Franciscan radical Peter John Olivi (1248–1298), who identified the mighty angel as Francis of Assisi, one of several apocalyptic identities Francis received from Franciscan commentators.[18] These examples notwithstanding, the christological interpretation remained primary.

Some sixteenth- and seventeenth-century Protestants (e.g., John Bale and Hugh Broughton) also diverged from the patristic and medieval consensus, seeing in the mighty angel a symbol of preachers of the gospel, especially the Reformers. However, one might view this interpretive strategy as simply an extension of the traditional christological reading, the angel as a figure of Christ intervening in history through his sixteenth-century servants.[19]

There is also some divergence in Eastern exegesis, which was far less prominent than in the West, with only two Greek commentaries surviv-

16. Alexander Minorita, *Expositio in Apocalypsim*, ed. Alois Wachtel (Weimar: Hermann Böhlaus Nachfolger, 1955), 155, 159.

17. On the Master Bertram altarpiece, see Claus M. Kauffmann, *An Altarpiece of the Apocalypse from Master Bertram's Workshop in Hamburg*, MM 25 (London: HMSO, Victoria and Albert Museum, 1968).

18. Robert E. Lerner, "The Medieval Return to the Thousand-Year Sabbath," in *The Apocalypse in the Middle Ages*, ed. Richard K. Emmerson and Bernard McGinn (Ithaca, NY: Cornell University Press, 1992), 60–61; Arthur W. Wainwright, *Mysterious Apocalypse* (Nashville: Abingdon, 1993), 54–57. St. Bonaventure famously identified Francis as the angel with "the seal of the living God" (Rev 7:2), while an anonymous Franciscan commentary on Revelation attributed to Alexander of Hales presents Francis as another John. See Ian Boxall, "Francis of Assisi as Apocalyptic Visionary," in *Revealed Wisdom: Studies in Apocalyptic in Honour of Christopher Rowland*, ed. John Ashton, AGJU 88 (Leiden: Brill, 2014), 259–61.

19. See Ian Boxall, "The Mighty Angel with the Little Scroll: British Perspectives on the Reception History of Revelation 10," in *The Book of Revelation: Currents in British Research on the Apocalypse*, ed. Garrick V. Allen, Ian Paul, and Simon P. Woodman, WUNT 411 (Tübingen: Mohr Siebeck, 2015), 254–56.

ing from the early centuries, both now dated to the sixth or early seventh century. Oecumenius presumes the mighty angel is merely an angel, the cloud signifying "the formlessness and invisibility of the holy angels," the rainbow conveying angelic brightness, "for they are angels of light."[20] Similarly, for Andreas of Caesarea, the cloud, rainbow, and light like the sun are symbols of this angel's virtues and "the brightness of its angelic nature and understanding."[21] The visual impact of this angelic interpretation is unclear, however. Canonical disputes about the Apocalypse in the East resulted in a paucity of Revelation-inspired iconography, at least in the Byzantine tradition, until the early modern period. The earliest Greek example of an Apocalypse cycle, the sixteenth-century frescoes in the Monastery of Dionysiou on Mount Athos, shows clear dependence on Dürer, whether directly or through his successors.

### Anglo-Norman Apocalypses: Abingdon, Getty, and Cloisters

Dürer's mighty angel may be fruitfully compared with a cluster of images from the thirteenth- and fourteenth-century Anglo-Norman Apocalypses, which are arguably more successful in conveying the subtlety and exegetical ambiguity of the angel seen by John of Patmos. These richly illuminated books, of which a significant number survive, represent a twofold shift in the visual reception of the Apocalypse: from monastic and liturgical use to lay (albeit aristocratic) and devotional usage, and from attention to unfolding narrative plot to contemplation of specific images (with or without attention to the corresponding biblical text or commentary excerpts, which in some cases may have been added to provide gravitas to the work).[22] The manuscripts fall mainly into two types: the Corpus-Lambeth group, whose images are accompanied by an anonymous French prose gloss, and those with excerpts from the *Expositio super septem visiones libri Apocalypsis* by Berengaudus accompanying the image and the biblical text

---

20. William C. Weinrich, trans., *Greek Commentaries on Revelation*, ACT (Downers Grove, IL: IVP Academic, 2011), 44.

21. Weinrich, *Greek Commentaries on Revelation*, 149.

22. Suzanne Lewis, *Reading Images: Narrative Discourse and Reception in the Thirteenth-Century Illuminated Apocalypse* (Cambridge: Cambridge University Press, 1995), 51; O'Hear, *Contrasting Images*, 22.

(subdivided into the Metz, Morgan, Westminster, and Trinity clusters).[23] The three examples discussed here all come from Berengaudus-type manuscripts, probably intended for private reading, and prepared by "teams of artists and scribes working under the aegis of theologically skilled, probably clerical, compilers."[24]

The precise identity of Berengaudus is disputed, though the majority view identifies him as an eleventh-century Benedictine monk inspired by the church reforms of Pope Gregory VII (1073–1085).[25] His Apocalypse commentary has a strongly christological and ecclesiological focus, evident in its complex allegorical interpretation of Rev 10. Following on from the first six trumpet plagues (Rev 8:6–9:21), interpreted as the persecution of the church by heretics, the vision of chapter 10 provides a welcome relief as Christ descends, clothed in the cloud of his flesh (i.e., this is a vision of the incarnation). The intertextual justification for interpreting the mighty angel (*angelus fortis*) as "our Lord Jesus Christ" is provided by reading Revelation alongside Ps 24:8 (Vulgate Ps 23:8): "The Lord who is strong and mighty [*fortis et potens*], the Lord mighty in battle." The rainbow around his head is a symbol of his mercy; his head, of his divinity. The pillar of fire that forms the angel's legs symbolizes the church; his two feet are either the two people, Israel and the Gentiles, united in the one column of the church, or the Old and New Testaments (Berengaudus's biblical text apparently has the singular *columna* instead of the expected plural *columnae*). The lion's roar is the message of the gospel. The seven thunders are the seven virtues, one indication of Berengaudus's concern for moral as well as christological interpretation.

Given Berengaudus's clear acceptance of the traditional identification of the mighty angel with Christ, the Anglo-Norman visualizations of this figure are striking for their diversity. Different manuscripts explore differ-

---

23. For the Latin text of Berengaudus, see PL 17:763–970, where it is misattributed to Ambrose.

24. O'Hear, *Contrasting Images*, 12.

25. On Berengaudus, see, e.g., Lewis, *Reading Images*, 40–43; O'Hear, *Contrasting Images*, 16–22; Richard K. Emmerson, *Apocalypse Illuminated: The Visual Exegesis of Revelation in Medieval Illustrated Manuscripts* (University Park: Pennsylvania State University Press, 2018), 112–27. For the alternative view that dates the commentary to the ninth century, identifying its author as the Carolingian Berengaudus of Ferrières, see Derk Visser, *Apocalypse as Utopian Expectation (800–1500): The Apocalypse Commentary of Berengaudus of Ferrières and the Relationship between Exegesis, Liturgy, and Iconography* (Leiden: Brill, 1996), 12–103.

ent emphases both in the biblical text and the Berengaudus commentary. However, there is a commonality regarding two features. First, the description of the angel as *amictum nube* is conveyed by the outline of a cloud formation behind his torso. Second, there is a tendency to gloss over the reference to legs like pillars or columns of fire, or to handle it in a less literal and more allusive fashion than the later Dürer or his Koberger model. Three examples will suffice to demonstrate this diversity of visual exegesis.

The first is in the Abingdon Apocalypse (Add. MS BL 42555, fol. 27v), variously dated to circa 1256–1262 and circa 1270–1275. Part of the Metz group, Abingdon combines the Latin text of Revelation with commentary in Anglo-Norman French translation on alternate pages. Although the majority of commentary glosses come from Berengaudus, a minority are derived from the Latin commentary of ninth-century exegete Haimo of Auxerre.[26]

Folio 27v (*John Takes the Book*, fig. 10.2) contains both the image and the Vulgate text of Rev 10:1–11. The image itself combines two scenes: to the left, John is commanded by an angelic mediator to take the book from the mighty angel (Rev 10:8); the command is fulfilled in the right-hand scene (illustrating Rev 10:9–11), in which the mighty angel dominates. The Abingdon illuminator has come closest to conveying this angel's christological aspect. Though his form is conventionally angelic (winged and haloed), he is not only bearded but also has a cross in his halo, mirroring Abingdon's earlier image of the enthroned Christ, depicting Rev 4 and 5 (fol. 6v). The difference in the faces of these two figures is apparently due to an attempt, only partially successful, to show how the angel's face shone like the sun.

The Abingdon Apocalypse has one additional surprising feature in its visualization of Rev 10. As if to underscore Berengaudus's interpretation of that passage as a vision of Christ's incarnation, interrupting visions of the seven trumpet plagues understood as the persecution of the church, Abingdon takes the unusual step of inserting (on the facing page) an image of the *Massacre of the Innocents and Flight into Egypt* from Matt 2:13–18 (fol. 28r; fig. 10.3).

The precise reason for this juxtaposition of apocalyptic vision and these two gospel narratives is not immediately clear. Their presence in the

---

26. Daron Burrows, ed., *Abingdon Apocalypse (British Library, Add. 24555)*, ANT (Oxford: Anglo-Norman Text Society, 2017). For the Latin text of Haimo, see PL 11:937–1220.

Fig. 10.2. Abingdon Apocalypse, *John Takes the Book* (ca. 1270–1275). Colors with gold on parchment; folio size 13 x 8 in. British Library, London, Add. MS 42555, fol. 27v. © The British Library Board.

Fig. 10.3. Abingdon Apocalypse, *Massacre of the Innocents and Flight into Egypt*, ca. 1270–1275. Colors with gold on parchment; folio size 13 x 8 in. British Library, London, Add. MS 42555, fol. 28r. © The British Library Board.

Anglo-Norman cycles is certainly not unprecedented. Berengaudus's commentary makes the connection between Matt 2:13–15 and Rev 12, where Herod is allegorized as the dragon pursuing the woman (interpreted as Mary) into the wilderness. Other Anglo-Norman Apocalypses, such as the Cloisters Apocalypse, produced in Normandy circa 1330, preface the Apocalypse proper with a cycle of scenes from Christ's infancy, culminating in the massacre and the flight.[27] The latter scene of the holy family's exile to Egypt functions as a smooth transition to the story of John, whose sojourn on Patmos was also considered an exile.

A clue as to Abingdon's unusual placement of these two infancy images alongside the text of Rev 10 is provided in the French gloss underneath the image of the massacre and the flight on folio 28r:

> *E je vi un autre aungele fort descendaunt del ciel, et cetera.* Li *aungele* est Jesu Crist, ki est messager de paternele volunté, kar li *aungele* aparut de *une nue afublé*, pur ce ke nostre Seingnur aparut entre gent en vesture de char, de ki le Prophete: "Estes vus, nostre Seingnur muntera sur une legere nue e entra en Egypte." Il munta sur la legere *nue* quant il prist char de la Virgine Marie senz grevaunce de peché.[28]

This gloss comes from the Haimo commentary rather than Berengaudus, although it concurs with the latter that the mighty angel is Jesus Christ, and the cloud symbolizes the flesh with which the incarnate Christ is clothed. It finds in the angelic cloud a reference to Isa 19:1: "Our Lord will ascend on a light cloud and enter into Egypt," the cloud being the sinless flesh of the Virgin Mary. Isaiah 19 is frequently connected in patristic and medieval exegesis with the flight into Egypt and the apocryphal story of the fall of the idols on the holy family's arrival (e.g., Eusebius, *Dem. ev.* 6.20; Rufinus, *Hist. mon.* 7.1; Ps.-Mt. 23). Though ordinarily connected to Rev 12:6, 14, the Abingdon illuminator sees it already being fulfilled in the arrival of Christ as the mighty angel of Rev 10.

A different emphasis is found in the Getty Apocalypse, formerly the Dyson Perrins Apocalypse, part of the Westminster group and probably produced in London circa 1255–1260 (MS Ludwig III.1).[29] Revelation 10 is spread across two images: *The Mighty Angel and John Forbidden to Write*

---

27. Emmerson, *Apocalypse Illuminated*, 153–54.
28. Burrows, *Abingdon Apocalypse*, 54.
29. On Getty, see Nigel J. Morgan, *Illuminating the End of Time: The Getty Apoca-*

(fol. 15, fig. 10.4), and *Saint John Eats the Book Received from the Angel* (fol. 15v), the second image giving due weight to the prophetic dimension that dominates the Dürer image. Getty's mighty angel, who has central place in both images, lacks both the beard and crossed nimbus of Abingdon. In other words, the christological interpretation of the Berengaudus commentary recedes into the background, and the focus is rather on the angel as angelic mediator, just one among several in the unfolding narrative of Rev 10–11.

Nonetheless, this angel remains the dominant figure, and the Getty illuminator has also sought to convey the angelic "feet like pillars of fire" by depicting red bare feet emerging from beneath his ankle-length robe. In the first of the two Getty images, meanwhile, John is a marginal figure on the right, engaged in a comic dispute with another angel, who snatches his quill from his hand to prevent him writing down the content of the seven thunders (represented as seven dog-like heads emerging from the cloud in the top right).

Our third example, the mighty angel in the fourteenth-century Cloisters Apocalypse stands somewhere in between the robustly christomorphic angel of Abingdon and the angelic form of Getty.[30] Cloisters (ca. 1330; Cloisters, MS MMA 68.174) is closely related to two other Apocalypse manuscripts of the period (Add. MS BL 17333; MS BNF lat. 14410); all three are derived from the Metz group, perhaps the famous Lambeth Apocalypse (ca. 1260; MS Lambeth Pal. 209).[31] Cloisters contains only the Vulgate text of Revelation, without the Berengaudus commentary.

The Cloisters Apocalypse traces the flow of the unfolding narrative of Rev 10–11 (the descent of the angel, John devouring the book, John commissioned to measure the temple of God). What is perhaps most interesting is how the angel's appearance changes as we move through the frames, as if to emphasize the multivalency of the vision. His first appearance, *The Angel with the Book* (fol. 16r; fig. 10.5), illustrating the text of Rev 10:1–9 placed beneath the image, stresses his christomorphic character. The angel is clean-shaven rather than bearded, but has the crossed halo

---

*lypse Manuscript; Facsimile Edition with a Commentary* (Los Angeles: J. Paul Getty Museum, 2011).

30. Florens Deuchler, Jeffrey M. Hoffeld, and Helmut Nickel, *The Cloisters Apocalypse: An Early Fourteenth-Century Manuscript in Facsimile*, 2 vols. (New York: Metropolitan Museum of Art, 1971).

31. Deuchler, Hoffeld, and Nickel, *Cloisters Apocalypse*, 2:10.

10. SEEING CHRIST'S ANGEL 275

Fig. 10.4. Getty Apocalypse, *The Mighty Angel and John Forbidden to Write*, ca. 1255–1260. Tempera colors, gold leaf, colored washes, pen and ink on parchment; 12 9/16 x 8 7/8 in. Getty Museum, Malibu, MS Ludwig III.1, fol. 15. Credit: Digital image courtesy of the Getty's Open Content Program.

Fig. 10.5. Cloisters Apocalypse, *The Angel with the Book*, ca. 1330. Tempera, gold, silver, and ink on parchment; folio size 12 1/8 x 9 1/16 in. The Cloisters, Metropolitan Museum of Art, New York, 68.174, fol. 16r.

used of Christ elsewhere, as in the image of the enthroned Christ depicting Rev 4–5 (fol. 5v).[32] So he is like Christ, but (*pace* Berengaudus) not Christ. Moreover, in the next image (fol. 16v), the mighty angel becomes even less christomorphic and more conventionally angelic, although he retains the fiery red feet of the preceding image, a fairly successful attempt to convey the angel's "feet like pillars of fire."

These three examples, displaying a remarkable diversity in visualizing the mighty angel, illustrate the dynamic relationship between biblical text, authoritative exegetical traditions, and artistic imagination, given the explicitly christological interpretation of the Berengaudus commentary. However, there is one consistent feature they share in common: that the descending angel looks not at John but directly forward, out of the page, toward the viewer. It is often noted how these Anglo-Norman Apocalypses served to draw the reader into the story of what John sees, making possible for a lay elite the life of contemplation hitherto reserved to monks and clergy, or perhaps even making possible a "spiritual pilgrimage" to the new Jerusalem, given the impossibility of pilgrimage to the earthly Jerusalem following the city's fall in 1244.[33] So then perhaps one of the most important considerations is what function this angel performs, gazing out of the page directly into the eyes of the attentive viewer.

## Jean Duvet

Some three hundred years after the earliest Anglo-Norman Apocalypses, French artist Jean Duvet illustrates the extraordinary influence of Albrecht Dürer's *Apocalypsis cum figuris*. Duvet is not alone among artists in the sixteenth century to be substantially indebted to Dürer. Other examples include Lucas Cranach the Elder's polemical woodcut illustrations for Luther's German New Testament of September 1522 (where for the first time the whore of Babylon wears the papal triple tiara), Matthias Gerung's woodcuts from circa 1530–1532, and the Dionysiou frescoes on Mount

---

32. The Lamb receiving the book is interpreted in Berengaudus's commentary as the incarnation, Christ receiving his humanity from his divinity (*Agnus ergo librum de dextra sedentis super thronum accepit; quia homo Christus a sua divinitate accepit*: PL 17:809C). The "Christlike" figure on the throne is both the divine Christ and God the Father ("He who has seen me has seen the Father").

33. Lewis, *Reading Images*, 32–34, 240.

Athos dated to 1547, their figures modified in line with Byzantine iconographical style.[34]

Jean Duvet, the earliest known French engraver, came from a family of goldsmiths from Langres in Burgundy and worked as goldsmith for two French kings, François II and Henri II. Duvet was born in Burgundy in 1485 and was active both in Langres and in nearby Dijon. He seems to have been living in Geneva between 1540 and 1556 (probably the result of religious persecution, since Protestant ideas had permeated his part of France). He was apparently back in France by the time his Apocalypse engravings were published.[35]

These twenty-three plates, probably produced between 1546 and 1555, were published in Lyon in 1561, under the title *Lapocalypse figuree par Jehan Duuet, iadis Orfevre des Rois, Francois premier de ce nom & Henri deuxieme*.[36] Apart from the clear influence of Dürer's Apocalypse woodcuts, Duvet is also indebted to Raphael, Marcantonio, and especially Mantegna, Italian Renaissance art having been introduced into France through the campaigns of François II.[37] The rather chaotic character of his images evokes the religious and political turmoil of the time during which they were produced. In the assessment of one critic: "The frenzied rush of Duvet's figures conveys something of the nightmare of the Apocalyptic visions, which is lacking in Dürer's more carefully thought out compositions, imaginative as they are."[38] Similarly, Christopher Rowland speaks

---

34. In the case of the Dionysiou frescoes, it is debated whether the influence of Dürer is direct or mediated through another German artist, such as Lucas Cranach the Elder, or the "Master IF." See Huguette Brunet-Dinard, "Le Maitre IF, inspirateur des fresques de l'Apocalypse de Dionysiou," *GBA* 6.44 (1954): 309-16, 363-65.

35. On Duvet's life, see, e.g., Michael Marqusee, "Introduction," in *The Revelation of St. John: Apocalypse Engravings by Jean Duvet*, MIB (New York: Paddington, 1976), 7-16; Colin Eisler, *The Master of the Unicorn: The Life and Work of Jean Duvet* (New York: Abaris Books, 1979), 1-34.

36. On the Apocalypse engravings, see Arthur E. Popham, "Jean Duvet," *PCQ* 8 (1921): 123-50; Henry P. Rossiter, "Duvet's Engravings of the Apocalypse," *BMFA* 50 (1952): 16-19; Henry S. Francis, "The Apocalypse of Jean Duvet," *BCMA* 41.3 (March 1954): 56-59; Eisler, *Master of the Unicorn*, 47-109; Frances Carey, ed., *The Apocalypse and the Shape of Things to Come* (Toronto: University of Toronto Press, 1999), 169-77; Christopher Rowland, "Imagining the Apocalypse," *NTS* 51 (2005): 304-5.

37. Marqusee, "Introduction," 8.

38. Popham, "Jean Duvet," 141.

of "a jumble of figures and the confusion of things earthly and heavenly,"[39] merging the terrestrial and celestial planes that Dürer strove so carefully to keep apart.

Duvet's plate illustrating Rev 10 needs to be viewed in the light of the opening plate, which depicts Duvet himself, seated at an altar-like desk on a Patmos-like island. On the desk in front of him is a copy of John's Apocalypse, together with a tablet that is the same shape as his Apocalypse engravings. Duvet, like Dürer before him, presents himself as an *alter Johannes*, his images mediating his own visionary apprehension of what John of Patmos once saw. The inscription on the tablet reads as follows: "Jean Duvet, goldsmith of Langres, aged seventy, has completed these histories in 1555." That this is the artistic endeavor of a man near the end of his life is underscored by a second inscription to the right, framed between the three Fates in a boat above and a swan with an arrow in its mouth below: "Death is upon me [literally 'the Fates press,' *fata premūt*] and my hands tremble, my eyes are already beginning to fail, yet the spirit remains victorious and I have completed my great work."[40] The aged artist now assumes the mantle of his namesake John of Patmos, who will be depicted in the plates that follow as a young man.[41]

The inspired artist is not completely devoid of human assistance, however. A third inscription at bottom left asserts, "The sacred mysteries contained in this and the other tablets following are derived from the divine Apocalypse of John and are closely adapted to the true letter of the text with the judgment of more learned men brought to bear." Colin Eisler has suggested that these more learned men might have included Duvet's contemporaries Canon Jean Lefèvre, humanist scholar Richard Roussat of Langres, poet Nicholas Bourbon, and Protestant theologian Antoine Dupinet, author of a treatise on the Apocalypse that was first published in Geneva in 1539.[42]

The frontispiece provides context for *The Angel Gives Saint John the Book to Eat*, the plate illustrating Rev 10 (fig. 10.6). As for Dürer, John's prophetic inspiration is foregrounded, as John devours the little book in the angel's hand. It is the angel, however, who now dominates. Albeit

---

39. Rowland, "Imagining the Apocalypse," 305.
40. Eisler, *Master of the Unicorn*, 47–48.
41. On Duvet as an exemplar of "visionary" visual exegesis, see O'Hear, *Contrasting Images*, 237.
42. Eisler, *Master of the Unicorn*, 48–49.

contorted, wings out of place, column-like legs off-balance, the angel is somehow more convincing than Dürer's disembodied figure. The cloud no longer replaces the torso. Rather, it clothes the torso, while also extending beyond the angel's body to provide a visual bridge between the figure of John and the heavenly altar that is the source of John's prophetic inspiration (and, by extension, Duvet's own artistic inspiration). The fire emerging from the top of the two pillar-legs conveys the impression of genuine flames. Both elements may have been suggested by the adaptation of Dürer's woodcut in *Das Newe Testament* (Wittenberg, 1522), issued by Hans Lufft.[43]

What does Duvet seek to convey by the mighty angel? There may be hints of an older christological interpretation, in the cruciform posture of his arms, the three sets of sunrays recalling the crossed-nimbus of some medieval antecedents, or the god-like character of his classical head, evoking an Apollo or an Adonis. The likeness to Apollo is particularly intriguing, given that commentators have often found possible echoes of Apollo elsewhere in the Apocalypse (e.g., 6:2; 12:1–6).[44] It may have been suggested here by the description of the angel's face "like the sun."[45] However, Duvet retains that textual ambiguity that allows this figure to be angelic, even if closely related to Christ or the one on the throne as messenger and mediator of prophetic inspiration. Duvet's mighty angel resembles the left-hand angel in Mantegna's *St. Bernardino of Siena between Two Angels* (1460; Pinacoteca di Brera, Milan), and St. Michael in his *Madonna della Vittoria* (1496; Louvre Museum, Paris). It is a very different figure from Duvet's "one like a son of man," clearly a Christ figure, who dominates his second engraving illustrating Rev 1.

## Nineteenth-Century Alternatives: William Blake, Benjamin West, and John Martin

The medieval tendency is to depict angels in human-like form, albeit with wings, and occasionally with features of the divine Christ. We have

---

43. Eisler, *Master of the Unicorn*, 101.

44. E.g., Allen Kerkeslager, "Apollo, Greco-Roman Prophecy, and the Rider on the White Horse in Rev 6.2," *JBL* 112 (1993): 116–21.

45. Eisler suggest that this may be the result of a humanistic reinterpretation of Rev 10:11 (*Master of the Unicorn*, 266).

Fig. 10.6. Jean Duvet, *The Angel Gives Saint John the Book to Eat*, 1561. Copper engraving, 15.3 x 20.9 in. Bibliothèque Nationale, Paris. Credit: INTERFOTO/Alamy Stock Photo.

also seen how, in the Anglo-Norman Apocalypses and even in Dürer, the mighty angel is no larger than the figure of John, underscoring that both have equally important roles to fulfill, though Duvet's more expansive angel, physically linking heaven and earth, may be hinting at a greater angelic prominence. The final examples to be considered are three nineteenth-century images that manage to evoke the sublime, otherworldly character of this angel (not least by emphasizing his extraordinary height), and one at least presenting a more modern problematization of the phenomenon of angelic vision. What is an angel? How can angels be seen? What are the ambiguities in claims to have seen an angel, and the alternative explanations?

William Blake's *And the Angel Which I Saw Lifted His Hand to Heaven* or *The Angel of the Revelation* (ca. 1803–1805; Metropolitan Museum of Art, New York; fig. 10.7), is one of a number of watercolors of images from Revelation that Blake painted between 1800 and 1805 for his friend Thomas Butts.[46] Compositionally, it recalls *The Great Red Dragon and the Beast from the Sea* (1805; National Gallery of Art, Washington, DC), depicting Rev 13:1–2, in the same series. As the title suggests, Blake presents the moment when the angel raises his right hand and swears that "there should be time no longer" (Rev 10:6 KJV). Blake gives full value to the King James Version's translation of ἄγγελον ἰσχυρὸν as "*mighty* angel." Blake's mighty angel is a powerful Colossus, dwarfing the small and somewhat androgynous figure of John at the bottom of the page (who appears less real, less corporeal, than the classically muscular, powerful young angel). Indeed, the angel is in the posture of the ancient Colossus of Rhodes, prints of which may have provided Blake with his model. Possible sources include the popular engraving by Maarten van Heemskerck (1570).[47]

For Blake, the mighty angel is Christ, the conquering hero, identified with the divine warrior on the white horse of Rev 19:11–16 and distinguished from most of Blake's other angels by his lack of wings.[48] The angel's massive size parallels other key players in the cosmic drama that Blake describes visually, who are equally gigantic in scale. There are strik-

---

46. See Christopher Rowland, *Blake and the Bible* (New Haven: Yale University Press, 2010), 224–28.

47. Morton D. Paley, *The Apocalyptic Sublime* (London: Yale University Press, 1986), 85.

48. On the latter point, see Harvey Stahl and Bruce Daryl Barone, eds., *William Blake: The Apocalyptic Vision* (Purchase, NY: Manhattanville College Press, 1974), 21.

Fig. 10.7. William Blake, *The Angel of the Revelation* (ca. 1803–1805). Watercolor, pen and black ink, over traces of graphite, 15 7/16 x 10 1/4 in. Metropolitan Museum of Art, New York, Rogers Fund, 14.81.1.

ing visual similarities between the angel and Blake's depiction of Albion, and also of Milton, showing the latter's place in a long line of prophets.[49] Blake's more allusive, imaginative approach is arguably more compelling than Dürer's overly literal treatment of the angel. The cloud is conveyed by a length of transparent cloth draped over his right shoulder, as well as the billowing cloud formation behind him. The flames emanating from his feet convey the energy implied in the metaphor "feet *like* pillars of fire." The explosion of sunrays behind his back function both for his rainbow-like halo and his face "as it were the sun" (Rev 10:1 KJV). By contrast, John's role, although crucial, is relegated to second place. One must look hard to see the tiny scroll laid out on the rocky outcrop of Patmos, which serves as the writing desk for the equally diminutive seer.

Blake's image exemplifies the capacity of visual art to evoke a profound emotional response. But visual exegesis can also function to exploit and magnify features that are less significant in the biblical source text, resulting in a novel, unexpected, or provocative reading of that text. This is particularly the case for a poet and visionary such as Blake, who emphasized the capacity of the Bible to stimulate the reader's imagination: "The Whole Bible is filld with Imaginations & Visions from End to End & not with Moral virtues that is the baseness of Plato & the Greeks & all Warriors."[50]

Blake's watercolor contains a feature that at first glance appears alien to the biblical text: seven horses and their riders in the cloud formation behind the angel's legs. This is almost certainly Blake's allusion to the seven thunders (Rev 10:3–4), which are generally treated as marginal to this text. (John hears them but then is immediately told not to write them down, so that their content remains obscure.) Blake not only gives this marginal element of Rev 10 greater prominence; he offers a particular solution to the puzzle as to what the seven thunders represent, by directly connecting them to the trumpet sequence that this chapter interrupts (we are in suspension between the sixth and seventh trumpets). The seven horsemen recall the four horsemen of the first four seals (6:1–8), plus the millions of demonic cavalry called forth in the previous chapter (9:13–19). Two of the four horsemen, famine and death, were depicted in a separate watercolor for Thomas Butts, *Death on a Pale Horse* (ca. 1800).

---

49. Joseph Anthony Wittreich, *Angel of Apocalypse: Blake's Idea of Milton* (Madison: University of Wisconsin Press, 1975), 17, 46.

50. William Blake, "Annotations to Berkeley," E664, quoted in Rowland, *Blake and the Bible*, 233.

For Blake, these seven horsemen are the seven trumpet-angels, now become fallen angels, contrasted with the mighty angel, who dominates the scene and to whom John's gaze is directed.[51] This is not far removed from one solution found in modern commentaries on the Apocalypse, whereby the seven thunders are interpreted as the continuation of the trumpet plagues, further judgments announced to John but interrupted by the announcement of this powerful angel and therefore not to be carried out.[52] But Blake makes the connection much more effectively and immediately by his visual commentary.

Arguably even more imposing is Benjamin West's stern angel in his *A Mighty Angel Standeth upon the Land and the Sea* (fig. 10.8), perhaps influenced by Blake's watercolor, and exhibited at the Royal Academy in 1798. West was born in Springfield, Pennsylvania, in 1738, moving to England in 1763, where he served two terms as president of the Royal Academy in London (1792–1805, 1806–1820). His *Mighty Angel* was one of several paintings on Revelation produced for William Beckford, intended to be housed in a Revelation Chamber at Beckford's home, Fonthill Abbey in Wiltshire (though the project was never realized).[53] That this figure is angelic rather than a manifestation of Christ is evident from its striking likeness to the archangel Michael in West's *St. Michael and the Dragon* (1797; Toledo Museum of Art, Toledo, Ohio), also painted for Beckford and exhibited at the Royal Academy at the same time.[54] John has disappeared from the scene entirely, allowing the angel the viewer's undivided attention. Nor has West attempted to visualize the feet "as pillars of fire," a detail that proved so intractable for Dürer and many of his successors.

The third nineteenth-century image seeks to visualize Revelation's angel in a manner very different from that of either Benjamin West or William Blake. John Martin was a visionary artist and social reformer, probably best known for his three massive apocalyptic canvases in Tate Britain in London (painted between 1851 and 1854).[55] His lithograph illustrating Rev 10, *The Angel with the Book* (fig. 10.9), was produced about

---

51. According to Wittreich, they are the seven angels, "all of them having fallen into error" (*Angel of Apocalypse*, 258 n. 40).
52. E.g., Koester, *Revelation*, 489.
53. Paley, *Apocalyptic Sublime*, 36–47.
54. For the image, see Paley, *Apocalyptic Sublime*, 42, pl. 19.
55. On Martin's visionary art, see, e.g., William Feaver, *The Art of John Martin*

Fig. 10.8. Benjamin West, *A Mighty Angel Standeth upon the Land and upon the Sea*, ca. 1797. Oil on paper, mounted on panel; 21 1/5 x 31 in. Location unknown. Credit: The Picture Art Collection / Alamy Stock Photo.

fifteen years earlier, in 1837, and is a much more tranquil scene than the Last Judgment triptych, and even his mezzotint *The Opening of the Seventh Seal* produced around the same time, which is compositionally very similar to his *Angel with the Book* (John standing on the same rocky outcrop of Patmos). The figure of John has his back to the viewer, typical of Martin's figures, who "look into the paintings, towards the action."[56]

But it is Martin's visualization of the angel himself that is most noteworthy. At first sight, John appears to be gazing up at the dazzling sunlight and a rather unusual cloud formation. It is only gradually that an angelic figure comes into focus, dwarfing the figure of John by its vast size. Martin seems to be problematizing in visual terms the nature of angelic vision, which was perhaps more pressing for Victorians than for the medieval illuminators of Abingdon, Getty, or Cloisters. How does one see an angel? And how can one be sure that what one sees is angelic, rather than the effect of sunlight and cloud on the human imagination? Martin's contemporary Christina Rossetti, for all her conventional piety, expresses the same question when commenting on Rev 10 in her "devotional" commentary on the Apocalypse, *The Face of the Deep*: "One notices a storm: another discerns an Angel. One hears thunder: another divines a message."[57] (The allusion there is to John 12:28–29.) Or one might recall William Blake's famous words in his *A Vision of the Last Judgment*:

> "What!" it will be questioned, "when the sun rises, do you not see a round disc of fire somewhat like a guinea!" Oh! no, no! I see an innumerable company of the heavenly host crying "Holy, holy, holy is the Lord God Almighty!" I question not my corporeal eye any more than I would question a window concerning a sight. I look through it, and not with it.[58]

To see and hear an angel requires a particular apocalyptic sensibility, which will always retain an element of ambiguity. The ambiguity may even extend to the identity of this figure, for the face of Martin's angel, albeit indistinct, is recognizably Christlike.

---

(Oxford: Clarendon, 1975); Paley, *Apocalyptic Sublime*, 122–54; Carey, *Apocalypse and the Shape*, 223–28; Martin Myrone, ed., *John Martin: Apocalypse* (London: Tate, 2011).

56. Feaver, *Art of John Martin*, 215.

57. Christina G. Rossetti, *The Face of the Deep: A Devotional Commentary on the Apocalypse*, 2nd ed. (London: SPCK, 1893), 275.

58. William Blake, *The Complete Poetry and Prose of William Blake*, ed. David V. Erdman (Berkeley: University of California Press, 1988), 565–66.

Fig. 10.9. Charles Wands after John Martin, *The Angel with the Book*, ca. 1839–1844. Engraving; 6 9/16 x 7 11/16 in. Victoria and Albert Museum, London, E.724-1968, Bequeathed by Thomas Balston through Art Fund. © Victoria and Albert Museum, London.

## Final Reflections

This chapter has sought to demonstrate some of the different possibilities that visual exegesis can make to understanding and responding to John's exegetically complex vision in Rev 10, complementing the necessary but not exhaustive role of textual exegesis found in Apocalypse commentaries. Visual art, for example, has the capacity to convey ambiguity and multivalency more effectively than written commentary, as it seeks to "transcend the rationally literal"[59] (though, as we have seen, this is not necessarily the case: extreme literalism can result in an image that is faintly ridiculous, as in the case of Dürer). The Anglo-Norman Apocalypses are far more successful in responding—in surprisingly different ways—both to

---

59. O'Hear and O'Hear, *Picturing the Apocalypse*, 4.

the christological dimensions of the mighty angel and the different angelic roles played by this character.

Second, visual art can function to prioritize particular moments in a complex narrative: for example, Dürer's prioritizing the moment when the newly commissioned prophet John devours the prophetic book, Blake's focus on the angel swearing an oath, or Martin capturing the moment when John on Patmos first sees the angel. Alternatively, it can present different stages in the narrative synchronically, as in the Anglo-Norman Apocalypses, juxtaposing the descent of the mighty angel with various heavenly commands to John. Third, visual images often exploit and magnify features that are less significant in the biblical source text, resulting in a novel or unforeseen reading of that text (Blake's introduction of the seven horsemen, as an unexpected commentary on the seven thunders, is a case in point).[60] Occasionally, as in the surprising juxtaposition of Rev 10 with the Matthean narrative of the massacre of the innocents and the flight into Egypt in the Abingdon Apocalypse, visual exegesis is able to open up quite complex intertextual relationships, uniting disparate biblical texts and biblical commentaries with their complex exegetical arguments, forging new connections and fresh interpretative possibilities for the viewer.

Finally, the immediacy of visual apprehension may be especially appropriate and effective for conveying the subject matter of a book such as John's Apocalypse, which presents itself as the literary mediation of a prior visionary experience.[61] When that subject matter concerns angels, or the angelic world, then the challenges and the possibilities are heightened still further.

## Works Cited

Alexander Minorita. *Expositio in Apocalypsim*. Edited by Alois Wachtel. Weimar: Hermann Böhlaus Nachfolger, 1955.

Blake, William. *The Complete Poetry and Prose of William Blake*. Edited by David V. Erdman. Berkeley: University of California Press, 1988.

---

60. See Rowland, *Imagining the Apocalypse*, 316–19; J. Cheryl Exum and Ela Nuţu, eds., *Between the Text and the Canvas: The Bible and Art in Dialogue*, BMW 13 (Sheffield: Sheffield Phoenix, 2007), 2.

61. See O'Hear, *Contrasting Images*, 199–236.

Boxall, Ian. "Francis of Assisi as Apocalyptic Visionary." Pages 253–66 in *Revealed Wisdom: Studies in Apocalyptic in Honour of Christopher Rowland*. Edited by John Ashton. AGJU 88. Leiden: Brill, 2014.

———. "The Mighty Angel with the Little Scroll: British Perspectives on the Reception History of Revelation 10." Pages 245–63 in *The Book of Revelation: Currents in British Research on the Apocalypse*. Edited by Garrick V. Allen, Ian Paul, and Simon P. Woodman. WUNT 411. Tübingen: Mohr Siebeck, 2015.

———. *The Revelation of St. John*. BNTC. Peabody, MA: Hendrickson, 2006.

Brighton, Louis Andrew. "The Angel of Revelation: An Angel of God and an Icon of Jesus Christ." PhD diss., Saint Louis University, 1991.

Brunet-Dinard, Huguette. "Le Maitre IF, inspirateur des fresques de l'Apocalypse de Dionysiou." *Gazette des Beaux-Arts* 6.44 (1954): 309–16, 363–65.

Burrows, Daron, ed. *The Abingdon Apocalypse (British Library, Add. 24555)*. ANT. Oxford: Anglo-Norman Text Society, 2017.

Carey, Frances, ed. *The Apocalypse and the Shape of Things to Come*. Toronto: University of Toronto Press, 1999.

Deuchler, Florens, Jeffrey M. Hoffeld, and Helmut Nickel. *The Cloisters Apocalypse: An Early Fourteenth-Century Manuscript in Facsimile*. 2 vols. New York: Metropolitan Museum of Art, 1971.

Eisler, Colin. *The Master of the Unicorn: The Life and Work of Jean Duvet*. New York: Abaris Books, 1979.

Emmerson, Richard K. *Apocalypse Illuminated: The Visual Exegesis of Revelation in Medieval Illustrated Manuscripts*. University Park: Pennsylvania State University Press, 2018.

Exum, J. Cheryl, and Ela Nuțu, eds. *Between the Text and the Canvas: The Bible and Art in Dialogue*. BMW 13. Sheffield: Sheffield Phoenix, 2007.

Feaver, William. *The Art of John Martin*. Oxford: Clarendon, 1975.

Francis, Henry S. "The Apocalypse of Jean Duvet." *BCMA* 41.3 (March 1954): 56–59.

Gieschen, Charles A. *Angelomorphic Christology: Antecedents and Early Evidence*. AGJU 42. Leiden: Brill, 1998.

Gumerlock, Francis X., ed. *Early Latin Commentaries on the Apocalypse*. Kalamazoo: Medieval Institute Publications, Western Michigan University, 2016.

Gundry, Robert H. "Angelomorphic Christology in the Book of Revelation." Pages 662–78 in *1994 Seminar Papers: One Hundred Thirtieth*

*Annual Meeting, November 19–22, 1994, the Chicago Hilton and Towers, Chicago, IL.* SBLSP 33. Atlanta: Scholars Press, 1994.

Kauffmann, Claus M. *An Altarpiece of the Apocalypse from Master Bertram's Workshop in Hamburg.* MM 25. London: HMSO, Victoria and Albert Museum, 1968.

Kerkeslager, Allen. "Apollo, Greco-Roman Prophecy, and the Rider on the White Horse in Rev 6.2." *JBL* 112 (1993): 116–21.

Koester, Craig R. *Revelation: A New Translation with Introduction and Commentary.* AYB 38A. New Haven: Yale University Press, 2014.

Kovacs, Judith, and Christopher Rowland. *Revelation: The Apocalypse of Jesus Christ.* BBC. Oxford: Blackwell, 2006.

Lerner, Robert E. "The Medieval Return to the Thousand-Year Sabbath." Pages 51–71 in *The Apocalypse in the Middle Ages.* Edited by Richard K. Emmerson and Bernard McGinn. Ithaca, NY: Cornell University Press, 1992.

Lewis, Suzanne. *Reading Images: Narrative Discourse and Reception in the Thirteenth-Century Illuminated Apocalypse.* Cambridge: Cambridge University Press, 1995.

Marqusee, Michael. "Introduction." Pages 7–16 in *The Revelation of St. John: Apocalypse Engravings by Jean Duvet.* MIB. New York: Paddington, 1976.

Morgan, Nigel J. *Illuminating the End of Time: The Getty Apocalypse Manuscript; Facsimile Edition with a Commentary.* Los Angeles: J. Paul Getty Museum, 2011.

Myrone, Martin, ed. *John Martin: Apocalypse.* London: Tate, 2011.

O'Hear, Natasha F. H. *Contrasting Images of the Book of Revelation in Late Medieval and Early Modern Art: A Case Study in Visual Exegesis.* OTM. Oxford: Oxford University Press, 2011.

O'Hear, Natasha, and Anthony O'Hear. *Picturing the Apocalypse: The Book of Revelation in the Arts over Two Millennia.* Oxford: Oxford University Press, 2015.

Paley, Morton D. *The Apocalyptic Sublime.* London: Yale University Press, 1986.

Panofsky, Erwin. *The Life and Art of Albrecht Dürer.* Princeton: Princeton University Press, 1955.

Popham, Arthur E. "Jean Duvet." *PCQ* 8 (1921): 123–50.

Rossetti, Christina G. *The Face of the Deep: A Devotional Commentary on the Apocalypse.* 2nd ed. London: SPCK, 1893.

Rossiter, Henry P. "Duvet's Engravings of the Apocalypse." *BMFA* 50 (1952): 16–19.
Rowland, Christopher. *Blake and the Bible*. New Haven: Yale University Press, 2010.
———. "Imagining the Apocalypse." *NTS* 51 (2005): 303–27.
Stahl, Harvey, and Bruce Daryl Barone, eds. *William Blake: The Apocalyptic Vision*. Purchase, NY: Manhattanville College Press, 1974.
Tyconius. *Exposition of the Apocalypse*. Translated by Francis X. Gumerlock. FC 134. Washington, DC: Catholic University of America Press, 2017.
Visser, Derk. *Apocalypse as Utopian Expectation (800–1500): The Apocalypse Commentary of Berengaudus of Ferrières and the Relationship between Exegesis, Liturgy, and Iconography*. Leiden: Brill, 1996.
Wainwright, Arthur W. *Mysterious Apocalypse*. Nashville: Abingdon, 1993.
Weinrich, William C., trans. *Greek Commentaries on Revelation*. Edited by Thomas C. Oden. ACT. Downers Grove, IL: IVP Academic, 2011.
Wittreich, Joseph Anthony. *Angel of Apocalypse: Blake's Idea of Milton*. Madison: University of Wisconsin Press, 1975.

## Contributors

**Ian Boxall** is Associate Professor of New Testament at the Catholic University of America, Washington, DC, and cochair of the SBL Bible and Visual Art program unit. His research interests include reception history, the Gospel of Matthew, and the book of Revelation. His recent publications include *Patmos in the Reception History of the Apocalypse* (2013), *Matthew through the Centuries* (2019), and *Christ in the Book of Revelation* (2021).

**James Clifton** is Director of the Sarah Campbell Blaffer Foundation and Curator in Renaissance and Baroque Painting at the Museum of Fine Arts, Houston. He has published extensively on early-modern European art and culture. His curated and cocurated exhibitions include *The Body of Christ in the Art of Europe and New Spain, 1150–1800* (1997); *Scripture for the Eyes: Bible Illustration in Netherlandish Prints of the Sixteenth Century* (2009); *Pleasure and Piety: The Art of Joachim Wtewael* (2015); and *Through a Glass Darkly: Allegory and Faith in Netherlandish Prints from Lucas van Leyden to Rembrandt* (2019). He was the chief script writer for two documentaries produced by the U.S. Conference of Catholic Bishops: "The Face: Jesus in Art" (2001) and "Picturing Mary" (2006). He coedited the volume *Imago exegetica: Visual Images as Exegetical Instruments, 1400–1700* (2013).

**David B. Gowler** is Pierce Professor of Religion at Oxford College of Emory University and Senior Faculty Fellow at the Center for Ethics at Emory University. He is the author of *Host, Guest, Enemy, and Friend: Portraits of the Pharisees in Luke and Acts* (2007); *What Are They Saying about the Parables?* (2nd ed., 2021); *What Are They Saying about the Historical Jesus?* (2007); *James through the Centuries* (2014); and *The Parables after Jesus: Their Imaginative Receptions across Two Millennia* (2020). He has also published dozens of articles, book chapters, public scholarship, and book reviews and is the editor or coeditor of over thirty books, including, with Kipton Jensen, *Howard Thurman: Sermons on the Parables* (2018).

**Jonathan Homrighausen**, a doctoral student in Hebrew Bible at Duke University, explores the intersection of biblical literature and its reception in the arts—especially calligraphy and lettering arts. He is the author of *Illuminating Justice: The Ethical Imagination of The Saint John's Bible* (2018), *Set Me as a Letterform: The Saint John's Bible, the Song of Songs, and The Word Made Flesh* (forthcoming), and articles in *Religion and the Arts*, *Image*, *Teaching Theology and Religion*, *Transpositions*, and *Visual Commentary on Scripture*. He is currently preparing a dissertation on Esther scrolls, visual storytelling, and the meanings of writing.

**Heidi J. Hornik** is Professor of Italian Renaissance and Baroque Art History and Department Chair at Baylor University. She is cochair of the SBL Bible and Visual Art program unit. This paper resulted from an earlier study initiated during her time as a Harvard Visiting Fellow in 2017 and presented in the Bible and Visual Arts session at the Society of Biblical Literature Annual Meeting in November 2017. Her *Michele Tosini and the Ghirlandaio Workshop in Cinquecento Florence* (2009), is the first biography on the Mannerist painter. Hornik and Mikeal C. Parsons coauthored the three-volume *Illuminating Luke* series (2003–2008) and *The Acts of the Apostles through the Centuries* (2020), and they coedited *Interpreting Christian Art* (2004). Her most recent solo-authored book is *The Art of Christian Reflection* (2018).

**Jeff Jay** is Byron K. Trippet Assistant Professor of Religion at Wabash College. His research focuses on early Jewish and Christian texts and their context in ancient Mediterranean cultures. His work encompasses gender and sexuality, critical theory, hermeneutics, religion and literature, and theater and the visual arts. He is the author of *The Tragic in Mark* (2014). His writing has appeared in *Journal of the History of Sexuality*, *Journal of Early Christian Studies*, *Journal for the Study of Judaism*, and *Ancient Judaism*, among other places.

**Christine E. Joynes** is Tutorial Fellow in Theology and Director of the Centre for Baptist Studies, Regent's Park College, Oxford; she also directs the Centre for Reception History of the Bible in the University of Oxford. Publications include, as editor, *Perspectives on the Passion: Encountering* *the Bible through the Arts* (2008) and *From the Margins 2: Biblical Women and their Afterlives* (2009).

**Yohana A. Junker** is Assistant Professor of Art, Religion, and Culture and Louisville Postdoctoral Fellow at the Claremont School of Theology. Her research probes the intersections of decolonial studies and ecology, paying special attention to contemporary Indigenous and diasporic art practices. In her writing, artmaking, and activism, she explores the human capacity to imagine and retrieve generative ways of being even in the face of impossibility. When she is not teaching, learning, or making art, you can find her writing on the poetics of resistance. She has contributed chapters to the forthcoming volumes *Georgetown Companion in Interreligious Studies* and *Religion and Sustainability: Interreligious Resources, Interdisciplinary Responses*. She is also coediting, with Aaron Rosen and Joelle Hathaway, *Modern and Contemporary Artists on Religion: A Global Sourcebook*. She is also a regular contributor to the Wabash Blog Series and the Feminist Studies in Religion Blog.

**Meredith Munson** is the Visiting Assistant Professor of Art History at Sam Houston State University. Meredith received a BA in art history at Baylor University, an MA in art history from Texas Christian University, and a PhD from the Graduate Theological Union in Berkeley. Her primary research interests concern twentieth-century American art and its connections with religion and spirituality. Meredith resides in Dallas, Texas, with her family.

**Ela Nuțu** holds a BA (Hons) in Theology from Manchester University and a PhD in Biblical Studies from Sheffield. Her doctoral work was interdisciplinary and focused on poststructural readings of John's Prologue and the concept of identity in biblical, cultural, and film studies. After her PhD, she held a postdoctoral research position at Sheffield, in the Centre for the Study of the Bible in the Modern World, during which she pursued her interest in the use, reception, and impact of the Bible through visual culture. Her current research continues to be predominantly interdisciplinary. She is particularly interested in theory, exploring different means of reading or interpreting biblical text, particularly the ways in which cultural trends affect a recycling of the Bible in terms of the creation of gender identity and ideology.

# Ancient Sources Index

Hebrew Bible/Old Testament

Genesis
9:16 — 85

Exodus
28:33–34 — 83

Numbers
13:23 — 83

Deuteronomy
8:8 — 83

2 Samuel
11 — 13–14
11:2–5 — 13
11:4 — 13

1 Kings
7:19 — 83
7:22 — 83
7:26 — 83
8:1–66 — 84, 85 (fig. 3.6)

2 Kings
25:17 — 83

Nehemiah
8:1–12 — 85

Psalms
23:1 — 193
24:8 — 269
111:2 — 48

Song of Songs
1:1 — 79
1:12–14 — 92
2:1 — 88, 91
2:1–2 — 50
2:7 — 79
2:13 — 93
2:14 — 93
3:1 — 70
3:1–4 — 92
3:1–5 — 70, 74
3:4 — 70
3:5 — 79
3:9 — 79
4:1 — 88
4:1–15 — 70, 77, 79
4:1–5:1 — 74, 77
4:3 — 82, 88
4:5 — 88
4:10–14 — 92
4:12 — 51–52, 70, 77–78
4:16 — 74, 77
5:1 — 50–51, 53, 55, 77
5:1–8:5 — 79
5:3 — 88
5:7–8 — 79
5:13 — 88, 91
6:1 — 51
6:3 — 79, 88
6:7 — 82
7:2 — 88
8:2 — 82

## Song of Songs (cont.)

| | |
|---|---|
| 8:4 | 79 |
| 8:6–7 | 79, 94, 95 (fig. 3.10) |
| 8:12 | 79 |

## Isaiah

| | |
|---|---|
| 6:1–13 | 84, 86 (fig. 3.7) |
| 19 | 273 |
| 19:1 | 273 |

## Ezekiel

| | |
|---|---|
| 2:1–3:4 | 262 |
| 3 | 93 |
| 40:1–48:35 | 85 |

## Daniel

| | |
|---|---|
| 12:4 | 264 |
| 13 (= Sus 1) | 197 |
| 14:36 (= Bel 1:36) | 113 |

### Deuterocanonical Books

## Bel and the Dragon

| | |
|---|---|
| 1:36 (= Dan 14:36) | 113 |

## Susanna

| | |
|---|---|
| 1 (= Dan 13) | 197 |

### Pseudepigrapha

## 4 Ezra

| | |
|---|---|
| 14:26 | 264 |
| 14:45–46 | 264 |

## Joseph and Aseneth

| | |
|---|---|
| 14–17 | 265 |

### Ancient Jewish Writers

## Josephus, *Antiquitates judaicae*

| | |
|---|---|
| 18.118 | 136 |
| 18.136 | 135 |

## Josephus, *Bellum judaicum*

| | |
|---|---|
| 5.212–214 | 88 |

### New Testament

## Matthew

| | |
|---|---|
| 2:13–15 | 273 |
| 2:13–18 | 270 |
| 2:13–23 | 202 |
| 6:28–29 | 49 |
| 9 | 137 |
| 13:1–23 | 163–64 |
| 14 | 103, 109, 135 |
| 14:1–12 | 135 |
| 14:5 | 136 |
| 14:6 | 136 |
| 14:7 | 136 |
| 14:8 | 136 |
| 14:9 | 136 |
| 14:12 | 137 |
| 14:22–33 | 109 |
| 14:24–32 | 110 |
| 14:28 | 112 |
| 14:28–31 | 107, 109, 112 |
| 14:29 | 113 |
| 14:30 | 114 |
| 14:31 | 114–15 |
| 16 | 121 |
| 16:18 | 114 |
| 16:18–19 | 131 |
| 18:10 | 265 |
| 25:1–13 | 182 |
| 25:31–46 | 202 |
| 26:20–30 | 254 |
| 26:26 | 265 |
| 27:55–56 | 88 |
| 28:1–10 | 115 |
| 28:9 | 127 |

## Mark

| | |
|---|---|
| 4:1–20 | 163–64 |
| 5 | 137 |
| 5:40 | 137 |
| 5:41 | 137 |
| 5:42 | 137 |
| 6:14–29 | 135 |
| 6:19–20 | 135 |
| 6:22 | 136 |

| | | | |
|---|---|---|---|
| 6:23 | 136 | John | |
| 6:24 | 136 | 1 | 94, 96 |
| 6:25 | 136 | 1:35–51 | 88, 231 |
| 6:26 | 136 | 1:38–39 | 231 |
| 6:29 | 137 | 2:1–12 | 252 |
| 6:33–44 | 78 | 2:22 | 235 |
| 6:45–52 | 109 | 3:11–15 | 115 |
| 8:1–10 | 78 | 5:20 | 231 |
| 10:38–39 | 235 | 6:15–21 | 109 |
| 14:17–26 | 254 | 6:56 | 234 |
| 14:22–25 | 233 | 9:25 | 129 |
| 15:40 | 88 | 10:11 | 235 |
| 16:1–8 | 115 | 10:15 | 235 |
| 16:7 | 122 | 10:17–18 | 235 |
| | | 11:1 | 129 |
| Luke | | 11:1–44 | 115 |
| 5:17–6:11 | 183 | 11:3 | 231–32 |
| 7 | 129 | 11:11 | 231 |
| 7:29–30 | 183 | 12:1–18 | 92 |
| 7:36–50 | 157, 183 | 12:2 | 232 |
| 7:37 | 129 | 12:16 | 235 |
| 8:2 | 157 | 12:28–29 | 287 |
| 8:4–15 | 163–64 | 13–17 | 210–11, 225, 237 |
| 10:25–37 | 181 | 13:1 | 235 |
| 10:38–42 | 129 | 13:1–17 | 234 |
| 14:12–24 | 202 | 13:3–4 | 235 |
| 15 | 182 | 13:4 | 235 |
| 15:1 | 183 | 13:7 | 235 |
| 15:2 | 182–83 | 13:8–11 | 235 |
| 15:4–7 | 182 | 13:12 | 235 |
| 15:8–10 | 182 | 13:14–16 | 235 |
| 15:11–32 | 181 | 13:18 | 225 |
| 15:13 | 182 | 13:21 | 226 |
| 15:29 | 183 | 13:23 | 209, 225–26, 231, 236 |
| 15:30 | 184 | 13:23–25 | 212, 233 |
| 15:31 | 183 | 13:25 | 209, 225, 227, 236 |
| 15:31–32 | 184 | 13:26 | 227 |
| 16:19–31 | 181 | 13:27–30 | 225, 227 |
| 22:14–38 | 254 | 13:34 | 233 |
| 22:62 | 131 | 13:34–35 | 225 |
| 23:44–49 | 88, 89 (fig. 3.8) | 14:26 | 235 |
| 23:49 | 88 | 15:1 | 233 |
| 24:1–12 | 115 | 15:1–7 | 233 |
| 24:13–32 | 254 | 15:1–17 | 233–34, 237 |
| | | 15:2 | 233 |

*Luke* (cont.)

| | |
|---|---|
| 15:4 | 233 |
| 15:4–5 | 233 |
| 15:5 | 233 |
| 15:7 | 233 |
| 15:9 | 233 |
| 15:9–17 | 225 |
| 15:10 | 233 |
| 15:12 | 233 |
| 15:12–15 | 235 |
| 15:13 | 234–35 |
| 15:13–15 | 231 |
| 15:16 | 233 |
| 15:18–16:4 | 225 |
| 16:27 | 231 |
| 17:11 | 233 |
| 17:21 | 233 |
| 17:23 | 233 |
| 18:15 | 230 |
| 19:25–27 | 88, 230 |
| 19:38–42 | 92 |
| 19:41 | 92 |
| 20 | 91 |
| 20:1 | 121 |
| 20:1–10 | 121 |
| 20:1–17 | 115 |
| 20:1–31 | 88, 90 (fig. 3.9) |
| 20:2 | 121 |
| 20:3–5 | 230 |
| 20:8 | 121 |
| 20:9 | 122 |
| 20:11 | 122 |
| 20:11–18 | 121, 129 |
| 20:12 | 122 |
| 20:13 | 123 |
| 20:14 | 123–24 |
| 20:15 | 125 |
| 20:16 | 125 |
| 20:17 | 103, 126 |
| 20:17–18 | 128 |
| 20:21–29 | 115 |
| 21:7 | 230 |
| 21:15–21 | 231 |
| 21:20 | 209, 212, 225, 233, 236 |
| 21:24 | 231 |

Acts

| | |
|---|---|
| 12:15 | 265 |

Romans

| | |
|---|---|
| 6:1–11 | 235 |

1 Corinthians

| | |
|---|---|
| 10:16 | 234 |
| 11:21–26 | 233 |

Hebrews

| | |
|---|---|
| 11:1 | 131 |

Revelation

| | |
|---|---|
| 1 | 265–66, 280 |
| 1:1 | 265 |
| 1:12–16 | 265 |
| 4 | 270 |
| 4–5 | 277 |
| 4:3 | 265 |
| 5 | 270 |
| 5:2 | 264 |
| 5:5 | 265 |
| 6:1–8 | 284 |
| 6:2 | 280 |
| 6:2–8 | 262 |
| 7:2 | 267 |
| 8:6–9:21 | 269 |
| 9:13–19 | 284 |
| 9:13–21 | 262 |
| 10 | 262, 264–65, 267, 269–70, 273, 279, 284–85, 287–89 |
| 10–11 | 274 |
| 10–20 | 266 |
| 10:1 | 266, 284 |
| 10:1–7 | 264 |
| 10:1–9 | 274 |
| 10:1–11 | 270 |
| 10:3 | 267 |
| 10:3–4 | 284 |
| 10:6 | 282 |
| 10:8 | 266, 270 |
| 10:8–11 | 262, 265 |
| 10:9–11 | 270 |
| 10:11 | 280 |

| | | | | |
|---|---|---|---|---|
| 12 | 266, 273 | Aristotle, *Rhetoric* | | |
| 12:1–6 | 280 | 3.1.6 [1404a] | | 208 |
| 12:6 | 273 | 3.11.2–4 [1411b–1412a] | | 208 |
| 12:14 | 273 | | | |
| 13:1–2 | 282 | Aulus Gellius, *Attic Nights* | | |
| 18:21 | 264 | 6.12.14–15 | | 230 |
| 19:10 | 265 | | | |
| 19:11–16 | 282 | Cicero, *In Catalinam* | | |
| 21:2–22:5 | 86 | 2.22–24 | | 230 |
| 22:8–9 | 265 | | | |
| | | [Demosthenes], *Eroticus* | | |

### Rabbinic Works

| | | | |
|---|---|---|---|
| | | 6 | 232 |
| | | 30 | 232 |
| m. Yad. | | | |
| 3:5 | 67 | Dio Cassius, *Historiae romanae* | |
| | | 79.16.5 | 230 |

### Early Christian Writings

Diogenes Laertius, *Lives and Opinions of Eminent Philosophers*

| | | | |
|---|---|---|---|
| Didache | | | |
| 9.2 | 233–34 | 2.19 | 231 |
| | | 2.23 | 231 |
| Eusebius, *Demonstration of the Gospel* | | 2.49 | 231 |
| 6.20 | 273 | 3.29–30 | 231 |
| | | 3.31 | 231 |
| Gospel of Pseudo-Matthew | | 4.19 | 231 |
| 23 | 273 | 4.21 | 231 |
| | | 4.22 | 231 |
| Justin Martyr, *Dialogue with Trypho* | | 4.29 | 231 |
| 49.4–5 | 137 | 4.41 | 231 |
| | | 5.3 | 231 |
| Rufinus, *Historia monachorum in Aegypto* | | 5.39 | 231 |
| 7.1 | 273 | 7.17 | 231 |
| | | 8.86 | 231 |

Tyconius of Carthage, *Exposition of the Apocalypse*

Eunapius, *Lives of Philosophers and Sophists*

| | | | |
|---|---|---|---|
| 10.1 | 266 | 502–503 | 232 |

Victorinus of Pettau, *Commentary on the Apocalypse*

Greek Anthology

| | | | |
|---|---|---|---|
| | | 5.17 | 230 |
| 10.1 | 266 | 5.25 | 230 |
| | | 5.51 | 232 |

### Greco-Roman Literature

| | | | |
|---|---|---|---|
| | | 5.107 | 230 |
| | | 5.116 | 230 |
| Apollodorus, *Bibliotheca* | | 5.136 | 230 |
| 1.5.3 | 83 | | |

## ANCIENT SOURCES INDEX

*Greek Anthology* (cont.)
   5.165                   230
   5.173                   230
   5.275                   230
   12.34                   230

Juvenal, *Satires*
   2.117–120

[Longinus], *On the lime*
   15.1–11               208

[Lucian], *Affairs of the Heart*
   54                     232

Lucian, *Dialogues of the Sea Gods*
   319                   232

Lucian, *Timon*
   41                     232

Lucian, *Zeus Rants*
   2                      232

Martial, *Epigrams*
   1.31                    230
   5.48                    230

Ovid, *Metamorphoses*
   5.536                   83

Persius, *Satirae*
   5                      231

Plato, *Symposium*
   180b                  232

Plutarch, *Amatorius*
   751A                  230
   765D                  232
   766A                  232

Quintilian, *Institutio Oratoria*
   4.2.63–65          208
   6.2.29–36          208
   8.3.62–72          208

   8.3.66                208
   9.1.27                208
   9.2.40                208

Sappho, *Fragments*
   132                   232

# Authors and Artists Index

| | | | |
|---|---|---|---|
| Adams, Doug | 164, 171 | Benton, Thomas Hart | 188, 190–204, 244 |
| Adams, Eston Dillon | 110 | | |
| Adams, Henry | 200 | Bercken, Erich von der | 107 |
| Aikema, Bernard | 166–67 | Berdini, Paolo | 3, 163, 165–67 |
| Alexander Minorita (of Bremen) | 266–67 | Bergognone, Ambrogio | 139 |
| Alexander of Hales | 267 | Berkel, Klaas van | 46 |
| Allori, Alessandro | 114 | Bernard, Émile | 174 |
| Altdorfer, Albrecht | 116 | Bernari, Carlo | 107 |
| Andreae, Bernard | 227 | Berry, Joanne | 213 |
| Apostolos-Cappadona, Diane | 130 | Berry, Wendell | 250 |
| Aquinas, Thomas | 137 | Bikker, Jonathan | 20, 22 |
| Arber, Agnes | 49 | Bilbro, Jeffrey | 68 |
| Armenini, Giovambattista | 141 | Bing, Peter | 230 |
| As-Vijvers, Anne Margreet W. | 56, 59 | Blake, William | 282, 283 (fig. 10.7), 284–85, 287, 289 |
| Astell, Ann W. | 51 | | |
| Babcock, James O. | 249 | Bloomquist, L. Gregory | 207, 209 |
| Baigell, Matthew | 200 | Blyth, Caroline | 30 |
| Baker, Jack R. | 68 | Bober, Jonathan | 109 |
| Bakhtin, Mikhail | 202 | Boer, Esther de | 129–30 |
| Bal, Mieke | 20, 32 | Boltraffio, Giovanni Antonio | 139 |
| Balch, David L. | 209 | Bonaiuto, Andrea di. *See* Firenze, Andrea da | |
| Bale, John | 267 | | |
| Balis, Arnout | 43–44, 50 | Bonaventure | 267 |
| Barnard, John | 78 | Bondone, Giotto di. *See* Giotto | |
| Barone, Bruce Daryl | 282 | Borcht, Pieter van der | 43 |
| Bartal, Ruth | 68 | Borromeo, Charles | 128 |
| Baruffaldi, Girolamo | 106 | Borromeo, Federico | 138, 159 |
| Bassano, Jacopo (da Ponte) | 165, 166 (fig. 6.1), 167, 177 | Bosch, Hieronymus | 184, 198, 262 |
| | | Boswell, John | 232 |
| Beard, Mary | 212–13 | Botticelli, Sandro | 84 |
| Beazley, J. D. | 219 | Bourbon, Nicholas | 279 |
| Beckford, William | 285 | Bourdichon, Jean | 16 (fig. 1.1), 17 |
| Benay, Erin E. | 115 | Bowron, Edgar Peters | 107 |
| Bennett, Jim | 56 | Boxall, Ian | 265, 267 |

Brenninkmeijer-de Rooij, Beatrijs 59
Brighton, Louis Andrew 265
Brigstocke, Hugh 168
Broughton, Hugh 267
Broun, Elizabeth 192
Brown, Raymond E. 234–35
Brueggemann, Walter 22
Brueghel, Jan (the Elder) 59
Brunet-Dinard, Huguette 278
Bruss, Jon Steffen 230
Bruyn, Nicolaas de 37, 43
Bry, Johann Theodor de 47–48, 52
Bucher, Christina 69
Bultmann, Rudolf 136
Buonarroti, Michelangelo. *See* Michelangelo
Buoninsegna, Duccio di. *See* Duccio
Burgard, Timothy 251
Burroughs, Polly 192, 197
Burrows, Daron 270, 273
Butler, Judith 11
Buytewech, Willem 17
Byron, George Gordon (Lord) 147
Cafà, Valeria 148
Calderhead, Christopher 68, 74–75, 78–79, 84, 91, 93–94
Calkins, Robert G. 82
Calvin, John 112
Cameron, Alan 230
Cano, Alonso 118, 119 (fig. 4.8), 127
Cantarella, Eva 228
Caracciolo, Giovanni Battista 118
Caravaggio, Michelangelo Merisi da 144
Carey, Frances 278, 287
Carpenter, Thomas H. 219
Carr, David M. 91
Cartwright, Ingrid 186
Castagno, Andrea del 255
Cavallini, Pietro 116
Cavallo, Adolfo Salvatore 83
Chagall, Marc 12, 23 (fig. 1.4), 24
Chemnitz, Martin 112
Chesneau, Ernest 171
Cipriani, Marina 227
Cixous, Hélène 19

Clarke, John R. 212–19
Clifton, James 56
Clusius, Carolus 43, 45–47
Cocca, Tiziana 213
Colbert, Thomas Burnell 250
Colgan, Emily 30
Collaert, Adriaen 37, 38 (fig. 2.1), 39 (fig. 2.2), 40 (fig. 2.3), 41 (fig. 2.4), 42 (fig. 2.5), 43–44, 46, 50–51, 55–56, 58 (fig. 2.9), 59, 61
Conova, Antonio 148
Conrad, Peter 160
Coote, Robert B. 207
Corn, Wanda M. 248
Correggio, Antonio Allegri da 118, 119 (fig. 4.7)
Cortona, Pietro da 118
Coulombe, Charles A. 112
Cowell, Norman D. 83
Cranach, Lucas (the Elder) 277–78
Crossan, John Dominic 136
Crowther-Heyck, Kathleen 50
Curry, John Steuart 191, 244
Da Vinci, Leonardo. *See* Vinci, Leonardo da
Daley, Brian E. 69
Danti, Vincenzo 141
David, Jan 51–56, 59
Davis, Ellen F. 87, 94
Davis, Thomas 177
Dekoninck, Ralph 52
Delacroix, Eugène 170, 174
Dennis, James M. 243
Dentzer, Jean-Marie 211, 227
Deuchler, Florens 274
Dewey, John 191
Diels, Ann 43–44, 50
Dodonaeus, Rembertus 43, 45–46, 49
D'Oench, Ellen 182, 186, 188, 198
Doss, Erika 201
Douglas, Mary 152
Dover, Kenneth J. 227, 229
Dow, Helen J. 174–76
Drost, Willem 17, 20, 21 (fig. 1.3), 22
Duccio (di Buoninsegna) 118

Dunbabin, Katherine M. D. 211–14, 218–19, 222–23, 229, 236
Dupinet, Antoine 279
Duran, Nicole Wilkinson 136
Dürer, Albrecht 116, 117 (fig. 4.5), 147, 186, 187 (fig. 7.2), 198, 261–62, 263 (fig. 10.1), 264–65, 268, 270, 274, 277–80, 282, 284–85, 288–89
Duvet, Jean 277–80, 281 (fig. 10.6), 282
Edwards, Katie B. 30
Eisler, Colin 278–80
El Greco 192
Elder, Nika 29
Ellis, Mary 197
Elsen-Novák, Gabriele 208–9
Emmerson, Richard K. 269, 273
Engammare, Max 52
Evans, R. Tripp 255–56
Exum, J. Cheryl 14–15, 20, 22, 69, 77, 91, 289
Fahy, Everett 108
Fanucci, Laura Kelly 88
Farrar, Margaret 251
Feaver, William 285, 287
Ferrari, Federico 20
Ferraro, Kathleen J. 31
Filippi, Sebastiano 106
Finney, Paul Corby 82
Firenze, Andrea da (di Bonaiuto) 110, 111 (fig. 4.3), 113–14
Fontana, Lavinia 118, 128
Fontana, Prospero 106
Fra Angelico 118
Fra Bartolomeo 116
Fraenger, William 184
Francis, Henry S. 278
Francis of Assisi 267
Fredericksen, Burton B. 107
Freedberg, David 60
Freeman, Margaret B. 83
Freud, Sigmund 152
Frymer-Kensky, Tikva 14
Furnish, Paul Victor 232
Gafney, Wilda 24–26, 29

Galle, Philips 37, 38 (fig. 2.1), 39 (fig. 2.2), 40 (fig. 2.3), 41 (fig. 2.4), 42 (fig. 2.5), 43–44, 46, 50–51, 55, 61
Galle, Theodoor 44, 51–53, 54 (fig. 2.7), 55
Gallop, Jane 154
Gambone, Robert L. 193–94, 197–98
Garofalo. See Tisi, Benvenuto
Garwood, Darrell 244, 256
Gauguin, Paul 175
Gaut, Berys 18–19
Gelder, J. G. van 43
Gemünden, Petra von 207–8
Genovese, Angelo 213
Gerard, John 46, 48–49
Germer, Renate 83
Gérôme, Jean-Léon 20, 29
Gerung, Matthias 277
Gheyn, Jacques de 47
Ghirlandaio, Domenico 255
Gieschen, Charles 265–66
Gillow, John 78
Giotto (di Bondone) 110, 116, 255–56
Girard, René 155–56, 160
Goethe, Johann Wolfgang von 147
Gogh, Vincent van 167, 174, 175 (fig. 6.4), 176, 179
Gombrich, Ernst H. 74, 78
Goodman, Nelson 12
Gowler, David B. 163, 171, 181–83, 186, 188, 196, 203–4
Grabar, Oleg 70, 94
Grafly, Dorothy 243
Graham, Nan Wood 247–49, 256
Groot, Irene de 50
Gruber, J. Richard 191, 199
Guest, Deryn 14
Gumerlock, Francis X. 266
Gundry, Robert H. 266
Halliday, Peter 94
Hamburger, Jeffrey 92, 94
Hannay, Margaret 130
Hänsel, Sylvaine 52
Harris, David 96
Harthan, John 17

## AUTHORS AND ARTISTS INDEX

Hartt, Frederick 84
Haskins, Susan 115, 129
Hauser, Christine 32
Heemskerck, Maarten van 18, 282
Herbert, Robert L. 170
Hoefnagel, Jacob 47
Hoefnagel, Joris 47
Hoffeld, Jeffrey M. 274
Holloway, R. Ross 227, 229
Homrighausen, Jonathan 68, 74, 84, 87–88, 92, 94
hooks, bell 11–12, 24–25
Hornik, Heidi J. 105, 114, 129
Hubbard, Thomas K. 230
Hughes, Robert 201
Hunt, Holman 171
Huysmans, Joris-Karl 135, 137
Hyland, Douglas 192
Illich, Ivan 93
Impelluso, Lucia 82
Jackson, Donald 67, 71 (fig. 3.1), 72–73 (fig. 3.2), 74, 75 (fig. 3.3), 76–79, 80 (fig. 3.4), 81 (fig. 3.5), 84, 85 (fig. 3.6), 86 (fig. 3.7), 87–88, 89 (fig. 3.8), 90 (fig. 3.9), 93–94, 95 (fig. 3.10), 96
Jacobs, Fredrika H. 141, 160
Janes, Regina 136, 156–57
Jansen, Cornelius 122
Janson, Anthony 168, 178
Janson, Horst 168, 178
Jarves, James Jackson 173
Jay, Jeff 230
Jeal, Roy R. 207–8
Jensen, Robin M. 13
Jewell, Edward Alden 243, 247
John of the Cross 70
Joly, Robert 231
Jones, Pamela M. 131, 138–39, 159–60
Jong, Erik A. de 50
Jong, Marijnke de 50
Jorink, Eric 46–47
Joynes, Christine E. 164
Kahl, Brigitte 210
Katsanis, Bobbi Dykema 92, 116
Kauffmann, Claus M. 164, 267
Kaufmann, Thomas DaCosta 56
Kaufmann, Virginia Roehrig 56
Keel, Othmar 70
Kemp, Martin 141
Kendrick, Laura 94
Kerkeslager, Allen 280
Kilmer, Martin F. 227
Kingsmill, Edmée 87
Knipping, John B. 129
Kobel, Esther 211, 225
Koberger, Anton 261–64
Koch, Ebba 44
Koenig, Sara M. 13–15
Koester, Craig R. 265, 285
Kondoleon, Christine 221–24
Koops, Robert 83, 88, 91
Kovacs, Judith 262
Kristeva, Julia 151–53
Kuhn, Annette 25
Laborie, Séverine 142
Lacan, Jacques 153–56
Lapide, Cornelius à 51–52, 105, 112–15, 118, 120–28, 131
Lear, Andrew 227
Lechte, John 151, 153
Leclercq, Jean 76
Leesberg, Marjolein 43–44, 50
Lefèvre, Jean 279
Lemli, Jozef 45
Lerner, Robert E. 267
Levi, Doro 222–24
Lévi-Strauss, Claude 156
Levine, Amy Jill 186
Lewis, Suzanne 268–69, 277
Lischer, Richard 181
Lissarrague, François 211, 220–22, 228
Lobelius, Mathias 43, 45, 48
Lomazzo, Giovanni Paolo 140
Longman, Tremper, III 70
Losty, Jeremiah P. 44
Lufft, Hans 280
Luini, Bernardino (del Lupino) 137–42, 143 (fig. 5.1), 144–45, 146 (fig. 5.2), 147 (fig. 5.3), 148 (fig. 5.4), 149 (figs.

5.5–5.6), 150–51, 152 (fig. 5.7), 153, 155, 157, 158 (fig. 5.8), 159–60
Luther, Martin 277
Maier, Harry O. 208
Maisch, Ingrid 115
Makron 219
Mandelbrote, Scott 56
Mannack, Thomas 219
Mantegna, Andrea 278, 280
Marcantonio 278
Marien, Mary Warner 28
Marling, Karal Ann 200–201
Marquand, Eleanor C. 83
Marqusee, Michael 278
Martin, John 285, 287, 288 (fig. 10.9)
Martin, Josef 226
Martin of Braga 128
Mason, James 137–38
Matter, E. Ann 68–69, 87, 92
Mayer, August L. 107
Mazzuoli, Giuseppe 106
McBride, Henry 243–44
McCall, Robert T. 148
McDonald, Julie Jensen 247, 249
Melion, Walter S. 52, 55, 61, 207
Melzi, Francesco de 140
Memling, Hans 17, 29
Mendonça, Melanie 219
Merriam, Susan 60
Mertens, Joan R. 219
Meyers, Carol L. 83
Michelangelo 147, 170
Michener, James 199
Mikuž, Jure 163
Millais, John Everett 167, 171, 172 (fig. 6.3), 173
Millet, Jean-François 167–68, 169 (fig. 6.2), 170–71, 174–76, 178–79
Milton, John 284
Mitchell, William J. T. 12, 202–3
Monaco, Lorenzo 255
Montano, Benito Arias 52, 61
Moore-Jumonville, Robert 75
Morgan, David 13
Morgan, Nigel J. 273

Mormando, Franco 105, 118, 126, 128, 130–31
Morrall, Andrew 49
Moser, Matthew A. Rothaus 76
Moyne, Jacques le 44–45
Muller, Marion 76
Mumford, Lewis 191
Munro, Jill M. 79, 82, 88
Murphy, Alexandra 168
Murphy, Roland E. 70
Murray, Linda 82, 91
Murray, Peter 82, 91
Musselman, Lytton John 83, 91
Myrone, Martin 287
Nancy, Jean-Luc 20
Napoli, Mario 227
Nazari, Vazrick 91
Nickel, Helmut 274
Nissen, Claus 43
North, Susan 45
Nouwen, Henri 203
Novák, Mirko 208–9
Novelli, Maria Angela 106, 108
Nunn, John F. 83
Nuțu, Ela 137, 144, 289
Nygard, Travis 245, 248
Nygren, Anders 232
Nygren, Christopher 146–47
Ogilvie, Brian W. 47
O'Grady, Lorraine 12, 24–27, 30, 32
O'Hear, Anthony 264, 288
O'Hear, Natasha F. H. 261–62, 264, 268–69, 279, 288–289
Olivi, Peter John 267
O'Malley, John W. 110
Opie, John 258
O'Reilly, Sally 30
Paley, Morton D. 282, 285, 287
Pallucchini, Rodolfo 107
Panofsky, Erwin 2–3, 210, 225, 261
Parsenios, George L. 211, 225–26, 236
Parsons, Mikeal C. 129, 181, 188
Passe, Crispijn de (the Younger) 43, 45–46, 49
Patella, Michael 68, 75, 78, 84–85, 91

Paton, W. R. 230
Peach, Lucinda Joy 31
Pearce, Susan 83
Penrose, Walter Duvall, Jr. 227, 229
Perry, E. Wood 165
Perugino, Pietro 116
Pirotte, Emmanuelle 76
Pissarro, Camille 170
Pissarro, Lucien 170
Polignac, François de 150
Pollock, Griselda 168, 170, 178
Pollock, Jackson 190, 198
Pontormo, Jacopo da 118
Pontrandolfo, Angela 227, 229
Popham, Arthur E. 278
Pouncey, Philip 108–9
Predis, Ambrogio de 142
Preziosi, Donald 12
Prieras, Sylvester 127
Promey, Sally M. 13
Proust, Marcel 251
Pulci, Antonia 188
Rafanelli, Lisa M. 115
Raimondi, Marcantonio. *See* Marcantonio
Raphael 278
Rearick, R. W. 165
Réau, Louis 164
Redd, Penelope 243
Rembrandt 17–18, 19 (fig. 1.2), 20, 185–86, 197–98
Renan, Ernst 177
Richlin, Amy 229, 231, 233
Richter, Jean Paul 141
Rijn, Rembrandt Harmenszoon van. *See* Rembrandt
Rikoon, J. Sanford 246
Rio, Alexis-François 138
Ripa, Cesare 83
Rivkin, Julie 153–56
Roberts, Brady 258
Robertson, Duncan 76–77
Robbins, Vernon K. 207
Robin, Jean 48
Rocha, Cristina 31
Roller, Matthew B. 212, 236

Rossetti, Christina G. 287
Rossi, Paola 107
Rossiter, Henry P. 278
Roty, Oscar 167, 176 (fig. 6.5), 177–79
Roussat, Richard 279
Rouveret, Agnès 227
Rowland, Christopher 262, 278–79, 282, 284, 289
Roy, Malini 44
Rubens, Peter Paul 59
Ruggeri, Ugo 106
Rupert of Deutz (Rupertus) 128
Ruskin, John 140–41, 171
Ryan, Michael 153–56
Sabatini, Lorenzo 106
Sadan, Ronah 46
Sadeler, Johannes 52, 55
Saiter, Johann Gottfried 253 (fig. 9.2)
Sakenfeld, Katharine Doob 14
Samacchini, Orazio 106
Scarsella, Ippolito (Scarsellino) 103, 104 (figs. 4.1–2), 105–20, 126, 131–32
Scarsella, Sigismondo 106
Schiller, Gertrud 164
Schiller, Johann Christoph Friedrich von 147
Schön, Erhard 164
Schongauer, Martin 69, 262
Schwartz, Gary 20
Segal, Sam 37, 45, 52
Seghers, Daniel 60 (fig. 2.10)
Segre, Ada 50
Sesto, Cesare da 139
Shearman, John 3
Sica, Maria 213
Silverman, Debora L. 176–77
Simpson, Lorna 12, 24–25, 27 (fig. 1.5), 28–30
Sink, Susan 68, 78, 84, 86, 91, 93–94
Sluijter, Eric Jan 17–18
Sontag, Susan 24
Sorenson, Lee 108
Spicq, Ceslaus 231–32
Stahl, Harvey 282
Steinbeck, John 199

Stokstad, Marilyn 79, 192
Suarez, Francisco 127
Sund, Judy 170, 174, 176
Surius, Laurentius 127
Swan, Claudia 47
Sweerts, Emmanuel 46
Tabernaemontanus, Jacobus 47
Taylor, John 45
Tietze, Hans 107
Tilborg, Sjef van 230
Tilghman, Benjamin C. 76, 82, 94
Tintoretto, Jacopo 106–8, 140, 197, 255
Tippens, Darryl 181
Tisi, Benvenuto (da Garofalo) 116, 117 (fig. 4.6)
Tissot, James 167, 171, 184
Titian 106, 118, 120 (fig. 4.9), 159
Toledo, Francisco de (Toletus) 127
Tomlin, Chris 91
Toynbee, J. M. C. 83
Train, Daniel 68
Truman, Harry 192
Urbino, Raffaello Sanzio da. See Raphael
Vallet, Pierre 48, 52
Van Gogh, Vincent. See Gogh, Vincent van
Vanderjagt, Arjo 46
Varone, Antonio 212–16
Vasari, Giorgio 137–38
Vecchio, Palma 22
Vecellio, Tiziano. See Titian
Velasco, Murillo 31
Velázquez, Diego 253, 254 (fig. 9.3)
Veldman, Ilja M. 44–45, 49
Venturi, Lionello 110
Vergara, Alejandro 18
Veronese, Paolo (Caliari) 106, 116, 197, 252–53
Vignau-Wilberg, Thea 47
Vinci, Leonardo da 139–42, 157, 256, 257 (fig. 9.4)
Visser, Derk 269
Voragine, Jacobus de 130
Vos, Maarten de 53, 55
Vries, Hans Vredeman de 50

Wachtel, Alexandra 43, 50
Wainwright, Arthur W. 267
Walker-Vadillo, Mónica 15
Wands, Charles 288 (fig. 10.9)
Waters, Sonia 118
Waterworth, James 112
Watt, Melinda 45
Waźbiński, Zygmunt 44
Wechsler, Judith Glatzer 68
Weems, Carrie Mae 12, 24, 28–30
Weinrich, William C. 268
Weinryb, Ittai 69
Weissenrieder, Annette 207, 210
Wendt, Friederike 207, 210
West, Benjamin 285, 286 (fig. 10.8)
Wetering, Ernst van de 186
Whatley, Mark 31
Wheelock, Arthur K., Jr. 59
Wierix, Johannes 46, 51–52, 53 (fig. 2.6), 55
Wilkins, David G. 84
Wilkins, Robert 188
Williams, Craig A. 229
Williamson, George C. 138–41, 144–45, 151
Winckelmann, Johann Joachim 147
Wischmeyer, Oda 232
Wit, Frederick de 43
Wittreich, Joseph Anthony 284–85
Wolff, Justin P. 192, 199, 201
Wood, Grant 191, 243, 244 (fig. 9.1), 245–52, 255–56, 257 (fig. 9.5), 258–59
Yanoviak, Eileen 91
Young, Victoria M. 87
Zeri, Federico 107
Zimmermann, Ruben 163
Zuffi, Stefano 167
Zug, John 247, 249

# Subject Index

Abingdon Apocalypse, 261, 270, 271 (fig. 10.2), 272 (fig. 10.3), 273–74, 287, 289
abjection, 151–53
abstract expressionism, 190
Academia Leonardo Vinci (Milan), 139
Accademia del Disegno, Ambrosian (Milan), 138
Adam and Eve, 53, 154
Adonis, 280
*Again* (Benton), 201
*agapān* (ἀγαπᾶν), New Testament meaning of, 231–32
Agros (Ἀγρός), 224, 226, 234
Ahab, king of Israel, 156
Aikema, Bernard, 166–67
Albion (Blake), 284
Alexander VI, Pope, 110, 113, 131
Alexander Minorita (of Bremen), 266–67
*Expositio in Apocalypsim*, 267
Alexander of Hales, 267
*Allegory of Modesty and Vanity* (Luini). See *Conversion of the Magdalene, The* (Luini)
Altdorfer, Albrecht, 116
*Noli Me Tangere*, 116
Ambrose of Milan, 112, 128, 269
Ambrosia, 222
Ambrosian Library (Milan), 150, 159
*American Gothic* (Wood), 191
"American Scene, The" (Benton), 195
*And the Angel Which I Saw Lifted His Hand to Heaven* (Blake). See *Angel of the Revelation, The* (Blake)
Andreas of Caesarea, 268

*Angel Gives Saint John the Book to Eat, The* (Duvet), 279–80, 281 (fig. 10.6), 282
*Angel of the Revelation, The* (Blake), 282, 283 (fig. 10.7), 284–85, 289
*Angel with the Book, The* (Cloisters Apocalypse), 274, 276 (fig. 10.5), 277
*Angel with the Book, The* (Wands/Martin), 285, 287, 288 (fig. 10.9)
angelomorphic Christology, 265–66
angels, 91, 130
  in Bel and the Dragon, 113
  in Ezek 3, 93
  in Rev 10 and its depictions, 262–89
  in the resurrection narratives, 121–25
Anglo-Norman Apocalypses, 268–77, 287–89. See also Abingdon Apocalypse; Cloisters Apocalypse; Getty Apocalypse;
*Annunciation to the Shepherds, The* (Bassano), 167
"answerability" (Bakhtin), 202
Anthony of Egypt, 150
Antioch (Syria), 225
Antioch on the Orontes (Turkey), 221–24, 234
Apocalypse of John. See Revelation, book of
*Apocalypsis cum figuris*, (Dürer), 261, 277
Apollo, 146–51, 280
Apollo Belvedere (*Pythian Apollo*), 147–50
Armenini, Giovambattista, 141
  *De'veri precetti della pittura*, 141
Art Institute of Chicago, 170, 190–91

-310-

## SUBJECT INDEX 311

Art Students League (New York), 190
Artemis, 149
Augustine of Hippo, 112, 114, 122, 126, 128
Bakery of the Chaste Lovers (Pompeii). See House of the Chaste Lovers (Pompeii)
*Baptism in Kansas* (Curry), 244
Barbara (Christian saint), 150
Baroque art, 103, 130
Baruffaldi, Girolamo, 106
  *Lives of the Ferrarese Painters and Sculptors, The,* 106
Bassano, Jacopo (da Ponte), 165–67, 177
  *Annunciation to the Shepherds, The* (Bassano), 167
  *Parable of the Sower, The* (Bassano), 165, 166 (fig. 6.1), 167, 177
Bathsheba, 11–32
*Bathsheba at Her Bath* (Rembrandt), 18, 19 (fig. 1.2), 20
*Bathsheba Bathing* (Bourdichon), 16 (fig. 1.1), 17
"Bathsheba Bathing" (Rouen book of hours), 17, 29
*Bathsheba in the Bath* (Memling), 17, 29
*Bathsheba Reading King David's Letter* (Buytewech), 17–18
*Bathsheba with David's Letter* (Drost), 20, 21 (fig. 1.3), 22
Beatus of Liébana, 266
Beckford, William, 285
Bede, 87, 266
Beloved Disciple, the, 209–10, 225–37
Benedict of Nursia, 267
Benedictine order, 67, 76, 87, 93, 269
Benton, Thomas Hart, 188, 190–204, 244
  *Again,* 201
  "American Scene, The," 195
  *Departure of the Joads, The,* 199, 200 (fig. 7.6)
  *Flanders' House, The,* 196
  *Holy Roller Camp Meeting,* 193
  *Lord Heal the Child,* 193
  *Lord Is My Shepherd, The,* 193
  *Meeting, The,* 195
  *Persephone,* 200–201
  *Prayer Meeting,* 195
  *Prodigal Son,* 188, 194 (fig. 7.5), 195–204
  *Social History of Missouri, A,* 190
  *Sunday Morning,* 195
  *Susanna and the Elders,* 197, 200–201, 244
  *Year of Peril,* 201
Berdini, Paolo, 3, 163, 165–67
Berengaudus (Benedictine monk), 268–70, 273–74, 277
  *Expositio super septem visiones libri Apocalypsis,* 268
Bergognone, Ambrogio, 139
Bernard of Clairvaux, 76–77, 93
Berry, Wendell, 250
  *Jayber Crow,* 250
*Bethsabée* (Gérôme), 20, 29
Bibliothèque Nationale (Paris), 262
Blake, William, 282, 284–85, 287, 289
  *Angel of the Revelation, The,* 282, 283 (fig. 10.7), 284–85, 289
  *Death on a Pale Horse,* 284
  *Great Red Dragon and the Beast from the Sea, The,* 282
  *Vision of the Last Judgment, A,* 287
Blanton Museum, 109
Boltraffio, Giovanni Antonio, 139
Bonaventure, 267
Book of Durrow, 76
Book of Kells, 76
books of hours
  Ghent-Bruges, 59
  Louis XII, 17
  "Mors Vincit Omnia," 57 (fig 2.8)
  Rouen, 17, 29
Borromeo, Charles, 128
Borromeo, Federico, 138, 159
Bosch, Hieronymus, 184, 198, 262
  *Pedlar, The,* 184
  *St. John the Evangelist on Patmos,* 262
Botticelli, Sandro, 84
  *Madonna of the Pomegranate,* 84

*Bouquet of Flowers* (Collaert/Galle), 37, 38 (fig. 2.1), 50
Bourbon, Nicholas, 279
Bourdichon, Jean, 16–17
　*Bathsheba Bathing*, 16 (fig. 1.1), 17
Bourges Cathedral, 188
Brera Pinacoteca (Milan), 150
British Museum, 108, 164
Brooklyn Museum (New York), 171
Brueghel, Jan (the Elder), 59
Bry, Johann Theodor de, 47–48, 52
　*Florilegium Novum*, 47–48, 52
Buonarroti, Michelangelo. *See* Michelangelo
Buoninsegna, Duccio di. *See* Duccio
Butts, Thomas, 282, 284
Buytewech, Willem, 17
　*Bathsheba Reading King David's Letter*, 17–18
Byron, George Gordon (Lord), 147
*Call of the Disciples* (Jackson), 88
calligraphy, 92–94, 96, 261
Cana, wedding at, 252–53
Canaan, 83
Cano, Alonso, 118–19, 127
　*Noli Me Tangere*, 119 (fig. 4.8), 127
Canterbury Cathedral, 164
Canticle of Canticles. *See* Song of Songs
Caracciolo, Giovanni Battista, 118
　*Noli Me Tangere*, 118
Caravaggio, Michelangelo Merisi da, 144
　*Salome with the Head of John the Baptist* (London), 144
　*Salome with the Head of John the Baptist* (Madrid), 144
Carracci, the, 106
Castagno, Andrea del, 255
　*Last Supper, The*, 255
Cathedral of Saint James at Compostela, 84
Catherine of Alexandria, 159
Cavallini, Pietro, 116
　*Noli Me Tangere*, 116
Chagall, Marc, 12, 23–24
　*David and Bathsheba*, 12, 23 (fig. 1.4), 24
Chartres Cathedral, 184, 188
chiaroscuro, 18, 140, 261
Christ. *See* Jesus
*Christ among the Doctors* (Luini), 150, 159
*Christ and Peter on the Sea of Galilee* (Firenze), 110, 111 (fig. 4.3), 113–14
*Christ and Saint Peter at the Sea of Galilee* (Scarsellino), 103, 104 (fig. 4.1), 105–9, 116, 118, 131–32
*Christ in the Attitude of Benediction* (Luini), 150, 159
*Christ in the Boat* (Delacroix), 174
*Christ Walking on the Water* (coin), 110, 111 (fig. 4.4), 112–14, 131
Chrysostom. *See* John Chrysostom
Cicero, 208, 214
City Art Museum (Saint Louis), 197
Clement of Alexandria, 131
Cloisters Apocalypse, 273–74, 276 (fig. 10.5), 287
Clusius, Carolus, 43, 45–47
Collaert, Adriaen, 37–44, 46, 50–51, 55–56, 58–59, 61
　*Bouquet of Flowers*, 37, 38 (fig. 2.1), 50
　*Florilegium*, 37–44, 46, 50–51, 55–56, 61
　*Lilies*, 42 (fig. 2.5)
　*Martyrologium Sanctarum Virginum*, 58 (fig. 2.9), 59
　*Roses*, 41 (fig. 2.4)
　*Saint Lucy*, 58 (fig. 2.9)
　*Sponsa and Sponsus*, 37, 40 (fig. 2.3), 45, 50–56
　*Title Plate*, 37, 39 (fig. 2.2), 50, 55
　*Virginis Mariae Vita*, 59
Cologne Bible, 261
Colossus of Rhodes, 282
Conova, Antonio, 148
　*Perseus with the Head of Medusa*, 148
*Conversion of the Magdalene, The* (Luini), 157, 158 (fig. 5.8), 159
*convivium*, 218

## SUBJECT INDEX

Correggio, Antonio Allegri da, 118–19
   *Noli Me Tangere*, 118, 119 (fig. 4.7)
Cortona, Pietro da, 118
   *Noli Me Tangere*, 118
Counter-Reformation, the, 105, 130–32
*Courtesan* (Vecchio), 22
crucifixion. *See* Jesus: crucifixion of
*Crucifixion* (Jackson), 88, 89 (fig. 3.8), 92
cubism, 190
Cupid, 146–47
Curry, John Steuart, 191, 244
   *Baptism in Kansas*, 244
   *Tragic Prelude—John Brown*, 191
Cyril of Alexandria, 122, 126
Da Vinci, Leonardo. *See* Vinci, Leonardo da
Dallas Museum of Fine Arts, 195
Dalziel brothers, the, 171–72
Danae, 232
*Das Newe Testament* (Lufft), 280
*Daughters of Revolution* (Wood), 247
David, Jan, 51–56, 59
   *Pancarpium Marianum*, 59
   *Paradisus Sponsi et Sponsae*, 51–56, 59
David, King of Israel, 13–24, 26, 48, 61
*David and Bathsheba* (Chagall), 12, 23 (fig. 1.4), 24
Davis, Thomas, 177
De Young Museum (San Francisco), 244, 251
*Death on a Pale Horse* (Blake), 284
Decadent art, 137, 142, 155
Delacroix, Eugène, 170, 174
   *Christ in the Boat*, 174
Delphic Python, 149
*Departure of the Joads, The* (Benton), 199, 200 (fig. 7.6)
*Departure of the Prodigal Son, The* (Rembrandt), 186
*De'veri precetti della pittura* (Armenini), 141
diaspora, Jewish, 85
*Die heimliche Offenbarung Johannis* (Dürer), 261

*Dinner for Threshers* (Wood), 243, 244 (fig. 9.1), 245–48, 250–51, 256, 257 (fig. 9.5), 258
Dionysiou frescoes (Mount Athos), 268, 277–78
Dionysus, 222–24
Dodonaeus, Rembertus, 43, 45–46, 49
Drost, Willem, 17, 20–22
   *Bathsheba with David's Letter*, 20, 21 (fig. 1.3), 22
Duccio, 118
   *Noli Me Tangere*, 118
Dupinet, Antoine, 279
Dürer, Albrecht, 116–17, 147, 186–87, 198, 261–65, 268, 270, 274, 277–80, 282, 284–85, 288–89
   *Apocalypsis cum figuris*, 261, 277
   *Die heimliche Offenbarung Johannis*, 261
   *Four Horsemen of the Apocalypse*, 262
   *Noli Me Tangere*, 116, 117 (fig. 4.5)
   *Prodigal Son amongst the Pigs, The*, 186, 187 (fig. 7.2)
   *St. John Devouring the Book*, 262, 263 (fig. 10.1), 264
Dust Bowl, the, 202, 251, 258
Duvet, Jean, 277–80, 282
   *Angel Gives Saint John the Book to Eat, The*, 279–80, 281 (fig. 10.6)
   *Lapocalypse figure par Jehan Duuet, iadis Orfevre des Rois, Francois premier de ce nom & Henri deuxieme*, 278

El Greco, 192
Elijah, 136, 156
Emmaus, Jesus's supper at, 124, 252–54
Ephesus, 225
Epiphanius, 128
Eros, 222
Etruscans, 228–229
Eucharist, 126, 233–34, 255
Euthymius, 122, 125, 127
*Executioner Presenting Herodias with the Head of John the Baptist, The* (Luini), 139, 142, 143 (fig. 5.1), 144–45

*Expositio in Apocalypsim* (Alexander Minorita), 267
Ezekiel, 84–85, 93
Ezra, 85
*Face of the Deep, The* (Rossetti), 287
Filippi, Sebastiano, 106
fin de siècle, 137, 142, 155, 160
Fine Arts Academy (Paris), 190
Firenze, Andrea da (di Bonaiuto), 110–11, 113–14
   *Christ and Peter on the Sea of Galilee*, 110, 111 (fig. 4.3), 113–14
Fitzwilliam Museum (Cambridge), 108
*Flanders' House, The* (Benton), 196
Flemish Apocalypse, 262
*Flight to Egypt* (Millet), 170
*Florilegium* (Collaert), 37–44, 46, 50–51, 55–56, 61
*Florilegium Novum* (de Bry), 47–48, 52
Fontana, Lavinia, 118, 128
   *Noli Me Tangere*, 118, 128
Fontana, Prospero, 106
*Four Horsemen of the Apocalypse* (Dürer), 262
Fra Angelico, 118
   *Noli Me Tangere*, 118
Fra Bartolomeo, 116
   *Noli Me Tangere*, 116
Francis of Assisi, 267
François II (King of France), 278
Freud, Sigmund, 152
*From Here I Saw What Happened and I Cried* (Weems), 29
Fronto, 233
Galle, Philips, 37–44, 46, 50–51, 55, 61
   *Bouquet of Flowers*, 37, 38 (fig. 2.1), 50
   *Lilies*, 42 (fig. 2.5)
   *Roses*, 41 (fig. 2.4)
   *Sponsa and Sponsus*, 37, 40 (fig. 2.3), 45, 50–56
   *Title Plate*, 37, 39 (fig. 2.2), 50, 55
Galle, Theodoor, 44, 51–55
   *Reciprocal Invitation of the Bride and Bridegroom to Their Respective Gardens* (Galle), 51–53, 54 (fig. 2.7)

*Garden of Desire* (Jackson), 70, 72–73 (fig. 3.2), 74, 75 (fig. 3.3)
*Garland of Flowers on a Carved Stone Medallion, A* (Seghers), 60 (fig. 2.10)
Garofalo. *See* Tisi, Benvenuto
Gauguin, Paul, 175
*Gaze I* (O'Grady), 26
*Gaze II* (O'Grady), 26
*Gazette des beaux-arts*, 171
Gérôme, Jean-Léon, 20, 29
   *Bethsabée*, 20, 29
Getty Apocalypse (Dyson Perrins Apocalypse), 273–74, 275 (fig. 10.4), 287
Ghent-Bruges school, 56, 59
Ghirlandaio, Domenico, 255
   *Last Supper, The*, 255
Giotto (di Bondone), 110, 116, 255–56
   *Last Supper, The*, 255
   *Navicella*, 110
Girard, René, 155–56, 160
God, 74, 86, 88, 109, 121, 126, 131, 156, 159, 183, 193–94, 197, 235, 254–55, 265–66, 274, 287
   creator, role as, 47–49
   *lectio divina* and, 76
   parable of the prodigal son and, 183–84, 203
   parable of the sheep and goats and, 202
   Revelation, depiction in, 264–65, 277
   *Saint John's Bible*, depiction in, 74, 79, 84–85, 86 (fig. 3.7)
   Song of Songs and, 67–68, 70, 87
   suprarational knowledge, object of, 49, 51, 61
   temple and, 87
*Godspell* (play/film), 188
Goethe, Johann Wolfgang von, 147
Gogh, Vincent van, 167, 174–76, 179
   *Sower, The* (Amsterdam), 174
   *Sower, The* (Otterlo), 167, 174, 175 (fig. 6.4), 176, 179
Gospel of Thomas. *See* Thomas, Gospel of
Gothic art, 244, 252, 256

*Grapes of Wrath, The* (Steinbeck), 199
Great Depression, 202, 244, 249, 251–52
*Great Red Dragon and the Beast from the Sea, The* (Blake). 282
Gregory I (The Great), Pope, 87, 93, 122, 124, 129
Gregory VII, Pope, 269
Gregory of Nyssa (Nyssen), 122
*Grimm's Fairy Tales*, 252
*Guarded Conditions* (Simpson), 27 (fig. 1.5), 28
Hades (god), 83, 201
Haimo of Auxerre, 270, 273
*Harvesters Resting* (Millet), 170
Heemskerck, Maarten van, 18, 282
Henri II (King of France), 278
Hera, 232
Hermitage (Saint Petersburg), 139
Herod I (The Great), 135, 202, 273
Herod II, 135
Herod Antipas, 109, 135–37, 142, 144–45, 147, 156–57
Herodias, 135–37, 142, 144, 153, 155–57, 160
*Herodias* (Luini [Florence]). *See Executioner Presenting Herodias with the Head of John the Baptist, The* (Luini)
Hiberno-Latin Reference Bible, 266
Hilary of Poitiers, 112
Hippolytus of Rome, 129
*Holy Family, The* (Luini), 158
*Holy Family with the Infant St John* (Luini), 158
*Holy Roller Camp Meeting* (Benton), 193
"Holy Roller Faith," 193–95
Holy Spirit, the, 114, 126
Homeric Hymn to Demeter, 83
*Hortorum Viridariorumque Elegantes & Multiplicis Formae* (de Vries), 50
*Hortus deliciarum*, 164
*Hortus Floridus* (de Passe), 43, 45–46
House of the Boat of Psyches (Antioch on the Orontes), 222, 224, 234
House of the Chaste Lovers (Pompeii), 212–19, 224, 234

fresco on east wall of triclinium of, 216–17
fresco on north wall of triclinium of, 215–16, 226–27
fresco on west wall of triclinium of, 214, 215 (fig. 8.1)
*I Am My Beloved's* (Jackson), 79, 80 (fig. 3.4)
iconic script, 92
*Iconologia* (Ripa), 83
Ignatius of Antioch, 225
impressionism, 190
*Infant Jesus Sleeping* (Luini), 158
intrinsic meaning, 2–3
Isaiah, 84
*Isaiah's Temple Vision* (Jackson), 84, 86 (fig. 3.7)
Israel (land), 87, 202
Israel (people)/Israelites, 68, 77, 85, 269
Jackson, Donald, 67, 71–81, 84–90, 93–96
*Call of the Disciples*, 88
*Crucifixion*, 88, 89 (fig. 3.8), 92
*Garden of Desire*, 70, 72–73 (fig. 3.2), 74, 75 (fig. 3.3)
*I Am My Beloved's*, 79, 80 (fig. 3.4)
*Isaiah's Temple Vision*, 84, 86 (fig. 3.7)
*Jacob's Ladder*, 91
*Loaves and Fishes*, 78
*Resurrection*, 88, 90 (fig. 3.9), 91–92
*Set Me as a Seal*, 79, 81 (fig. 3.5), 94, 95 (fig. 3.10)
*Solomon's Temple*, 84, 85 (fig. 3.6)
*Song of Solomon, The*, 70, 71 (fig. 3.1), 74, 87
*Word Made Flesh*, 94
*Jacob's Ladder* (Jackson), 91
Jairus, 137, 157
Jansen, Cornelius, 122
*Jayber Crow* (Berry), 250
Jefferson, Thomas, 252
Jerome, 112, 126
Jerusalem, 79, 85, 277
Jesus (Christ), 47, 88, 91–92, 103, 129–30, 136, 143, 145, 158, 160, 176–78,

183, 197, 202, 232, 255–56, 265, 267, 277, 280, 285
Abingdon Apocalypse, depiction in, 270
angel of Rev 10, identification with, 266, 269–70, 273, 282
ascension of, 110, 128
Beloved Disciple and, 209–10, 225–37
*Christ and Peter on the Sea of Galilee* (Firenze), depiction in, 111 (fig. 4.3), 114
*Christ and Saint Peter at the Sea of Galilee* (Scarsellino), depiction in, 103, 104 (fig. 4.1), 107, 116, 118, 131–32
*Christ Walking on the Water* (coin), depiction in, 110, 111 (fig. 4.4), 113
Cloisters Apocalypse, depiction in, 276–77
*Crucifixion* (Jackson), depiction in, 88, 89 (fig. 3.8)
crucifixion of, 88, 91–92, 159, 201
Emmaus, supper at, 124, 252–54
Farewell Discourse(s) of (in John), 210, 225, 233–34
flight into Egypt of, 202, 270, 272 (fig. 10.3), 273, 289
Last Supper of, 245, 252, 254–55, 258, 265
*Last Supper* paintings, depictions in, 255–56
Luini's paintings, depictions in, 150, 158–59
Madonna and Child paintings, depictions in, 84
*Marriage Feast at Cana* (Saiter/ Veronese), depiction in, 253 (fig. 9.2)
Mary Magdalene and, 128–29, 157
miracles of, 164
  raising Jairus's daughter, 137, 157
  turning water to wine, 252–53
  walking on water, 103, 109–15
*Noli Me Tangere* paintings, depictions in, 104 (fig. 4.2), 115–16, 117 (figs. 4.5–6), 118, 119 (figs. 4.7–8), 120 (fig. 4.9)
parables of, 163–65, 178, 181, 197, 203
  good Samaritan, 181
  lost coin, 182
  lost sheep, 182
  prodigal son, 129, 181–204
  rich man and Lazarus, 181
  sheep and goats, 202
  sower, 163–79
  wise and foolish virgins, 181–82
Peter's denial of, 131
*Reciprocal Invitation of the Bride and Bridegroom to Their Respective Gardens* (Galle), depiction in, 51–53, 54 (fig. 2.7), 55
*Resurrection* (Jackson), depiction in, 88, 90 (fig. 3.9)
resurrection of, 88, 91–92, 103, 115–28
Revelation, depiction in, 265
*Saint John's Bible, The*, depictions in, 69, 88, 91, 94
Song of Songs and, 51, 68–69
*Sponsa and Sponsus* (Collaert), depiction in, 40 (fig. 2.3), 50, 55–56
*Supper at Emmaus* (Velázquez), depiction in, 254 (fig. 9.3)
*Unicorn Tapestries, The*, depiction in, 83
vine metaphor of, 233–34
washing the feet of his disciples, 234–36
*Word Made Flesh* (Jackson), depiction in, 94
Jezebel, 156
John, son of Zebedee, 121–22
John Chrysostom, 112, 115, 122, 124, 127–28
John of Patmos, 86, 262, 264–68, 270, 273–74, 277, 279–80, 282, 284–85, 287–89
John of the Cross, 70
*John Takes the Book* (Abingdon Apocalypse), 270, 271 (fig. 10.2)

John the Baptist, 109, 135–37, 155–57
  in Luini's paintings, 143–45, 151
Joseph, husband of Mary, 202
Joseph of Arimathea, 92, 125
Josephus, Flavius, 88, 135–36, 157
Judas Iscariot, 225, 227, 254–56, 259
Julius II, Pope, 149
Justin, Byzantine Emperor, 266
Justin Martyr, 137
Justinian, Byzantine Emperor, 266
Kansas City Art Institute, 190, 198
Koberger, Anton, 261–64
*kourotrophos*, 151
Kristeva, Julia, 151–53
Kunsthistorisches Museum (Vienna), 151
kylix (Makron), 219, 220 (fig. 8.3), 221 (fig. 8.4), 224, 226
*La Vie de Notre Seigneur Jesus Christ* (Tissot), 171
Lacan, Jacques, 153–56
Lambeth Apocalypse, 274
Lapide, Cornelius à, 51–52, 105, 112–15, 118, 120–28, 131
*Lapocalypse figuree par Jehan Duuet, iadis Orfevre des Rois, Francois premier de ce nom & Henri deuxieme* (Duvet), 278
Last Judgment triptych (Martin), 285, 287
Last Supper, Jesus's, 245, 252, 254–55, 258, 265
*Last Supper, The* (Castagno), 255
*Last Supper, The* (da Vinci), 139, 256, 257 (fig. 9.5)
*Last Supper, The* (Ghirlandaio), 255
*Last Supper, The* (Giotto), 255
*Last Supper, The* (Monaco) 255
*Last Supper, The* (Tintoretto), 255
Lazarus, 115, 129, 232
*lectio divina*, 69, 74–77, 87, 92–93, 96
Lefèvre, Jean (Canon), 279
Leochares, 149
Leontius of Byzantium, 126
Leto, 149

Lévi-Strauss, Claude, 156
*Lilies* (Collaert/Galle), 42 (fig. 2.5)
Lindisfarne Gospels, 76
*Lives of the Ferrarese Painters and Sculptors, The* (Baruffaldi), 106
*Loaves and Fishes* (Jackson), 78
Lobelius, Mathias, 43, 45, 48
*Lord Heal the Child* (Benton), 193
*Lord Is My Shepherd, The* (Benton), 193
Louis XII, King of France and Naples, 139, 142
Louvre, 18, 20, 141–42, 145, 158
Lucian of Samosata, 232
Lufft, Hans, 280
  *Das Newe Testament*, 280
Luini, Bernardino (del Lupino), 137–53, 155, 157–60
  *Christ among the Doctors*, 150, 159
  *Christ in the Attitude of Benediction*, 150, 159
  *Conversion of the Magdalene, The*, 157, 158 (fig. 5.8), 159
  *Executioner Presenting Herodias with the Head of John the Baptist, The*, 139, 142, 143 (fig. 5.1), 144–45
  *Holy Family, The*, 158
  *Holy Family with the Infant St John*, 158
  *Infant Jesus Sleeping*, 158
  *Madonna and Child with Saints Catherine and Barbara*, 141–42, 145, 159
  *Madonna of the Rose Bush* (*Madonna of the Rose Hedge*), 139, 141–42, 145
  *Magdalene, The*, 159
  *Modesty and Vanity*, 157
  *Salome Receiving the Head of the Baptist* (Madrid), 145, 147 (fig. 5.3), 149 (fig. 5.6)
  *Salome with the Head of John the Baptist* (Vienna), 151, 152 (fig. 5.7), 155, 157–58
  *Salome with the Head of Saint John the Baptist* (Boston), 145, 147, 148 (fig. 5.4), 149 (fig. 5.5)

*Salome with the Head of St. John the Baptist* (Paris), 145, 146 (fig. 5.2)
*St. Catherine*, 139, 142
*Susanna*, 151
*Vanity and Modesty*, 139
*Virgin on a Throne with Saints, The*, 150
Luther, Martin, 277
Lycurgus, 222
Madonna and Child paintings, 84
*Madonna and Child with Saints Catherine and Barbara* (Luini), 141–42, 145, 159
*Madonna della Vittoria* (Mantegna), 280
*Madonna of the Pomegranate* (Botticelli), 84
*Madonna of the Rocks* (da Vinci). See *Virgin of the Rocks*
*Madonna of the Rose Bush (Madonna of the Rose Hedge)* (Luini), 139, 141–42, 145
*Madonna of the Rose Garden* (Schongauer), 69
*Magdalene, The* (Luini), 159
Makron, 219
Mannerism, 103, 106, 114, 129, 192
*manque-à-être*, 153–55
Mantegna, Andrea, 278, 280
  *Madonna della Vittoria*, 280
  *St. Bernardino of Siena between Two Angels*, 280
Marcantonio, 278
Marcus Aurelius, 233
*Marriage Feast at Cana* (Saiter/Veronese), 253 (fig. 9.2)
Martha, 129, 157, 159
Martin, John, 285, 287
  *Angel with the Book, The*, 285, 287, 288 (fig. 10.9)
  Last Judgment triptych, 285, 287
  *Opening of the Seventh Seal*, 287
Martin of Braga, 128
*Martyrologium Sanctarum Virginum* (Collaert), 58 (fig. 2.9), 59
Mary, mother of Jesus, 55, 59, 88, 91, 202, 273

  Luini's paintings, depiction in, 141–42, 145, 150, 158
  Madonna and Child paintings, depiction in, 69, 84, 139
  Song of Songs and, 51–52, 68–69
  wedding at Cana and, 252
Mary Magdalene, 50, 88, 105
  *Call of the Disciples* (Jackson), depiction in, 88
  Counter-Reformation and, 129–32
  Johannine resurrection narrative and, 92, 103, 115–28
  Luini's paintings, depiction in, 157–60
  *Noli Me Tangere* paintings, depiction in, 103, 104 (fig. 4.2), 115–16, 117 (figs. 4.5–6), 118, 119 (figs. 4.7–8), 120 (fig. 4.9), 127–28, 132
  *Resurrection* (Jackson), depiction in, 88, 91
Mary of Bethany, 92, 129, 157, 159
*Massacre of the Innocents and Flight into Egypt* (Abingdon Apocalypse), 270, 272 (fig. 10.3), 273, 289
Master Bertram, 267
Mazzuoli, Giuseppe, 106
Medici family, 37, 44
*Meeting, The* (Benton), 195
Memling, Hans, 17, 29
  *Bathsheba in the Bath*, 17, 29
#MeToo movement, 30
Metropolitan Museum of Art (New York), 219, 282
Michael (archangel), 266, 280
Michelangelo, 147, 170
*Mighty Angel and John Forbidden to Write, The* (Getty Apocalypse), 273–74, 275 (fig. 10.4)
*Mighty Angel Standeth upon the Land and upon the Sea, A* (West), 285, 286 (fig. 10.8)
Millais, John Everett, 167, 171–73
  *Parables of Our Lord and Saviour Jesus Christ, The*, 167, 171–72
  *Sower, The*, 167, 171, 172 (fig. 6.3), 173

Millet, Jean-François, 167–71, 174–76, 178–79
 *Sower, The* (1847–1848), 169
 *Sower, The* (1850), 167–68, 169 (fig. 6.2), 170–71, 174–76, 178–79
Milton, John, 284
*mimesis*, 155, 160
miracles. *See* Jesus: miracles of
*Modesty and Vanity* (Luini), 157
Monaco, Lorenzo, 255
 *Last Supper, The*, 255
Morgan Picture Bible, 15
*"Mors Vincit Omnia" Hours. See* books of hours
*Musaeum* (Borromeo), 138
Museé d'Orsay (Paris), 176
Museo Archeologico Nazionale (Naples), 216
Muses, the, 150
Museum Boijmans Van Beuningen (Rotterdam), 184
Museum of Fine Arts (Boston), 145, 170
Museum of Fine Arts (Budapest), 141, 159
National Gallery (London), 108, 139, 141, 144, 150, 159, 169
National Gallery of Art (Washington, DC), 109, 159, 262, 282
National Museum of Wales (Cardiff), 169
*Navicella* (Giotto), 110
*navicella* theme, 110
Nelson-Atkins Museum (Kansas City), 201
new Jerusalem, 86
Nicaea, Second Council of (787), 110, 112
Nicodemus, 115
Noah, 85
*Noli Me Tangere* (Altdorfer), 116
*Noli Me Tangere* (Cano), 119 (fig. 4.8), 127
*Noli Me Tangere* (Caracciolo), 118
*Noli Me Tangere* (Cavallini), 116
*Noli Me Tangere* (Correggio), 118, 119 (fig. 4.7)
*Noli Me Tangere* (Cortona), 118
*Noli Me Tangere* (Duccio), 118
*Noli Me Tangere* (Dürer), 116, 117 (fig. 4.5)
*Noli Me Tangere* (Fontana), 118, 128
*Noli Me Tangere* (Fra Angelico), 118
*Noli Me Tangere* (Fra Bartolomeo), 116
*Noli Me Tangere* (Perugino), 116
*Noli Me Tangere* (Pontormo), 118
*Noli Me Tangere* (Scarsellino), 103, 104 (fig. 4.2), 105, 116, 118, 120, 132
*Noli Me Tangere* (Tisi [da Garofalo]), 117 (fig. 4.6)
*Noli Me Tangere* (Titian), 118, 120 (fig. 4.9)
*Noli Me Tangere* (Veronese), 116
Nygren, Anders, 232
Oecumenius, 268
O'Grady, Lorraine, 12, 24–27, 30, 32
 *Gaze I*, 26
 *Gaze II*, 26
Oinos (Οἶνος), 224
Olivi, Peter John, 267
*Opening of the Seventh Seal* (Martin), 287
Opōra (Ὀπώρα), 223–24, 226, 234
*Opōra, Agros, and Oinos at Dinner* (mosaic), 221–22, 223 (fig. 8.5), 226
Origen, 112, 120, 123–24
Palacio Real (Madrid), 144
*Pancarpium Marianum* (David), 59
Panofsky, Erwin, 2–3, 210, 225, 261
*Parable of the Prodigal Son, The, No. I: The Departure* (Tissot), 185
*Parable of the Prodigal Son, The, No. II: In Foreign Climes* (Tissot), 185 (fig. 7.1)
*Parable of the Prodigal Son, The, No. III: The Return* (Tissot), 185
*Parable of the Prodigal Son, The, No. IV: The Fatted Calf* (Tissot), 185
*Parable of the Sower, The* (Bassano), 165, 166 (fig. 6.1), 167, 177
parables. *See* Jesus: parables of
*Parables of Our Lord and Saviour Jesus Christ, The* (Dalziel/Millais), 167, 171–72

*Paradisus Sponsi et Sponsae* (David), 51–56, 59
Passe, Crispijn de (the Younger), 43, 45–46, 49
   *Hortus Floridus*, 43, 45–46
Patmos, 86, 262, 268, 273, 279, 284, 287, 289
Paul, 233
*Pedlar, The* (Bosch), 184
Pentecost, 59, 110, 114
*Perseus with the Head of Medusa* (Conova), 148
Persephone, 83, 201
*Persephone* (Benton), 200–201
Perugino, Pietro, 116
   *Noli Me Tangere*, 116
Peter, 87, 103, 105, 129–31
   *Christ and Peter on the Sea of Galilee* (Firenze), depiction in, 111 (fig. 4.3), 114
   *Christ and Saint Peter at the Sea of Galilee* (Scarsellino), depiction in, 103, 104 (fig. 4.1), 106–7, 116, 131–32
   *Christ Walking on the Water* (coin), depiction in, 111 (fig. 4.4), 113
   Johannine Last Supper and, 226–27, 235
   Johannine resurrection narrative and, 121–22, 124, 230
   Matthean walking on water narrative and, 103, 107, 109–15
Pharisees, 183
Pissarro, Camille, 170
Pissarro, Lucien, 170
*Play of the Prodigal Son, The* (Pulci), 188
pointillism, 190
Pollock, Jackson, 190, 198
Pompeii, 212–19, 224
Pompeiian fresco (attribution unknown), 216, 217 (fig. 8.2)
Pontormo, Jacopo da, 118
   *Noli Me Tangere*, 118
Prado (Madrid), 145, 158
*Prayer Meeting* (Benton), 195

*Prefer, Refuse, Decide* (Simpson), 29
Pre-Raphaelite Brotherhood, 171
Primasius of Hadrumetum, 266
Princely Collection (Liechtenstein), 151
"Prodigal Son, The" (Wilkins), 188
*Prodigal Son* (Benton), 188, 194 (fig. 7.5), 195–204
*Prodigal Son amongst the Pigs, The* (Dürer), 186, 187 (fig. 7.2)
Proust, Marcel, 251
Psalms, book of, 84, 93
Pseudo-Athanasius, 124
Pseudo-Justin, 127
Psyche, 222
Pulci, Antonia, 188
   *Play of the Prodigal Son, The*, 188
Quakers, 252, 255
*Rape of Persephone, The* (Benton). See *Persephone* (Benton)
Raphael, 278
*Reciprocal Invitation of the Bride and Bridegroom to Their Respective Gardens* (Galle), 51–53, 54 (fig. 2.7)
Reformation, the, 13, 130
Reformers, the, 103, 130, 267
regionalism, 190–91, 193, 198, 248–50
Rembrandt, 17–18, 19 (fig. 1.2), 20, 185–86, 197–98
   *Bathsheba at Her Bath*, 18, 19 (fig. 1.2), 20
   *Departure of the Prodigal Son, The*, 186
   *Return of the Prodigal Son, The* (1636), 187–88, 189 (figs. 7.3–4)
   *Return of the Prodigal Son, The* (1667–1669), 186–87
   *Self-Portrait with Saskia in the Guise of the Prodigal Son*, 185
Renaissance art, 83–84, 129, 138, 244, 252, 255–56, 263, 278
Renan, Ernst, 177
   *Vie de Jésus*, 177
resurrection, of Jesus. See Jesus: resurrection of
*Resurrection* (Jackson), 88, 90 (fig. 3.9), 91–92

"Return from Bohemia" (Wood), 246–47, 252
*Return of the Prodigal Son, The* (Rembrandt [1636]), 187–88, 189 (figs. 7.3–4)
*Return of the Prodigal Son, The* (Rembrandt [1667–1669]), 186–87
Revelation, book of, 68, 85–86, 261–89
"Revolt against the City" (Wood), 249
Rijksmuseum (Amsterdam), 174
Rijn, Rembrandt van. *See* Rembrandt
*ritrare*, 141
Romanos the Melodist, 188
Romantic art, 140
*Roses* (Collaert/Galle), 41 (fig. 2.4)
Rossetti, Christina, 287
  *Face of the Deep, The*, 287
Roty, Oscar, 167, 176–79
  *Sower, The*, 167, 176 (fig. 6.5), 177–79
Roussat, Richard, 279
Rubens, Peter Paul, 59
Rupert of Deutz (Rupertus), 128
Royal Academy of Arts (London), 285
*Ruth and Boaz* (Millet). *See Harvesters Resting* (Millet)
Sabatini, Lorenzo, 106
*Sacra Parallela*, 15
*Saint John Eats the Book Received from the Angel* (Getty Apocalypse), 274,
Saint John's Abbey, 67, 84, 87, 93
*Saint John's Bible, The*, 67–97
  butterflies in, 79, 91–92
  lace in, 69, 77, 79, 82, 84, 87–88, 91
  lilies in, 69, 79, 82, 88, 91
  pomegranates in, 82–87
*Saint Lucy* (Collaert), 58 (fig. 2.9)
Salome (daughter of Herodias), 135–37, 155–57, 160
  in Caravaggio's paintings, 144
  in Luini's paintings, 142–51, 153, 155, 157–58, 160
*Salome* (Luini [Florence]). *See Executioner Presenting Herodias with the Head of John the Baptist, The* (Luini)

*Salome Receiving the Head of the Baptist* (Luini [Madrid]), 145, 147 (fig. 5.3), 149 (fig. 5.6)
*Salome with the Head of John the Baptist* (Caravaggio [London]), 144
*Salome with the Head of John the Baptist* (Caravaggio [Madrid]), 144
*Salome with the Head of John the Baptist* (Luini [Vienna]), 151, 152 (fig. 5.7), 155, 157–58
*Salome with the Head of Saint John the Baptist* (Luini [Boston]), 145, 147, 148 (fig. 5.4), 149 (fig. 5.5)
*Salome with the Head of St. John the Baptist* (Luini [Paris]), 145, 146 (fig. 5.2)
Salon (Paris), 168
Samacchini, Orazio, 106
San Diego Museum of Art, 157
*Satyricon* (Petronius), 230
Scarsella, Ippolito (Scarsellino), 103–20, 126, 131–32
  *Christ and Saint Peter at the Sea of Galilee*, 103, 104 (fig. 4.1), 105–9, 116, 118, 131–32
  *Noli Me Tangere*, 103, 104 (fig. 4.2), 105, 116, 118, 120, 132
Schiller, Johann Christoph Friedrich von, 147
Schongauer, Martin, 69, 262
  *St. John on Patmos*, 262
Sciarra Colonna Palace, 139
Sea of Galilee, 103, 107, 114
Seghers, Daniel, 60
  *Garland of Flowers on a Carved Stone Medallion, A*, 60 (fig. 2.10)
*Self-Portrait with Saskia in the Guise of the Prodigal Son* (Rembrandt), 185
"Semeur" (Tissot), 171
*Set Me as a Seal* (Jackson), 79, 81 (fig. 3.5), 94, 95 (fig. 3.10)
Sforza, Ludovico (Il Moro), Duke of Milan, 139
Silenus, 223–24
Simon the Pharisee, 183
Simpson, Lorna, 12, 24–25, 27–30

*Guarded Conditions*, 27 (fig. 1.5), 28
*Prefer, Refuse, Decide*, 29
*Waterbearer*, 29
*You're Fine*, 28
*Social History of Missouri, A* (Benton), 190
Society of Jesus, 105
Solomon, 79, 84
*Solomon's Temple* (Jackson), 84, 85 (fig. 3.6)
Son of Man, 265, 280
*Song of Solomon, The* (Jackson), 70, 71 (fig. 3.1), 74, 87
Song of Songs, 37, 45, 50–56, 67–97
*Sower, The* (Millais), 167, 171, 172 (fig. 6.3), 173
*Sower, The* (Millet [1847–1848]), 169
*Sower, The* (Millet [1850]), 167–68, 169 (fig. 6.2), 170–71, 174–76, 178–79
*Sower, The* (Roty), 167, 176 (fig. 6.5), 177–79
*Sower, The* (van Gogh [Amsterdam]), 174
*Sower, The* (van Gogh [Otterlo]), 167, 174, 175 (fig. 6.4), 176, 179
Spicq, Ceslaus, 231–32
*Spirited Horses, No. 2* (Joseph Hoover & Sons), 248
*Sponsa and Sponsus* (Collaert/Galle), 37, 40 (fig. 2.3), 45, 50–56
*St. Bernardino of Siena between Two Angels* (Mantegna), 280
*St. Catherine* (Luini), 139, 142
*St. John Devouring the Book* (Dürer), 262, 263 (fig. 10.1), 264
*St. John on Patmos* (Schongauer), 262
*St. John the Evangelist on Patmos* (Bosch), 262
*St. Michael and His Angels Fighting and Casting out the Red Dragon and His Angels* (West), 285
Staatlichen Museen (Berlin), 262
Steinbeck, John, 199
  *Grapes of Wrath, The*, 199
stigmata, 116
*Suite de l'enfant prodigue: En pays étranger* (Tissot), 184

*Sunday Morning* (Benton), 195
*Supper at Emmaus, The* (Velázquez), 253, 254 (fig. 9.3)
Susanna, 151, 197–98
*Susanna* (Luini), 151
*Susanna and the Elders* (Benton), 197, 200–201, 244
*symposium*, 209, 218–20, 225–26, 228–29
synchronism, 190
Synoptic Gospels, 164, 233, 252, 254
Tate Britain (London), 285
temple, the (Jerusalem), 69, 77, 82–85, 87
Tertullian, 112
Theophylact, 122, 125, 127, 137
Thomas, 115, 127
Thomas, Gospel of, 164
Tintoretto, Jacopo, 106–8, 140, 197, 255
  *Last Supper, The*, 255
Tisi, Benvenuto (da Garofalo), 116–17
  *Noli Me Tangere*, 117 (fig. 4.6)
Tissot, James, 167, 171, 184
  *La Vie de Notre Seigneur Jesus Christ*, 171
  *Parable of the Prodigal Son, The, No. I: The Departure*, 185
  *Parable of the Prodigal Son, The, No. II: In Foreign Climes*, 185 (fig. 7.1)
  *Parable of the Prodigal Son, The, No. III: The Return*, 185
  *Parable of the Prodigal Son, The, No. IV: The Fatted Calf*, 185
  "Semeur," 171
  *Suite de l'enfant prodigue: En pays étranger*, 184
Titian, 106, 118, 120, 159
  *Noli Me Tangere*, 118, 120 (fig. 4.9)
*Title Plate* (Collaert/Galle), 37, 39 (fig. 2.2), 50, 55
Toledo, Francisco de (Toletus), 127
Toledo Museum of Art (Ohio), 285
Tomb of the Diver (Paestum), 227
  fresco on north wall of, 228 (fig. 8.6)
  fresco on south wall of, 228, 229 (fig. 8.7)
Torah, the, 85

*Tragic Prelude—John Brown* (Curry), 191
Trent, Council of, 103, 110, 112, 129
Truman, Harry, 192
Trygaeus, 224
Twelve, the, 88
Tyconius of Carthage, 266
Uffizi Gallery, 142, 144–45
*Unicorn Tapestries, The*, 83
*Vagabond, The* (Bosch). See *Pedlar, The* (Bosch)
Van Gogh, Vincent. See Gogh, Vincent van
*Vanity and Modesty* (Luini), 139
Vatican Museums, 149
Vecchio, Palma, 22
　*Courtesan*, 22
Vecellio, Tiziano. See Titian
Velázquez, Diego, 253
　*Supper at Emmaus, The*, 253, 254 (fig. 9.3)
Veronese, Paolo (Caliari), 106, 116, 197, 252–53
　*Marriage Feast at Cana*, 253 (fig. 9.2)
　*Noli Me Tangere*, 116
*Vie de Jésus* (Renan), 177
Vinci, Leonardo da, 139–42, 157, 256–57
　*Last Supper, The*, 139, 256, 257 (fig. 9.5)
　*Virgin of the Rocks* (London), 141–42
　*Virgin of the Rocks* (Paris), 141–42
vine imagery, in early Christianity, 233–34
*Virgin and Child in the Enclosed Garden, The* (Wierix), 51–52, 53 (fig. 2.6), 55
Virgin Mary. See Mary, mother of Jesus
*Virgin of the Rocks* (da Vinci [London]), 141–42
*Virgin of the Rocks* (da Vinci [Paris]), 141–42
*Virgin on a Throne with Saints, The* (Luini), 150
*Virginis Mariae Vita* (Collaert), 59
*visio divina*, 77
*Vision of the Last Judgment, A* (Blake), 287

visual exegesis, 3, 68–69, 210, 237, 264, 270, 279, 284, 288–89
Vries, Hans Vredeman de, 50
　*Hortorum Viridariorumque Elegantes & Multiplicis Formae*, 50
Vulgate, 126, 142, 264, 269–70, 274
*Waterbearer* (Simpson), 29
*Wednesday Evening* (Benton). See *Prayer Meeting* (Benton)
Weems, Carrie Mae, 12, 24, 28–30
　*From Here I Saw What Happened and I Cried*, 29
West, Benjamin, 285
　*Mighty Angel Standeth upon the Land and upon the Sea, A*, 285, 286 (fig. 10.8)
　*St. Michael and His Angels Fighting and Casting out the Red Dragon and His Angels*, 285
Whitney Museum of American Art (New York), 255
Wierix, Johannes, 46, 51–53, 55
　*Virgin and Child in the Enclosed Garden, The*, 51–52, 53 (fig. 2.6), 55
Wilkins, Robert, 188
　"Prodigal Son, The," 188
*Winnower, The* (Millet), 169
womanist interpretation, 25–32
Wood, Grant, 191, 243–52, 255–59
　*American Gothic*, 191, 243
　*Daughters of Revolution*, 247
　*Dinner for Threshers*, 243, 244 (fig. 9.1), 245–48, 250–51, 256, 257 (fig. 9.5), 258
　"Return from Bohemia," 246–47, 252
　"Revolt against the City," 249
Wood, Hattie Weaver, 258
Wood, Maryville, 255–56, 258–59
Word, the (christological title), 94
*Word Made Flesh* (Jackson), 94
*Year of Peril* (Benton), 201
*You're Fine* (Simpson), 28
Zeus, 232